Shojo Beat

My love STORY!!

5

Art / Story

KAZUNE KAWAHARA

ARUKO

MY love STORY!!

5
CONTENTS

STORY Thus Far...

Takeo Goda, a first-year high school student, is a hot-blooded guy who is 6'6" tall and weighs 265 pounds. Boys look up to him, but the girls he falls in love with all end up liking his handsome best friend, Makoto Sunakawa! All that changes when Takeo saves Rinko Yamato from a groper on the train, and she becomes his girlfriend.

Takeo and gang meet a guy named Hayato Oda who's in love with Makoto's sister, Ai—but she has no interest in Oda whatsoever! Oda wants Ai to tell Takeo her feelings for him, but Ai chooses to keep the truth to herself in part because she knows how close Takeo and Yamato are.

Takeo has always thought of himself as unpopular, but then another girl, a classmate named Mariya Saijo, starts to realize just how great he is. Once she discovers that Takeo has a girlfriend, however, she settles for telling Takeo that she likes him— as a person...

Chapter 16

3

Chapter 17

49

Chapter 18

91

Chapter 19

135

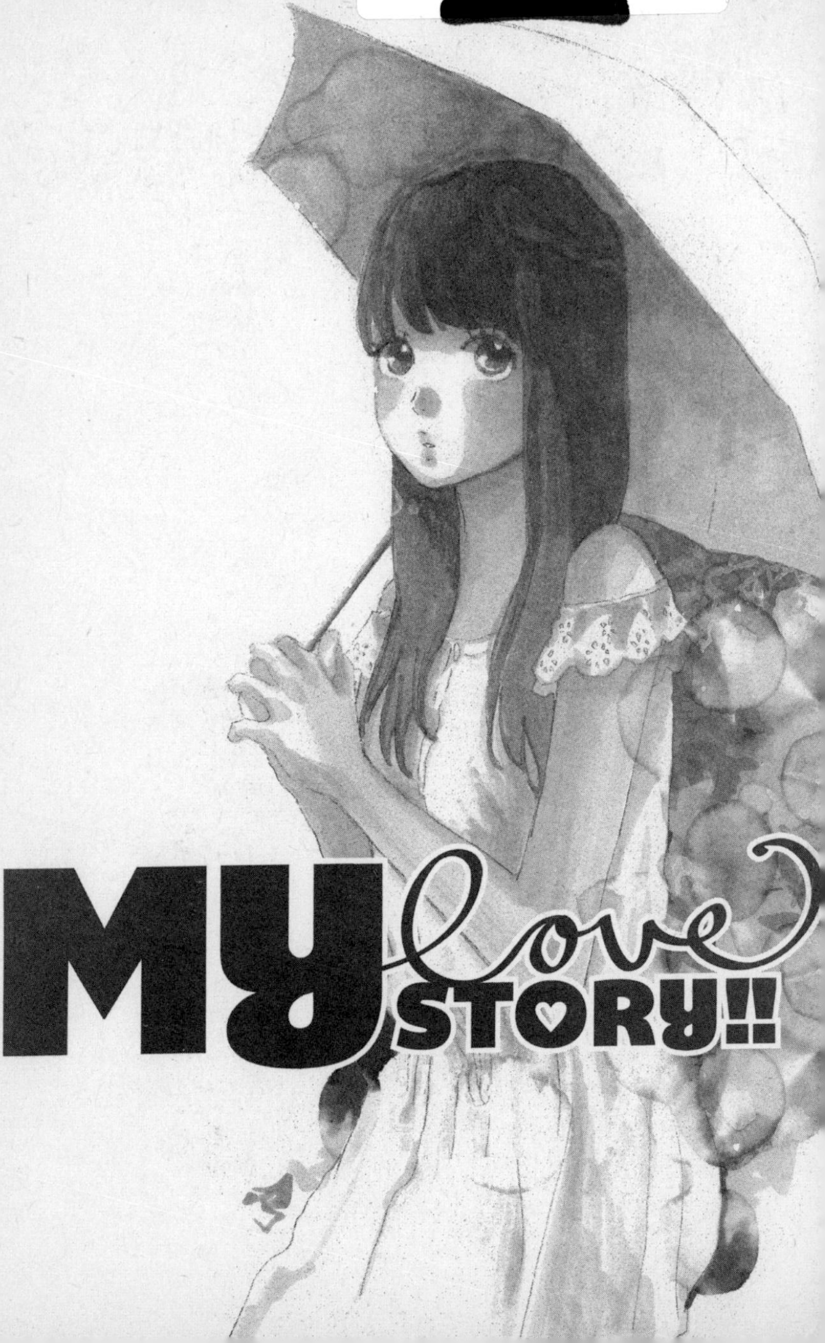
MY love STORY!!

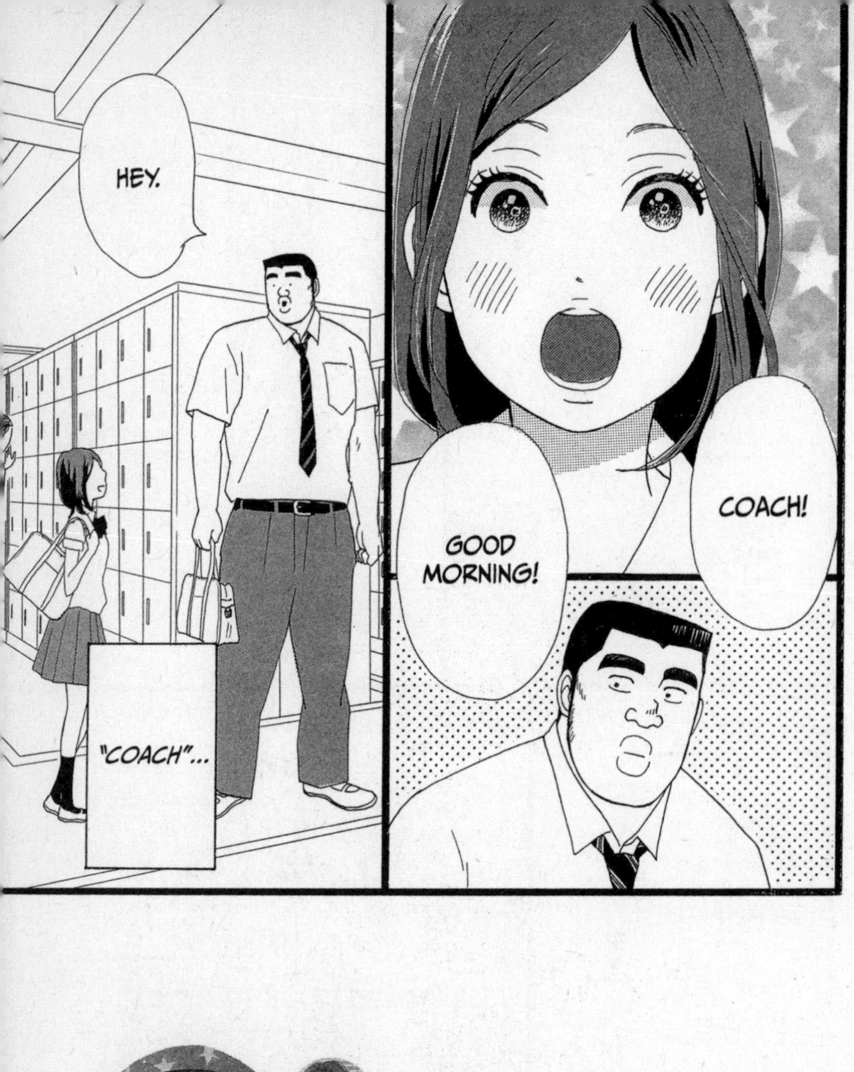
COACH!
GOOD MORNING!
HEY.
"COACH"...

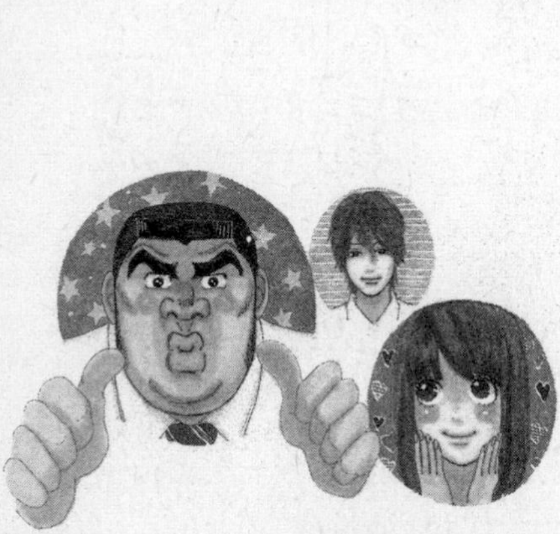

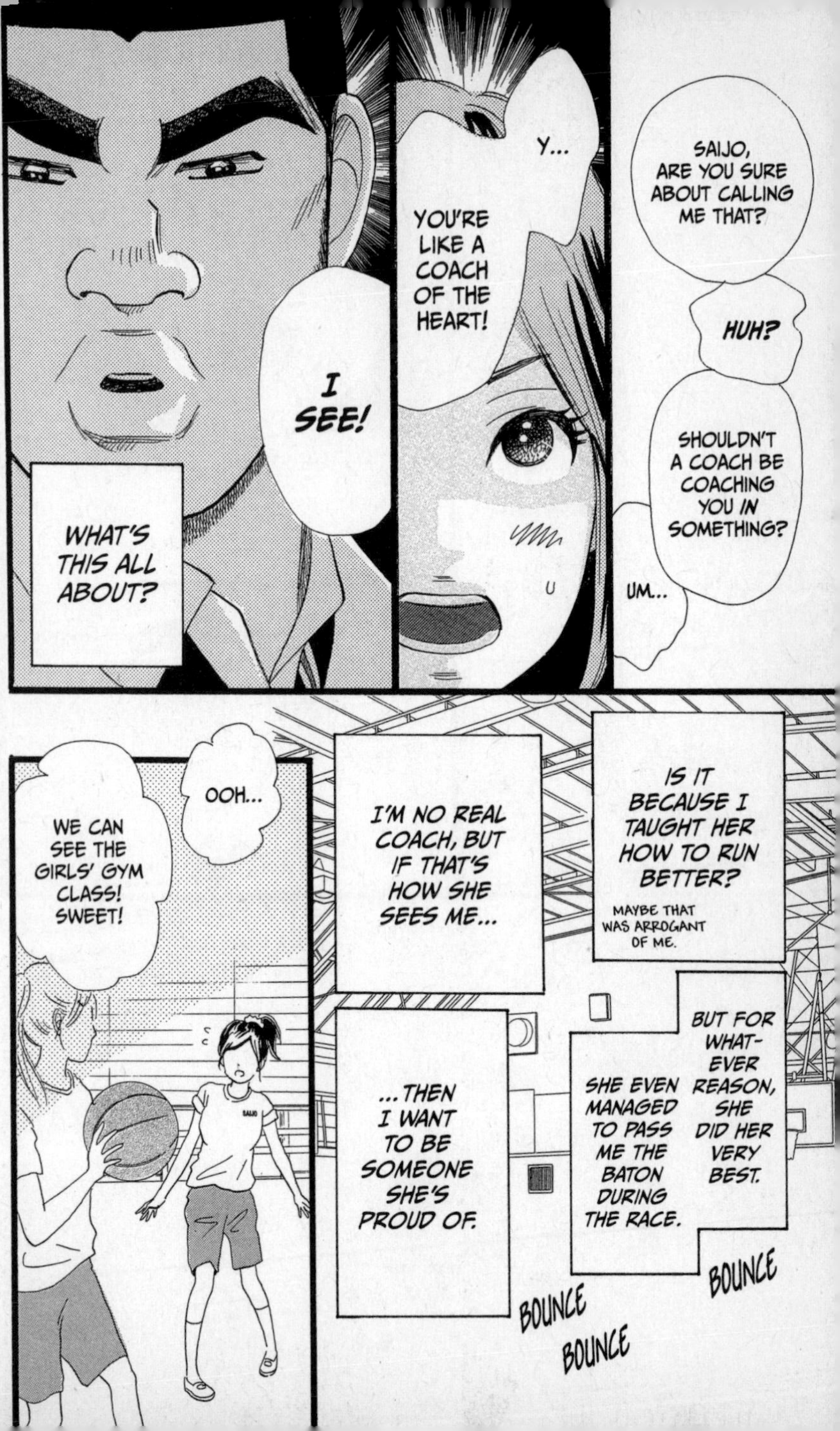
SAIJO, ARE YOU SURE ABOUT CALLING ME THAT?
HUH?
SHOULDN'T A COACH BE COACHING YOU IN SOMETHING?
UM...
Y...
YOU'RE LIKE A COACH OF THE HEART!
I SEE!
WHAT'S THIS ALL ABOUT?
IS IT BECAUSE I TAUGHT HER HOW TO RUN BETTER?
MAYBE THAT WAS ARROGANT OF ME.
BUT FOR WHAT-EVER REASON, SHE DID HER VERY BEST.
SHE EVEN MANAGED TO PASS ME THE BATON DURING THE RACE.
I'M NO REAL COACH, BUT IF THAT'S HOW SHE SEES ME...
...THEN I WANT TO BE SOMEONE SHE'S PROUD OF.
BOUNCE
BOUNCE
BOUNCE
OOH...
WE CAN SEE THE GIRLS' GYM CLASS! SWEET!

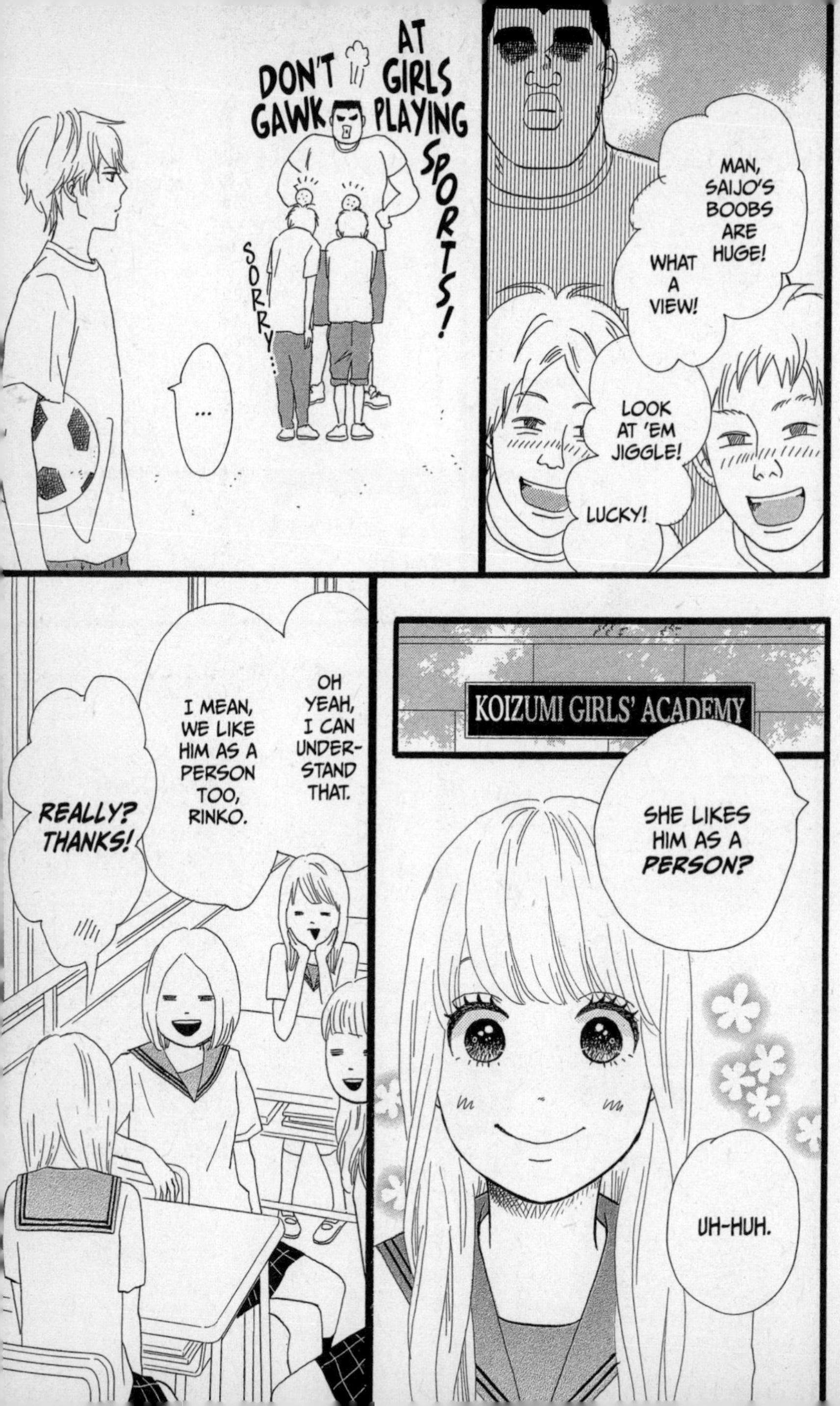
MAN, SAIJO'S BOOBS ARE HUGE!
WHAT A VIEW!
LOOK AT 'EM JIGGLE!
LUCKY!
DON'T GAWK AT GIRLS PLAYING SPORTS!
SORRY...
...
KOIZUMI GIRLS' ACADEMY
SHE LIKES HIM AS A *PERSON?*
UH-HUH.
OH YEAH, I CAN UNDER-STAND THAT.
I MEAN, WE LIKE HIM AS A PERSON TOO, RINKO.
REALLY? THANKS!

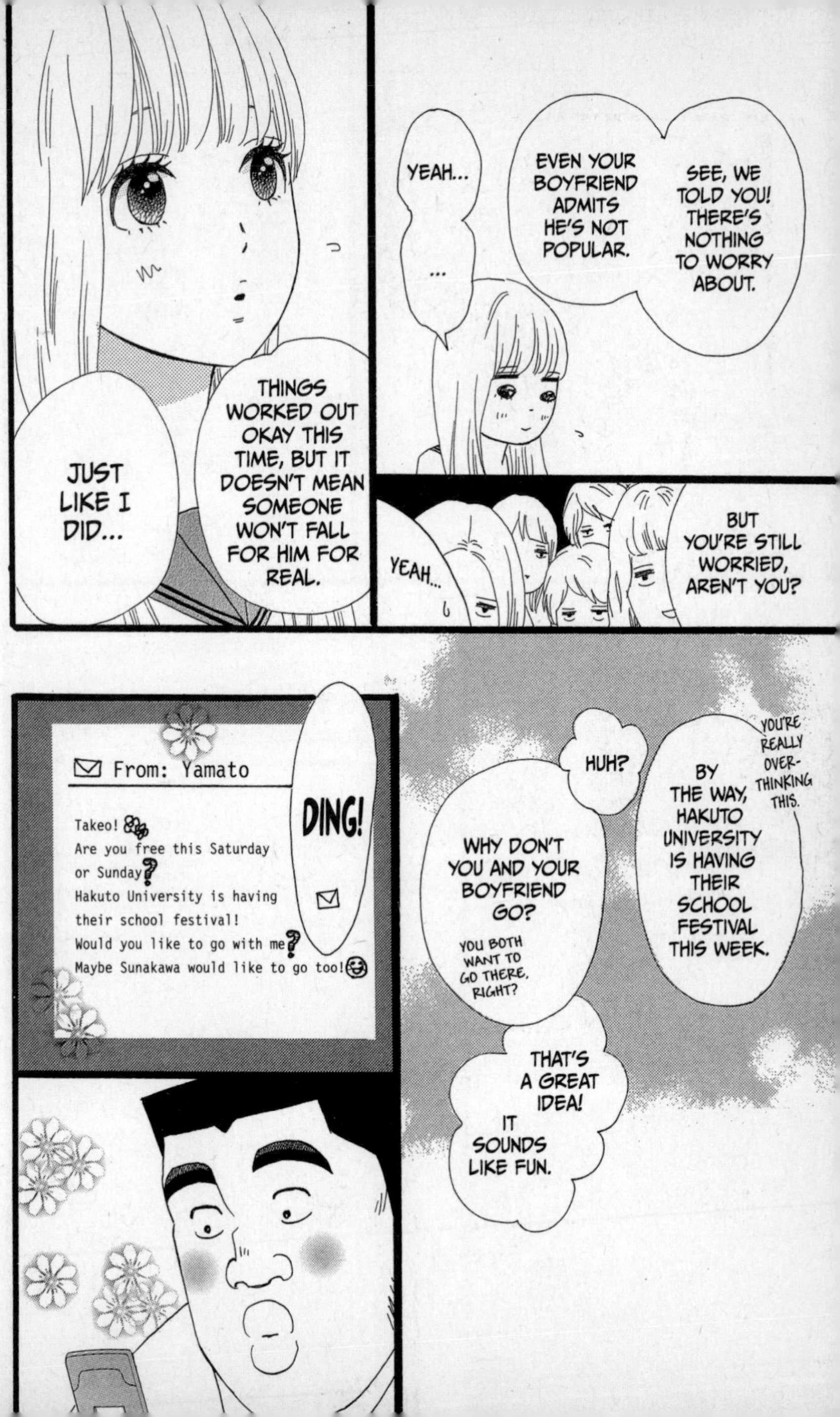
SEE, WE TOLD YOU! THERE'S NOTHING TO WORRY ABOUT.
EVEN YOUR BOYFRIEND ADMITS HE'S NOT POPULAR.
YEAH... ...
BUT YOU'RE STILL WORRIED, AREN'T YOU?
YEAH...
THINGS WORKED OUT OKAY THIS TIME, BUT IT DOESN'T MEAN SOMEONE WON'T FALL FOR HIM FOR REAL.
JUST LIKE I DID...
YOU'RE REALLY OVER-THINKING THIS.
BY THE WAY, HAKUTO UNIVERSITY IS HAVING THEIR SCHOOL FESTIVAL THIS WEEK.
HUH?
WHY DON'T YOU AND YOUR BOYFRIEND GO?
YOU BOTH WANT TO GO THERE, RIGHT?
THAT'S A GREAT IDEA!
IT SOUNDS LIKE FUN.
DING!
From: Yamato
Takeo!
Are you free this Saturday or Sunday?
Hakuto University is having their school festival!
Would you like to go with me?
Maybe Sunakawa would like to go too!

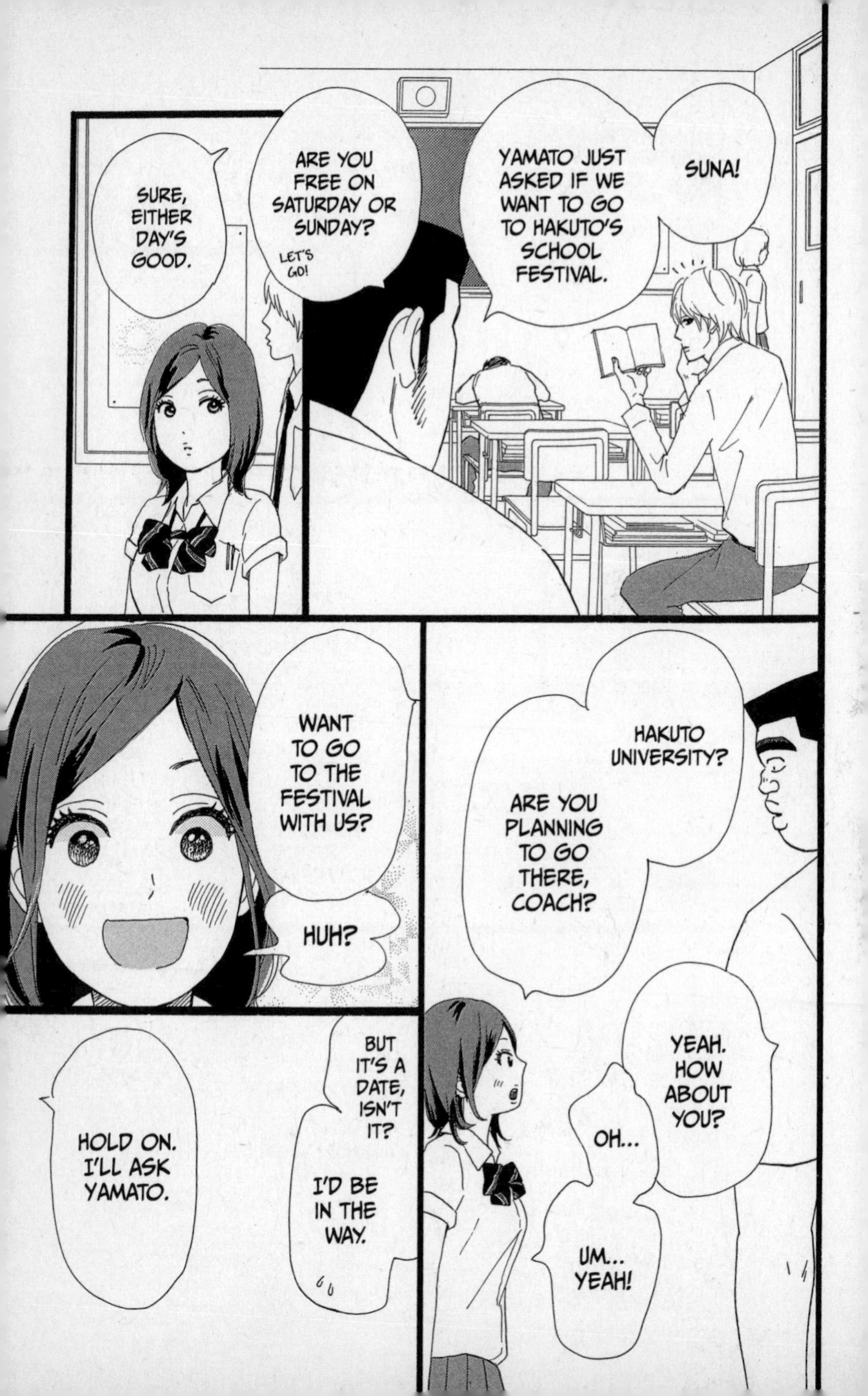

SUNA!
YAMATO JUST ASKED IF WE WANT TO GO TO HAKUTO'S SCHOOL FESTIVAL.
ARE YOU FREE ON SATURDAY OR SUNDAY?
LET'S GO!
SURE, EITHER DAY'S GOOD.
HAKUTO UNIVERSITY?
ARE YOU PLANNING TO GO THERE, COACH?
WANT TO GO TO THE FESTIVAL WITH US?
HUH?
YEAH. HOW ABOUT YOU?
OH...
UM... YEAH!
BUT IT'S A DATE, ISN'T IT?
I'D BE IN THE WAY.
HOLD ON. I'LL ASK YAMATO.

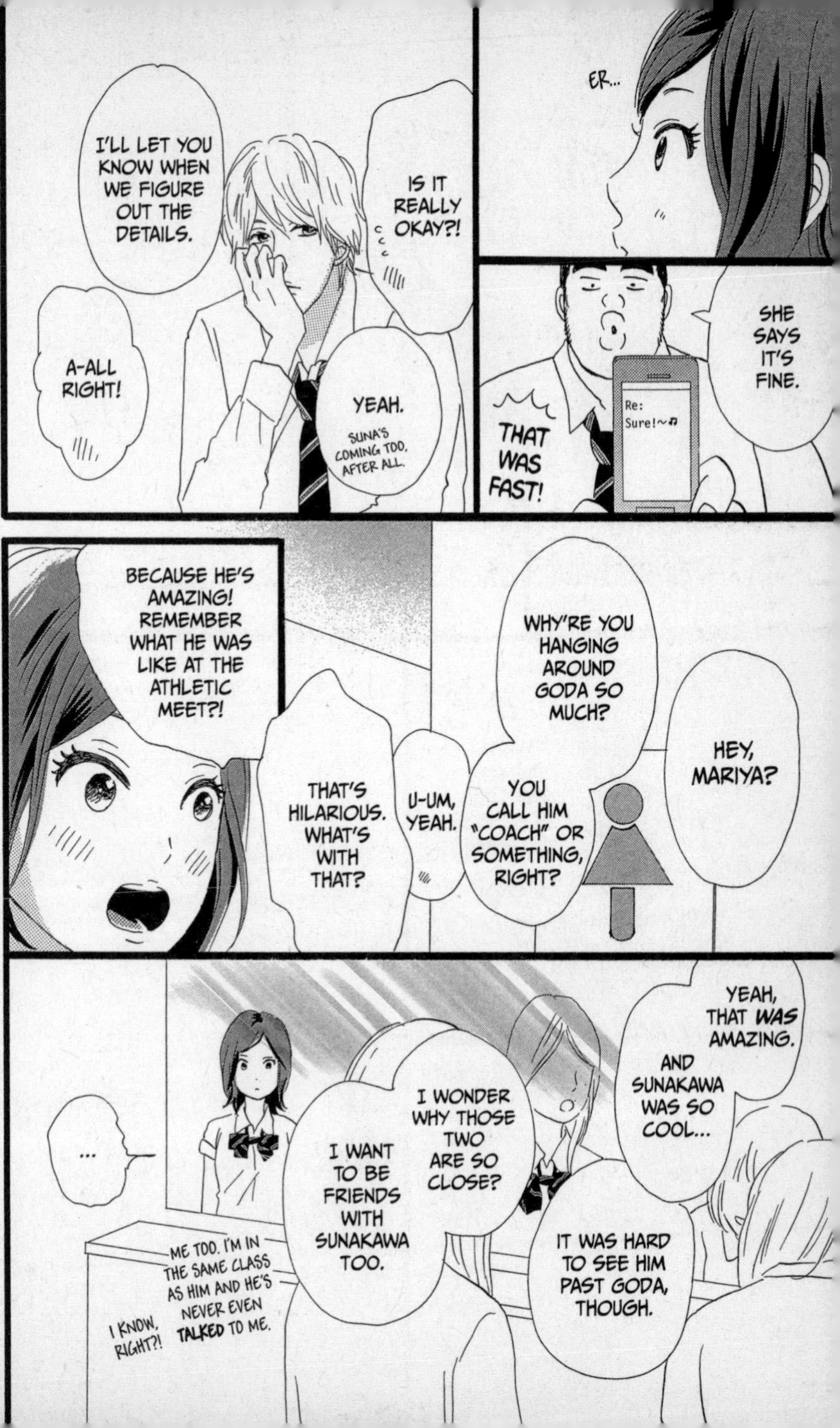
ER...
SHE SAYS IT'S FINE.
Re: Sure!~♪
THAT WAS FAST!
IS IT REALLY OKAY?!
I'LL LET YOU KNOW WHEN WE FIGURE OUT THE DETAILS.
YEAH.
SUNA'S COMING TOO, AFTER ALL.
A-ALL RIGHT!
HEY, MARIYA?
WHY'RE YOU HANGING AROUND GODA SO MUCH?
YOU CALL HIM "COACH" OR SOMETHING, RIGHT?
U-UM, YEAH.
THAT'S HILARIOUS. WHAT'S WITH THAT?
BECAUSE HE'S AMAZING! REMEMBER WHAT HE WAS LIKE AT THE ATHLETIC MEET?!
YEAH, THAT *WAS* AMAZING.
AND SUNAKAWA WAS SO COOL...
I WONDER WHY THOSE TWO ARE SO CLOSE?
IT WAS HARD TO SEE HIM PAST GODA, THOUGH.
I WANT TO BE FRIENDS WITH SUNAKAWA TOO.
ME TOO. I'M IN THE SAME CLASS AS HIM AND HE'S NEVER EVEN **TALKED** TO ME.
I KNOW, RIGHT?!
...

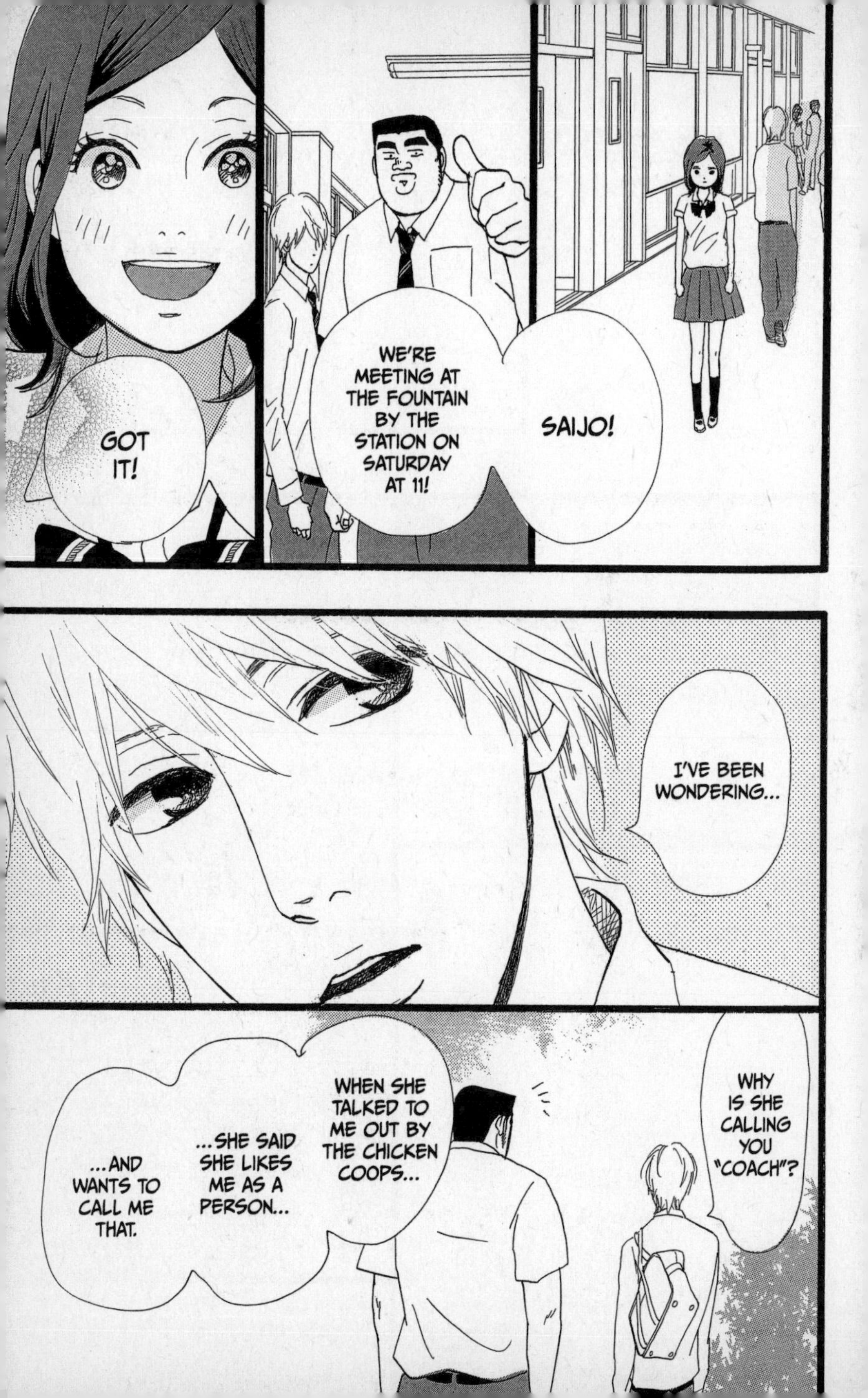
SAIJO!
WE'RE MEETING AT THE FOUNTAIN BY THE STATION ON SATURDAY AT 11!
GOT IT!
I'VE BEEN WONDERING...
WHY IS SHE CALLING YOU "COACH"?
WHEN SHE TALKED TO ME OUT BY THE CHICKEN COOPS...
...SHE SAID SHE LIKES ME AS A PERSON...
...AND WANTS TO CALL ME THAT.

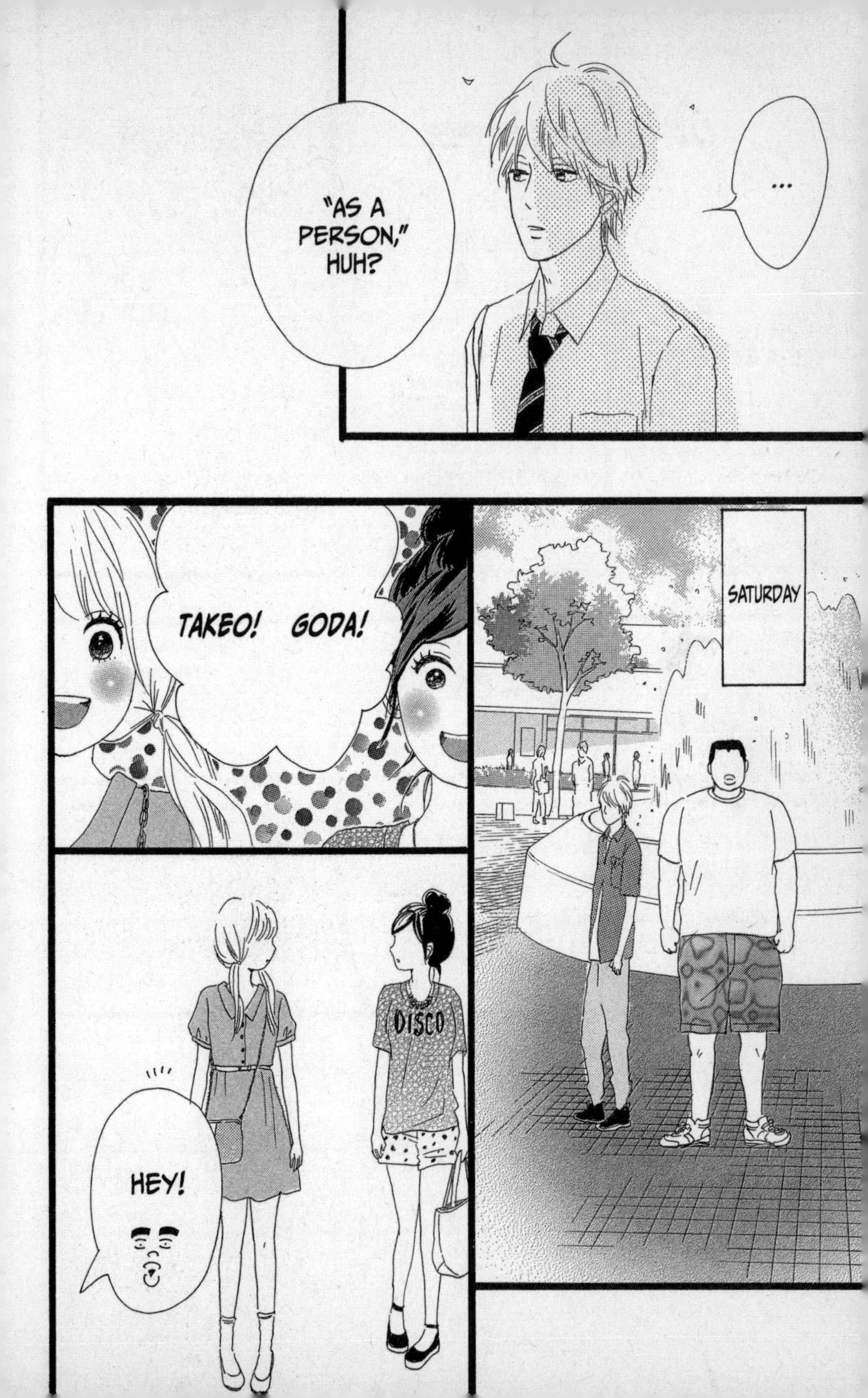
...
"AS A PERSON," HUH?
SATURDAY
TAKEO! GODA!
HEY!

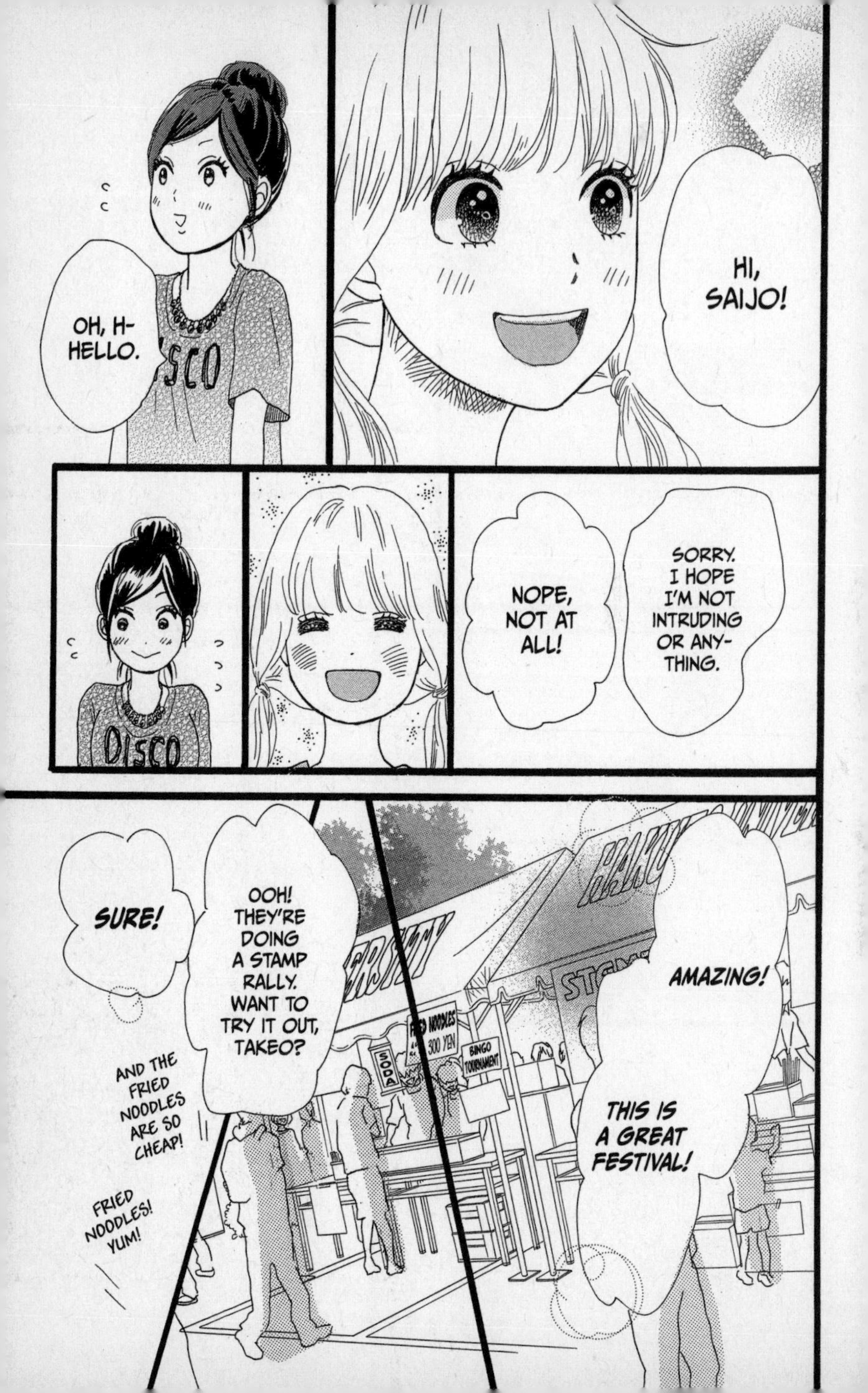

HI, SAIJO!
OH, H-HELLO.
SORRY. I HOPE I'M NOT INTRUDING OR ANY-THING.
NOPE, NOT AT ALL!
AMAZING!
THIS IS A GREAT FESTIVAL!
BINGO TOURNAMENT
FRIED NOODLES 300 YEN
SODA
OOH! THEY'RE DOING A STAMP RALLY. WANT TO TRY IT OUT, TAKEO?
SURE!
AND THE FRIED NOODLES ARE SO CHEAP!
FRIED NOODLES! YUM!

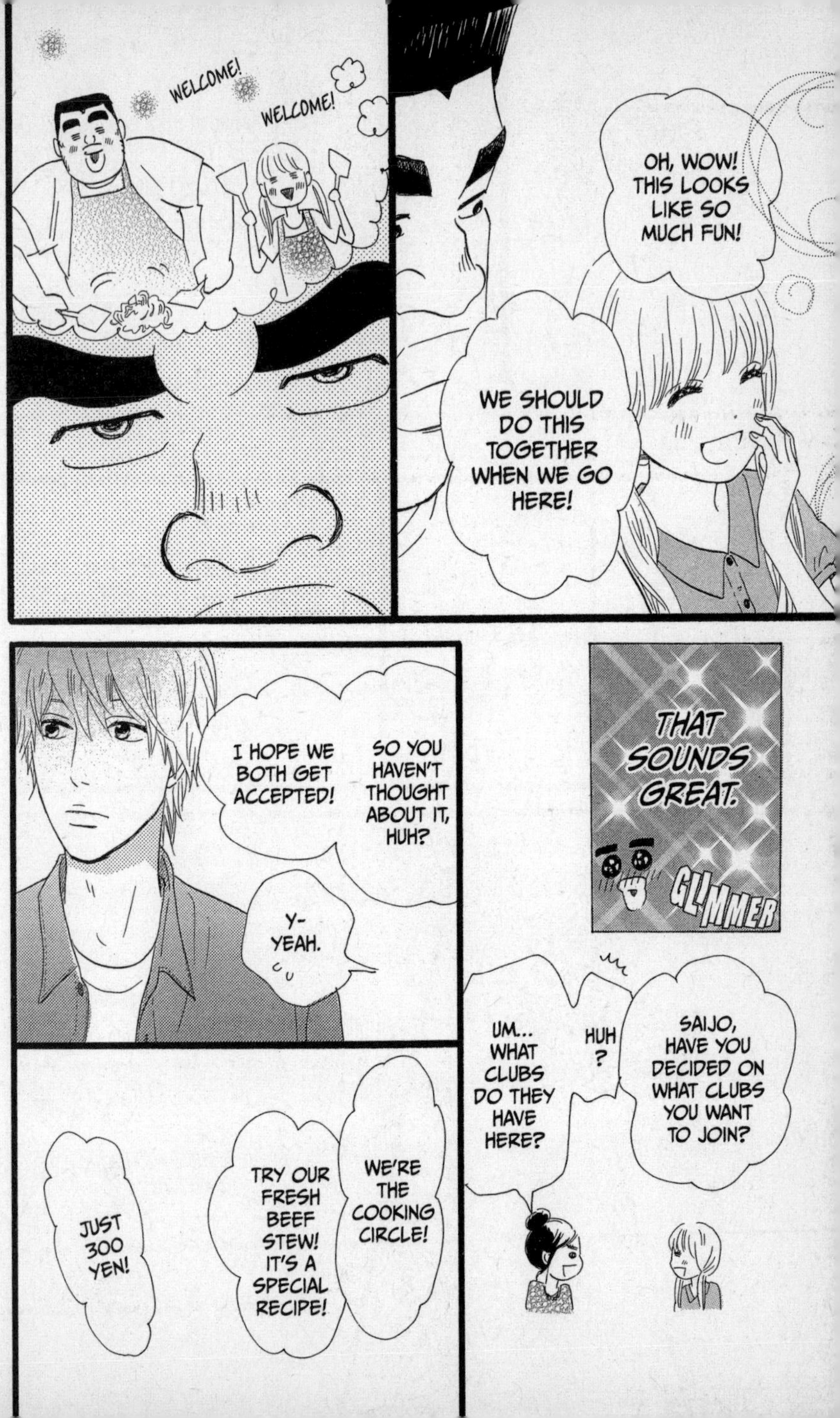
OH, WOW! THIS LOOKS LIKE SO MUCH FUN!
WE SHOULD DO THIS TOGETHER WHEN WE GO HERE!
WELCOME!
WELCOME!
THAT SOUNDS GREAT.
GLIMMER
SO YOU HAVEN'T THOUGHT ABOUT IT, HUH?
I HOPE WE BOTH GET ACCEPTED!
Y-YEAH.
SAIJO, HAVE YOU DECIDED ON WHAT CLUBS YOU WANT TO JOIN?
HUH?
UM... WHAT CLUBS DO THEY HAVE HERE?
WE'RE THE COOKING CIRCLE!
TRY OUR FRESH BEEF STEW! IT'S A SPECIAL RECIPE!
JUST 300 YEN!

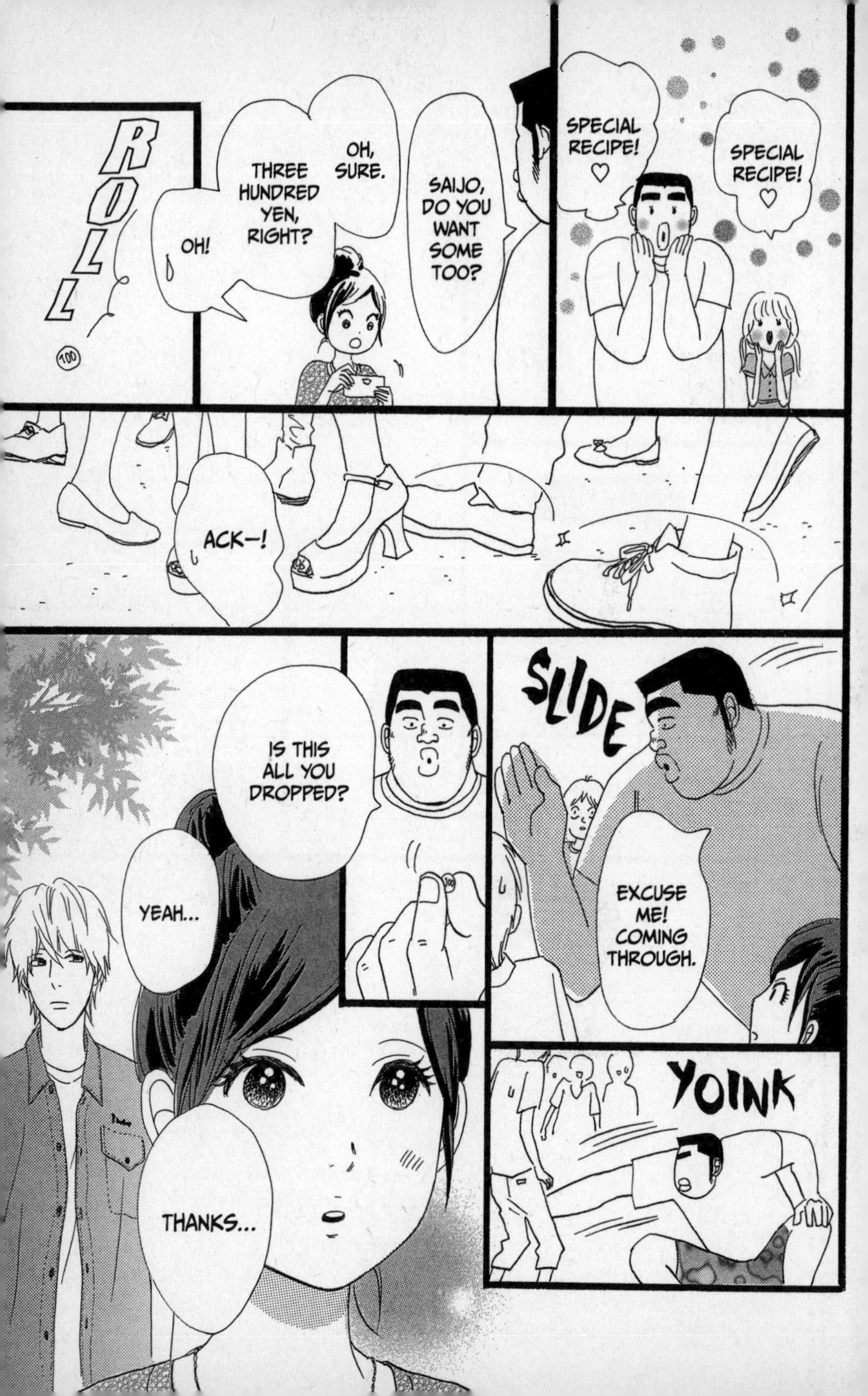
SPECIAL RECIPE! ♡
SPECIAL RECIPE! ♡
SAIJO, DO YOU WANT SOME TOO?
OH, SURE.
THREE HUNDRED YEN, RIGHT?
OH!
ROLL
100
ACK—!
SLIDE
EXCUSE ME! COMING THROUGH.
YOINK
IS THIS ALL YOU DROPPED?
YEAH...
THANKS...

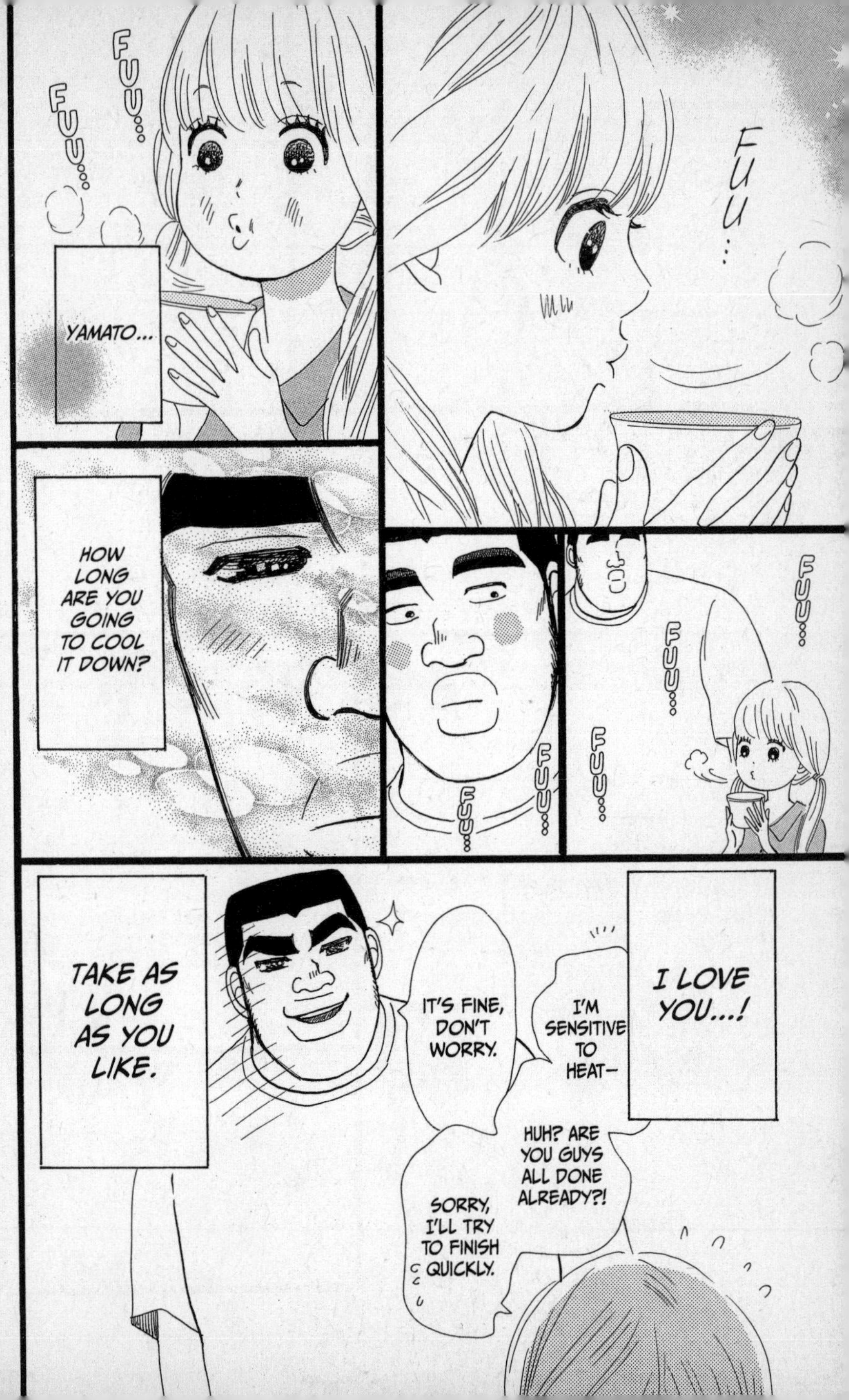
FUU...
FUU...
FUU...
YAMATO...
FUU...
FUU...
FUU...
FUU...
FUU...
HOW LONG ARE YOU GOING TO COOL IT DOWN?
I LOVE YOU...!
I'M SENSITIVE TO HEAT—
HUH? ARE YOU GUYS ALL DONE ALREADY?!
IT'S FINE, DON'T WORRY.
SORRY, I'LL TRY TO FINISH QUICKLY.
TAKE AS LONG AS YOU LIKE.

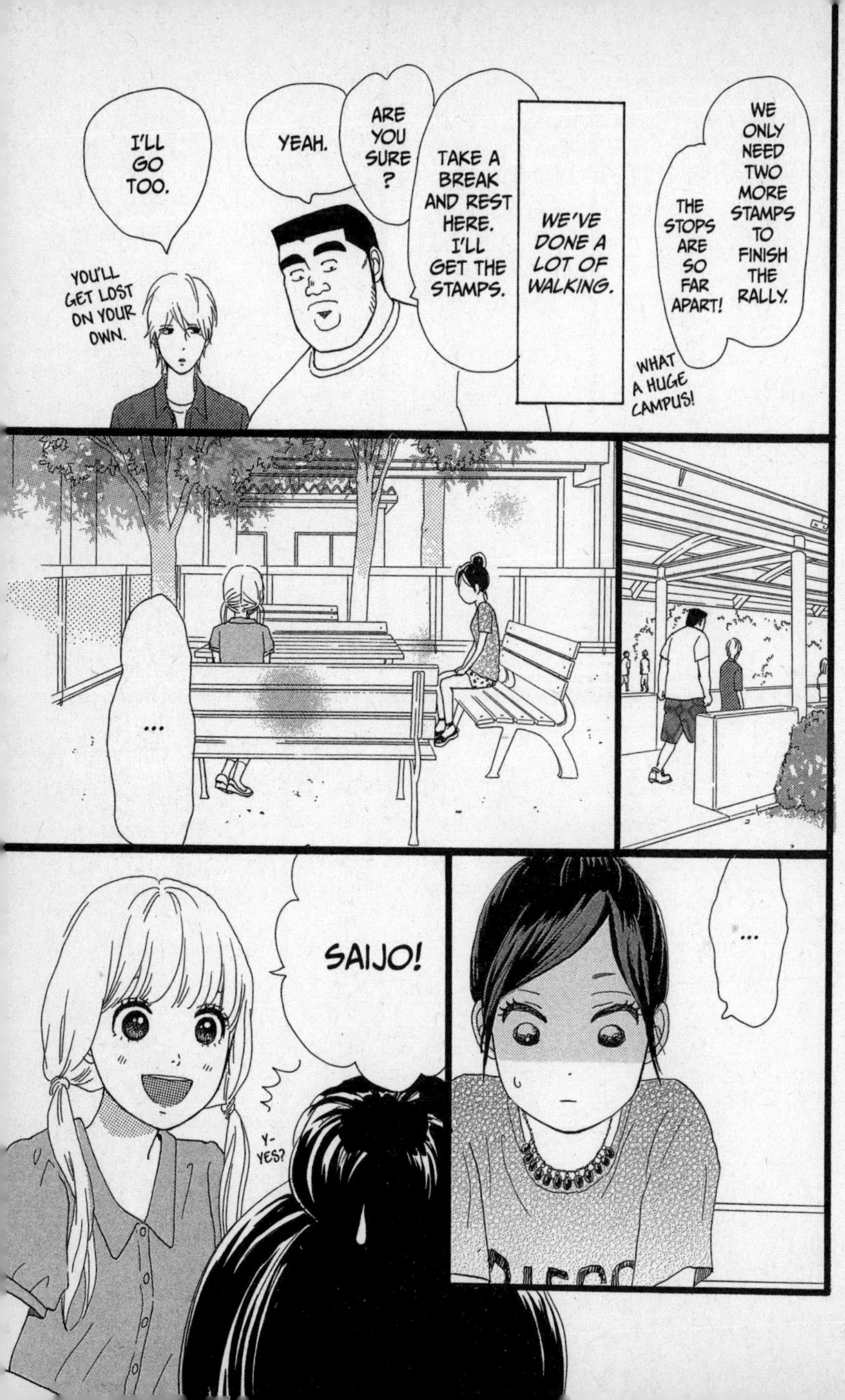
WE ONLY NEED TWO MORE STAMPS TO FINISH THE RALLY.
THE STOPS ARE SO FAR APART!
WHAT A HUGE CAMPUS!
WE'VE DONE A LOT OF WALKING.
TAKE A BREAK AND REST HERE. I'LL GET THE STAMPS.
ARE YOU SURE?
YEAH.
I'LL GO TOO.
YOU'LL GET LOST ON YOUR OWN.
...
...
SAIJO!
Y-YES?

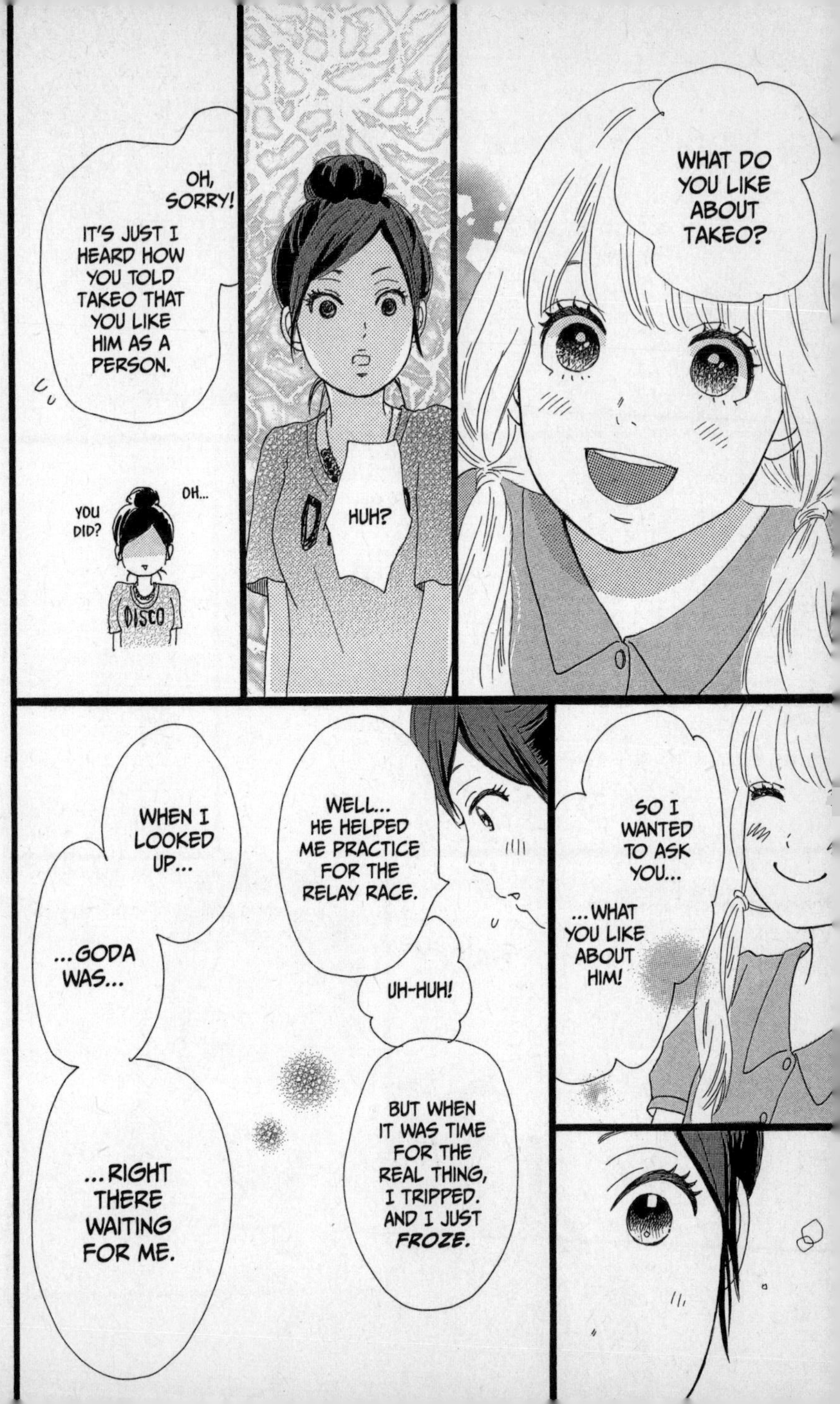
WHAT DO YOU LIKE ABOUT TAKEO?
HUH?
OH, SORRY!
IT'S JUST I HEARD HOW YOU TOLD TAKEO THAT YOU LIKE HIM AS A PERSON.
OH...
YOU DID?
SO I WANTED TO ASK YOU...
...WHAT YOU LIKE ABOUT HIM!
WELL... HE HELPED ME PRACTICE FOR THE RELAY RACE.
UH-HUH!
BUT WHEN IT WAS TIME FOR THE REAL THING, I TRIPPED. AND I JUST *FROZE*.
WHEN I LOOKED UP...
...GODA WAS...
...RIGHT THERE WAITING FOR ME.

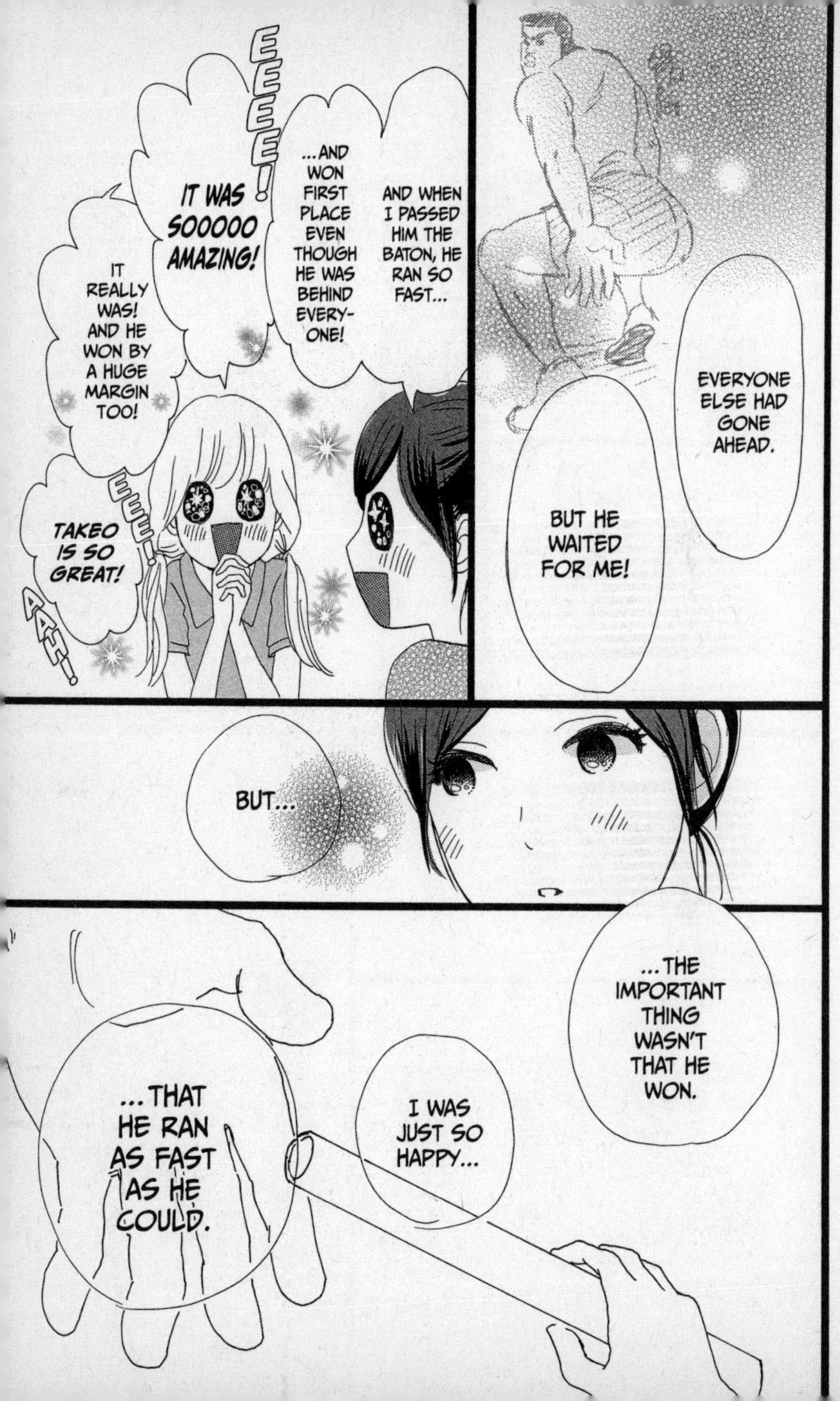
EVERYONE ELSE HAD GONE AHEAD.
BUT HE WAITED FOR ME!
AND WHEN I PASSED HIM THE BATON, HE RAN SO FAST...
...AND WON FIRST PLACE EVEN THOUGH HE WAS BEHIND EVERY-ONE!
EEEEE!
IT WAS SOOOOO AMAZING!
IT REALLY WAS! AND HE WON BY A HUGE MARGIN TOO!
EEE!
TAKEO IS SO GREAT!
AAH!
BUT...
...THE IMPORTANT THING WASN'T THAT HE WON.
I WAS JUST SO HAPPY...
...THAT HE RAN AS FAST AS HE COULD.

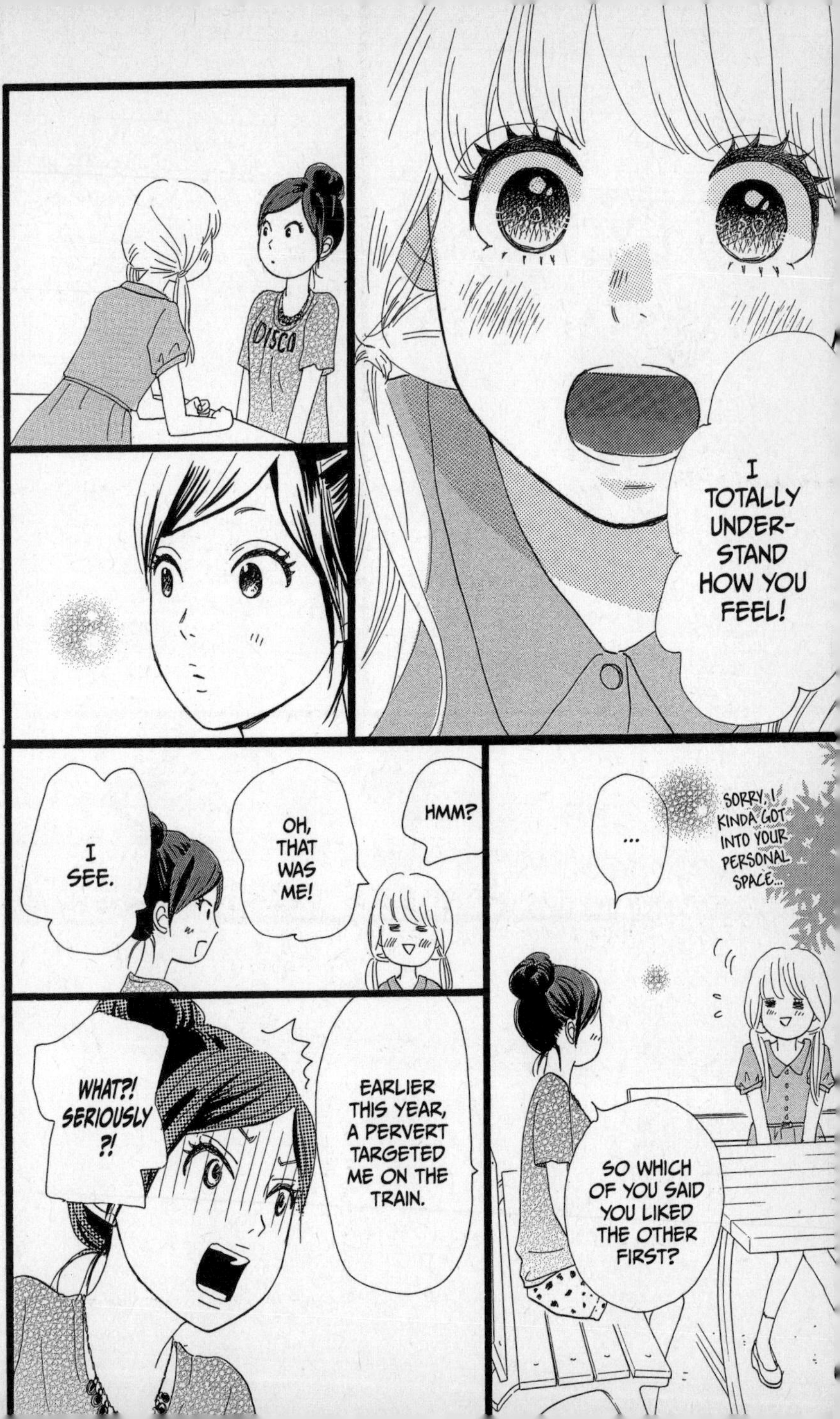
I TOTALLY UNDERSTAND HOW YOU FEEL!
SORRY, I KINDA GOT INTO YOUR PERSONAL SPACE...
...
SO WHICH OF YOU SAID YOU LIKED THE OTHER FIRST?
HMM?
OH, THAT WAS ME!
I SEE.
EARLIER THIS YEAR, A PERVERT TARGETED ME ON THE TRAIN.
WHAT?! SERIOUSLY?!

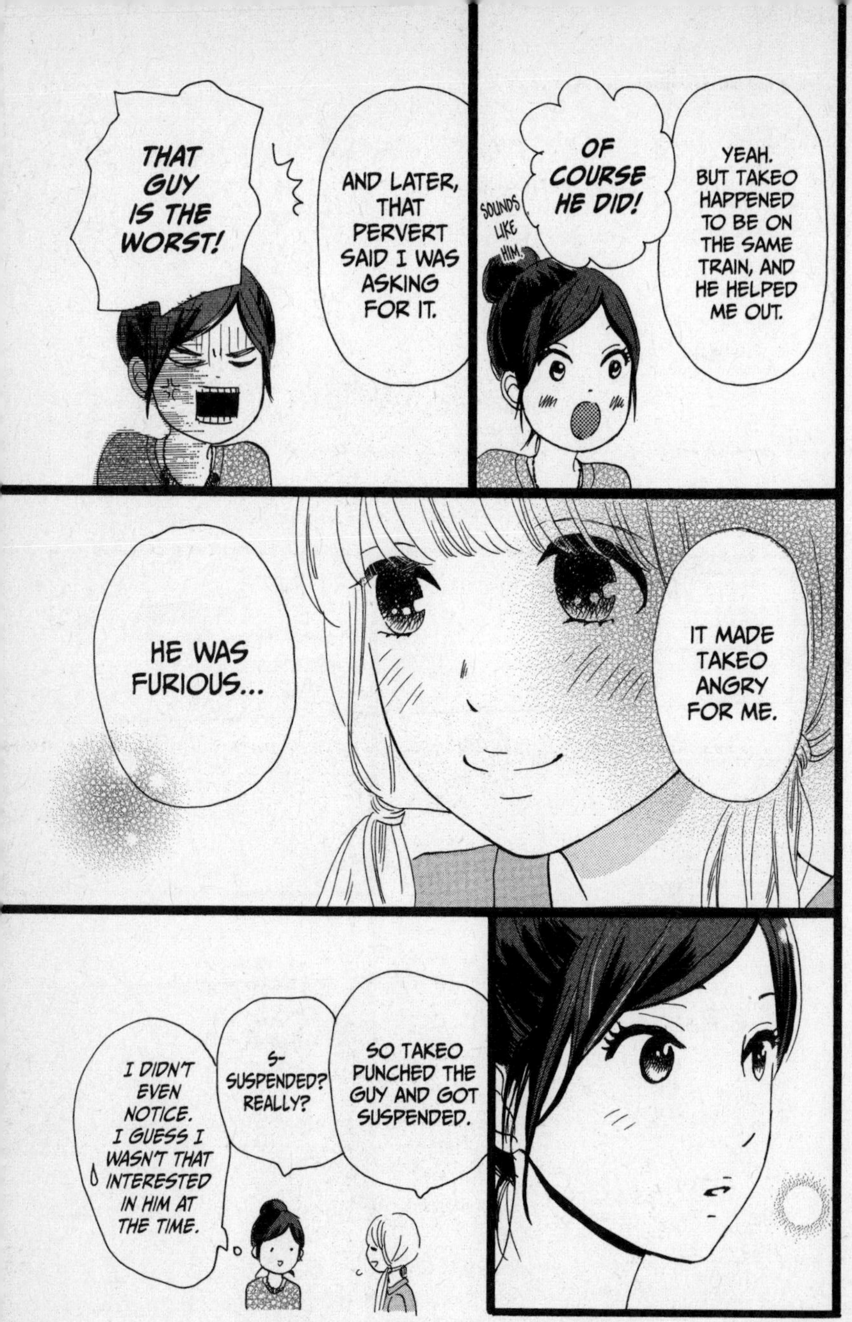
YEAH. BUT TAKEO HAPPENED TO BE ON THE SAME TRAIN, AND HE HELPED ME OUT.
OF COURSE HE DID!
SOUNDS LIKE HIM.
AND LATER, THAT PERVERT SAID I WAS ASKING FOR IT.
THAT GUY IS THE WORST!
IT MADE TAKEO ANGRY FOR ME.
HE WAS FURIOUS...
SO TAKEO PUNCHED THE GUY AND GOT SUSPENDED.
S-SUSPENDED? REALLY?
I DIDN'T EVEN NOTICE. I GUESS I WASN'T THAT INTERESTED IN HIM AT THE TIME.

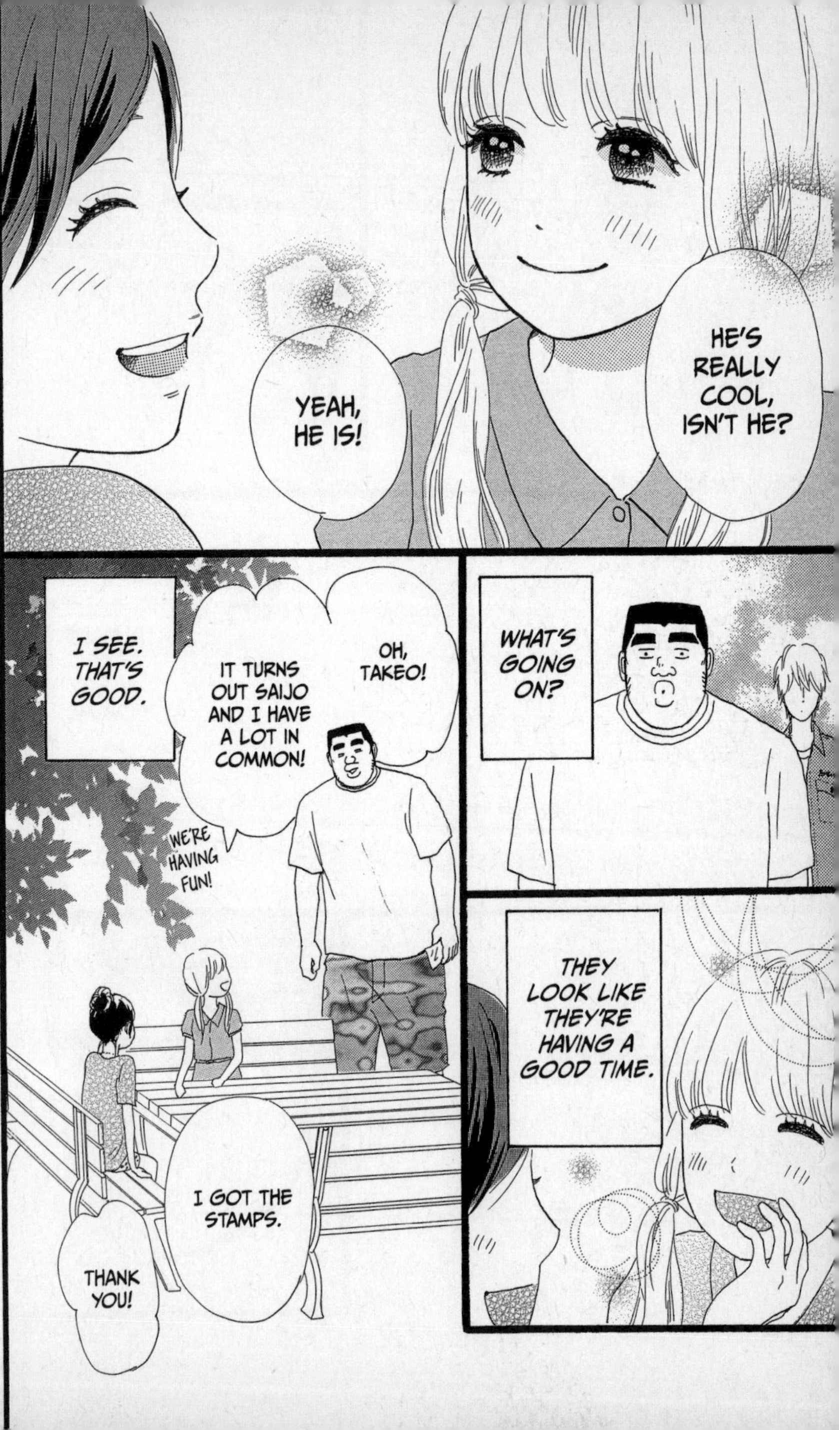
HE'S REALLY COOL, ISN'T HE?
YEAH, HE IS!
WHAT'S GOING ON?
THEY LOOK LIKE THEY'RE HAVING A GOOD TIME.
OH, TAKEO!
IT TURNS OUT SAIJO AND I HAVE A LOT IN COMMON!
WE'RE HAVING FUN!
I SEE. THAT'S GOOD.
I GOT THE STAMPS.
THANK YOU!

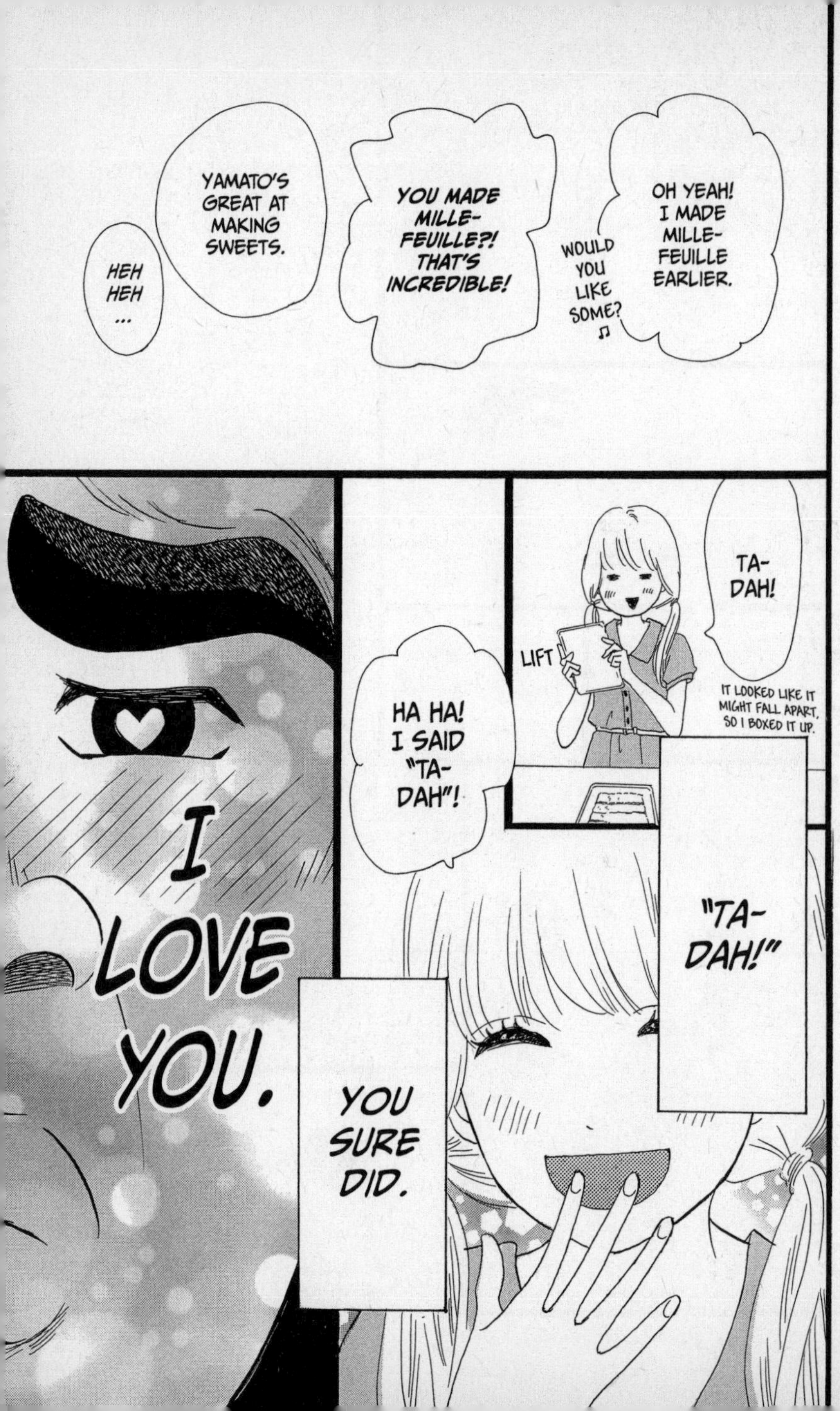
OH YEAH! I MADE MILLE-FEUILLE EARLIER.
WOULD YOU LIKE SOME? ♫
YOU MADE MILLE-FEUILLE?! THAT'S INCREDIBLE!
YAMATO'S GREAT AT MAKING SWEETS.
HEH HEH ...
TA-DAH!
LIFT
IT LOOKED LIKE IT MIGHT FALL APART, SO I BOXED IT UP.
HA HA! I SAID "TA-DAH"!
"TA-DAH!"
YOU SURE DID.
I LOVE YOU.

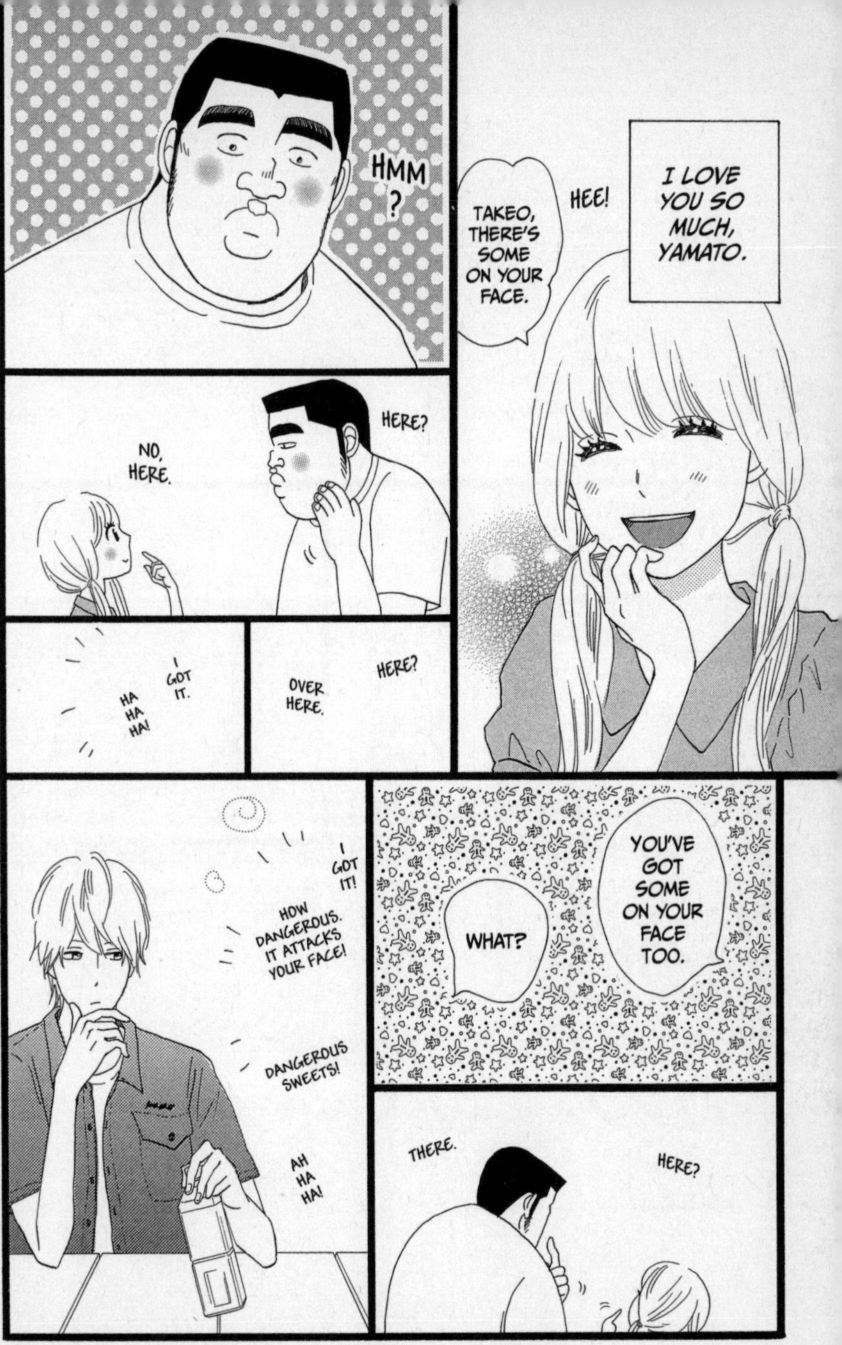
I LOVE YOU SO MUCH, YAMATO.
HEE!
TAKEO, THERE'S SOME ON YOUR FACE.
HMM ?
HERE?
NO, HERE.
HERE?
OVER HERE.
I GOT IT.
HA HA HA!
YOU'VE GOT SOME ON YOUR FACE TOO.
WHAT?
HERE?
THERE.
I GOT IT!
HOW DANGEROUS. IT ATTACKS YOUR FACE!
DANGEROUS SWEETS!
AH HA HA!

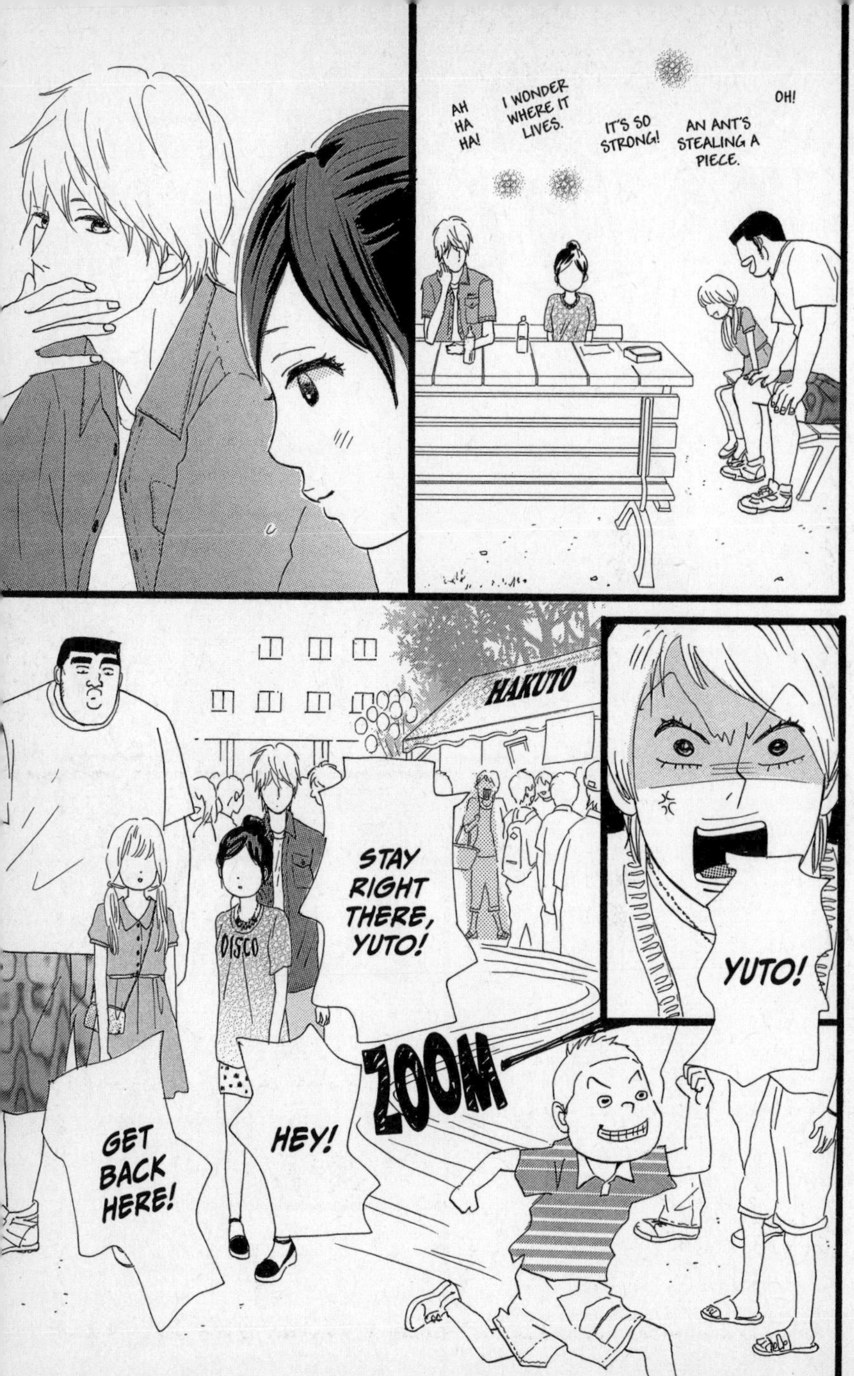
OH!
AN ANT'S STEALING A PIECE.
IT'S SO STRONG!
I WONDER WHERE IT LIVES.
AH HA HA!
YUTO!
HAKUTO
STAY RIGHT THERE, YUTO!
ZOOM
HEY!
GET BACK HERE!

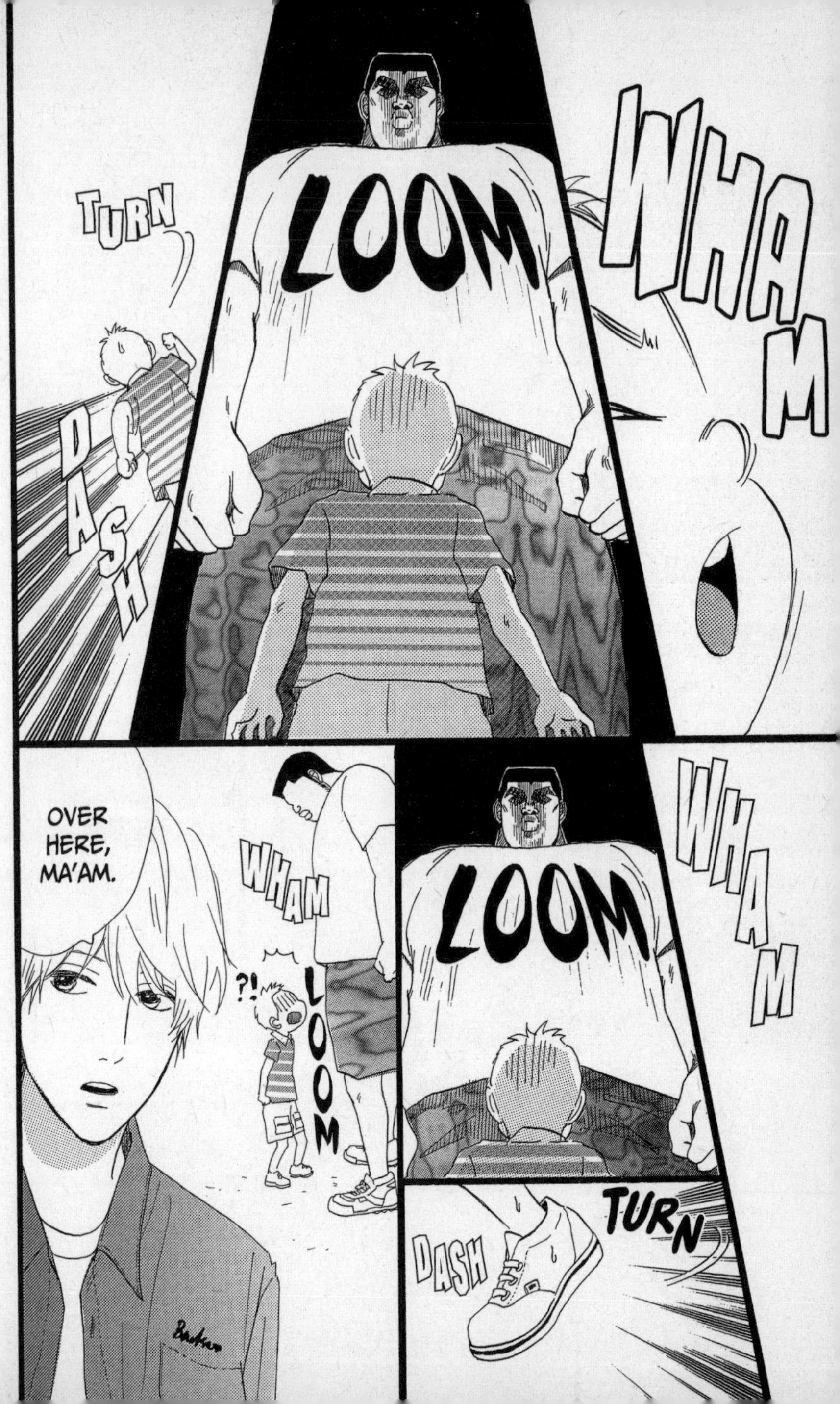
WHAM
LOOM
TURN
DASH
WHAM
LOOM
TURN
DASH
WHAM
?!
LOOM
OVER HERE, MA'AM.

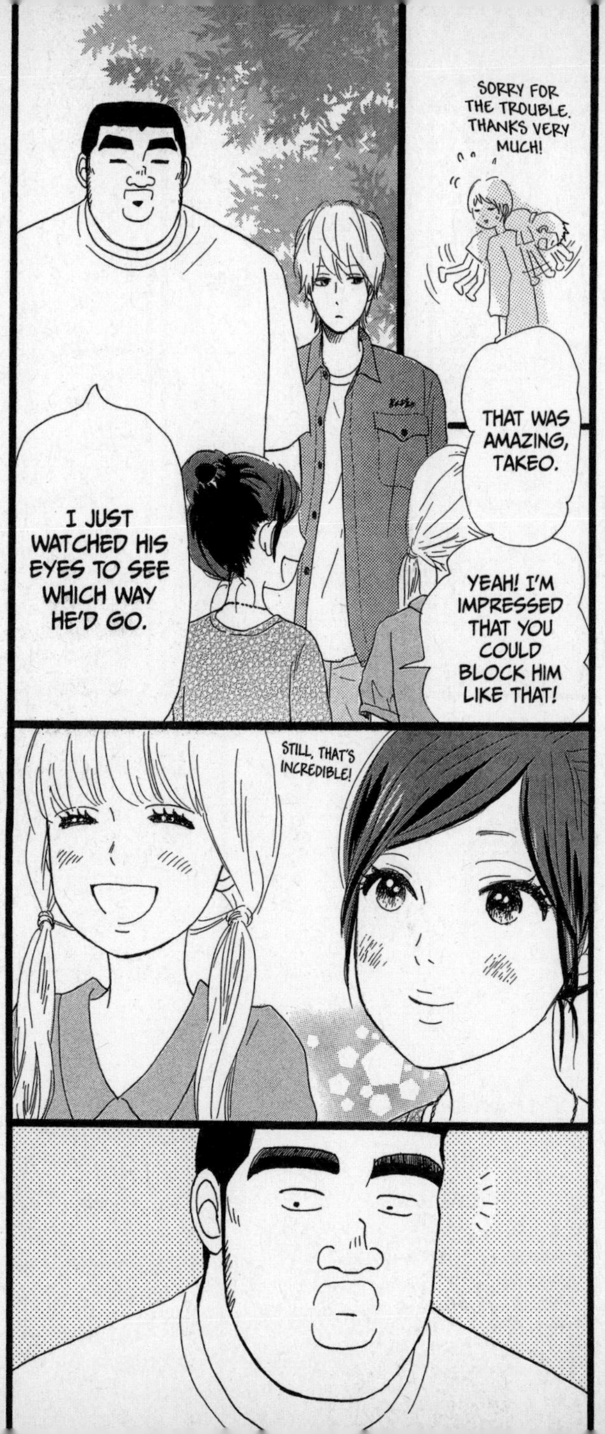
SORRY FOR THE TROUBLE. THANKS VERY MUCH!
THAT WAS AMAZING, TAKEO.
YEAH! I'M IMPRESSED THAT YOU COULD BLOCK HIM LIKE THAT!
I JUST WATCHED HIS EYES TO SEE WHICH WAY HE'D GO.
STILL, THAT'S INCREDIBLE!

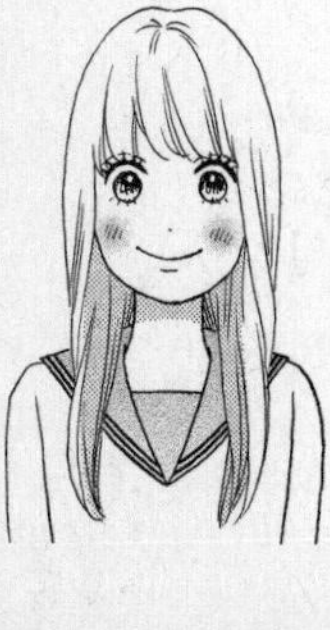

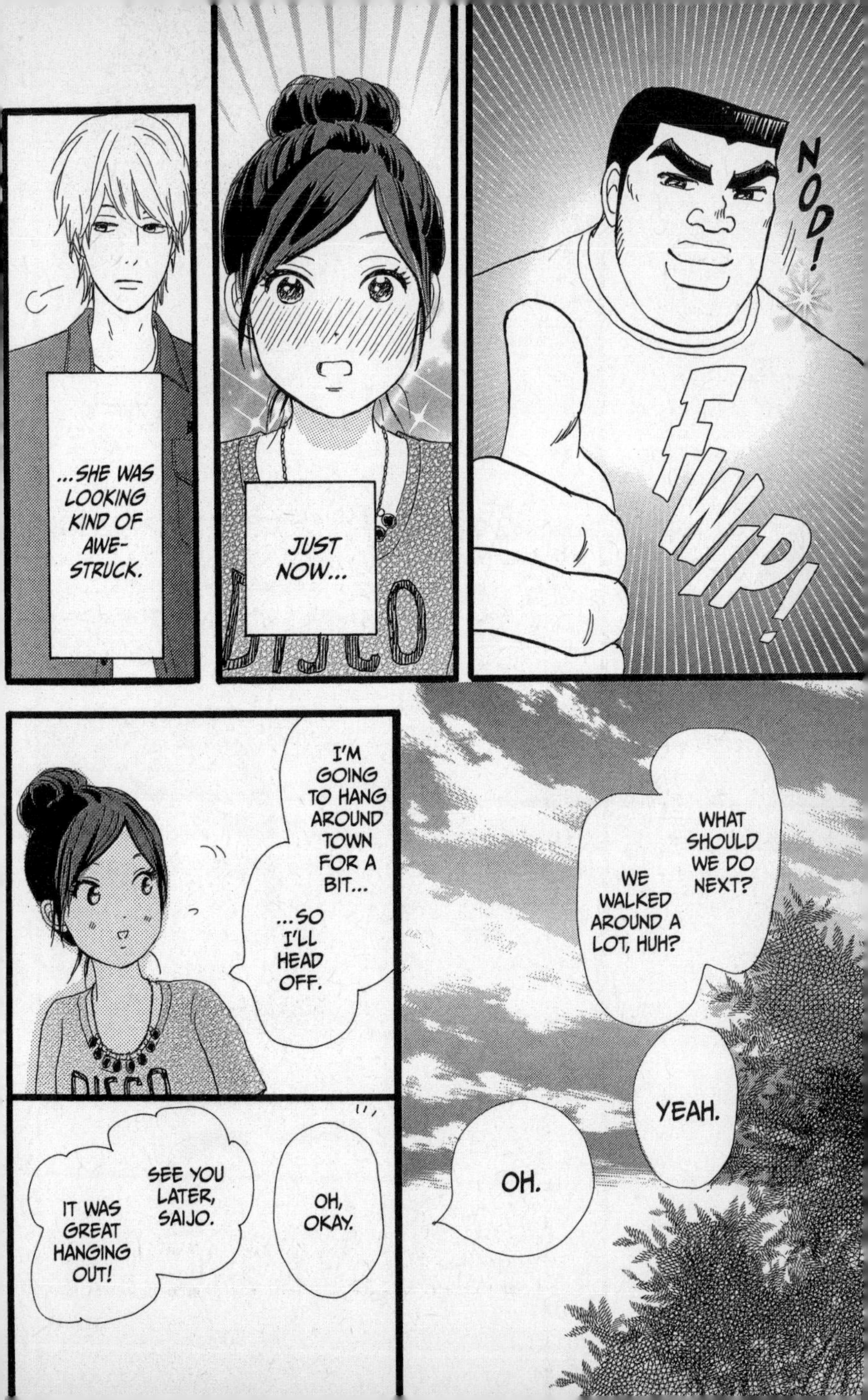
NOD!
FWIP!
JUST NOW...
...SHE WAS LOOKING KIND OF AWE-STRUCK.
WHAT SHOULD WE DO NEXT?
WE WALKED AROUND A LOT, HUH?
YEAH.
OH.
I'M GOING TO HANG AROUND TOWN FOR A BIT...
...SO I'LL HEAD OFF.
OH, OKAY.
SEE YOU LATER, SAIJO.
IT WAS GREAT HANGING OUT!

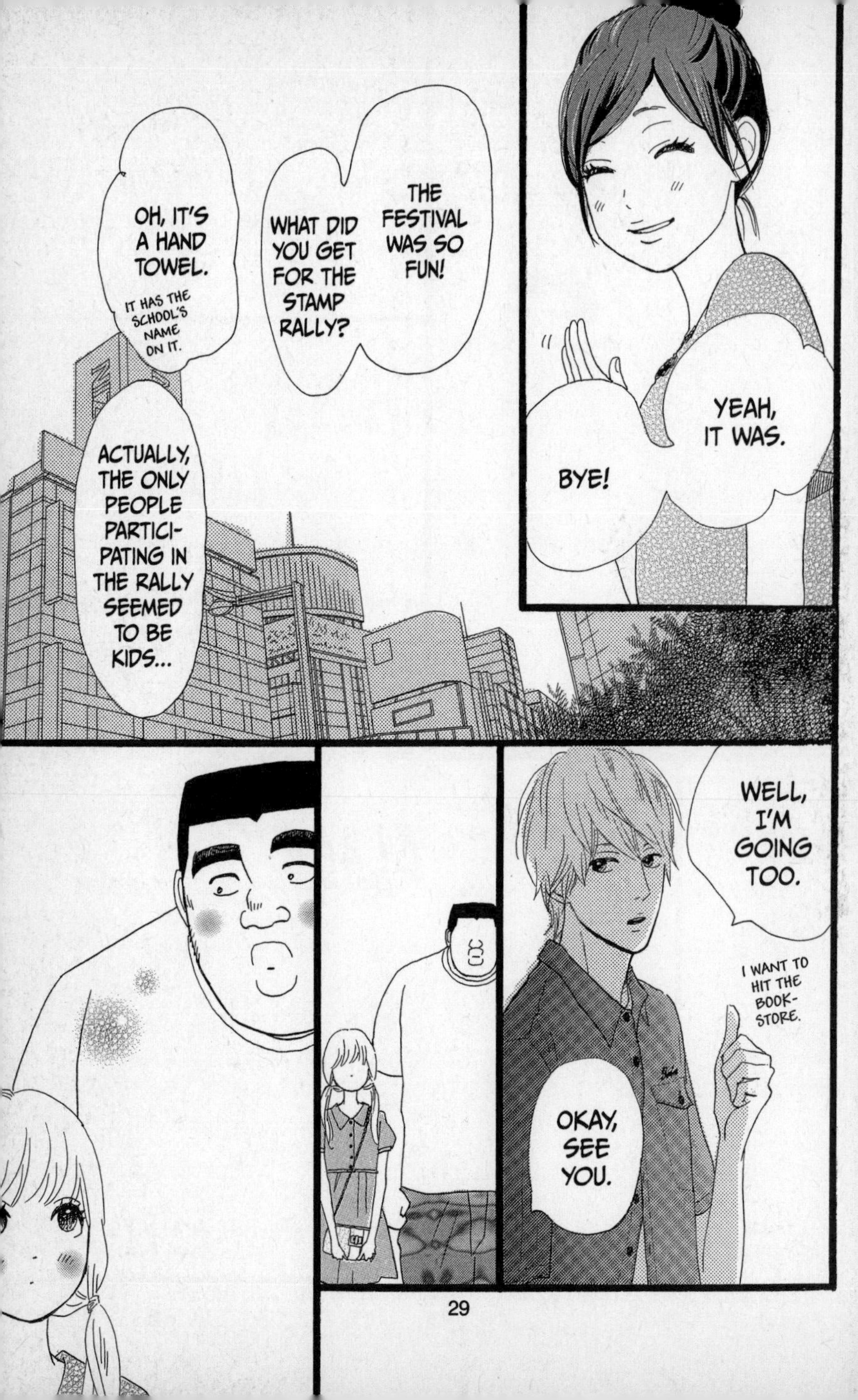
YEAH, IT WAS.
BYE!
THE FESTIVAL WAS SO FUN!
WHAT DID YOU GET FOR THE STAMP RALLY?
OH, IT'S A HAND TOWEL.
IT HAS THE SCHOOL'S NAME ON IT.
ACTUALLY, THE ONLY PEOPLE PARTICI-PATING IN THE RALLY SEEMED TO BE KIDS...
WELL, I'M GOING TOO.
I WANT TO HIT THE BOOK-STORE.
OKAY, SEE YOU.

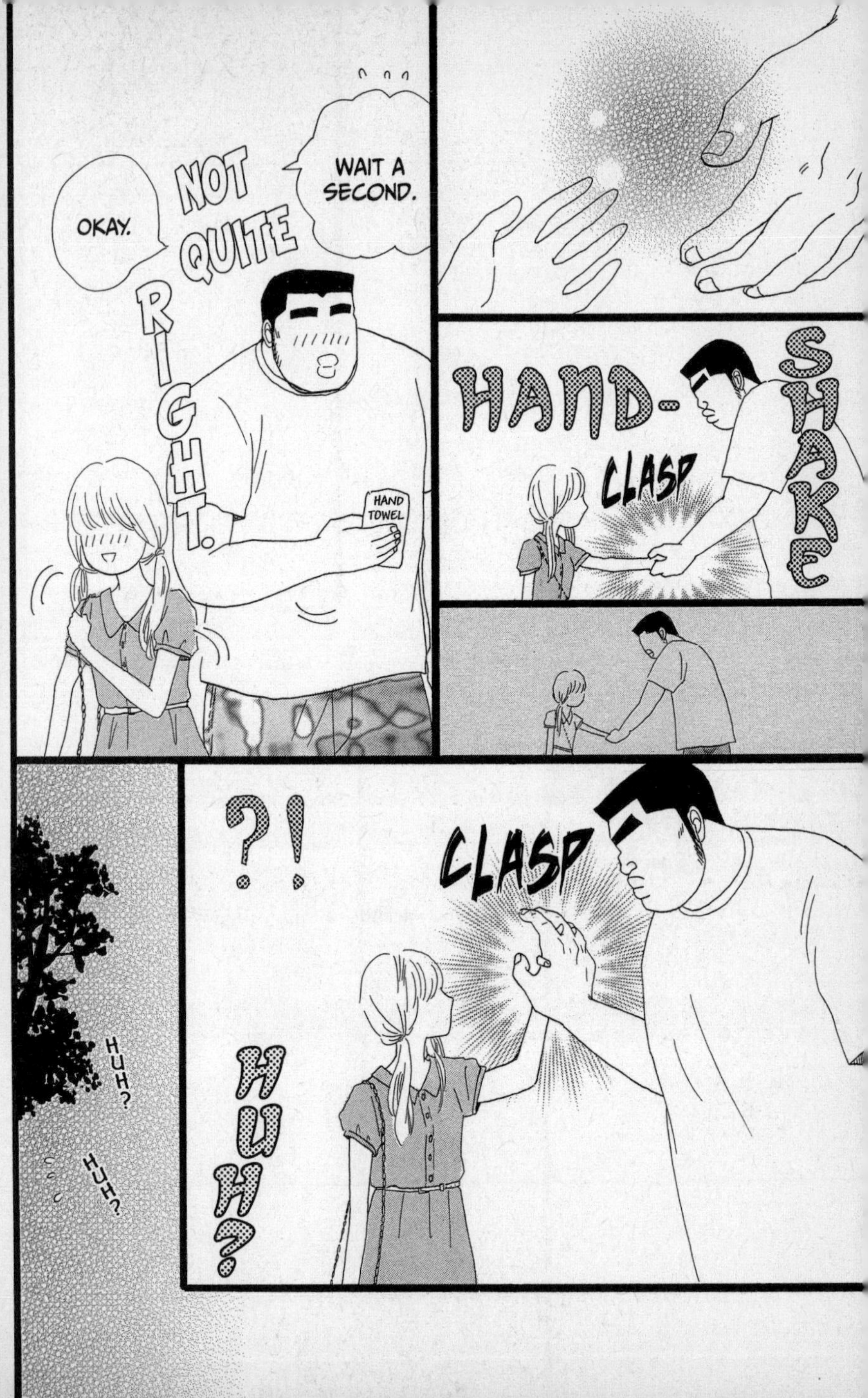
HAND-SHAKE
CLASP
WAIT A SECOND.
NOT QUITE RIGHT.
OKAY.
HAND TOWEL
CLASP
?!
HUH?
HUH?
HUH?

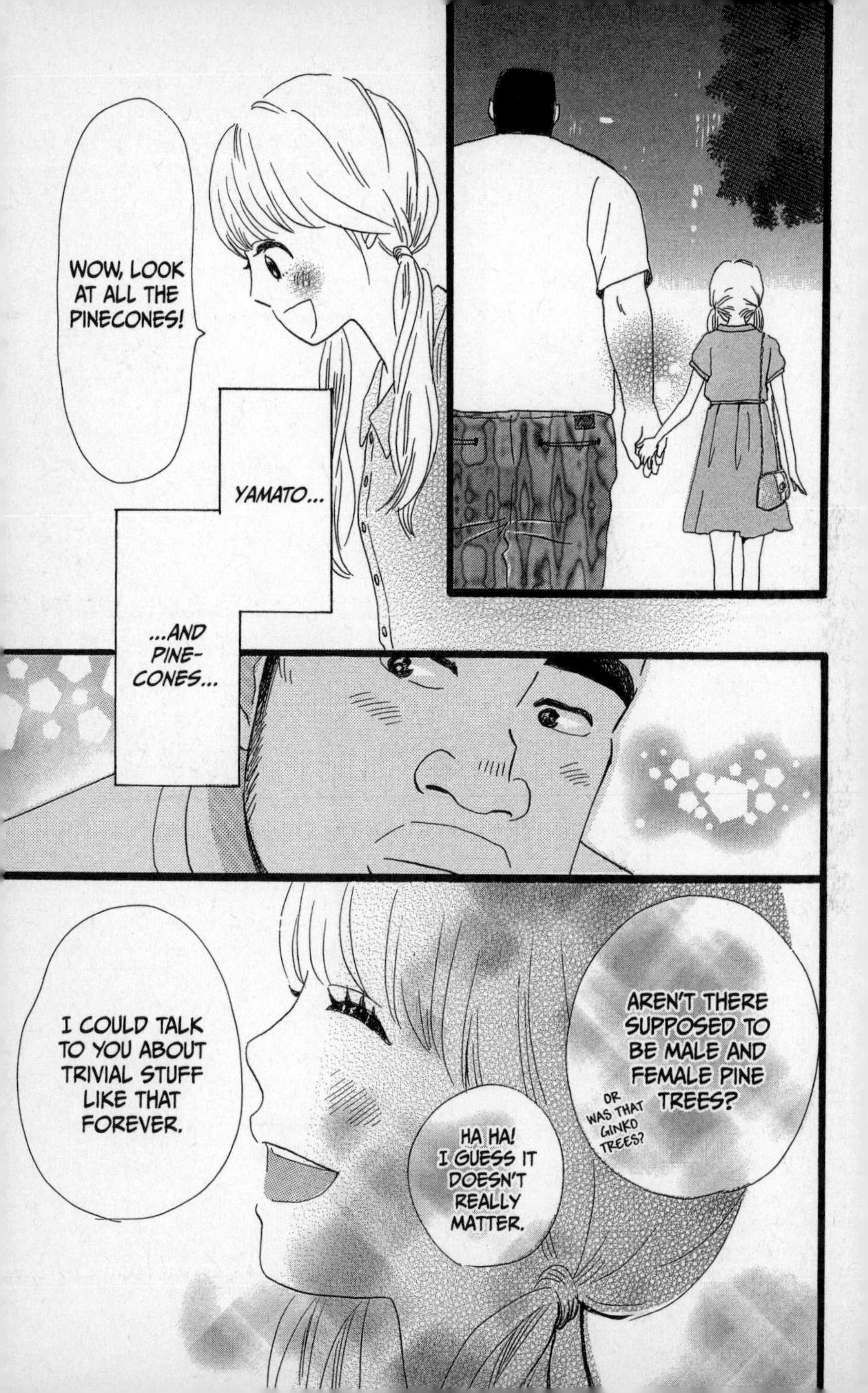
WOW, LOOK AT ALL THE PINECONES!
YAMATO...
...AND PINE-CONES...
AREN'T THERE SUPPOSED TO BE MALE AND FEMALE PINE TREES?
OR WAS THAT GINKO TREES?
HA HA! I GUESS IT DOESN'T REALLY MATTER.
I COULD TALK TO YOU ABOUT TRIVIAL STUFF LIKE THAT FOREVER.

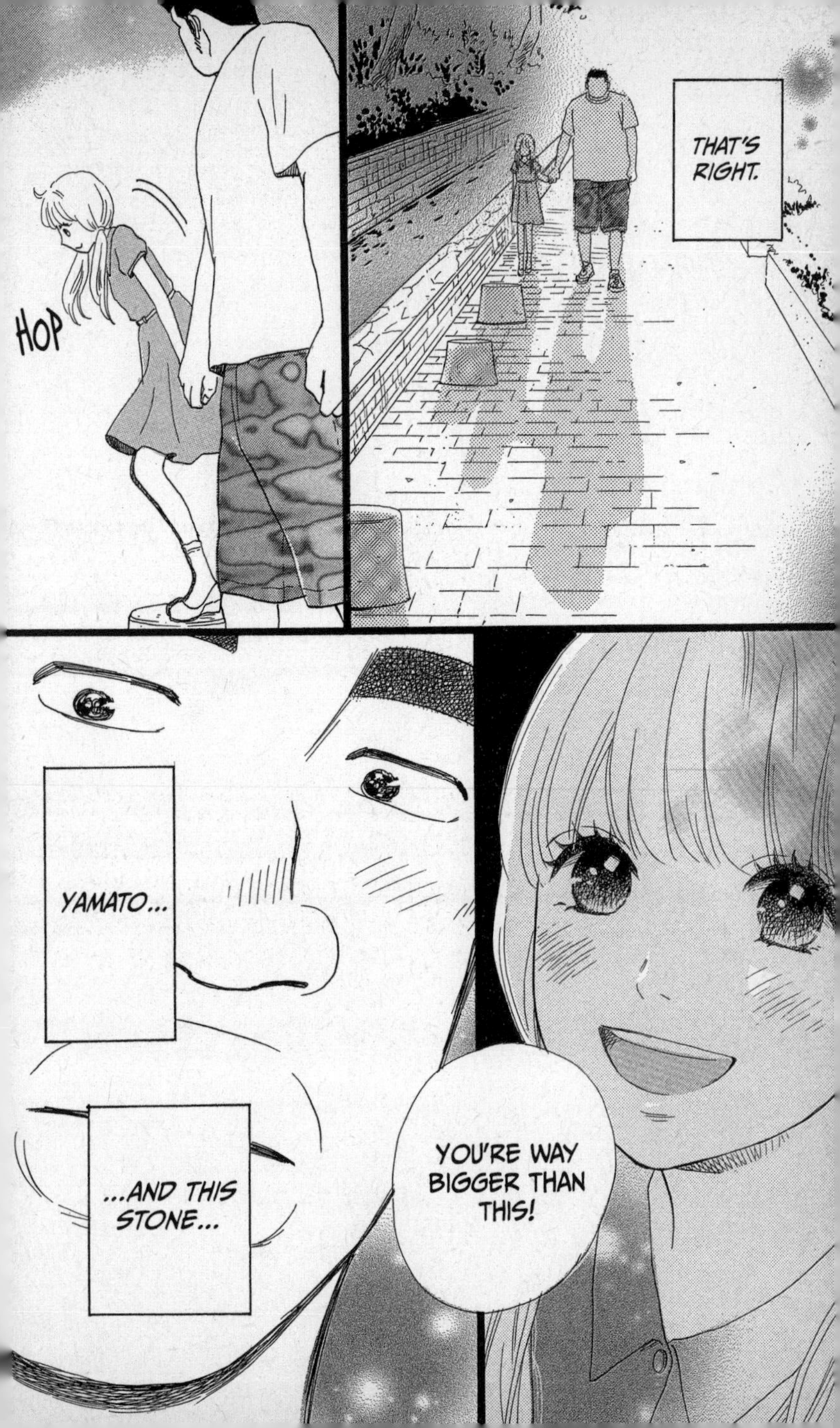
THAT'S RIGHT.
HOP
YOU'RE WAY BIGGER THAN THIS!
YAMATO...
...AND THIS STONE...

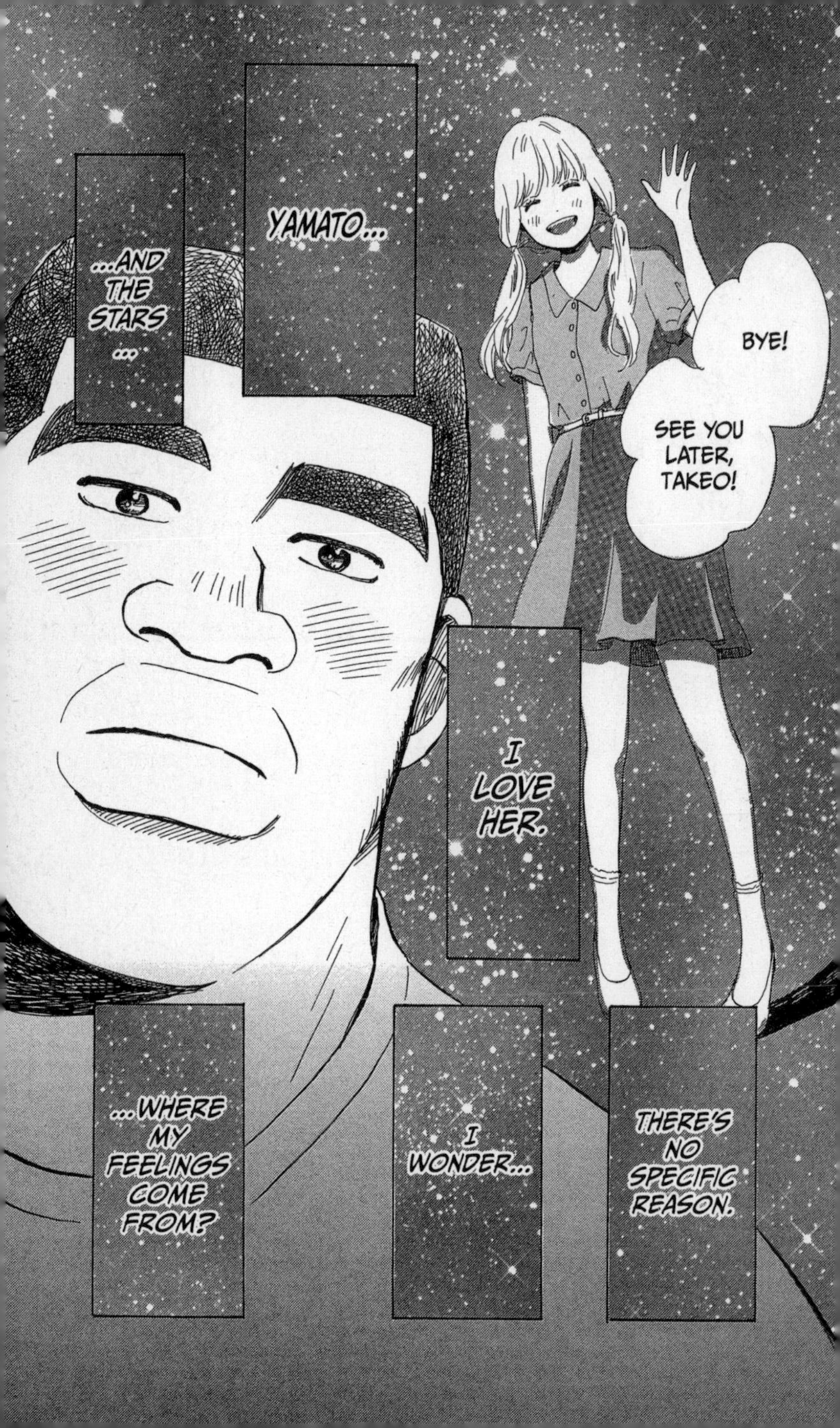
BYE!
SEE YOU LATER, TAKEO!
YAMATO...
...AND THE STARS...
I LOVE HER.
THERE'S NO SPECIFIC REASON.
I WONDER...
...WHERE MY FEELINGS COME FROM?

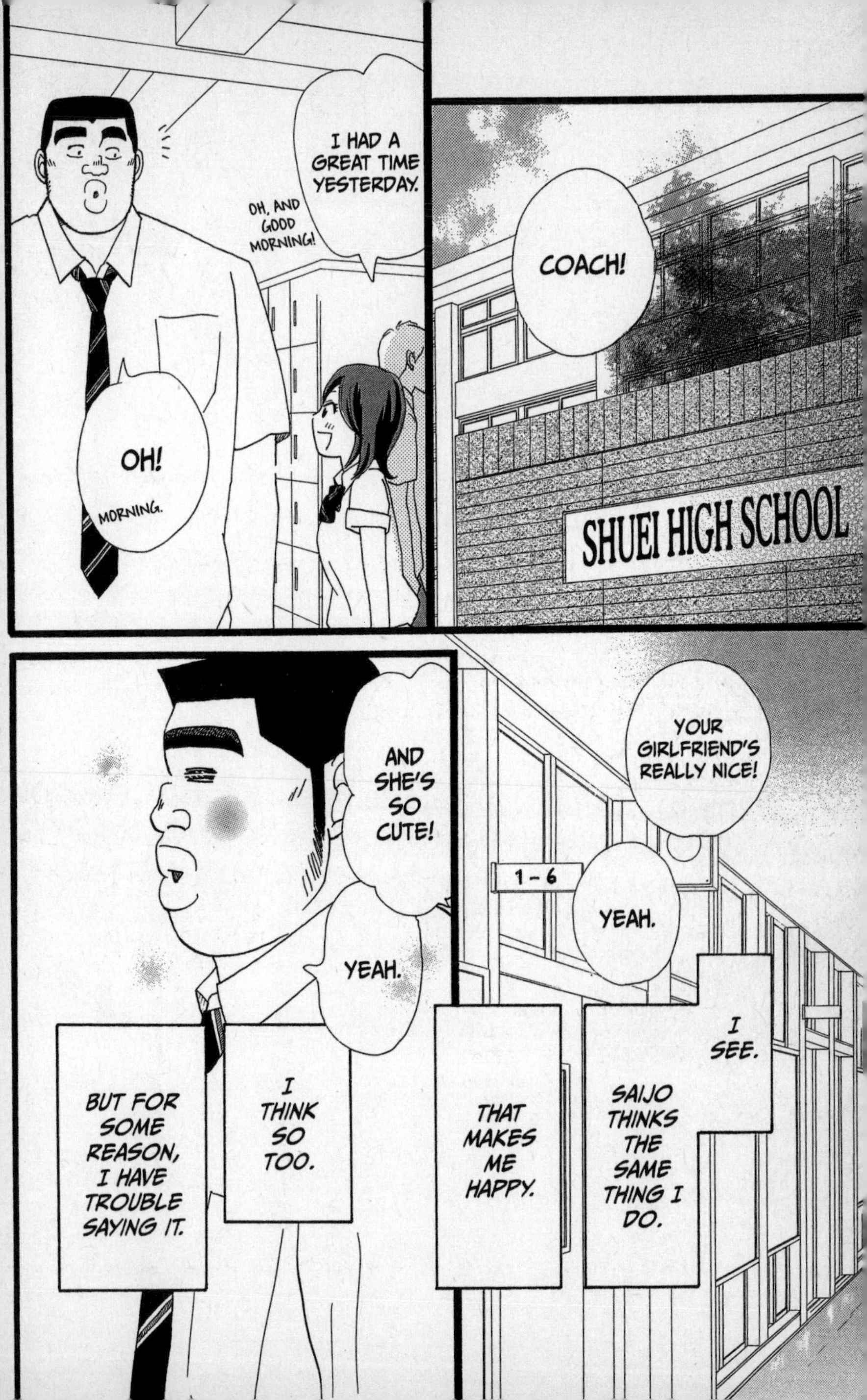
COACH!
SHUEI HIGH SCHOOL
I HAD A GREAT TIME YESTERDAY.
OH, AND GOOD MORNING!
OH!
MORNING.
YOUR GIRLFRIEND'S REALLY NICE!
1-6
YEAH.
I SEE.
SAIJO THINKS THE SAME THING I DO.
THAT MAKES ME HAPPY.
AND SHE'S SO CUTE!
YEAH.
I THINK SO TOO.
BUT FOR SOME REASON, I HAVE TROUBLE SAYING IT.

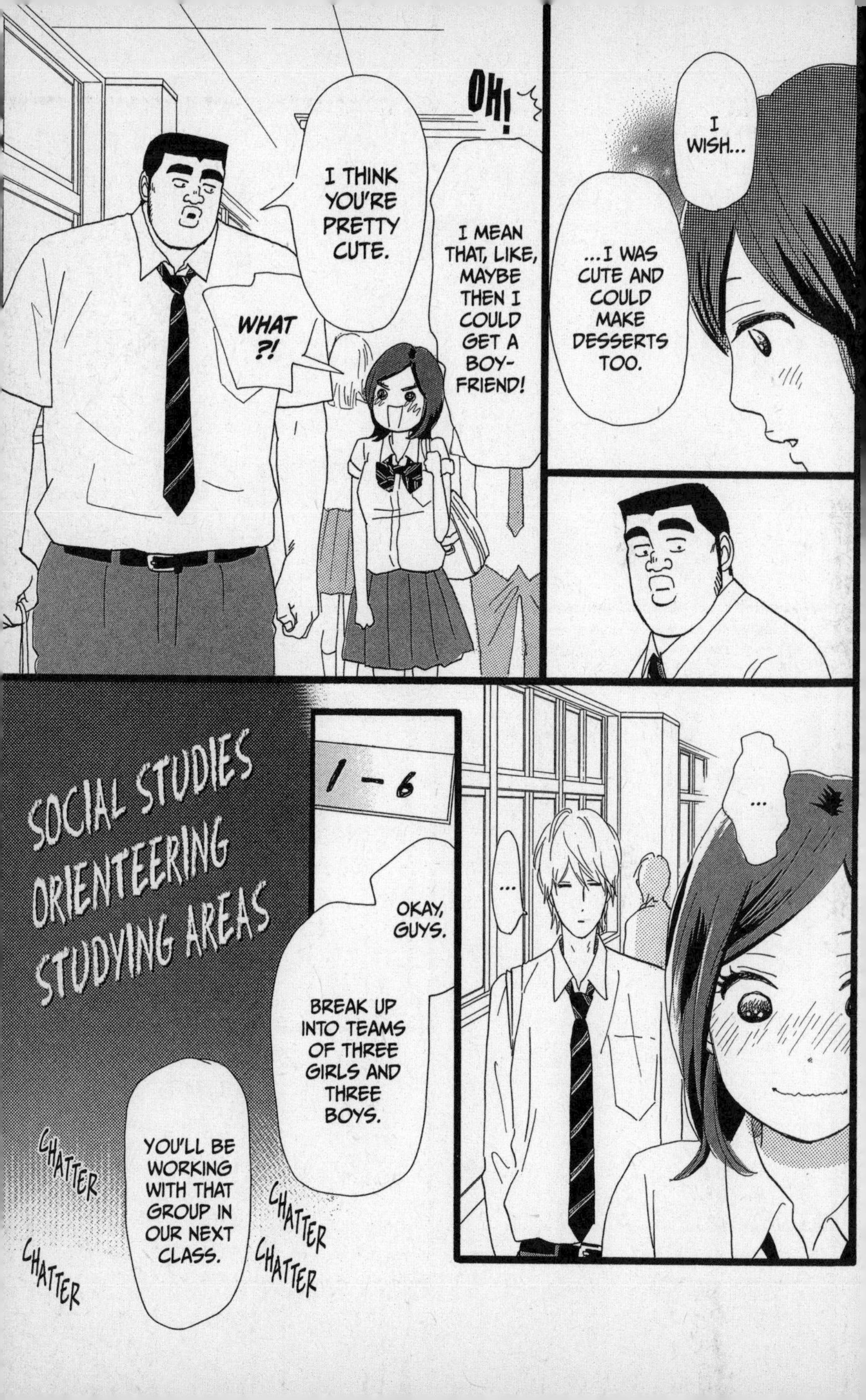
I WISH...
...I WAS CUTE AND COULD MAKE DESSERTS TOO.
OH!
I MEAN THAT, LIKE, MAYBE THEN I COULD GET A BOY-FRIEND!
I THINK YOU'RE PRETTY CUTE.
WHAT ?!
...
1-6
...
OKAY, GUYS.
BREAK UP INTO TEAMS OF THREE GIRLS AND THREE BOYS.
SOCIAL STUDIES ORIENTEERING STUDYING AREAS
YOU'LL BE WORKING WITH THAT GROUP IN OUR NEXT CLASS.
CHATTER
CHATTER
CHATTER
CHATTER

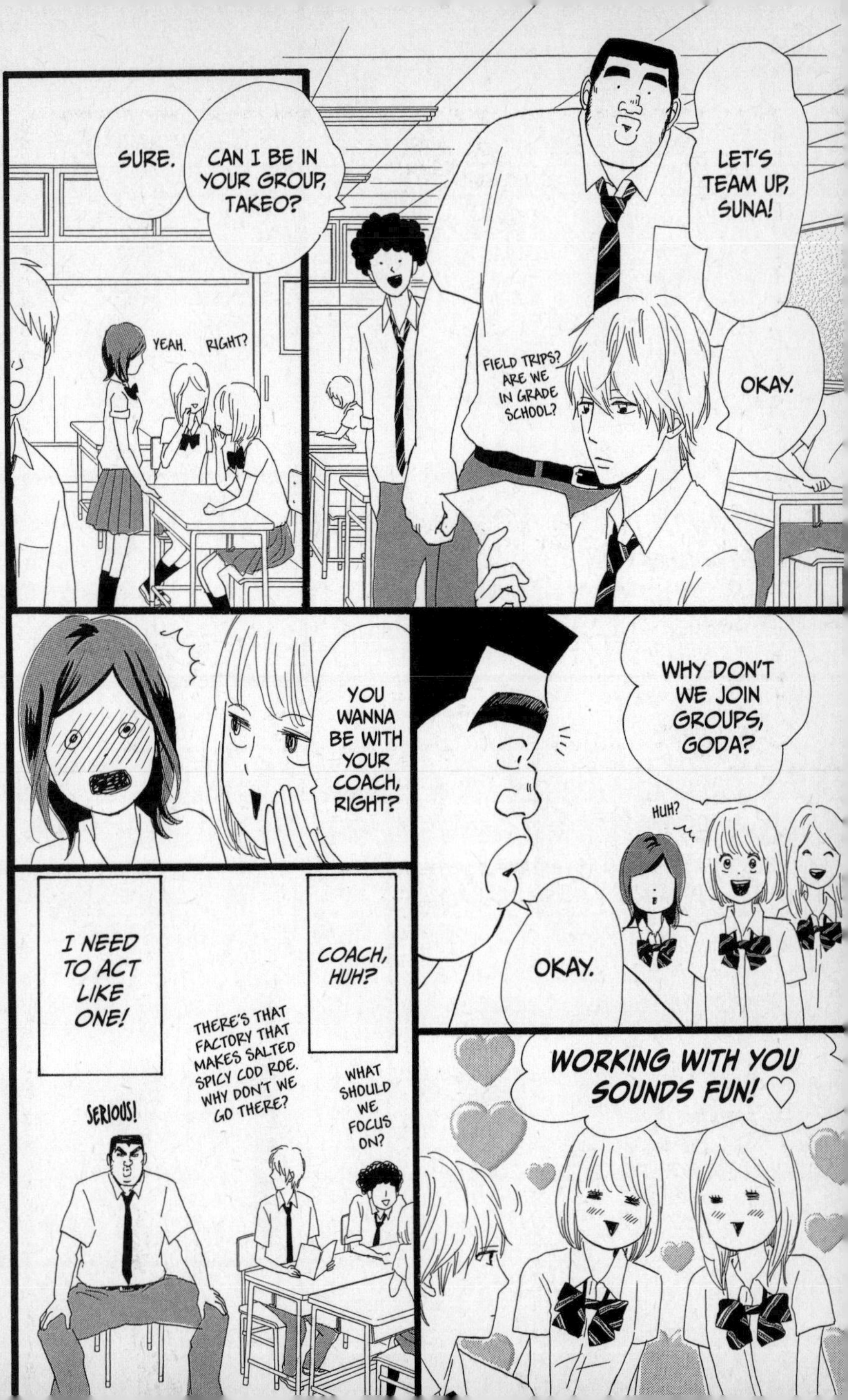
LET'S TEAM UP, SUNA!
OKAY.
FIELD TRIPS? ARE WE IN GRADE SCHOOL?
CAN I BE IN YOUR GROUP, TAKEO?
SURE.
RIGHT?
YEAH.
WHY DON'T WE JOIN GROUPS, GODA?
HUH?
OKAY.
WORKING WITH YOU SOUNDS FUN! ♡
YOU WANNA BE WITH YOUR COACH, RIGHT?
COACH, HUH?
I NEED TO ACT LIKE ONE!
WHAT SHOULD WE FOCUS ON?
THERE'S THAT FACTORY THAT MAKES SALTED SPICY COD ROE. WHY DON'T WE GO THERE?
SERIOUS!

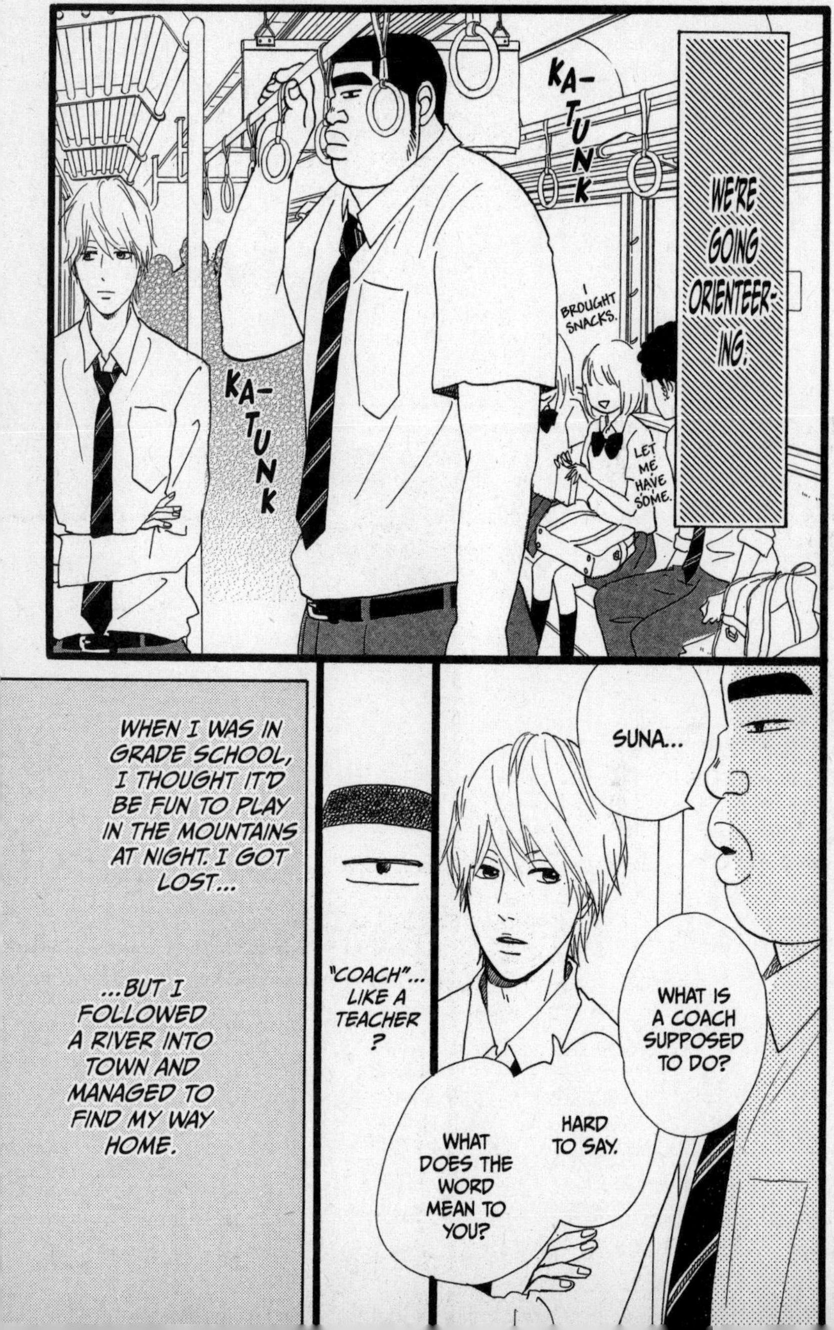
WE'RE GOING ORIENTEER-ING.
KA-TUNK
I BROUGHT SNACKS.
LET ME HAVE SOME.
KA-TUNK
SUNA...
WHAT IS A COACH SUPPOSED TO DO?
HARD TO SAY.
WHAT DOES THE WORD MEAN TO YOU?
"COACH"... LIKE A TEACHER?
WHEN I WAS IN GRADE SCHOOL, I THOUGHT IT'D BE FUN TO PLAY IN THE MOUNTAINS AT NIGHT. I GOT LOST...
...BUT I FOLLOWED A RIVER INTO TOWN AND MANAGED TO FIND MY WAY HOME.

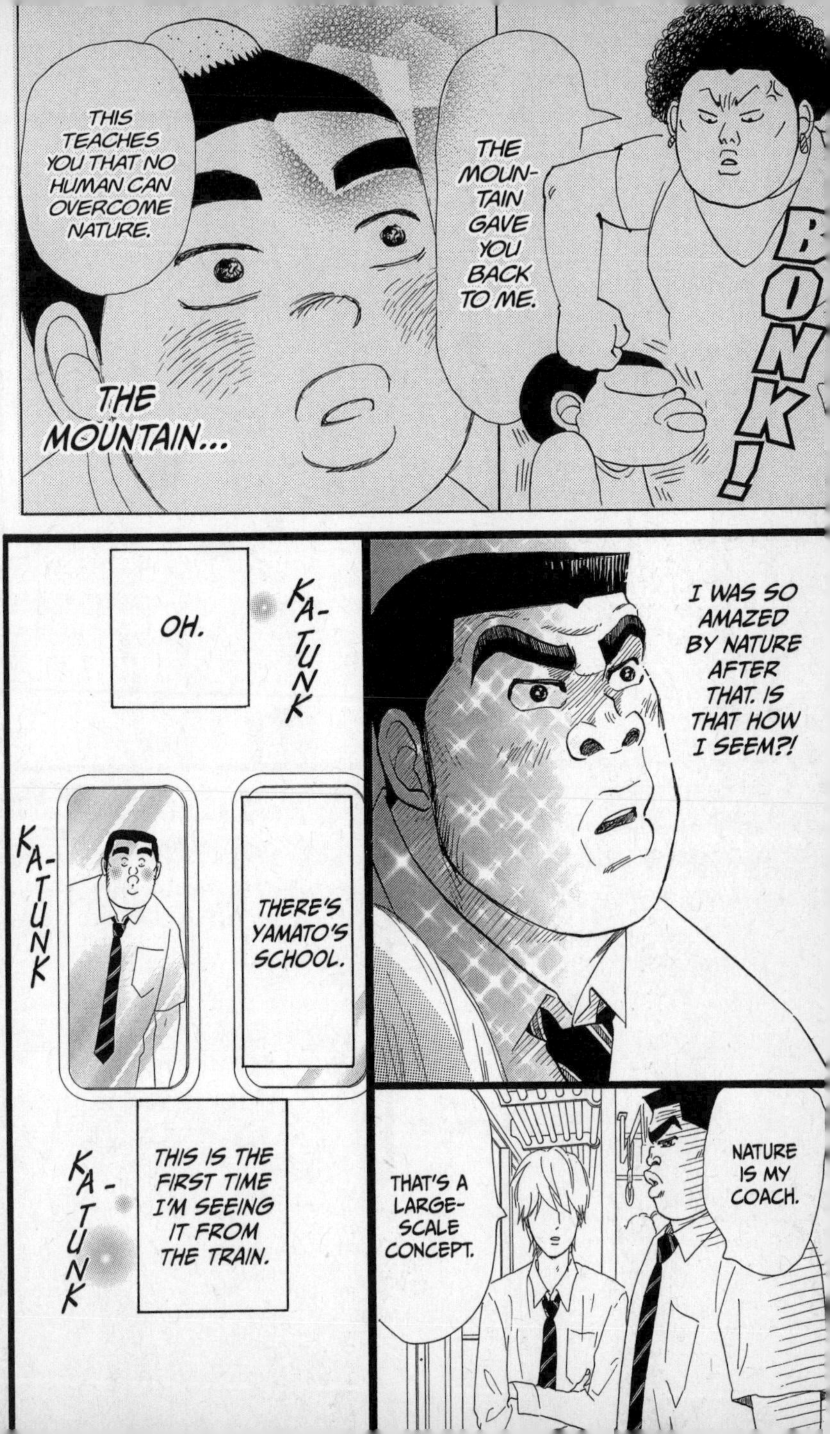
THE MOUNTAIN GAVE YOU BACK TO ME.
BONK!
THIS TEACHES YOU THAT NO HUMAN CAN OVERCOME NATURE.
THE MOUNTAIN...
I WAS SO AMAZED BY NATURE AFTER THAT. IS THAT HOW I SEEM?!
NATURE IS MY COACH.
THAT'S A LARGE-SCALE CONCEPT.
KA-TUNK
OH.
THERE'S YAMATO'S SCHOOL.
KA-TUNK
KA-TUNK
THIS IS THE FIRST TIME I'M SEEING IT FROM THE TRAIN.

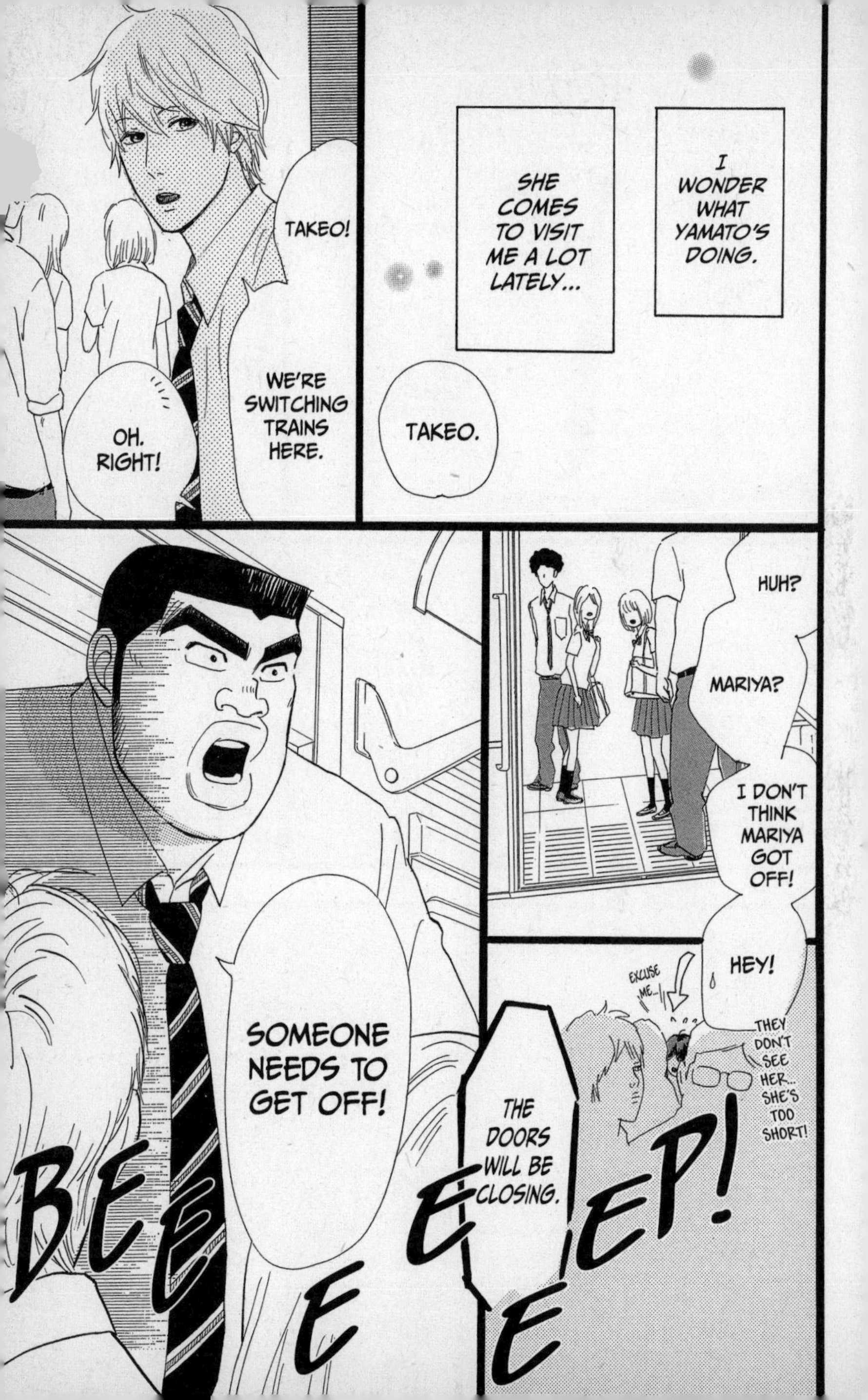
I WONDER WHAT YAMATO'S DOING.
SHE COMES TO VISIT ME A LOT LATELY...
TAKEO.
TAKEO!
WE'RE SWITCHING TRAINS HERE.
OH. RIGHT!
HUH?
MARIYA?
I DON'T THINK MARIYA GOT OFF!
HEY!
EXCUSE ME...
THEY DON'T SEE HER... SHE'S TOO SHORT!
THE DOORS WILL BE CLOSING.
SOMEONE NEEDS TO GET OFF!
BEEEEEEP!

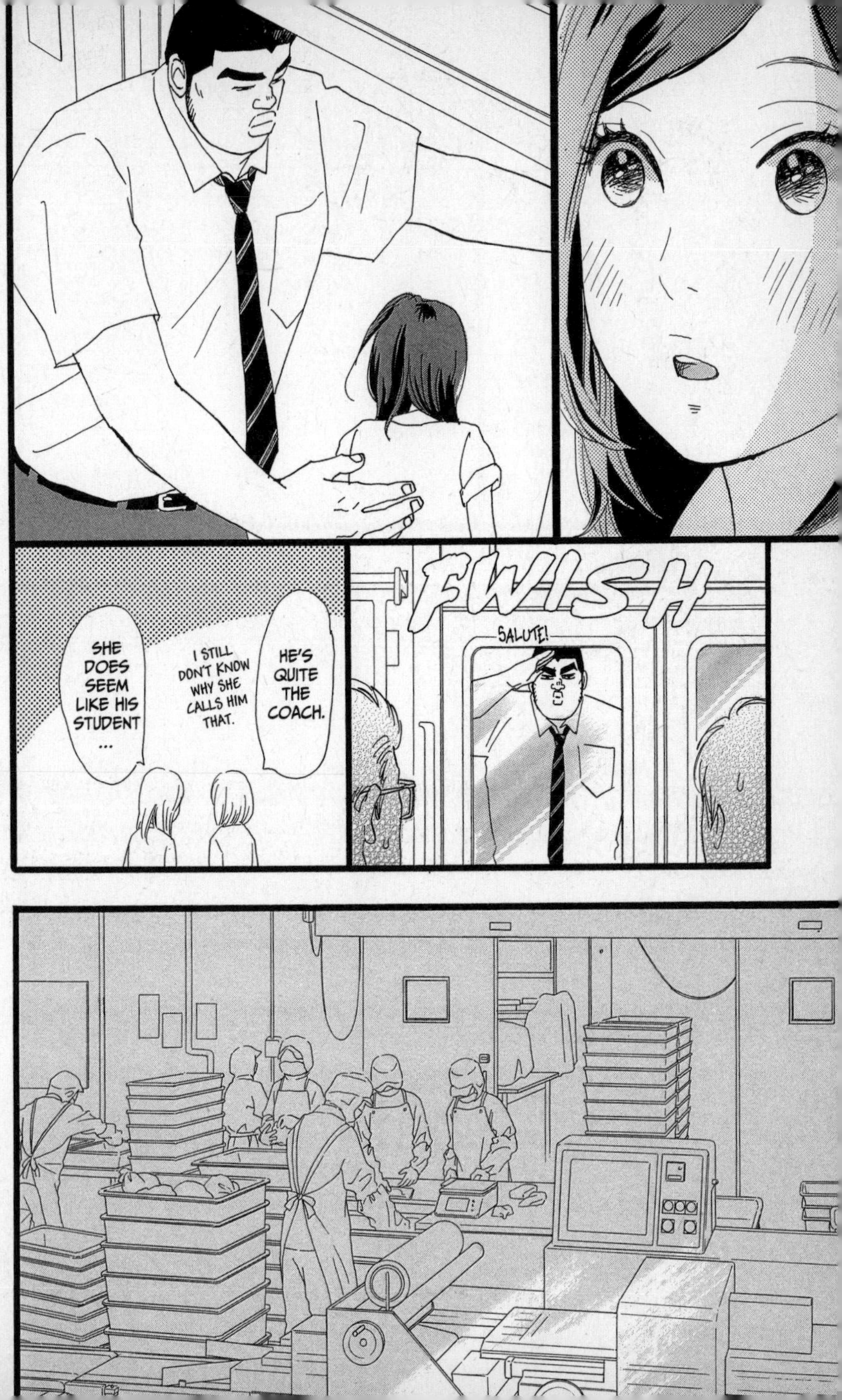
FWISH
SALUTE!
HE'S QUITE THE COACH.
I STILL DON'T KNOW WHY SHE CALLS HIM THAT.
SHE DOES SEEM LIKE HIS STUDENT ...

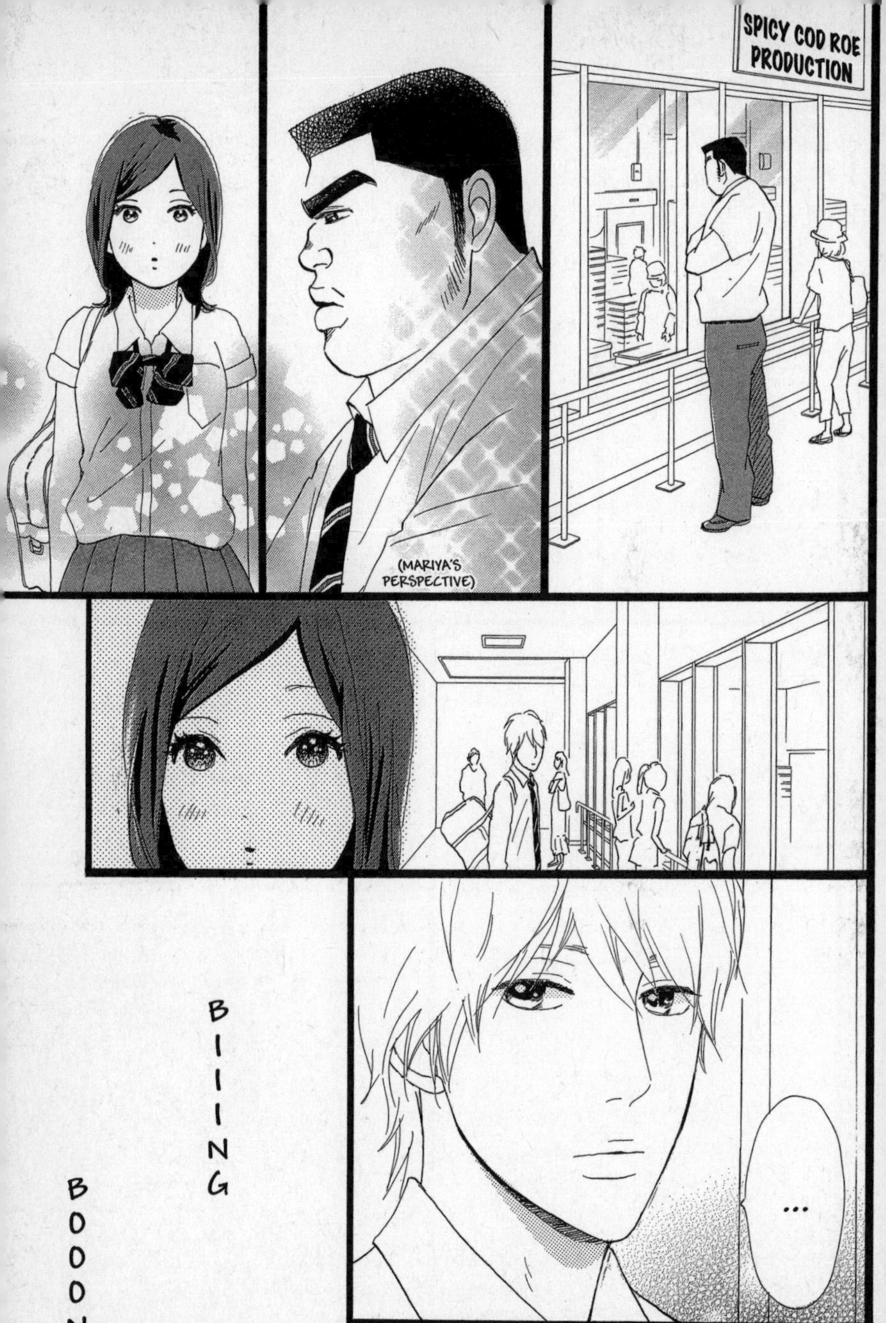
SPICY COD ROE PRODUCTION
(MARIYA'S PERSPECTIVE)
...
BIIING
BOOONG

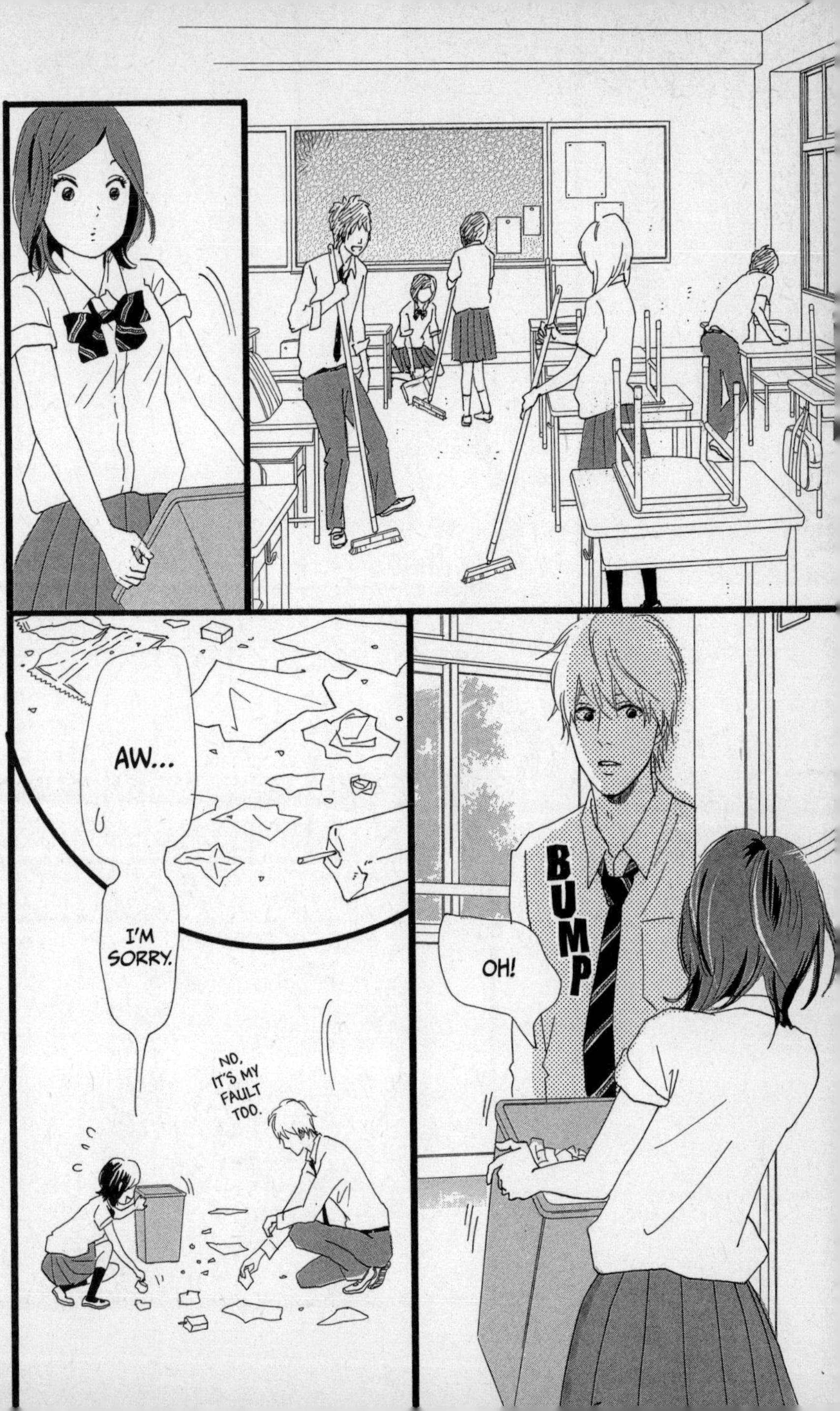
BUMP
OH!
AW...
I'M SORRY.
NO, IT'S MY FAULT TOO.

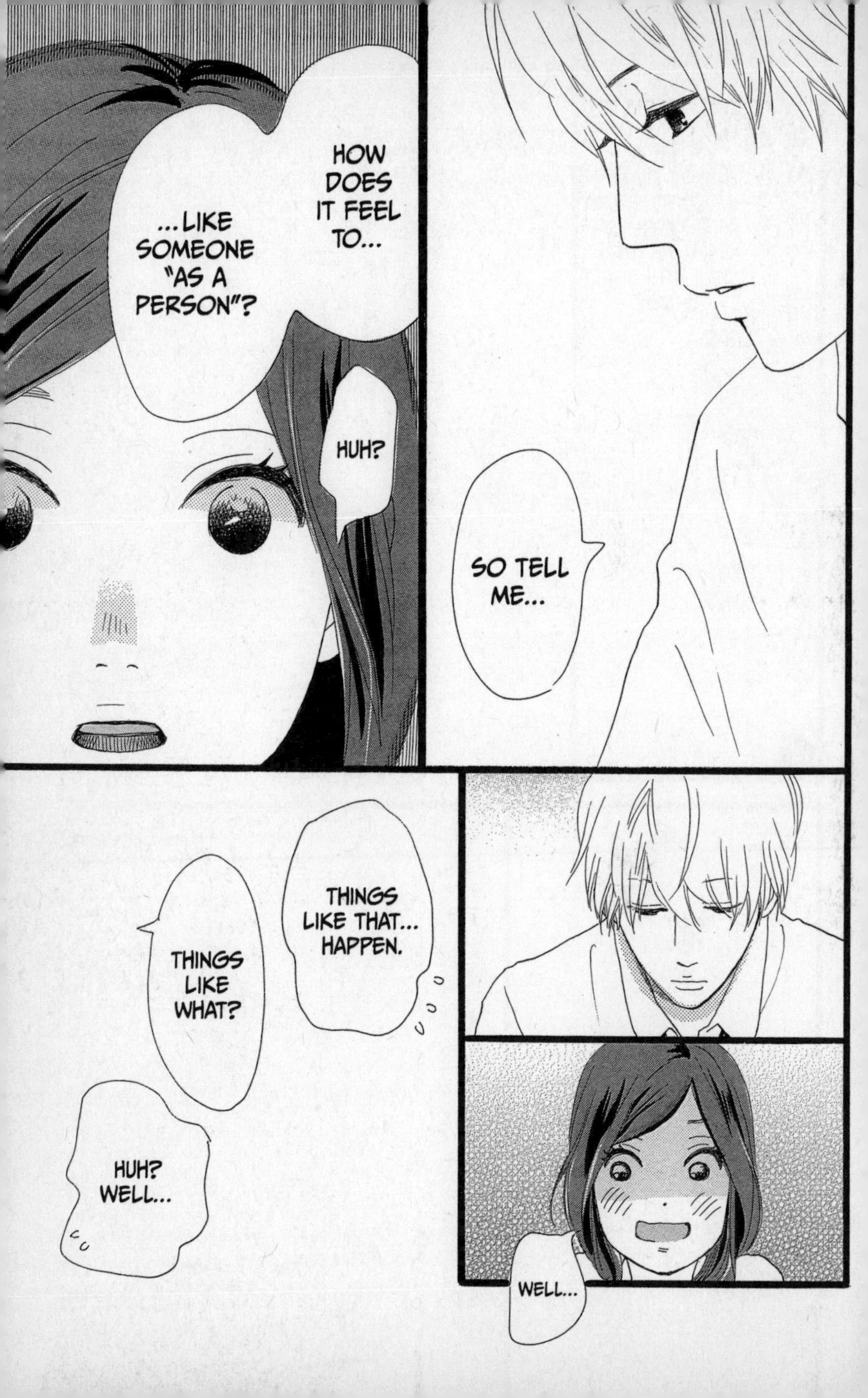
SO TELL ME...
HOW DOES IT FEEL TO...
...LIKE SOMEONE "AS A PERSON"?
HUH?
WELL...
THINGS LIKE THAT... HAPPEN.
THINGS LIKE WHAT?
HUH? WELL...

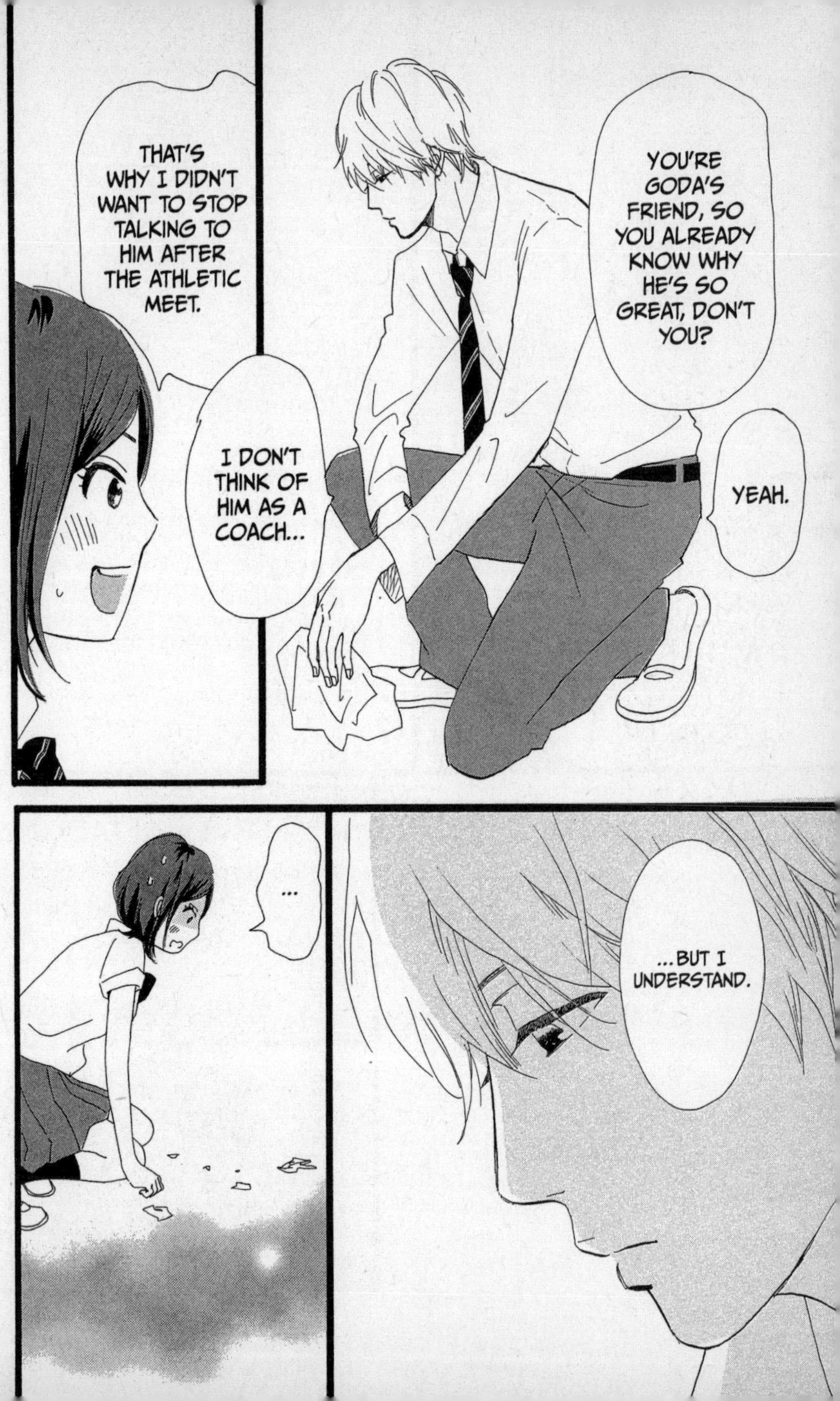
YOU'RE GODA'S FRIEND, SO YOU ALREADY KNOW WHY HE'S SO GREAT, DON'T YOU?
YEAH.
I DON'T THINK OF HIM AS A COACH...
THAT'S WHY I DIDN'T WANT TO STOP TALKING TO HIM AFTER THE ATHLETIC MEET.
...BUT I UNDERSTAND.
...

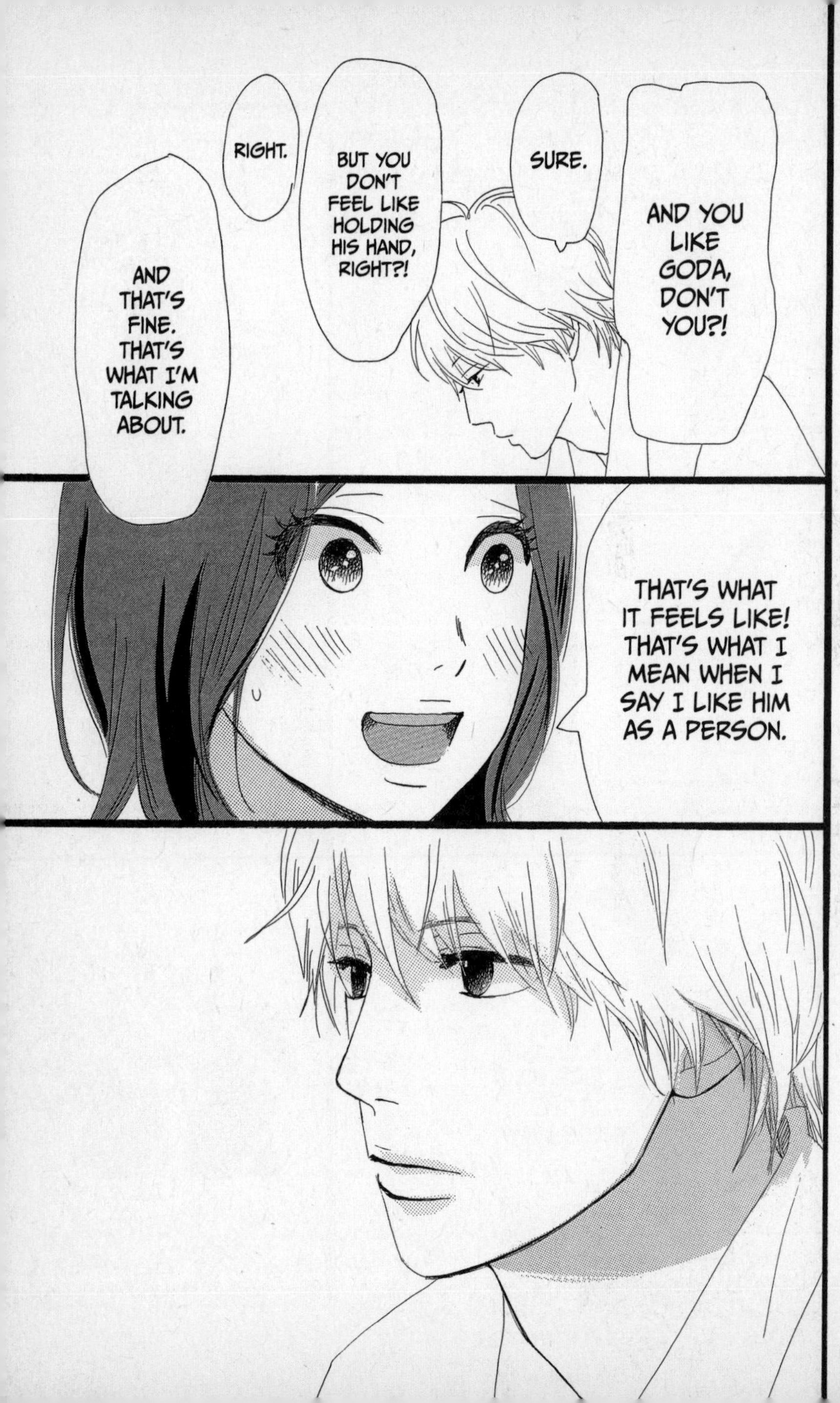
AND YOU LIKE GODA, DON'T YOU?!
SURE.
BUT YOU DON'T FEEL LIKE HOLDING HIS HAND, RIGHT?!
RIGHT.
AND THAT'S FINE. THAT'S WHAT I'M TALKING ABOUT.
THAT'S WHAT IT FEELS LIKE! THAT'S WHAT I MEAN WHEN I SAY I LIKE HIM AS A PERSON.

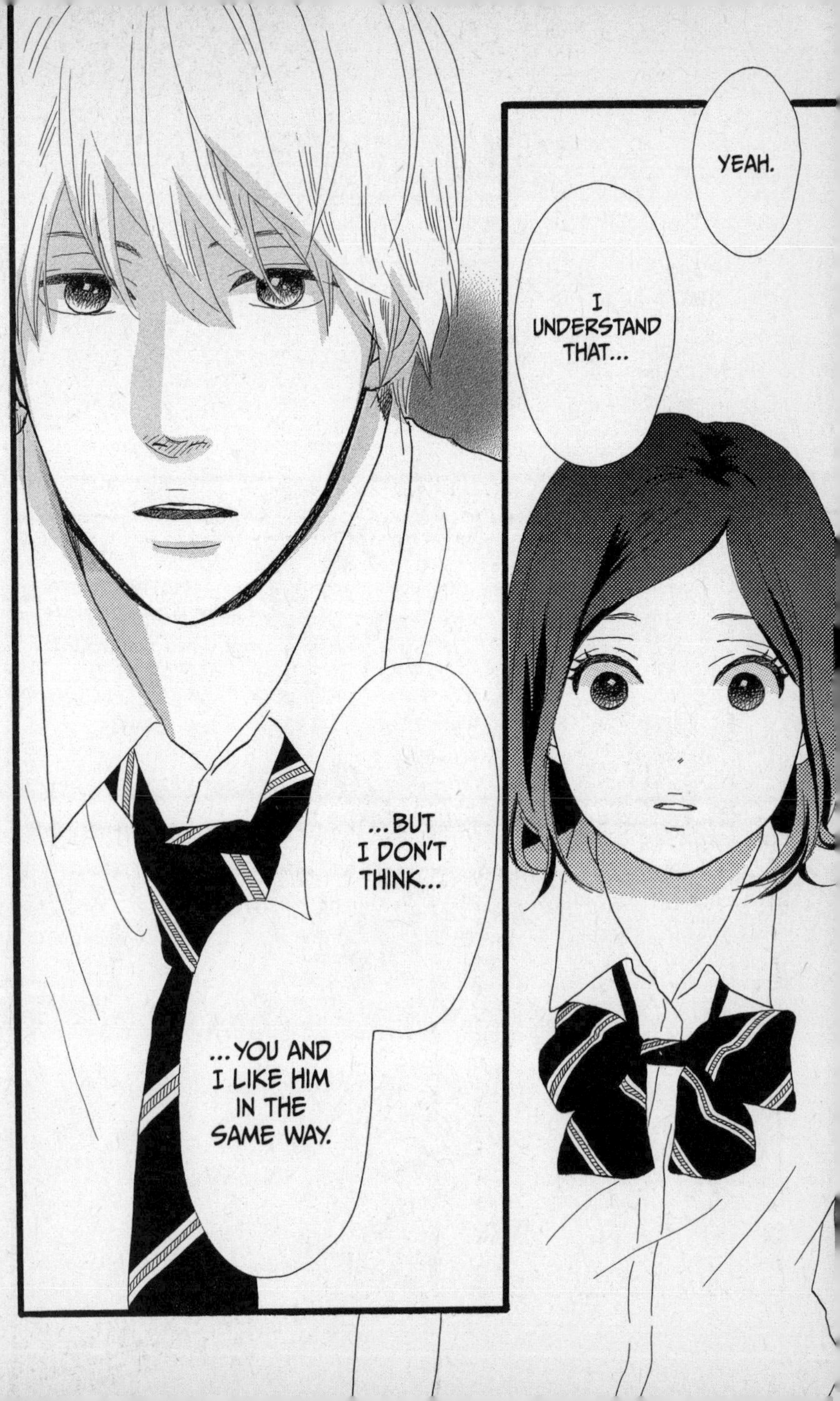
YEAH.
I UNDERSTAND THAT...
...BUT I DON'T THINK...
...YOU AND I LIKE HIM IN THE SAME WAY.

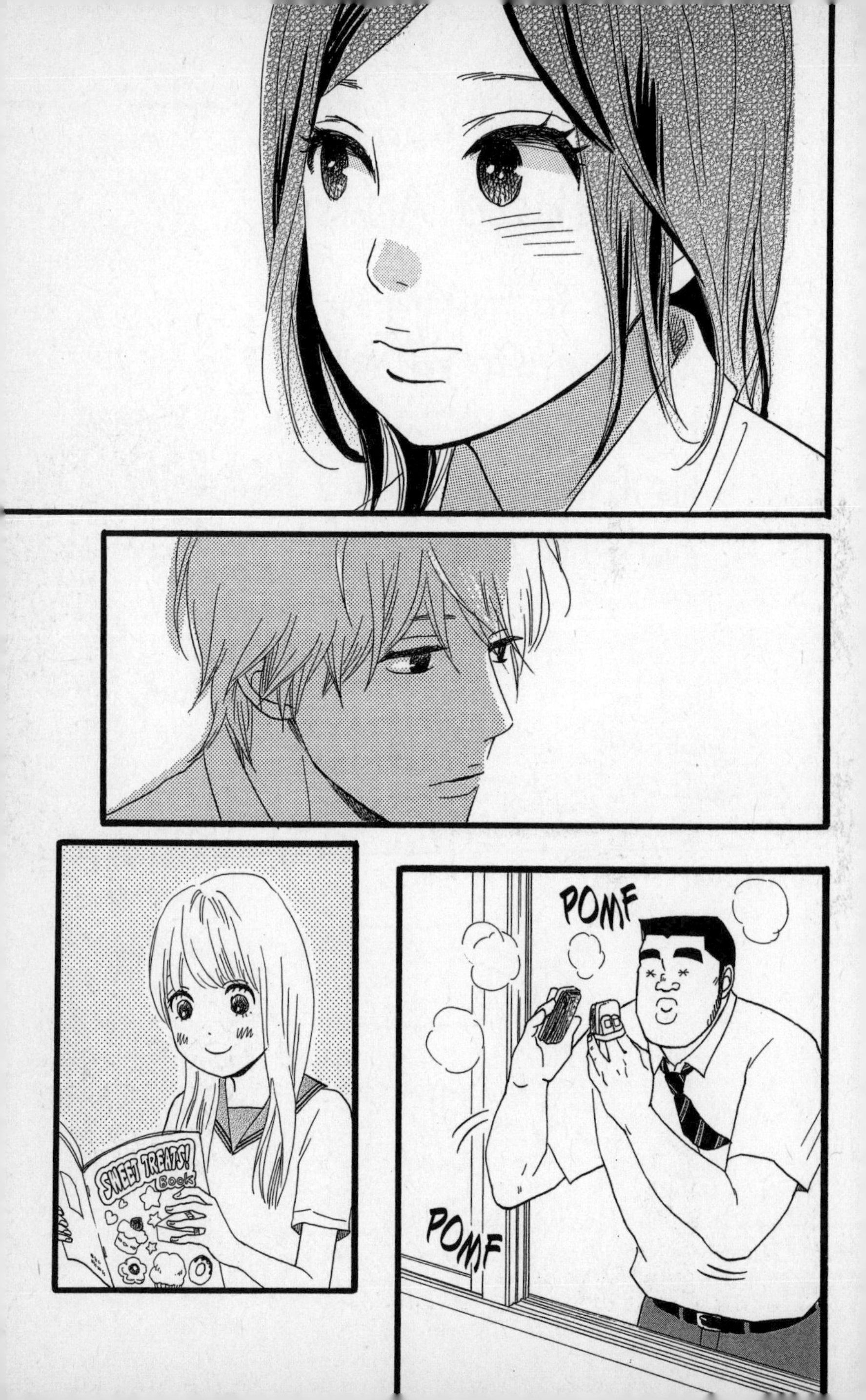
POMF
POMF
SWEET TREATS!
Book

Hi, this is Aruko!

Thanks for picking up *My Love Story!!* volume 5. I had a great time with Takeo and his friends in 2013. I hope 2014 is every bit as wonderful.

Please keep reading! ♡

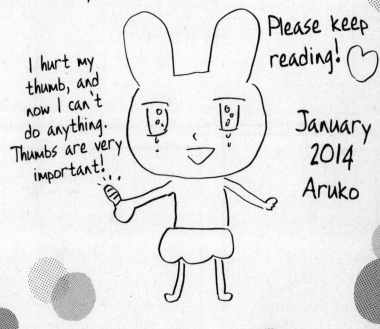

I hurt my thumb, and now I can't do anything. Thumbs are very important!

January 2014
Aruko

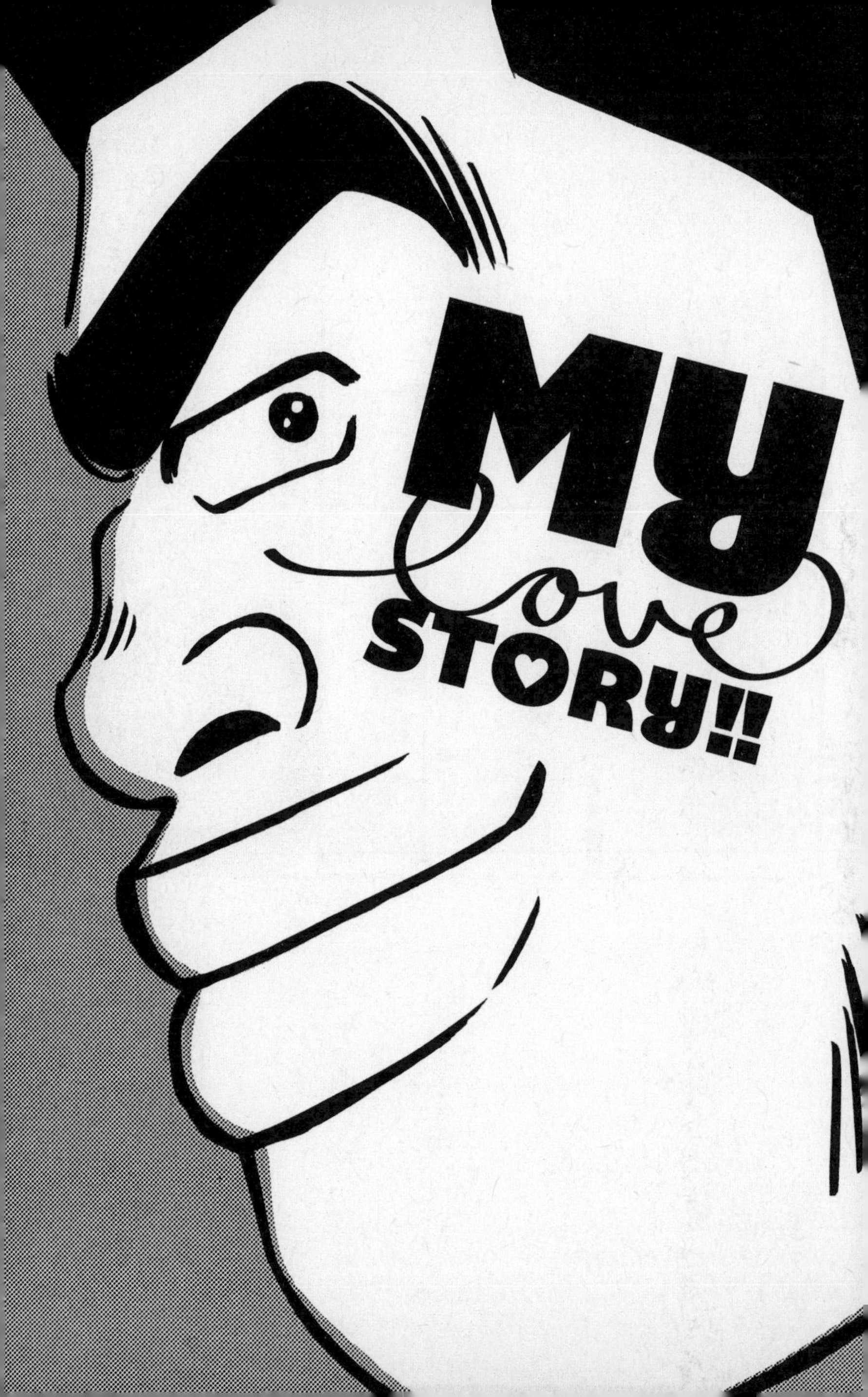
MY
Love
STORY!!

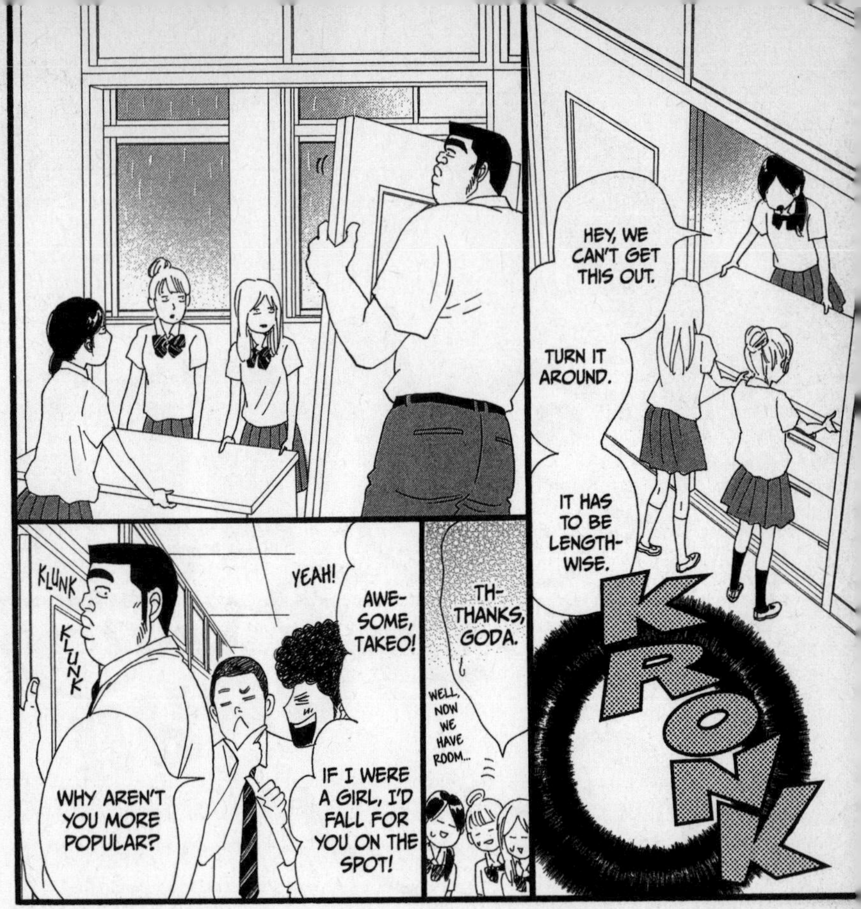
HEY, WE CAN'T GET THIS OUT.
TURN IT AROUND.
IT HAS TO BE LENGTH-WISE.
KRONK
TH-THANKS, GODA.
WELL, NOW WE HAVE ROOM...
YEAH!
AWE-SOME, TAKEO!
KLUNK
KLUNK
IF I WERE A GIRL, I'D FALL FOR YOU ON THE SPOT!
WHY AREN'T YOU MORE POPULAR?

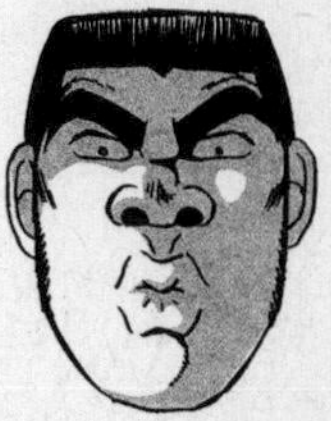

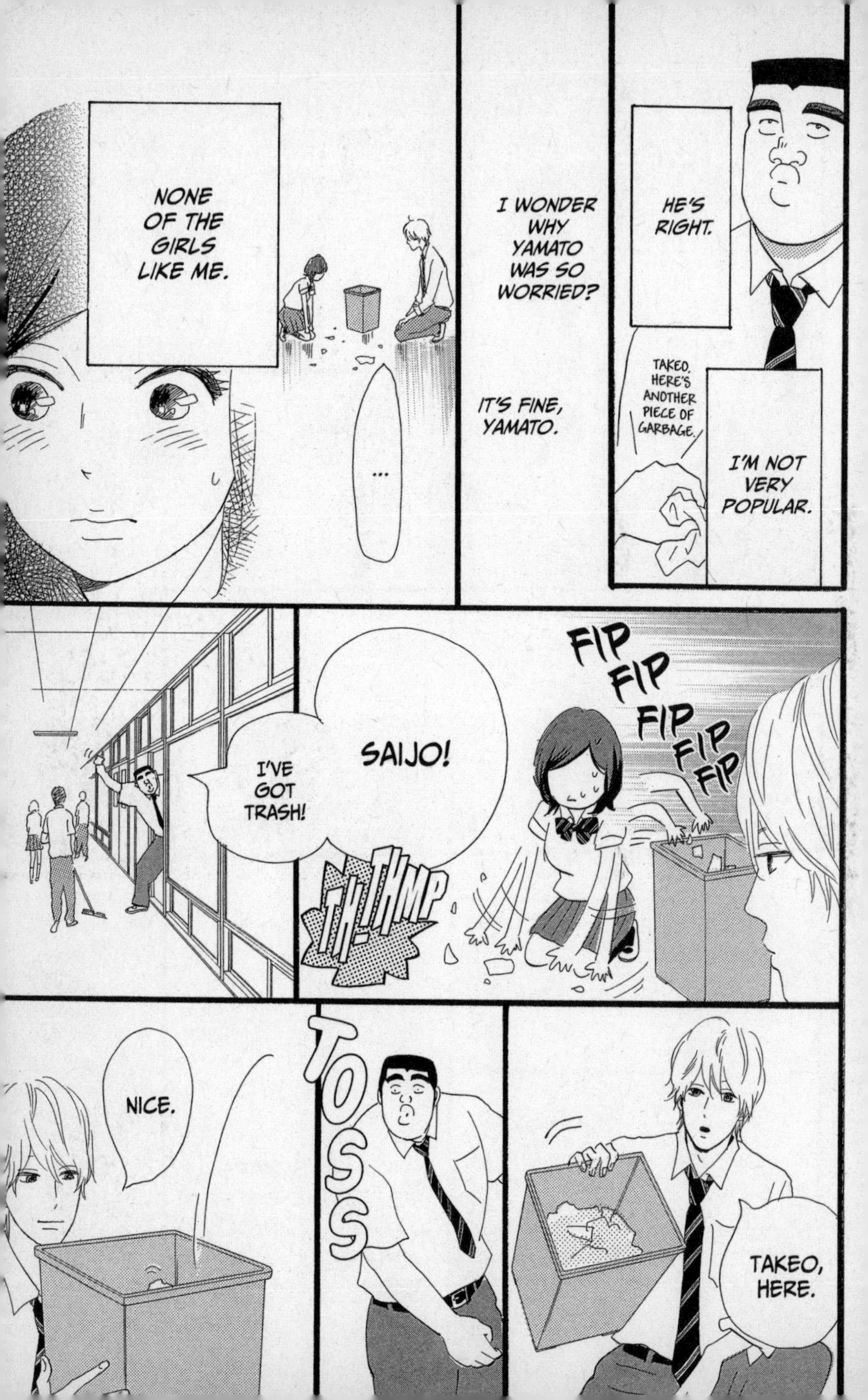
HE'S RIGHT.
TAKEO, HERE'S ANOTHER PIECE OF GARBAGE.
I'M NOT VERY POPULAR.
I WONDER WHY YAMATO WAS SO WORRIED?
IT'S FINE, YAMATO.
NONE OF THE GIRLS LIKE ME.
...
FIP FIP FIP FIP FIP
SAIJO!
I'VE GOT TRASH!
TH! THMP
TAKEO, HERE.
TOSS
NICE.

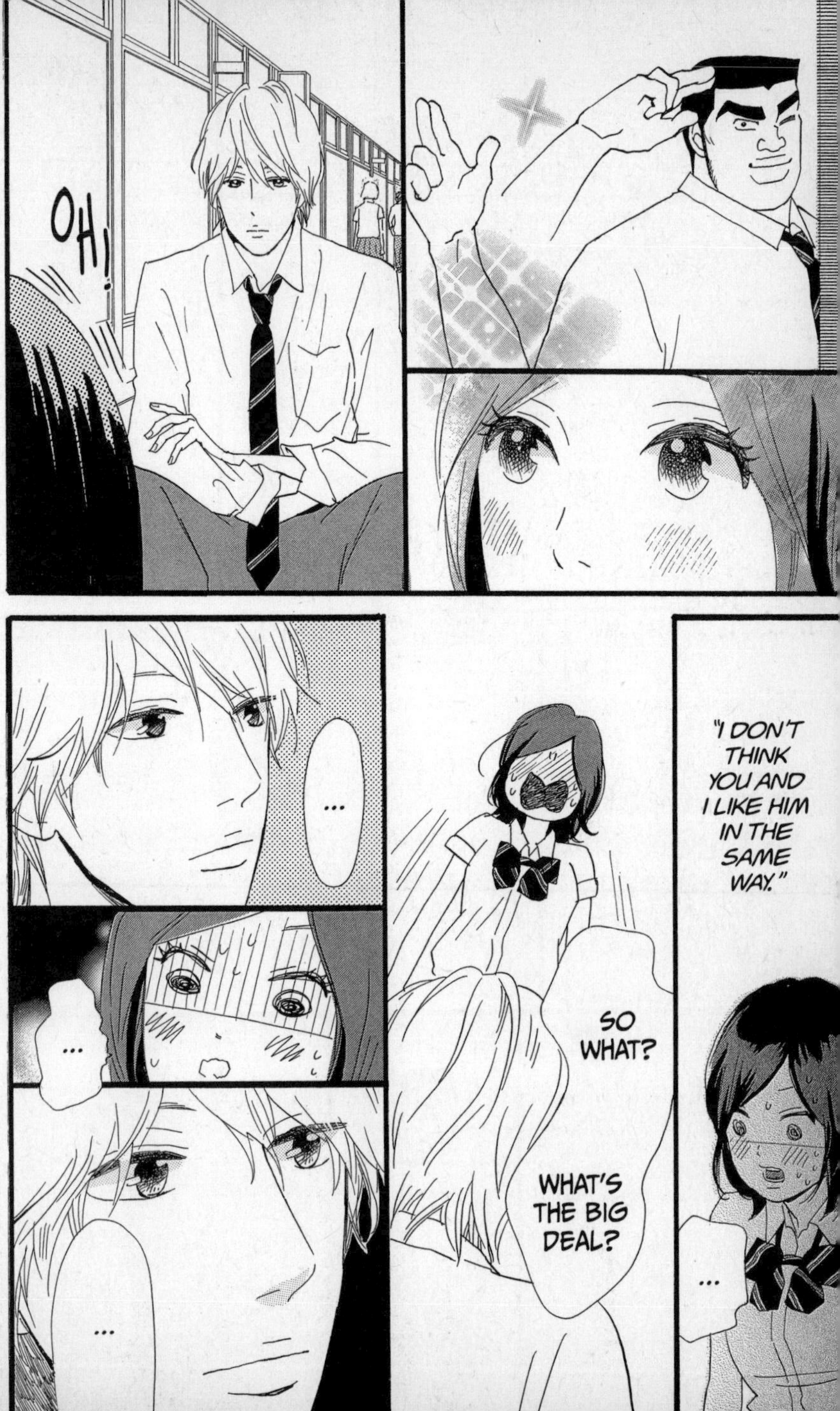
OH!
"I DON'T THINK YOU AND I LIKE HIM IN THE SAME WAY."
...
SO WHAT?
WHAT'S THE BIG DEAL?
...
...
...

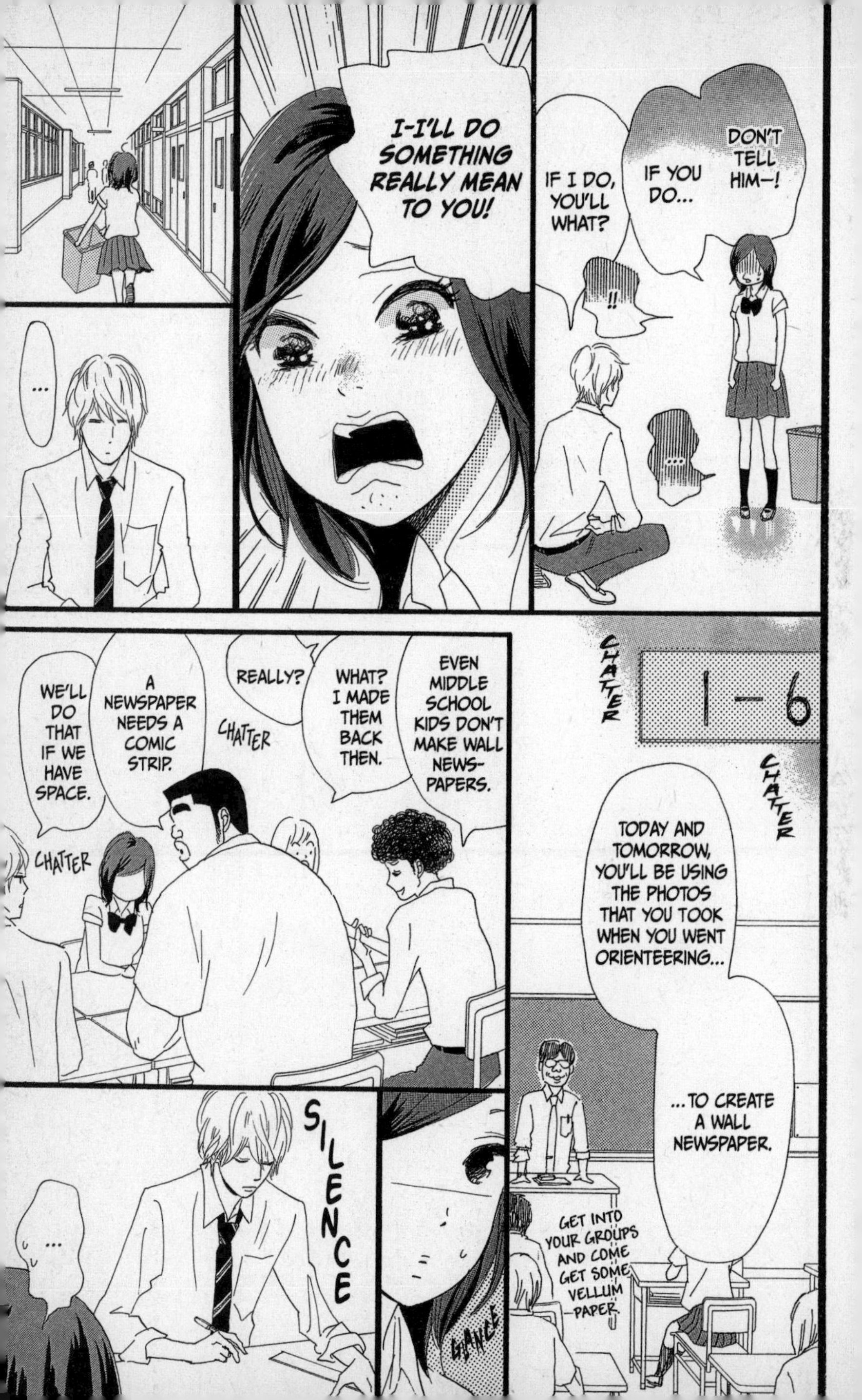
DON'T TELL HIM—!
IF YOU DO...
IF I DO, YOU'LL WHAT?
!!
...
I-I'LL DO SOMETHING REALLY MEAN TO YOU!
...
CHATTER
1-6
CHATTER
TODAY AND TOMORROW, YOU'LL BE USING THE PHOTOS THAT YOU TOOK WHEN YOU WENT ORIENTEERING...
...TO CREATE A WALL NEWSPAPER.
GET INTO YOUR GROUPS AND COME GET SOME VELLUM PAPER.
EVEN MIDDLE SCHOOL KIDS DON'T MAKE WALL NEWSPAPERS.
WHAT? I MADE THEM BACK THEN.
REALLY?
CHATTER
A NEWSPAPER NEEDS A COMIC STRIP.
WE'LL DO THAT IF WE HAVE SPACE.
CHATTER
GLANCE
SILENCE
...

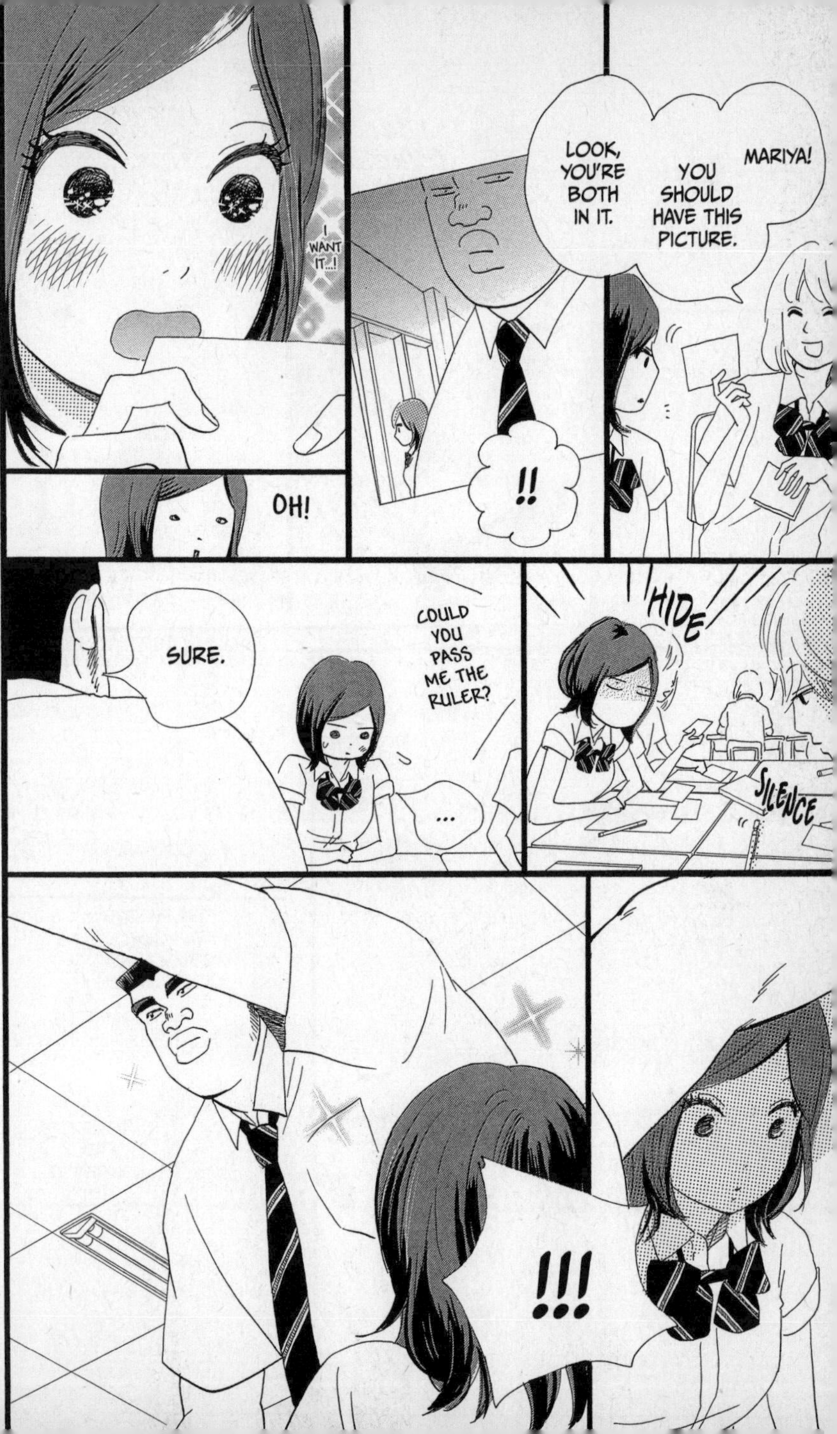
MARIYA! YOU SHOULD HAVE THIS PICTURE. LOOK, YOU'RE BOTH IN IT.
!!
I WANT IT...!
OH!
HIDE
SILENCE
COULD YOU PASS ME THE RULER?
...
SURE.
!!!

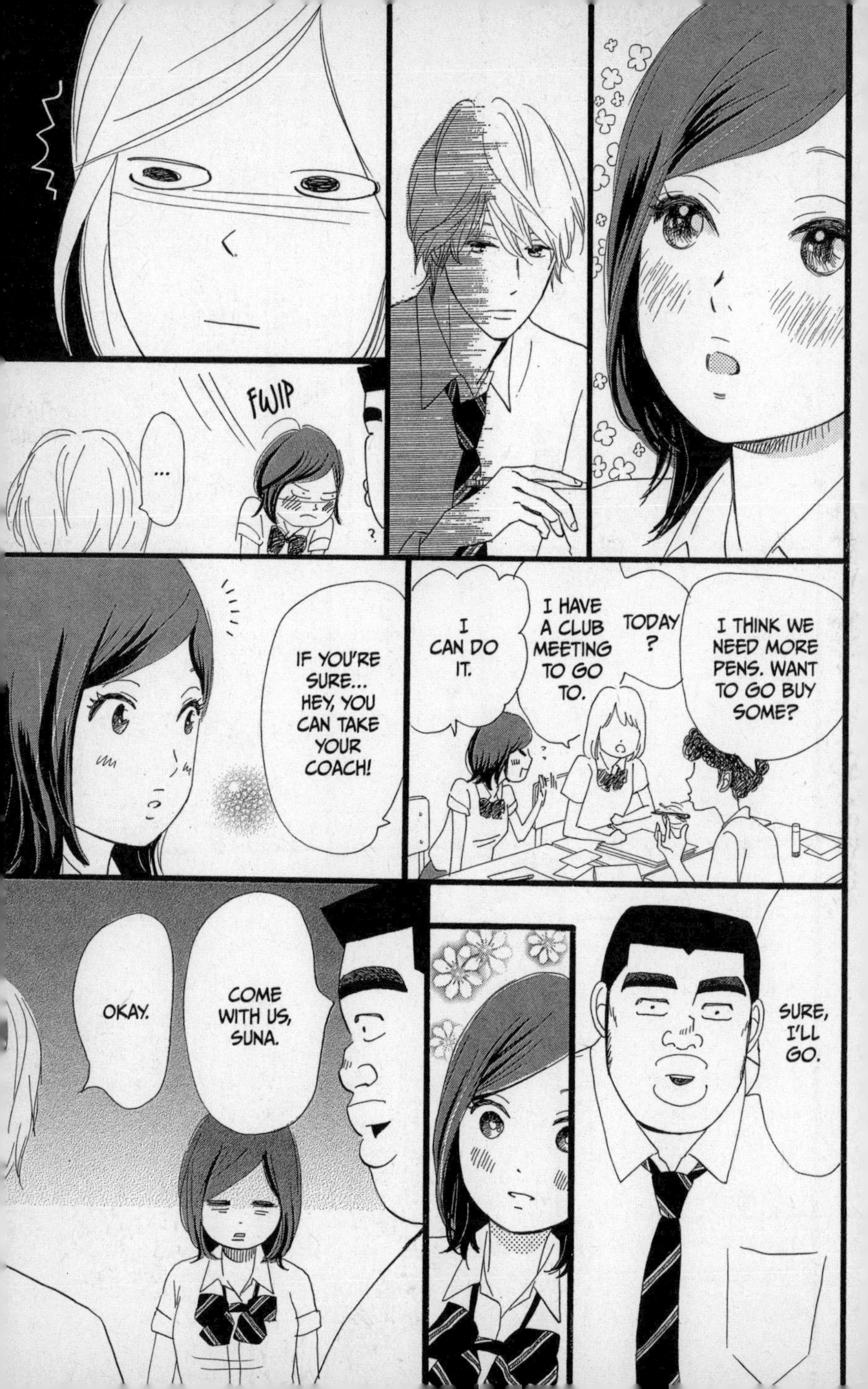
FWIP
...
?
I THINK WE NEED MORE PENS. WANT TO GO BUY SOME?
TODAY?
I HAVE A CLUB MEETING TO GO TO.
I CAN DO IT.
IF YOU'RE SURE... HEY, YOU CAN TAKE YOUR COACH!
SURE, I'LL GO.
COME WITH US, SUNA.
OKAY.

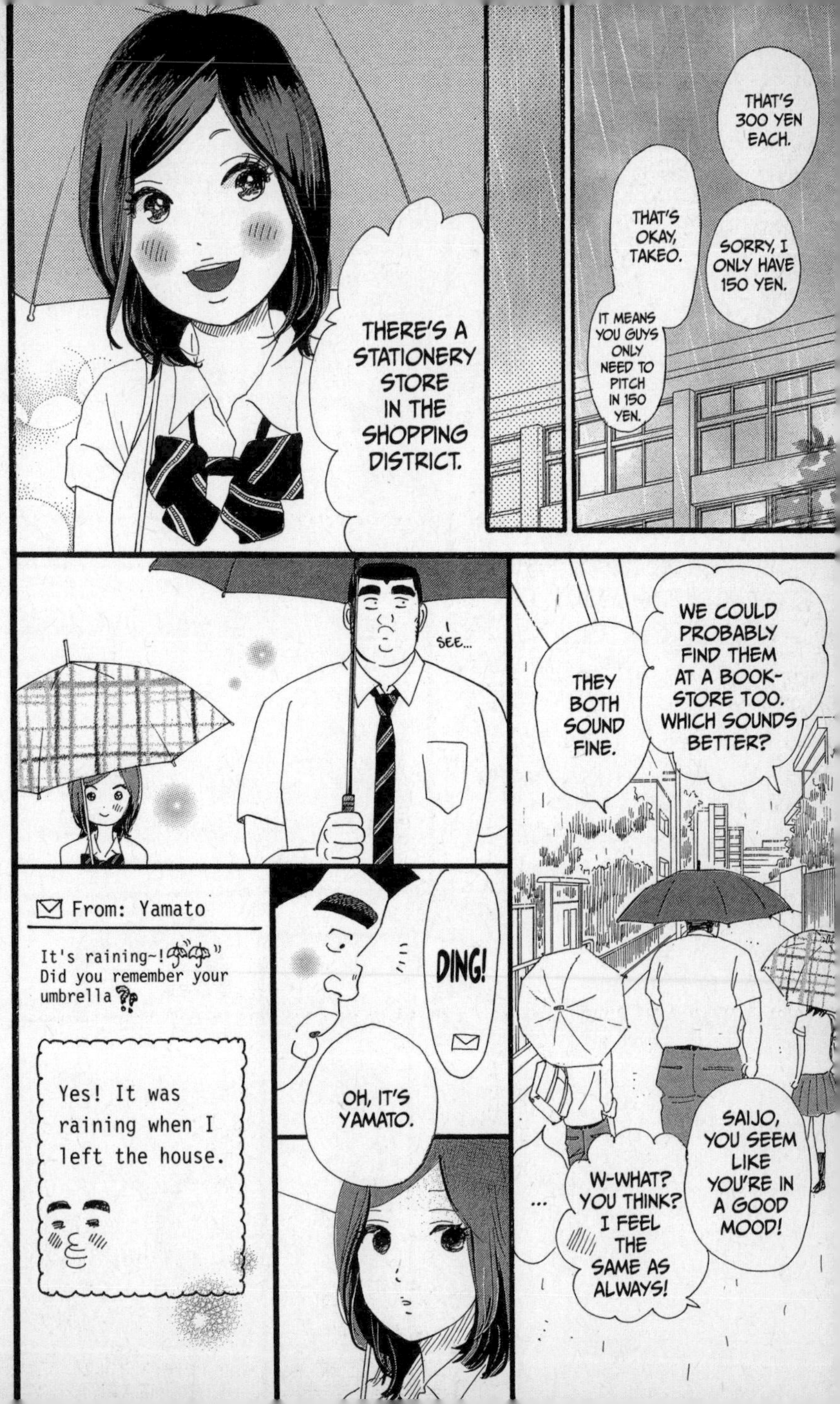
THAT'S 300 YEN EACH.
SORRY, I ONLY HAVE 150 YEN.
THAT'S OKAY, TAKEO.
IT MEANS YOU GUYS ONLY NEED TO PITCH IN 150 YEN.
THERE'S A STATIONERY STORE IN THE SHOPPING DISTRICT.
WE COULD PROBABLY FIND THEM AT A BOOK-STORE TOO. WHICH SOUNDS BETTER?
THEY BOTH SOUND FINE.
SAIJO, YOU SEEM LIKE YOU'RE IN A GOOD MOOD!
W-WHAT? YOU THINK? I FEEL THE SAME AS ALWAYS!
...
I SEE...
DING!
OH, IT'S YAMATO.
From: Yamato
It's raining~! Did you remember your umbrella?!
Yes! It was raining when I left the house.

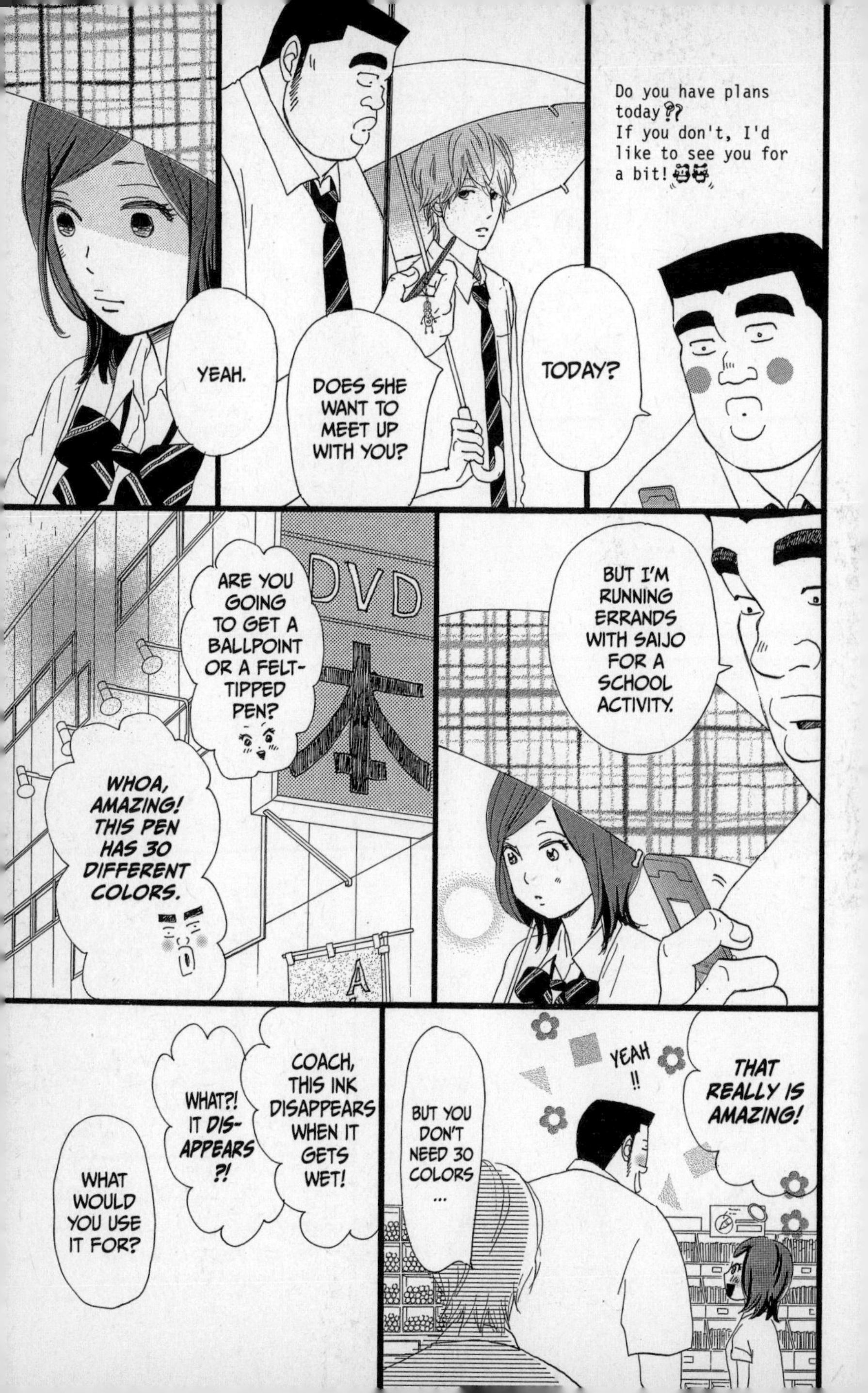
Do you have plans today?? If you don't, I'd like to see you for a bit!
TODAY?
DOES SHE WANT TO MEET UP WITH YOU?
YEAH.
BUT I'M RUNNING ERRANDS WITH SAIJO FOR A SCHOOL ACTIVITY.
DVD
ARE YOU GOING TO GET A BALLPOINT OR A FELT-TIPPED PEN?
WHOA, AMAZING! THIS PEN HAS 30 DIFFERENT COLORS.
THAT REALLY IS AMAZING!
YEAH!!
BUT YOU DON'T NEED 30 COLORS...
COACH, THIS INK DISAPPEARS WHEN IT GETS WET!
WHAT?! IT DISAPPEARS?!
WHAT WOULD YOU USE IT FOR?

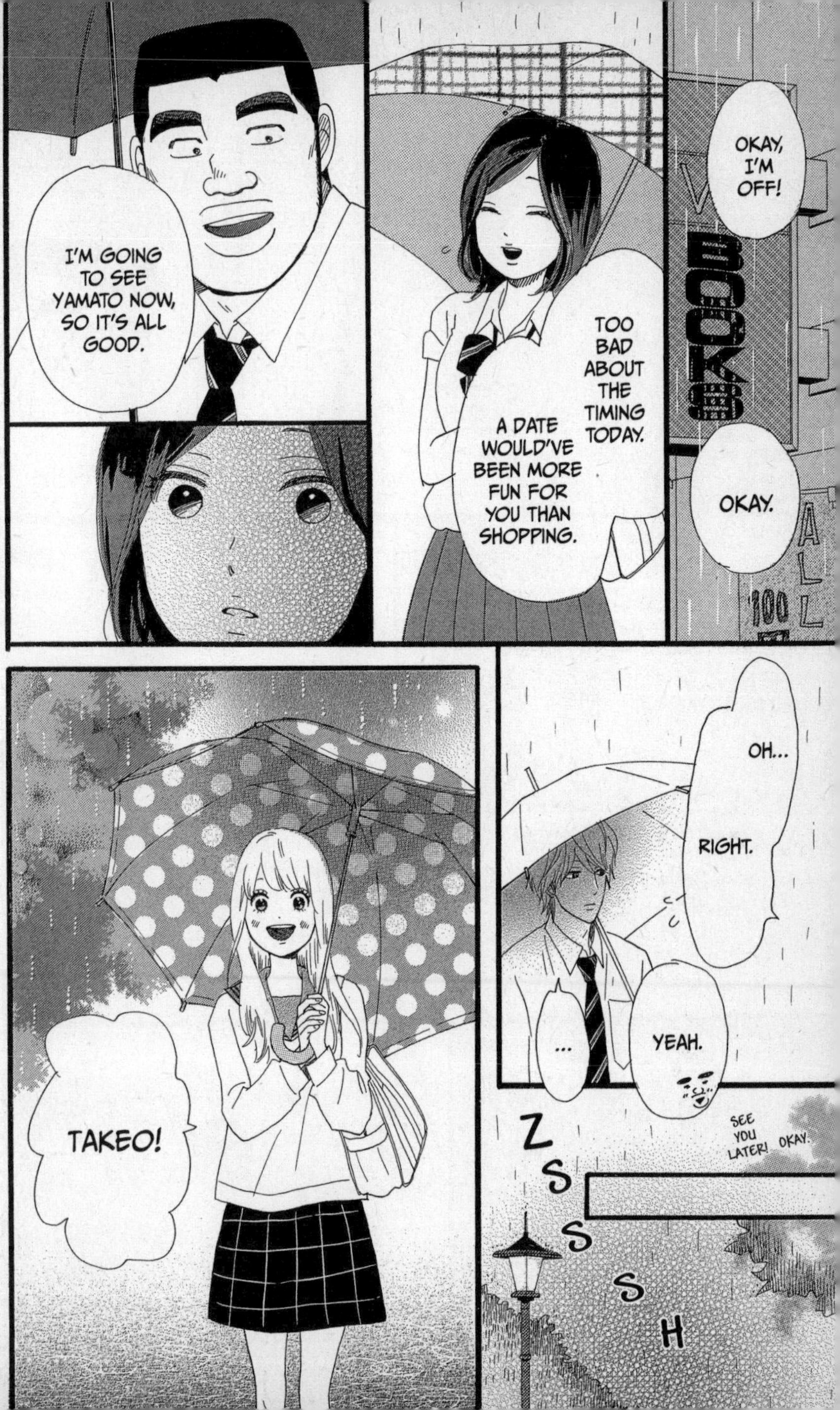
OKAY, I'M OFF!
TOO BAD ABOUT THE TIMING TODAY. A DATE WOULD'VE BEEN MORE FUN FOR YOU THAN SHOPPING.
OKAY.
I'M GOING TO SEE YAMATO NOW, SO IT'S ALL GOOD.
OH... RIGHT.
...
YEAH.
SEE YOU LATER!
OKAY.
ZSSSH
TAKEO!

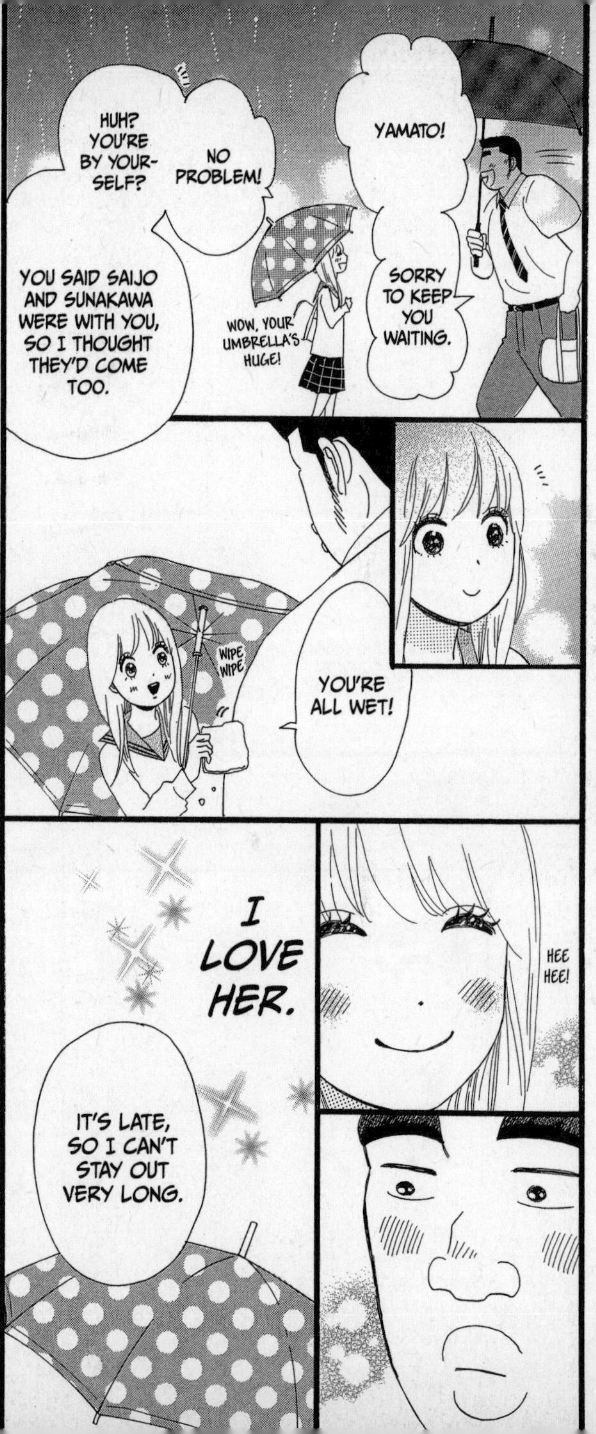
YAMATO!
SORRY TO KEEP YOU WAITING.
WOW, YOUR UMBRELLA'S HUGE!
NO PROBLEM!
HUH? YOU'RE BY YOUR-SELF?
YOU SAID SAIJO AND SUNAKAWA WERE WITH YOU, SO I THOUGHT THEY'D COME TOO.
YOU'RE ALL WET!
WIPE WIPE
HEE HEE!
I LOVE HER.
IT'S LATE, SO I CAN'T STAY OUT VERY LONG.

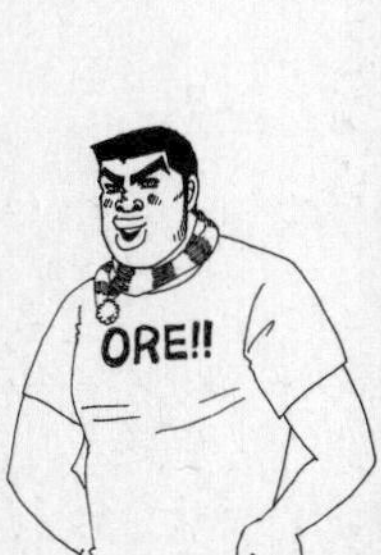
ORE!!

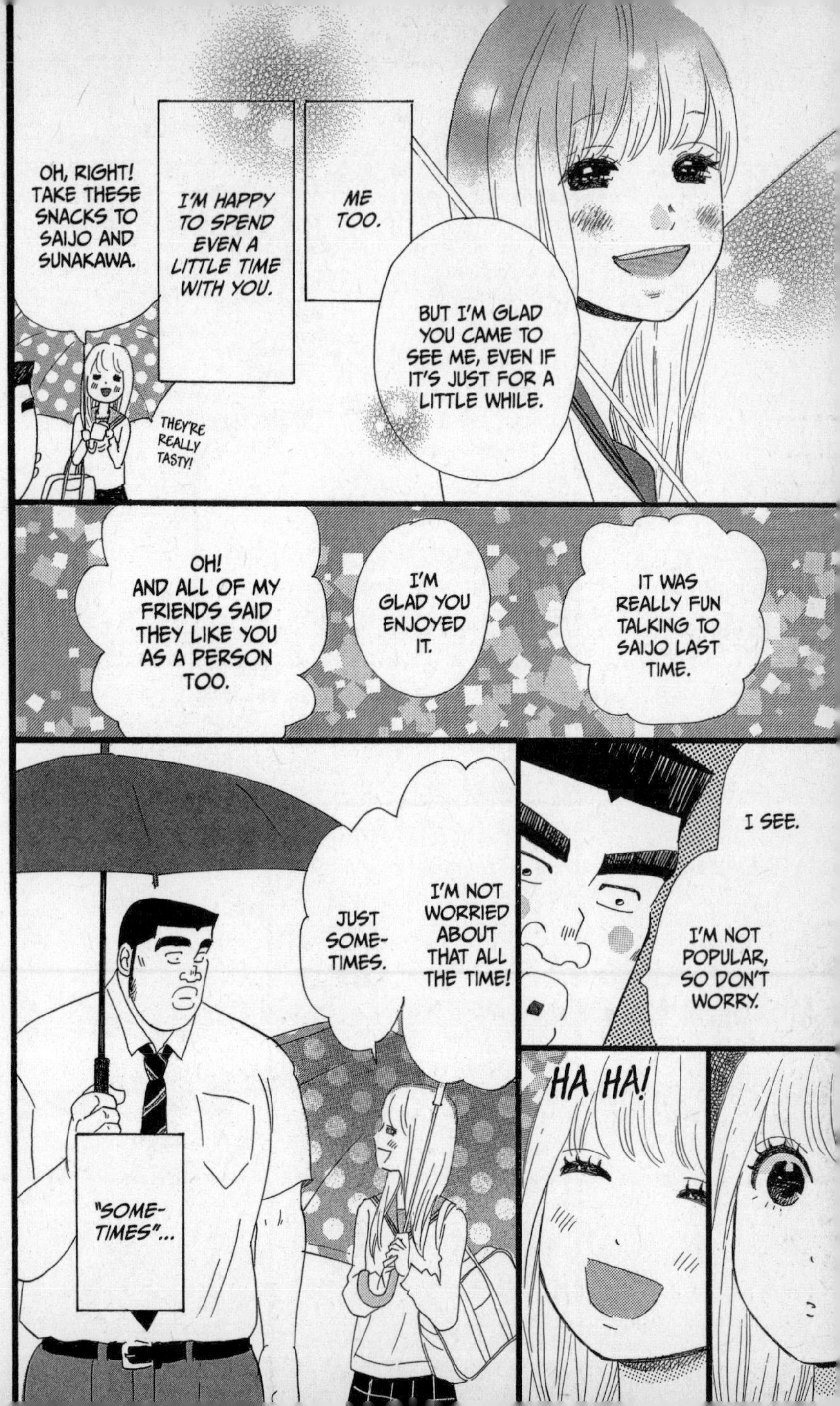
BUT I'M GLAD YOU CAME TO SEE ME, EVEN IF IT'S JUST FOR A LITTLE WHILE.
ME TOO.
I'M HAPPY TO SPEND EVEN A LITTLE TIME WITH YOU.
OH, RIGHT! TAKE THESE SNACKS TO SAIJO AND SUNAKAWA.
THEY'RE REALLY TASTY!
IT WAS REALLY FUN TALKING TO SAIJO LAST TIME.
I'M GLAD YOU ENJOYED IT.
OH! AND ALL OF MY FRIENDS SAID THEY LIKE YOU AS A PERSON TOO.
I SEE.
I'M NOT POPULAR, SO DON'T WORRY.
HA HA!
I'M NOT WORRIED ABOUT THAT ALL THE TIME!
JUST SOME-TIMES.
"SOME-TIMES"...

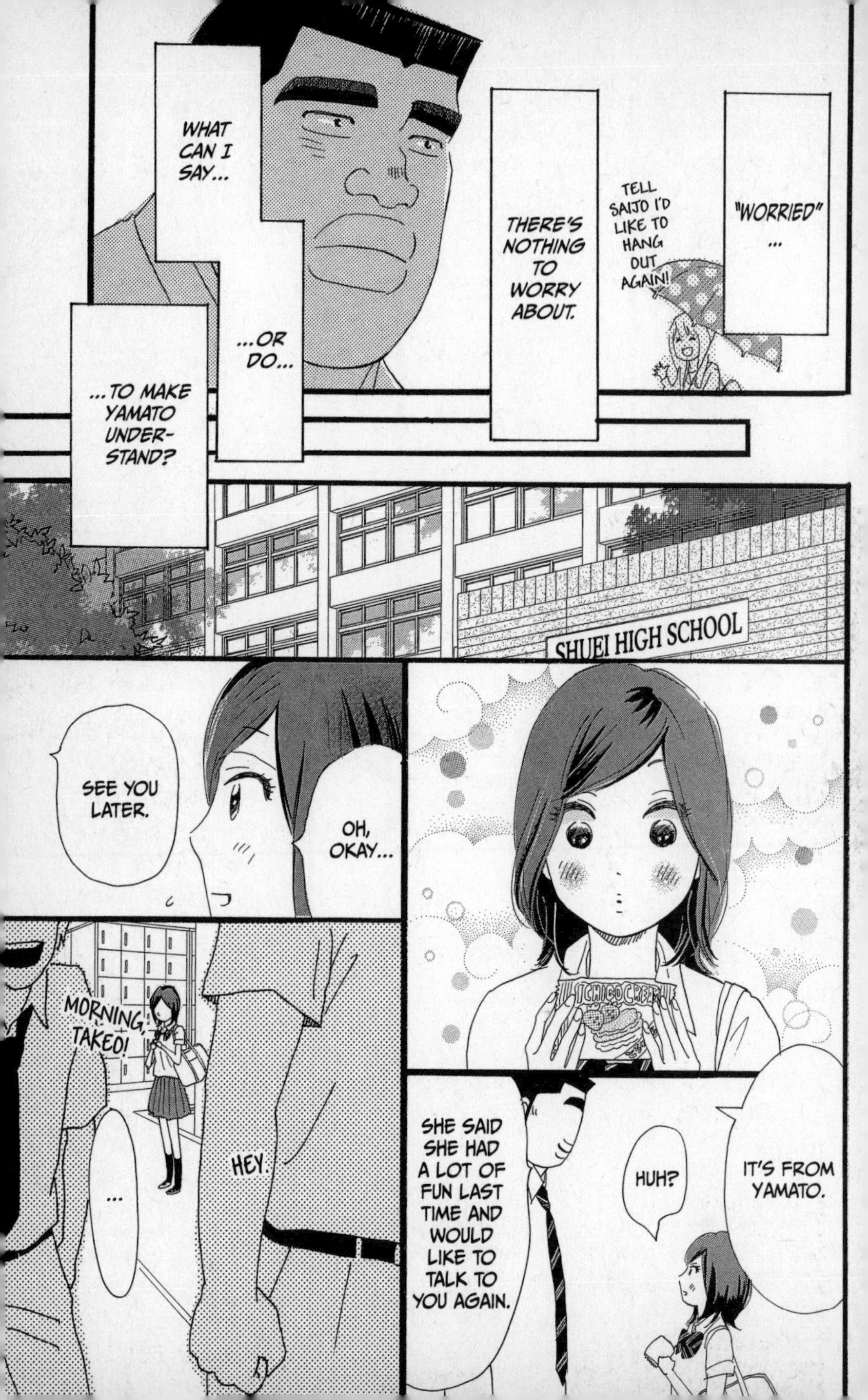
"WORRIED" ...
TELL SAIJO I'D LIKE TO HANG OUT AGAIN!
THERE'S NOTHING TO WORRY ABOUT.
WHAT CAN I SAY...
...OR DO...
...TO MAKE YAMATO UNDER-STAND?
SHUEI HIGH SCHOOL
IT'S FROM YAMATO.
HUH?
SHE SAID SHE HAD A LOT OF FUN LAST TIME AND WOULD LIKE TO TALK TO YOU AGAIN.
OH, OKAY...
SEE YOU LATER.
MORNING, TAKEO!
HEY.
...

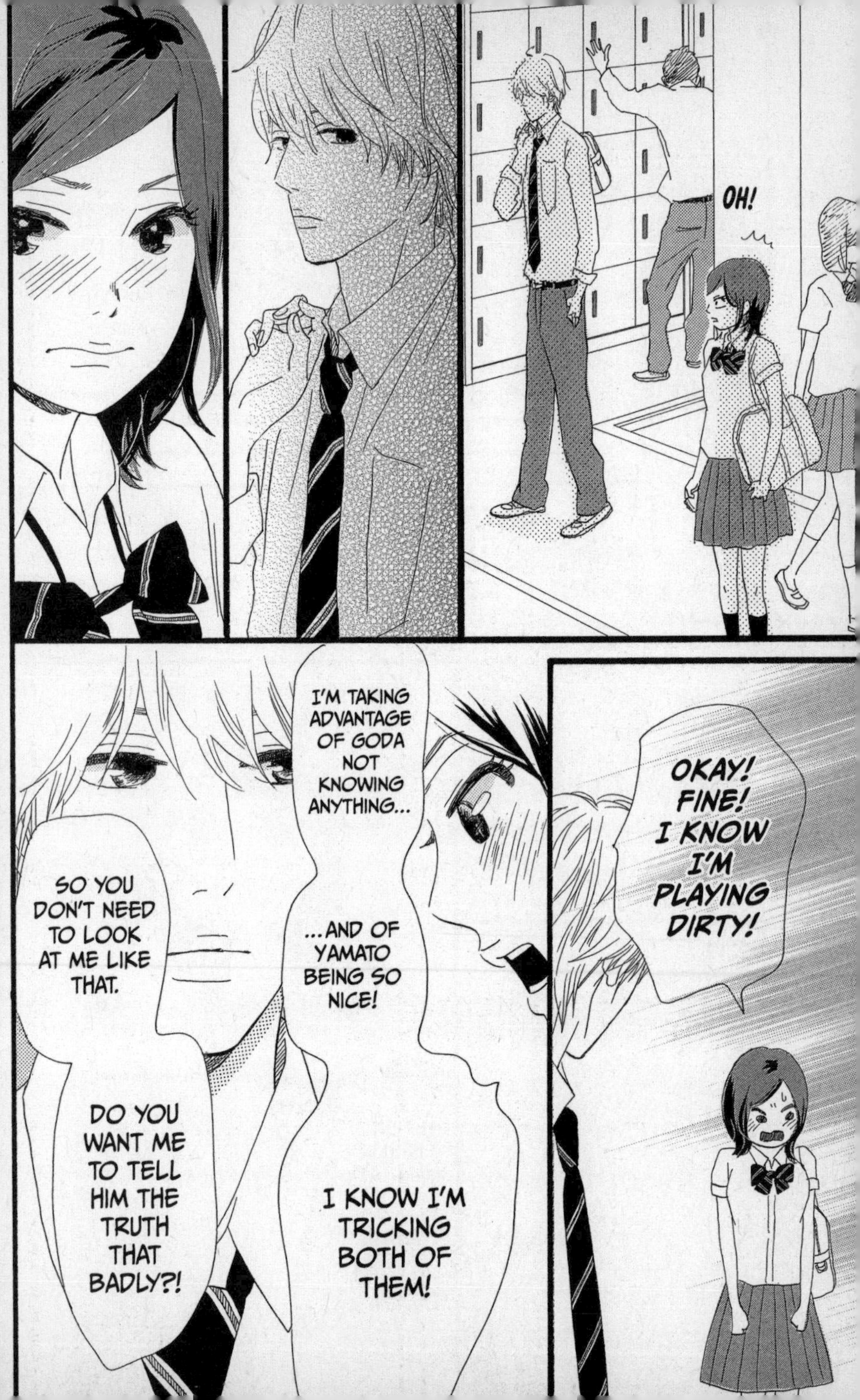
OH!
OKAY! FINE! I KNOW I'M PLAYING DIRTY!
I'M TAKING ADVANTAGE OF GODA NOT KNOWING ANYTHING...
...AND OF YAMATO BEING SO NICE!
I KNOW I'M TRICKING BOTH OF THEM!
SO YOU DON'T NEED TO LOOK AT ME LIKE THAT.
DO YOU WANT ME TO TELL HIM THE TRUTH THAT BADLY?!

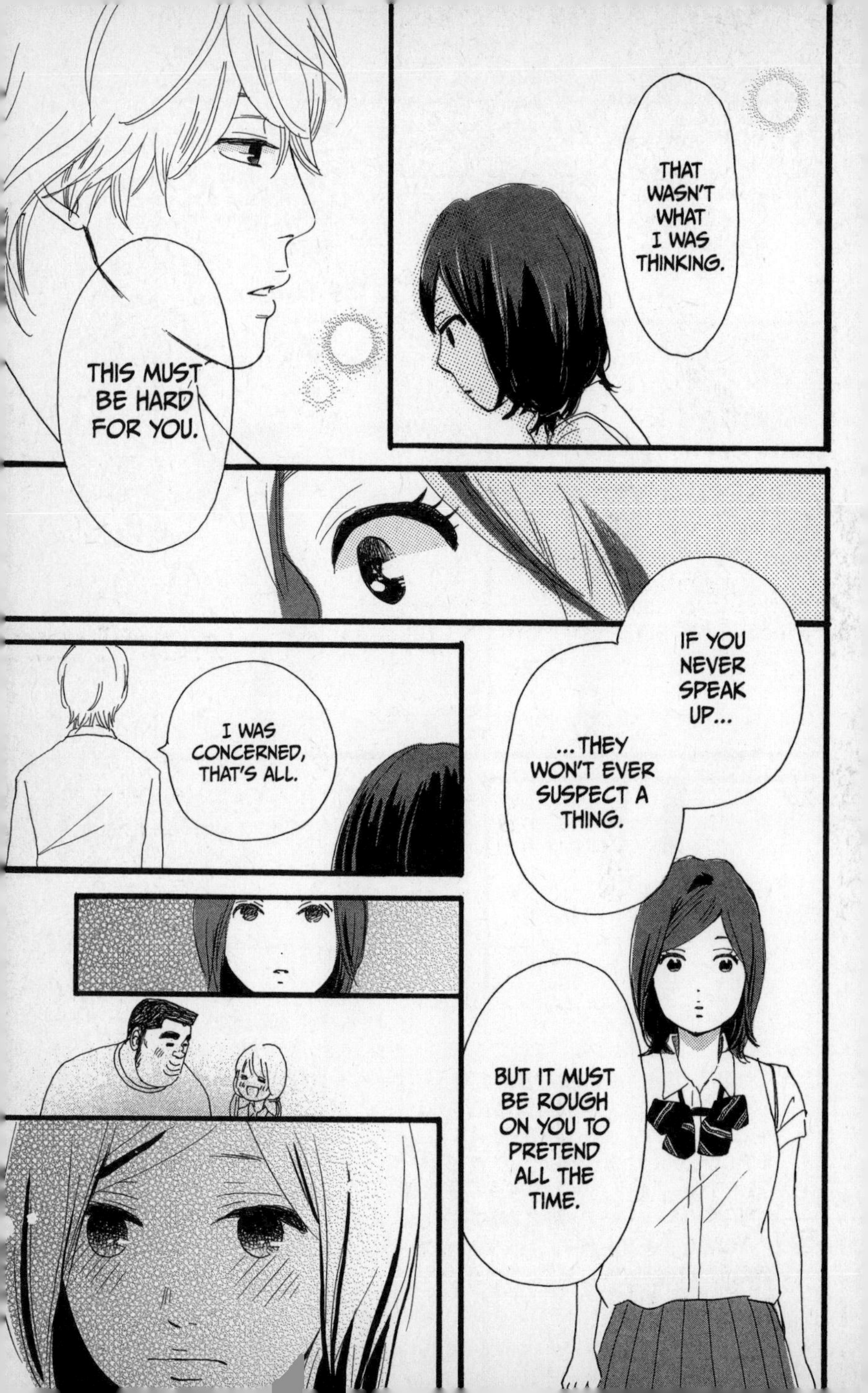
THAT WASN'T WHAT I WAS THINKING.
THIS MUST BE HARD FOR YOU.
IF YOU NEVER SPEAK UP...
...THEY WON'T EVER SUSPECT A THING.
BUT IT MUST BE ROUGH ON YOU TO PRETEND ALL THE TIME.
I WAS CONCERNED, THAT'S ALL.

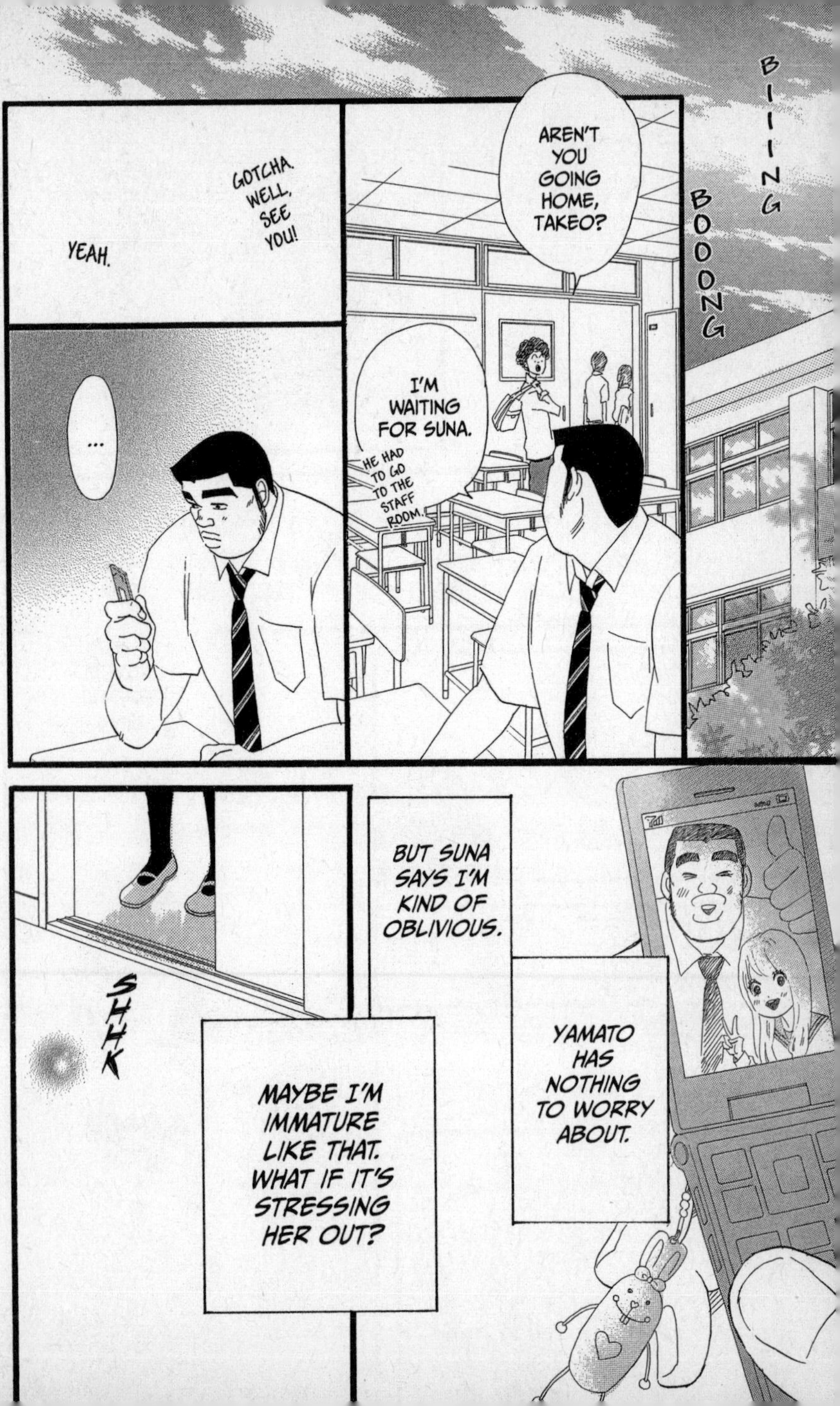
BIIING
BOOONG
AREN'T YOU GOING HOME, TAKEO?
I'M WAITING FOR SUNA.
HE HAD TO GO TO THE STAFF ROOM.
GOTCHA. WELL, SEE YOU!
YEAH.
...
YAMATO HAS NOTHING TO WORRY ABOUT.
BUT SUNA SAYS I'M KIND OF OBLIVIOUS.
MAYBE I'M IMMATURE LIKE THAT. WHAT IF IT'S STRESSING HER OUT?
SHHK

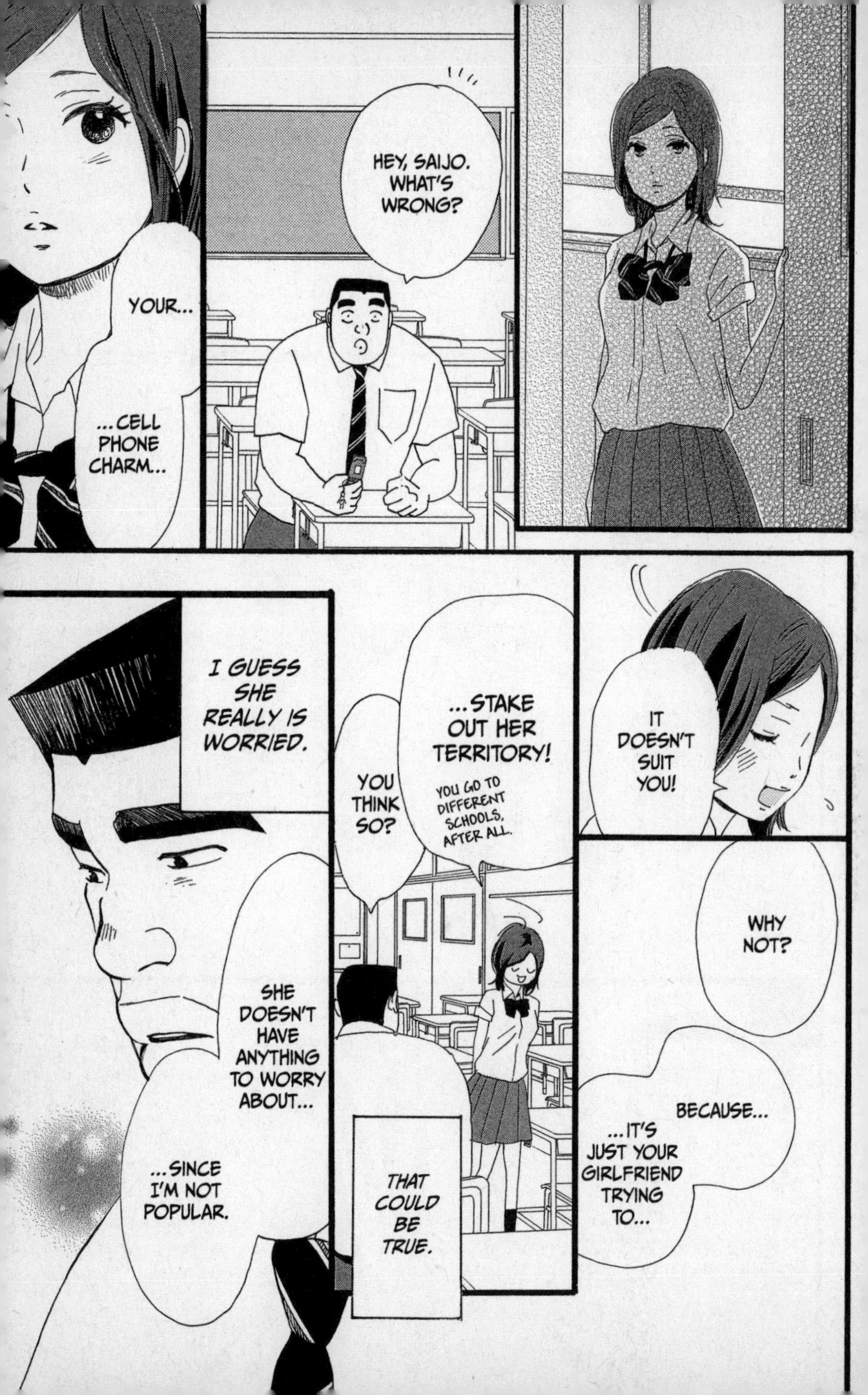
HEY, SAIJO. WHAT'S WRONG?
YOUR...
...CELL PHONE CHARM...
IT DOESN'T SUIT YOU!
WHY NOT?
BECAUSE...
...IT'S JUST YOUR GIRLFRIEND TRYING TO...
...STAKE OUT HER TERRITORY!
YOU GO TO DIFFERENT SCHOOLS, AFTER ALL.
YOU THINK SO?
THAT COULD BE TRUE.
I GUESS SHE REALLY IS WORRIED.
SHE DOESN'T HAVE ANYTHING TO WORRY ABOUT...
...SINCE I'M NOT POPULAR.

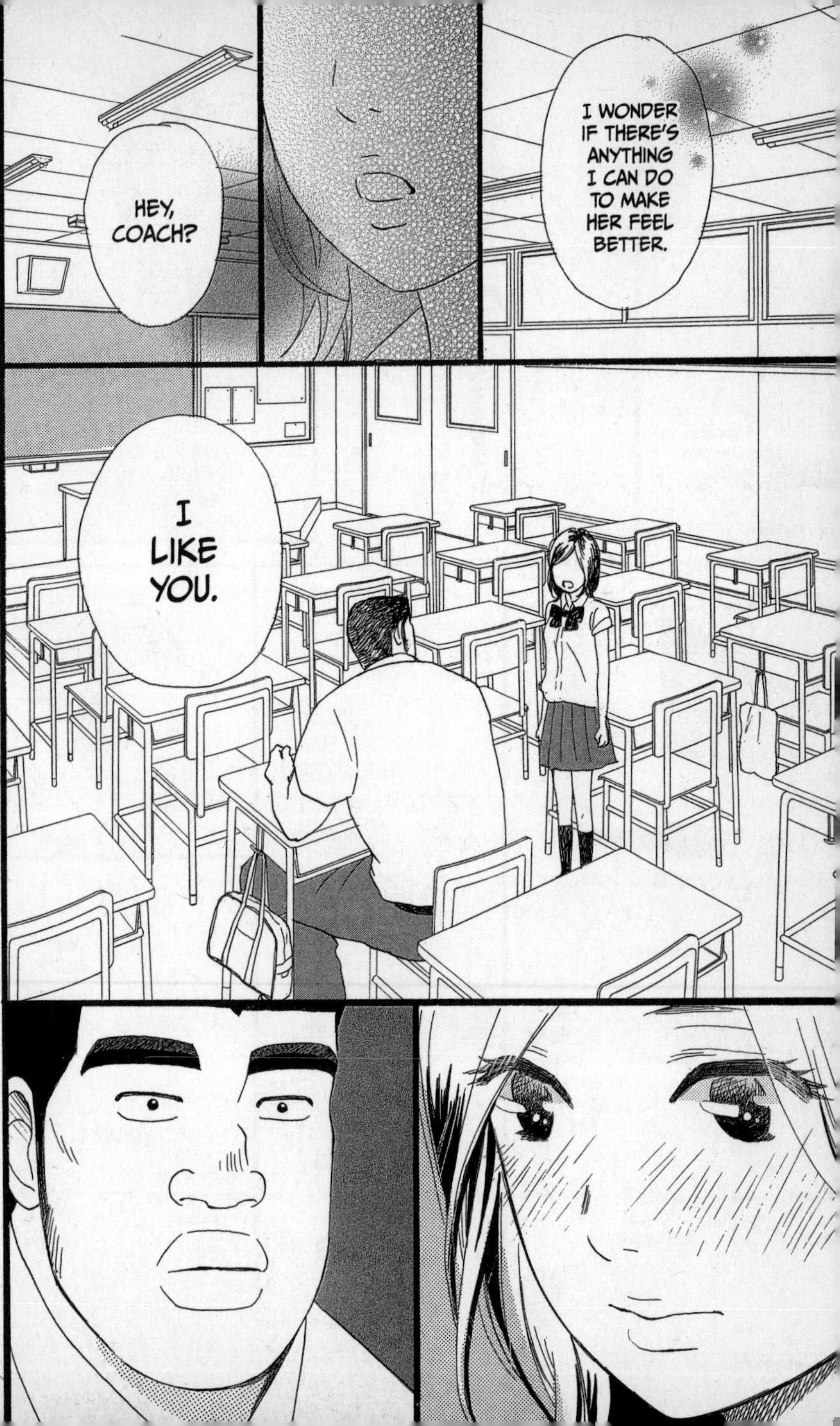
I WONDER IF THERE'S ANYTHING I CAN DO TO MAKE HER FEEL BETTER.
HEY, COACH?
I LIKE YOU.

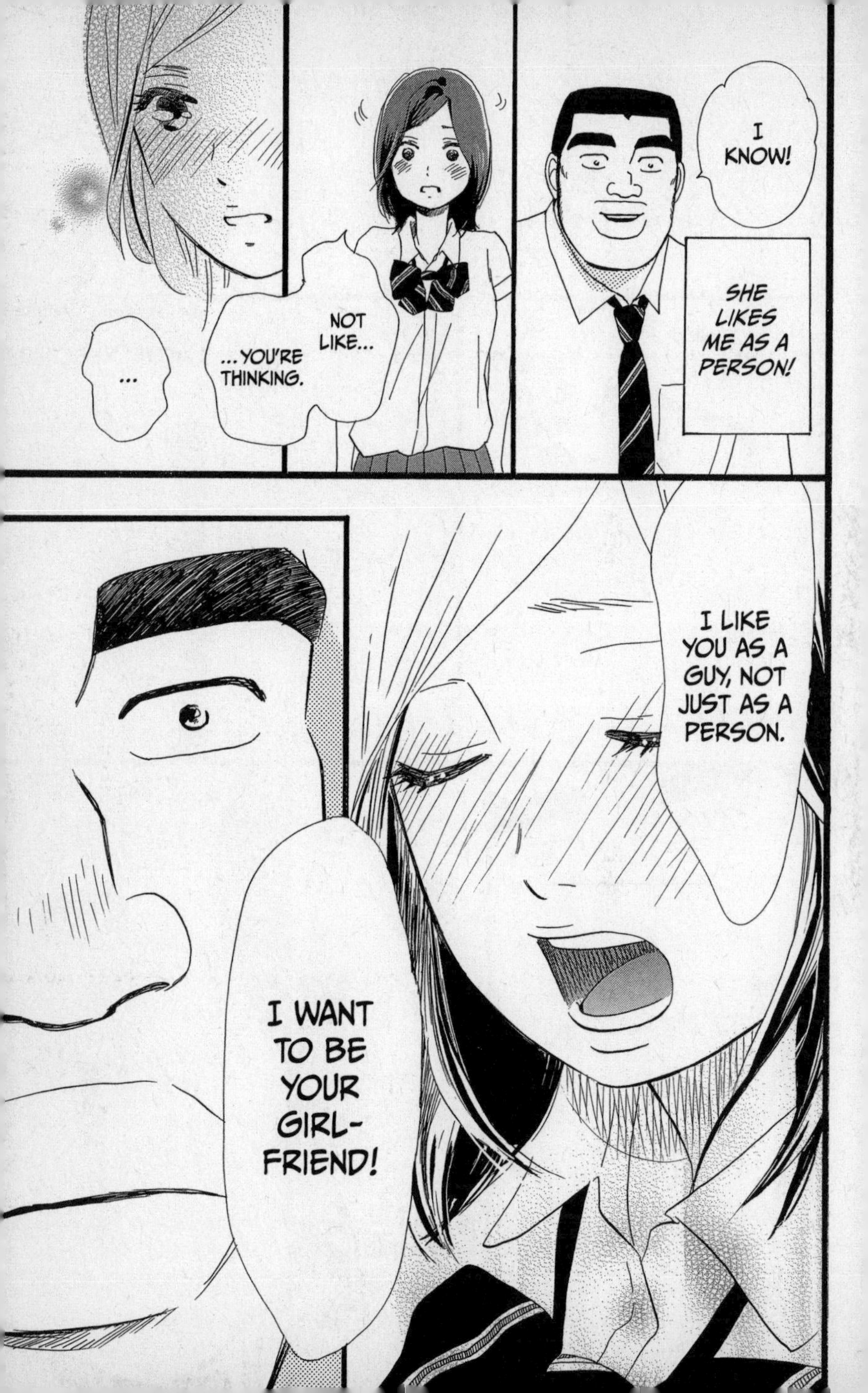
I KNOW!
SHE LIKES ME AS A PERSON!
NOT LIKE...
...YOU'RE THINKING.
...
I LIKE YOU AS A GUY, NOT JUST AS A PERSON.
I WANT TO BE YOUR GIRL-FRIEND!

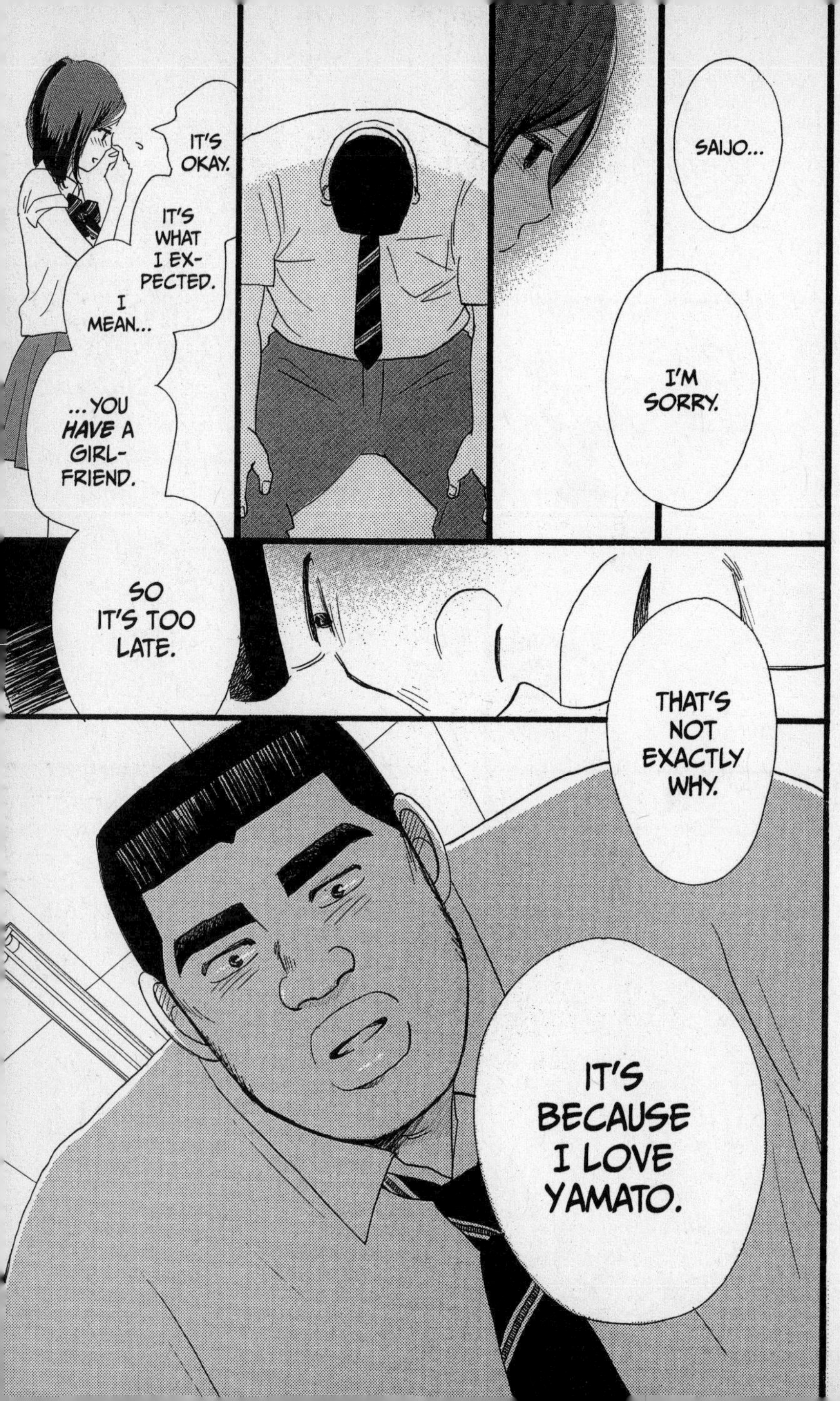
SAIJO...
I'M SORRY.
IT'S OKAY.
IT'S WHAT I EX-PECTED.
I MEAN...
...YOU *HAVE* A GIRL-FRIEND.
SO IT'S TOO LATE.
THAT'S NOT EXACTLY WHY.
IT'S BECAUSE I LOVE YAMATO.

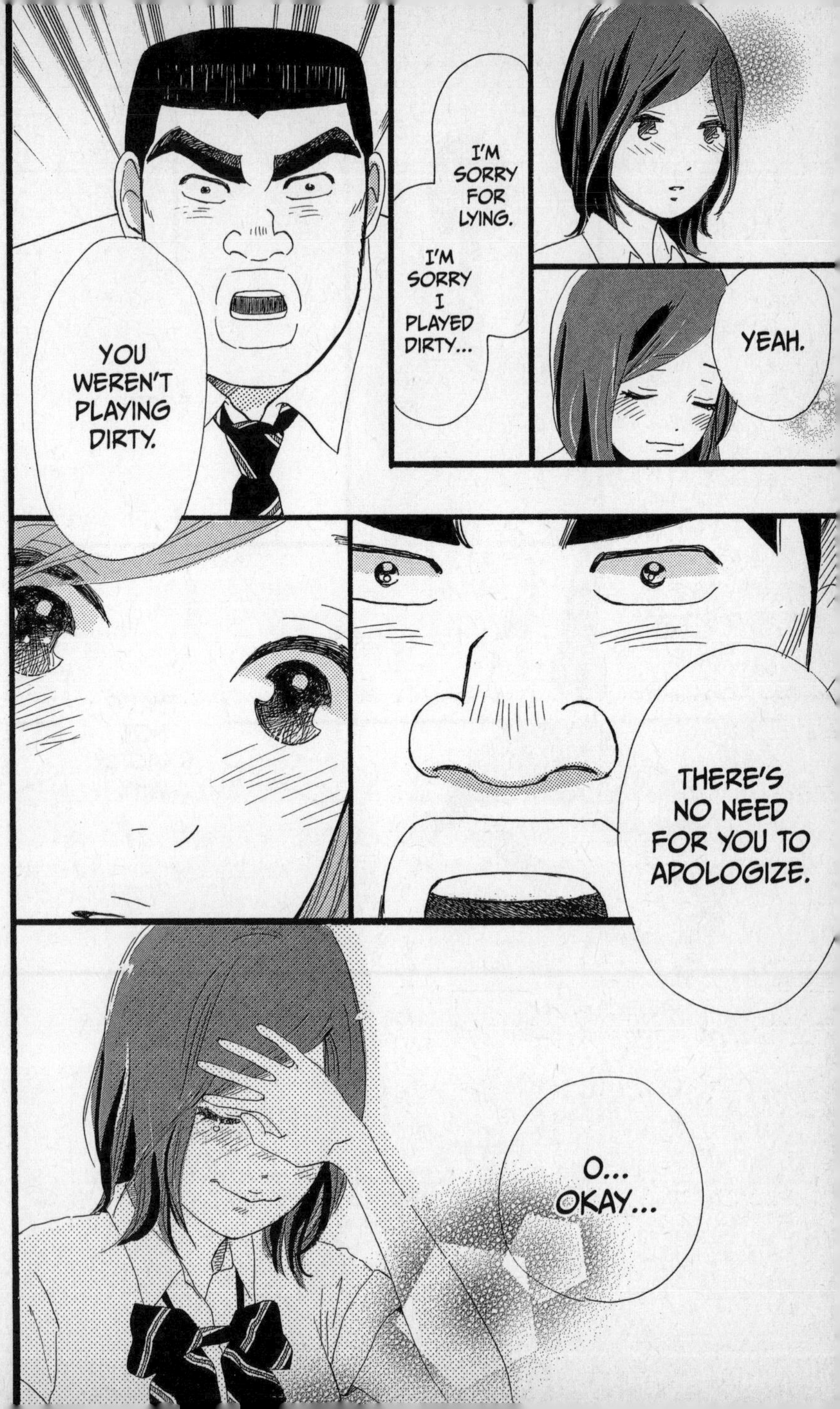
I'M SORRY FOR LYING.
I'M SORRY I PLAYED DIRTY...
YEAH.
YOU WEREN'T PLAYING DIRTY.
THERE'S NO NEED FOR YOU TO APOLOGIZE.
O... OKAY...

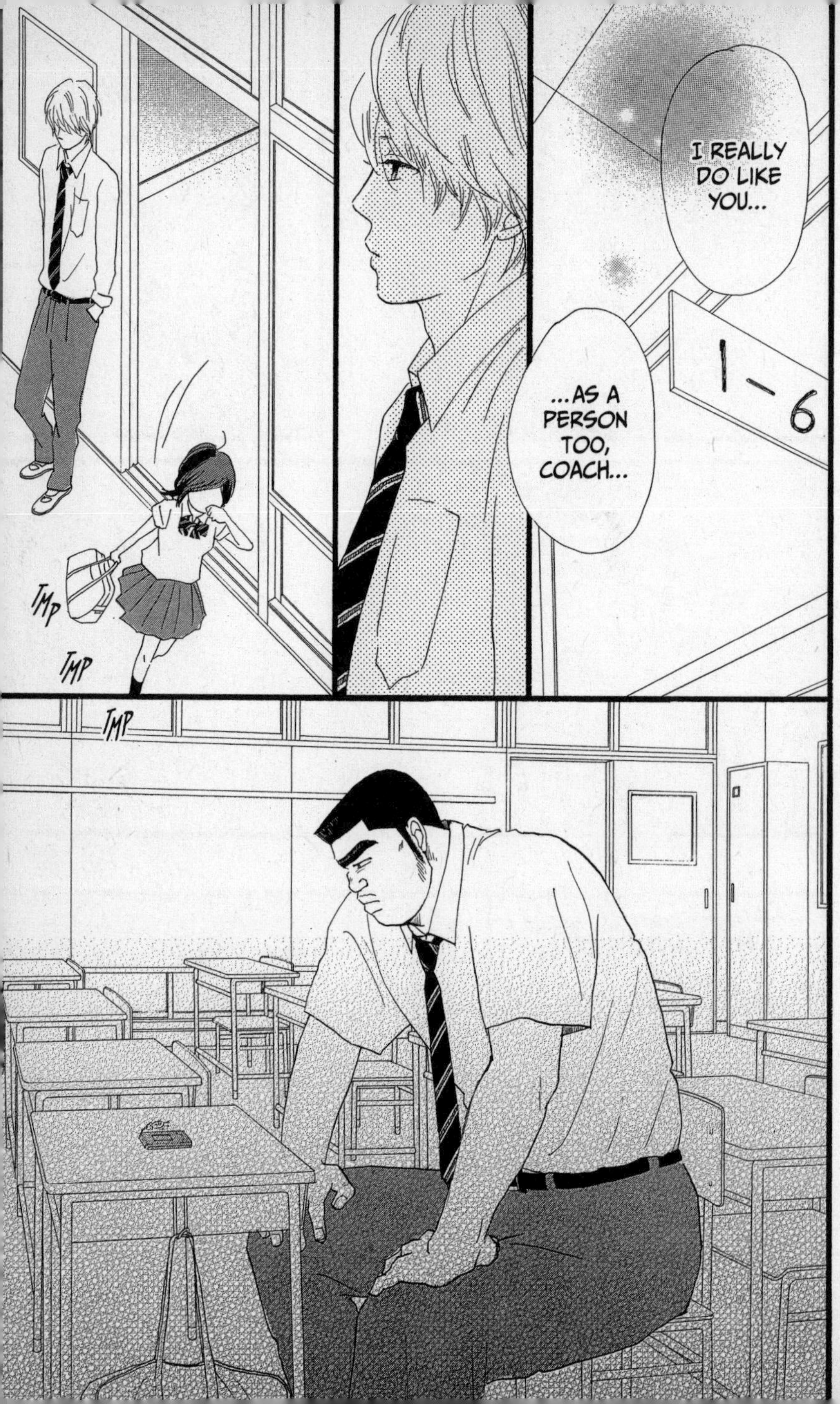
I REALLY DO LIKE YOU...
...AS A PERSON TOO, COACH...
1-6
TMP
TMP
TMP

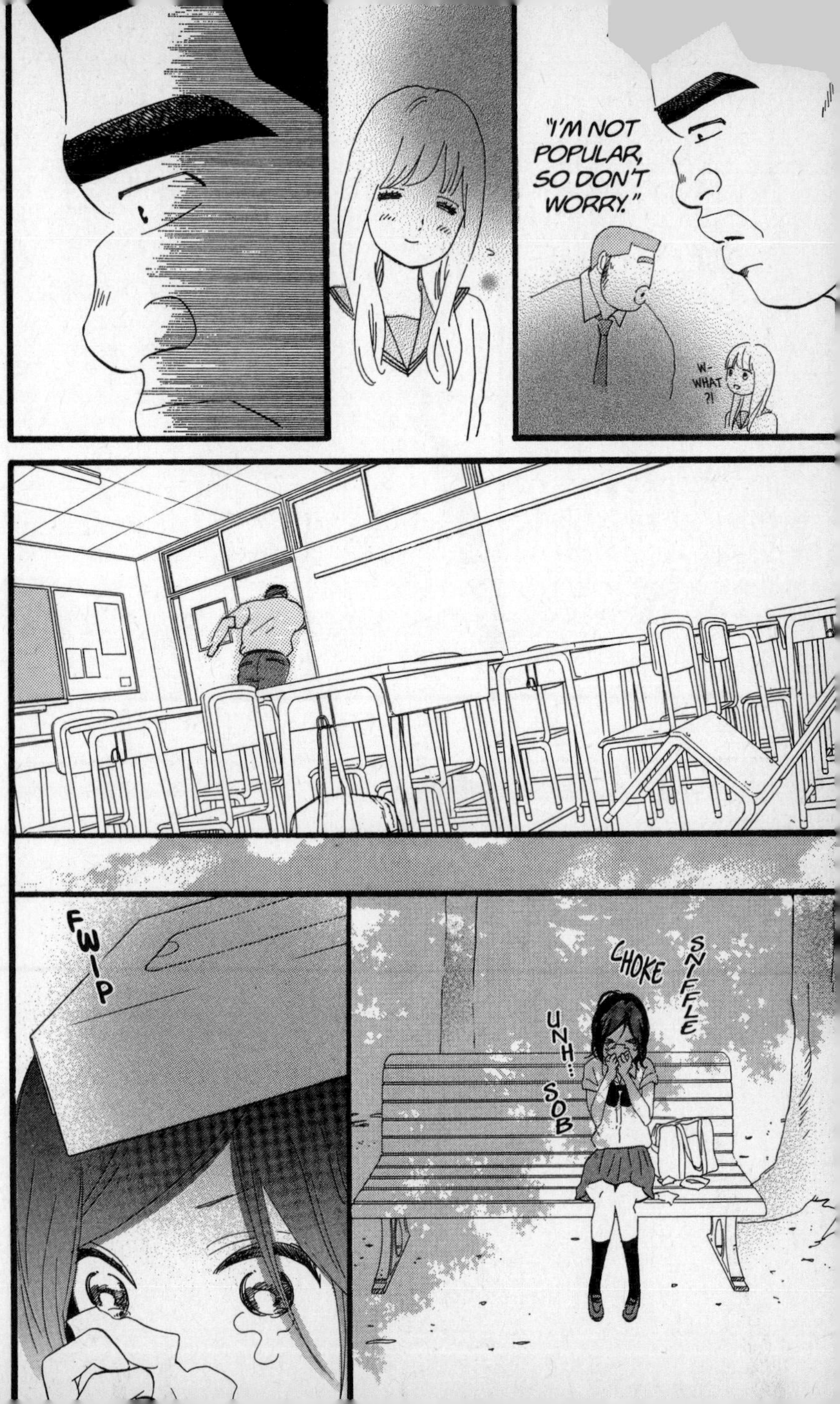
"I'M NOT POPULAR, SO DON'T WORRY."
W-WHAT?!
CHOKE
SNIFFLE
UNH...
SOB
FWIP

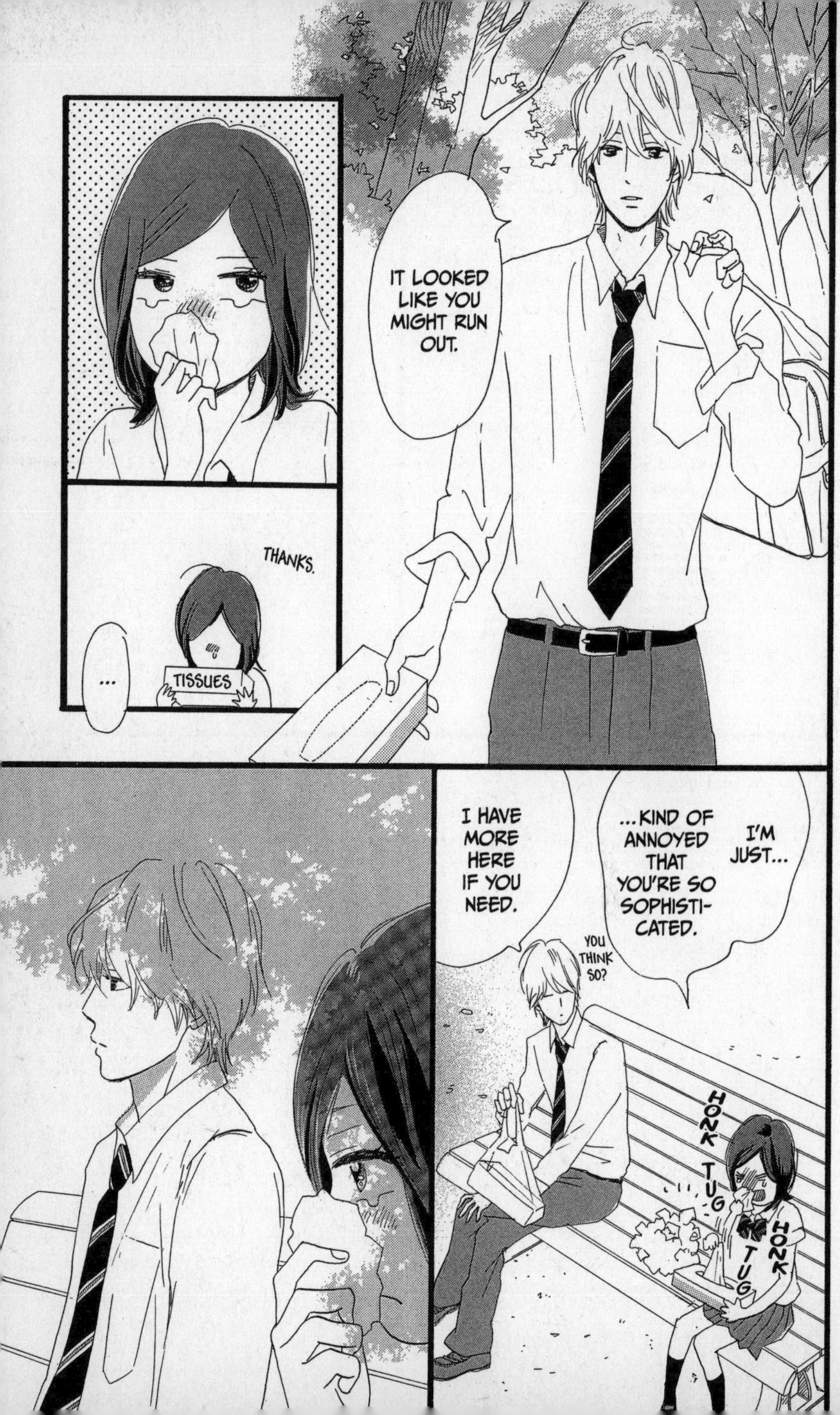
IT LOOKED LIKE YOU MIGHT RUN OUT.
THANKS.
TISSUES
...
I'M JUST...
...KIND OF ANNOYED THAT YOU'RE SO SOPHISTICATED.
I HAVE MORE HERE IF YOU NEED.
YOU THINK SO?
HONK
TUG
HONK
TUG

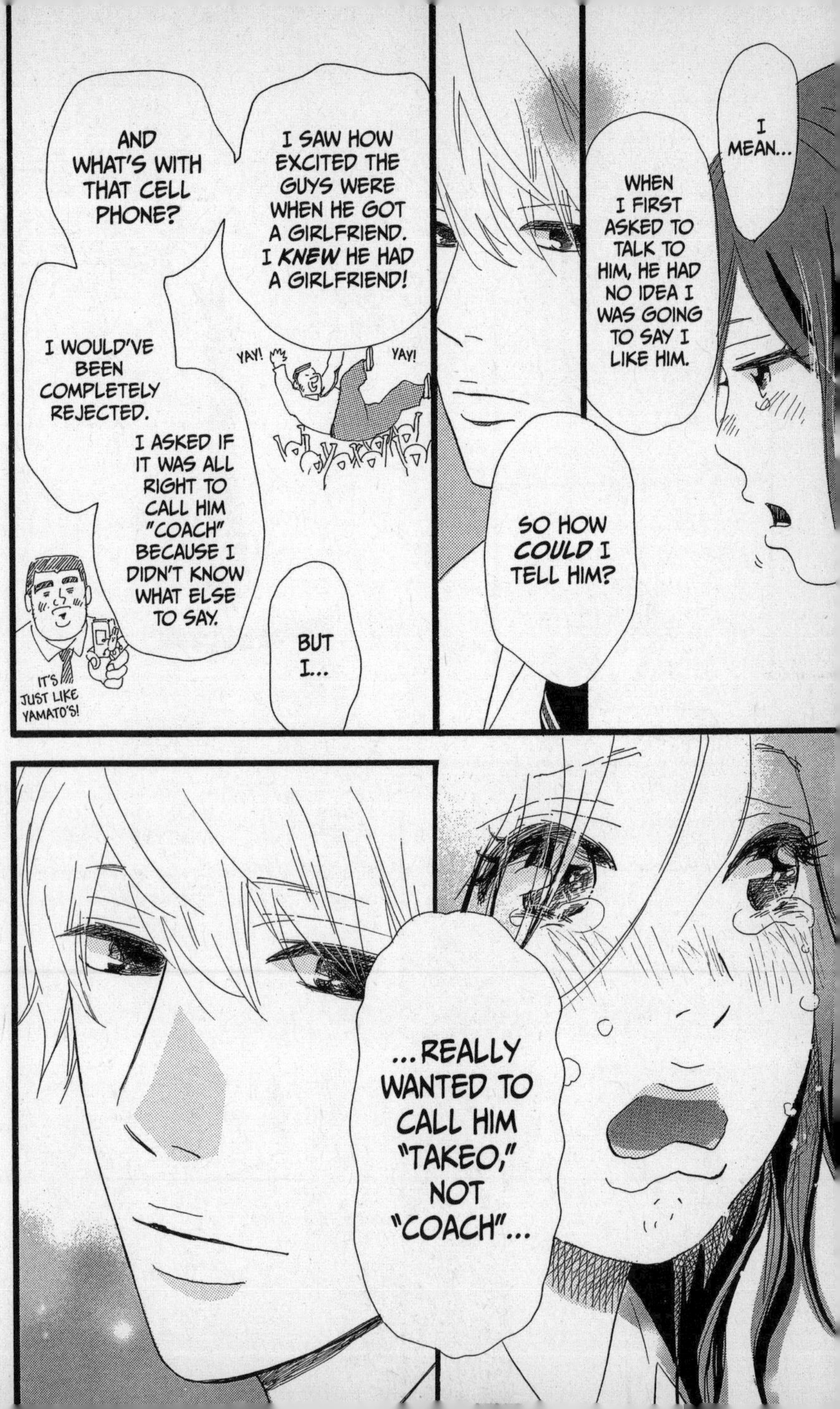
I MEAN...
WHEN I FIRST ASKED TO TALK TO HIM, HE HAD NO IDEA I WAS GOING TO SAY I LIKE HIM.
SO HOW COULD I TELL HIM?
I SAW HOW EXCITED THE GUYS WERE WHEN HE GOT A GIRLFRIEND. I KNEW HE HAD A GIRLFRIEND!
YAY!
YAY!
AND WHAT'S WITH THAT CELL PHONE?
IT'S JUST LIKE YAMATO'S!
I WOULD'VE BEEN COMPLETELY REJECTED.
I ASKED IF IT WAS ALL RIGHT TO CALL HIM "COACH" BECAUSE I DIDN'T KNOW WHAT ELSE TO SAY.
BUT I...
...REALLY WANTED TO CALL HIM "TAKEO," NOT "COACH"...

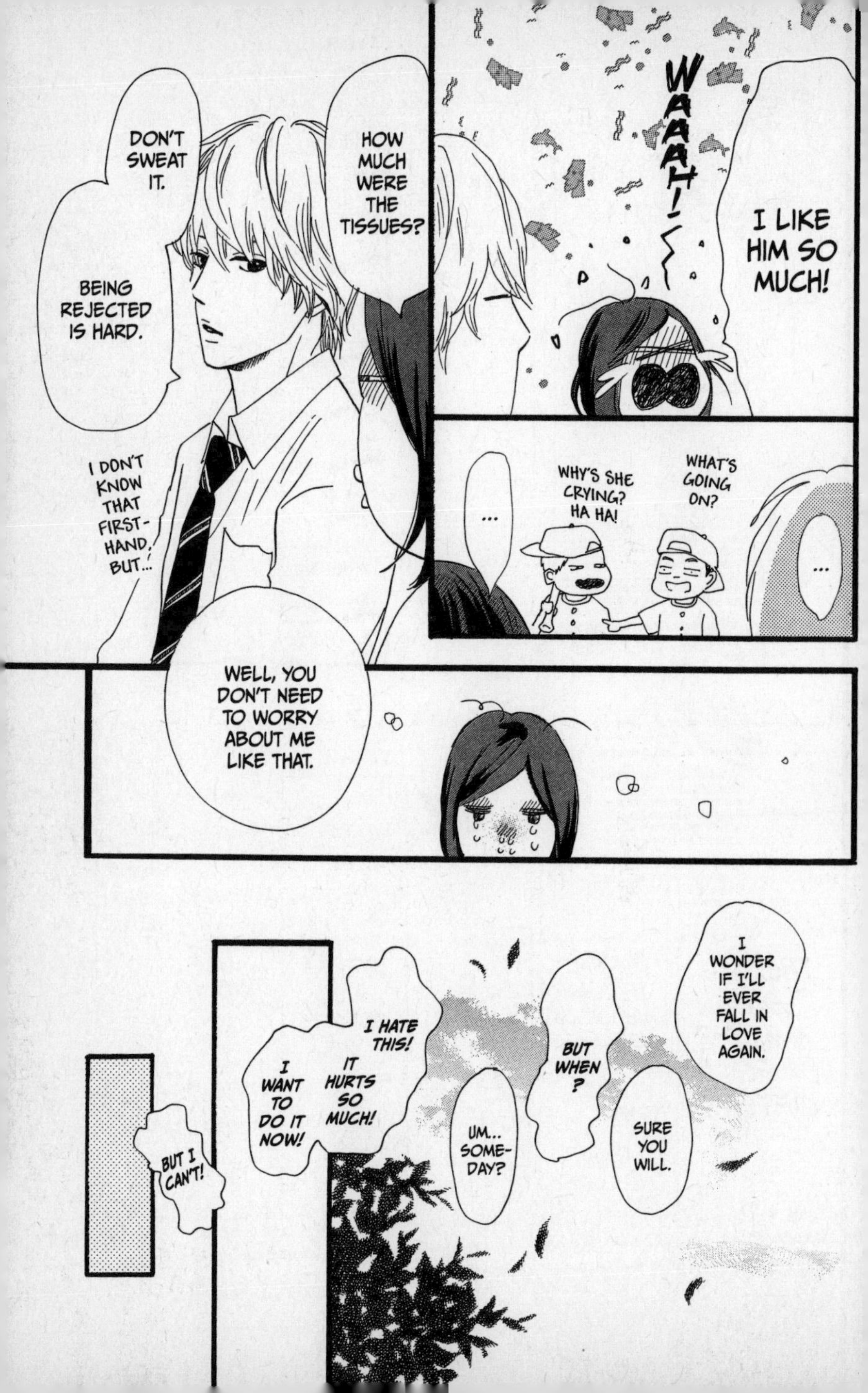
I LIKE HIM SO MUCH!
WAAAH!
WHAT'S GOING ON?
...
WHY'S SHE CRYING? HA HA!
...
HOW MUCH WERE THE TISSUES?
DON'T SWEAT IT.
BEING REJECTED IS HARD.
I DON'T KNOW THAT FIRST-HAND, BUT...
WELL, YOU DON'T NEED TO WORRY ABOUT ME LIKE THAT.
I WONDER IF I'LL EVER FALL IN LOVE AGAIN.
SURE YOU WILL.
BUT WHEN?
UM... SOME-DAY?
I HATE THIS!
IT HURTS SO MUCH!
I WANT TO DO IT NOW!
BUT I CAN'T!

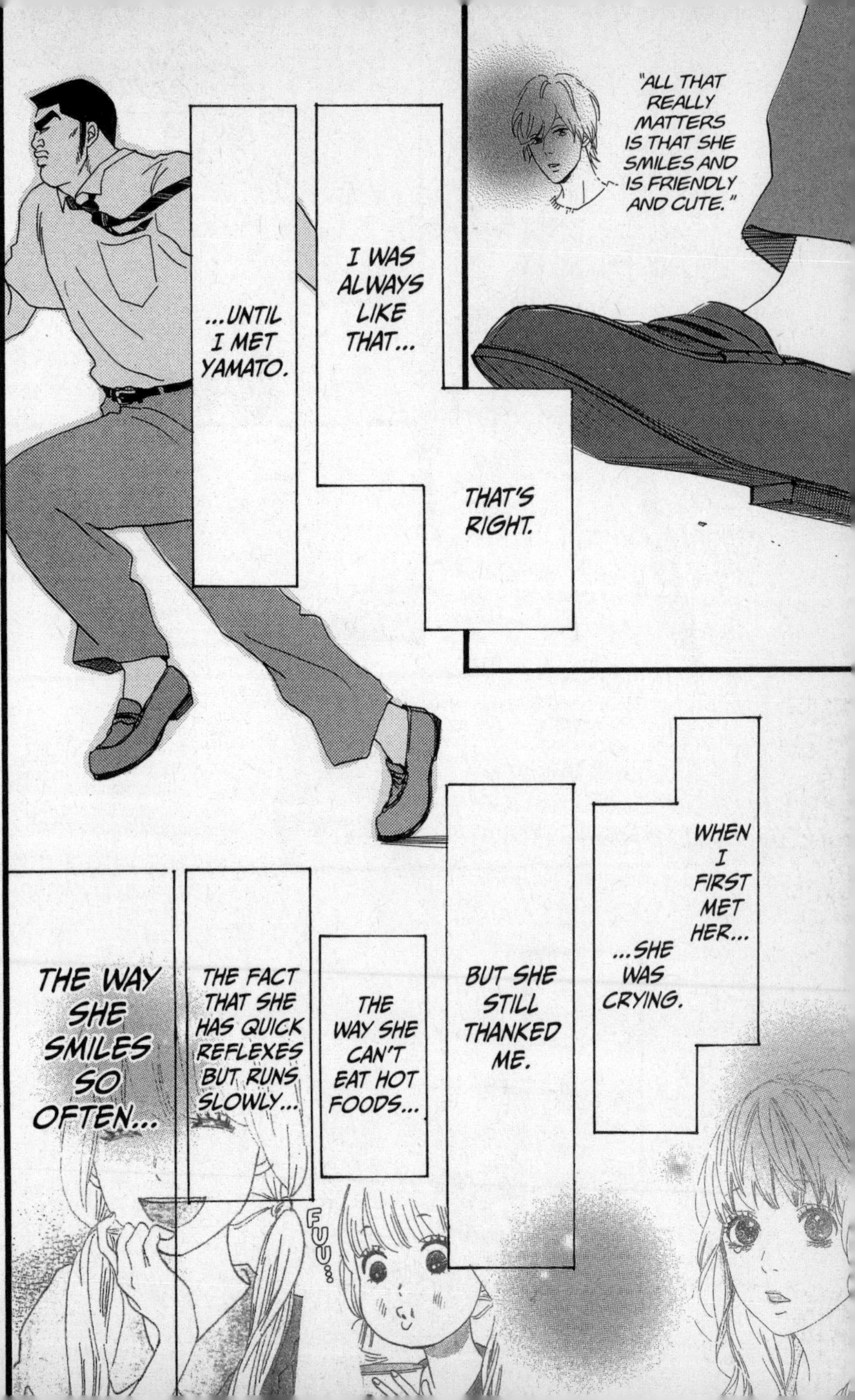
"ALL THAT REALLY MATTERS IS THAT SHE SMILES AND IS FRIENDLY AND CUTE."
THAT'S RIGHT.
I WAS ALWAYS LIKE THAT...
...UNTIL I MET YAMATO.
WHEN I FIRST MET HER...
...SHE WAS CRYING.
BUT SHE STILL THANKED ME.
THE WAY SHE CAN'T EAT HOT FOODS...
FUU...
THE FACT THAT SHE HAS QUICK REFLEXES BUT RUNS SLOWLY...
THE WAY SHE SMILES SO OFTEN...

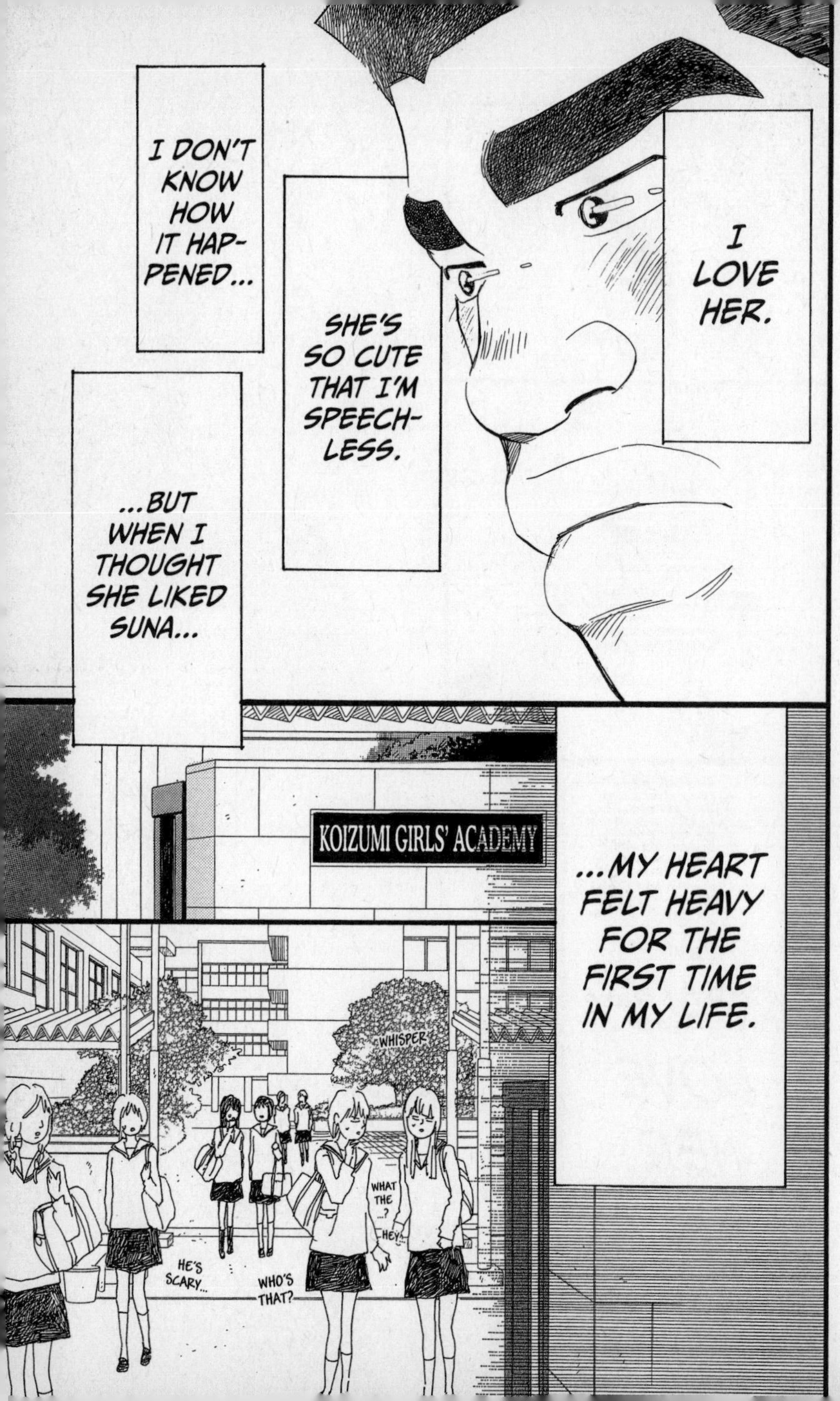
I LOVE HER.
SHE'S SO CUTE THAT I'M SPEECHLESS.
I DON'T KNOW HOW IT HAPPENED...
...BUT WHEN I THOUGHT SHE LIKED SUNA...
...MY HEART FELT HEAVY FOR THE FIRST TIME IN MY LIFE.
KOIZUMI GIRLS' ACADEMY
WHISPER
WHAT THE ...?
HEY
WHO'S THAT?
HE'S SCARY...

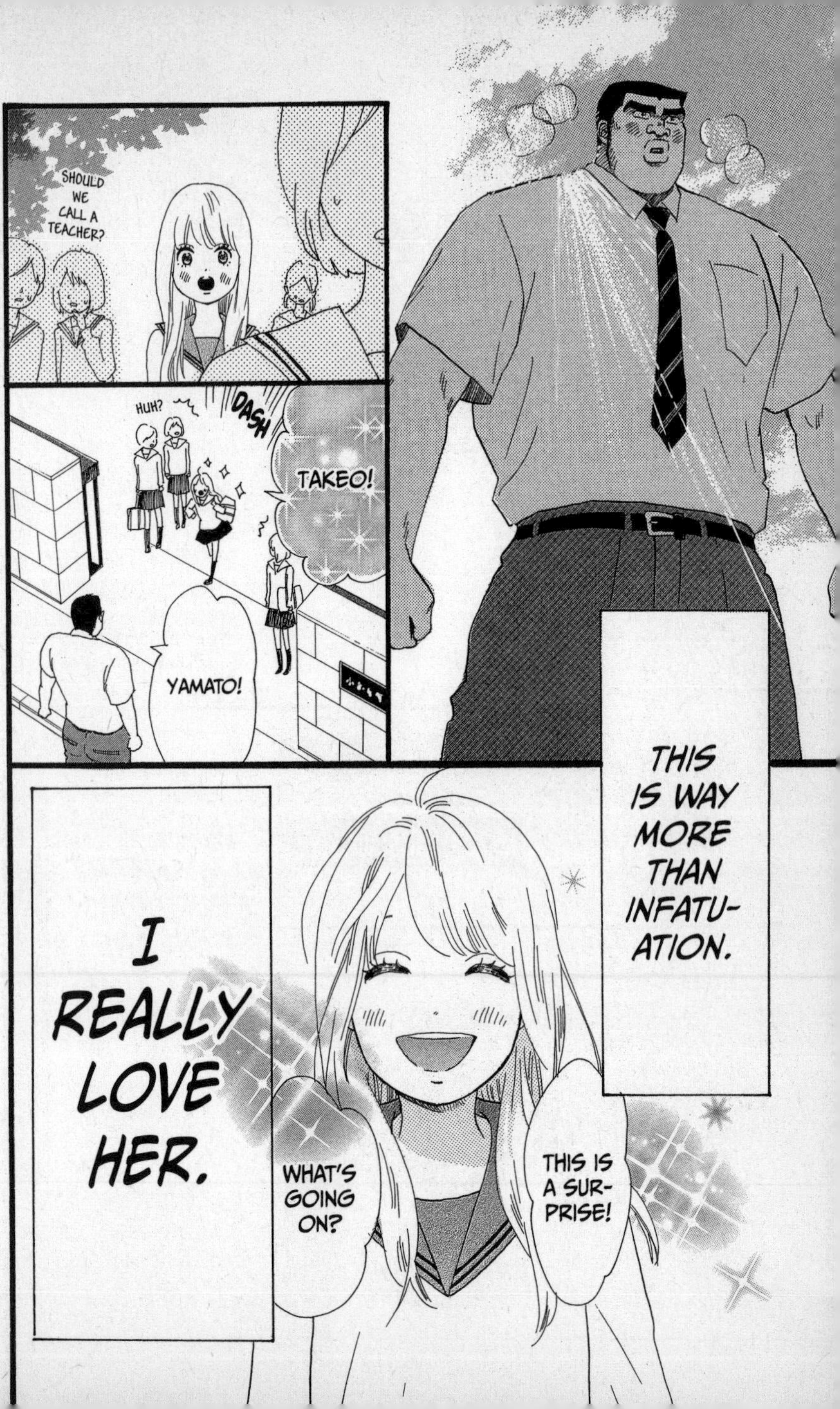
SHOULD WE CALL A TEACHER?
DASH
TAKEO!
HUH?
YAMATO!
THIS IS WAY MORE THAN INFATU-ATION.
THIS IS A SUR-PRISE!
WHAT'S GOING ON?
I REALLY LOVE HER.

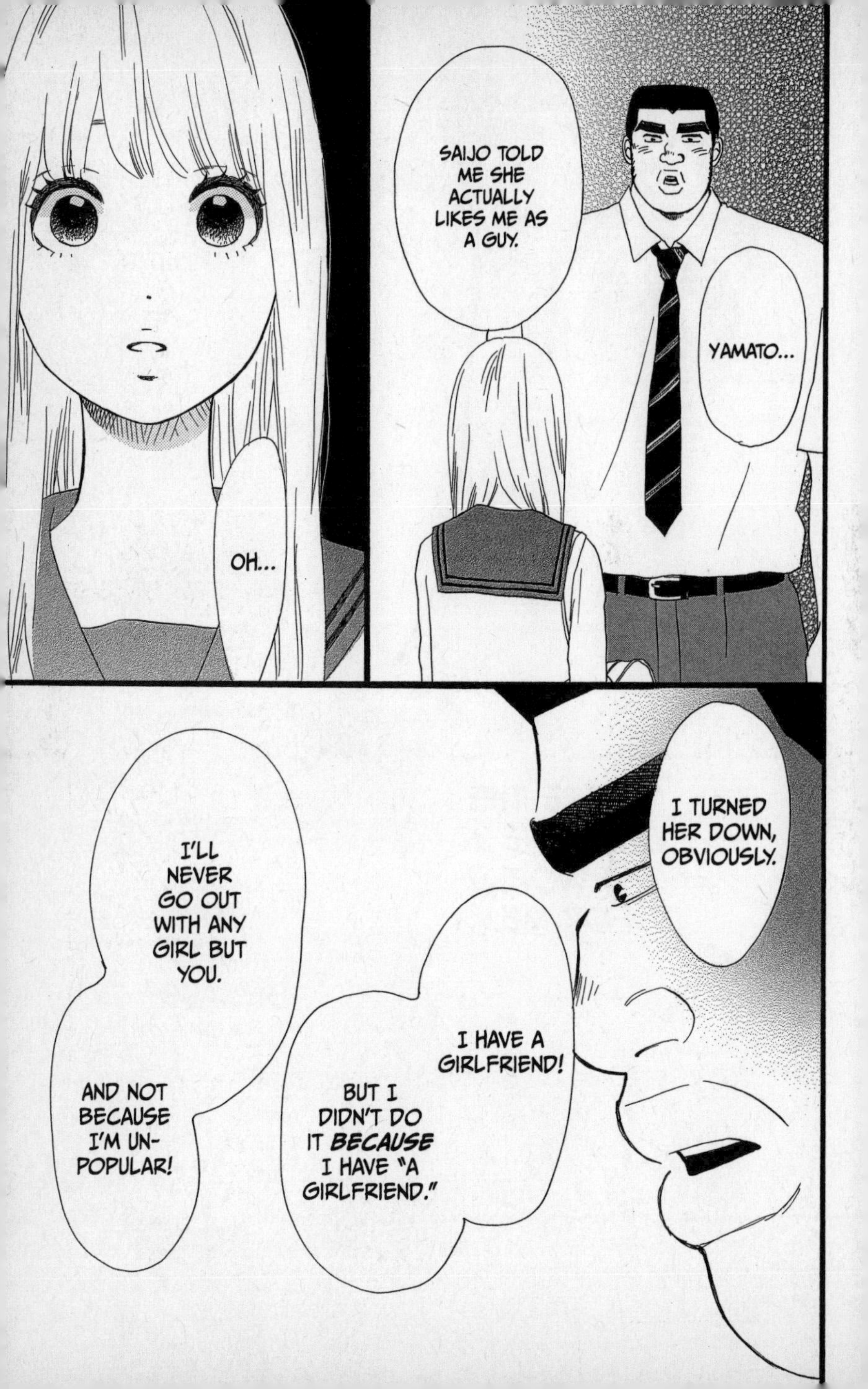
SAIJO TOLD ME SHE ACTUALLY LIKES ME AS A GUY.
YAMATO...
OH...
I TURNED HER DOWN, OBVIOUSLY.
I HAVE A GIRLFRIEND!
BUT I DIDN'T DO IT *BECAUSE* I HAVE "A GIRLFRIEND."
I'LL NEVER GO OUT WITH ANY GIRL BUT YOU.
AND NOT BECAUSE I'M UN-POPULAR!

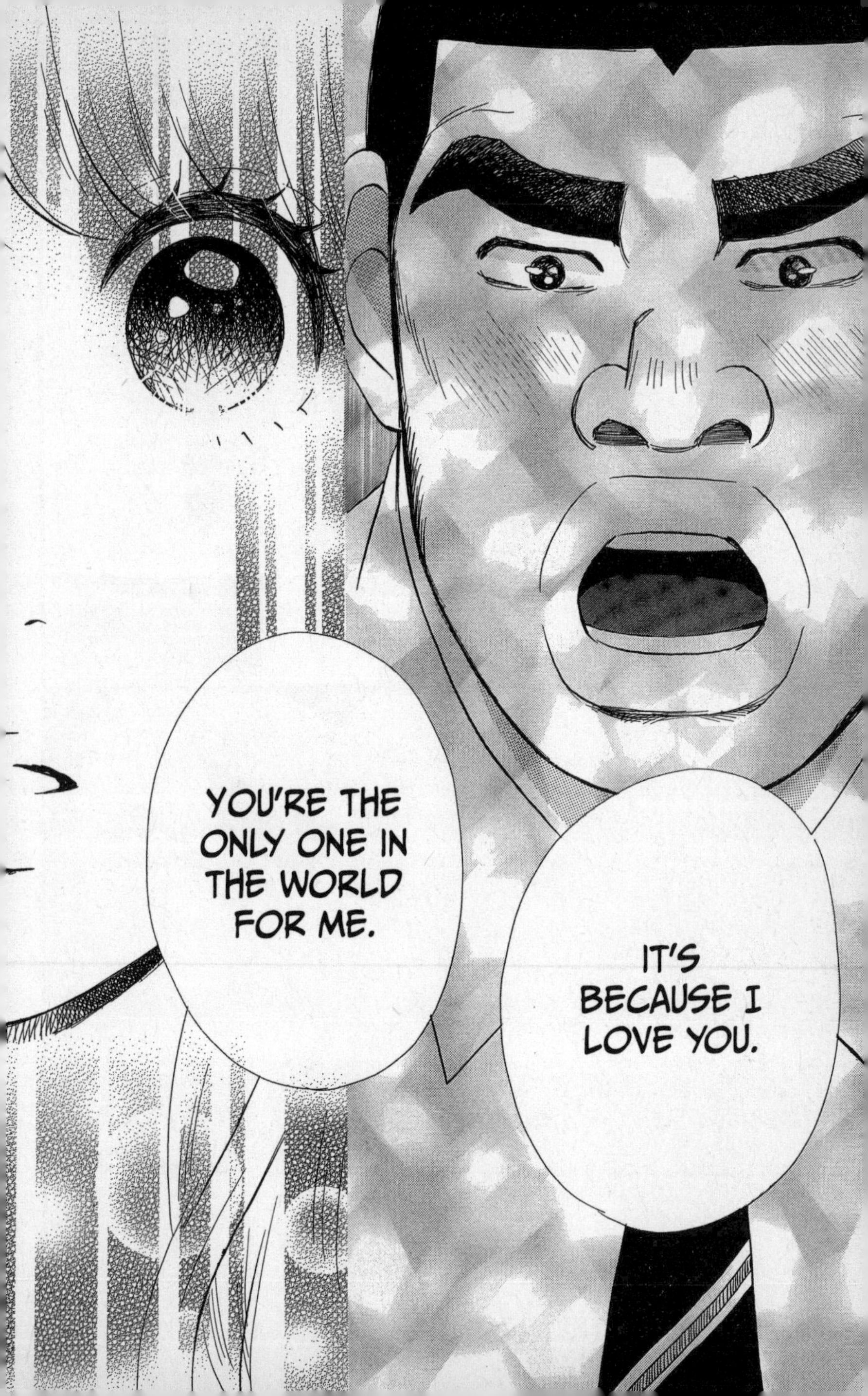
IT'S BECAUSE I LOVE YOU.
YOU'RE THE ONLY ONE IN THE WORLD FOR ME.

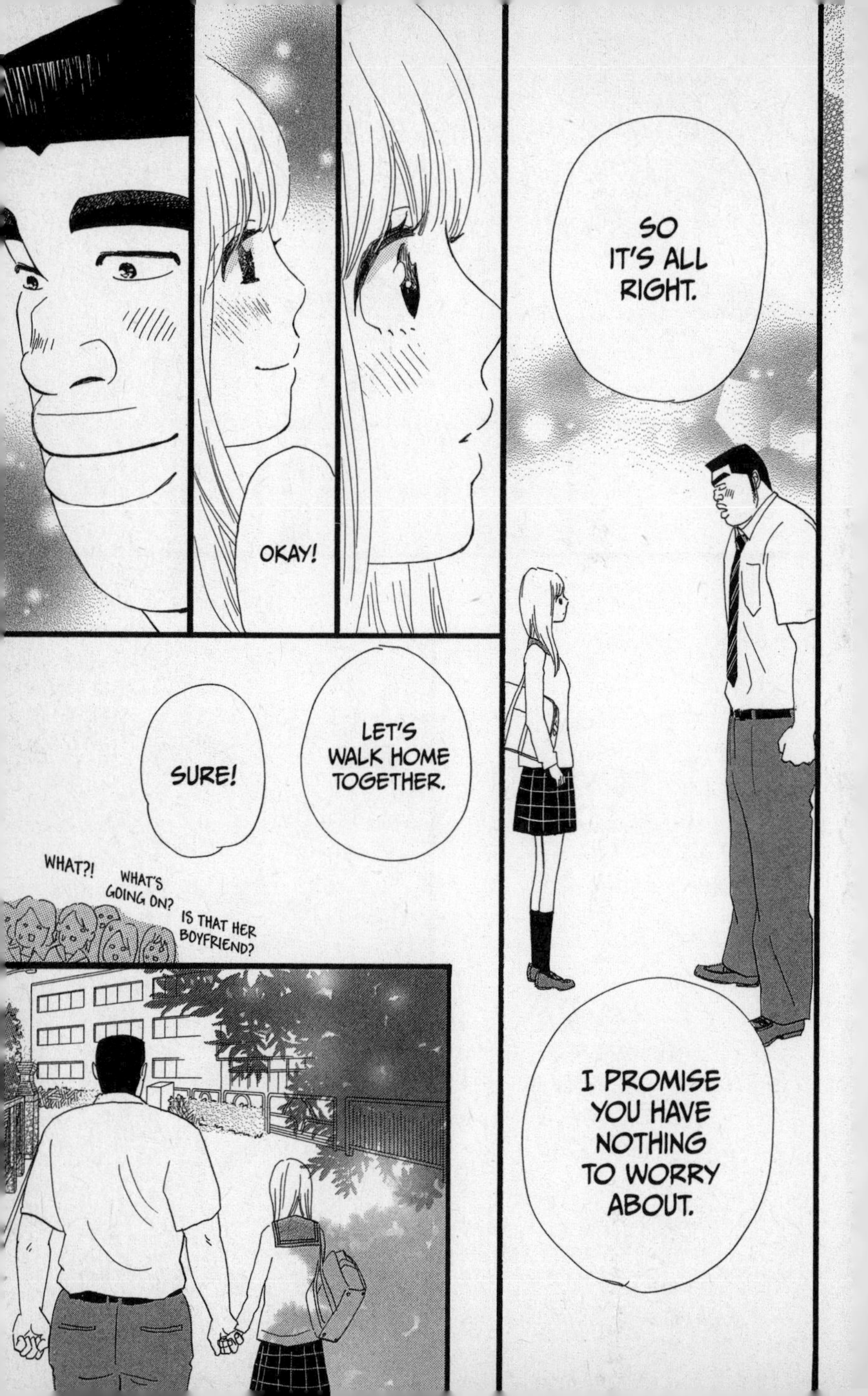
SO IT'S ALL RIGHT.
I PROMISE YOU HAVE NOTHING TO WORRY ABOUT.
OKAY!
LET'S WALK HOME TOGETHER.
SURE!
IS THAT HER BOYFRIEND?
WHAT'S GOING ON?
WHAT?!

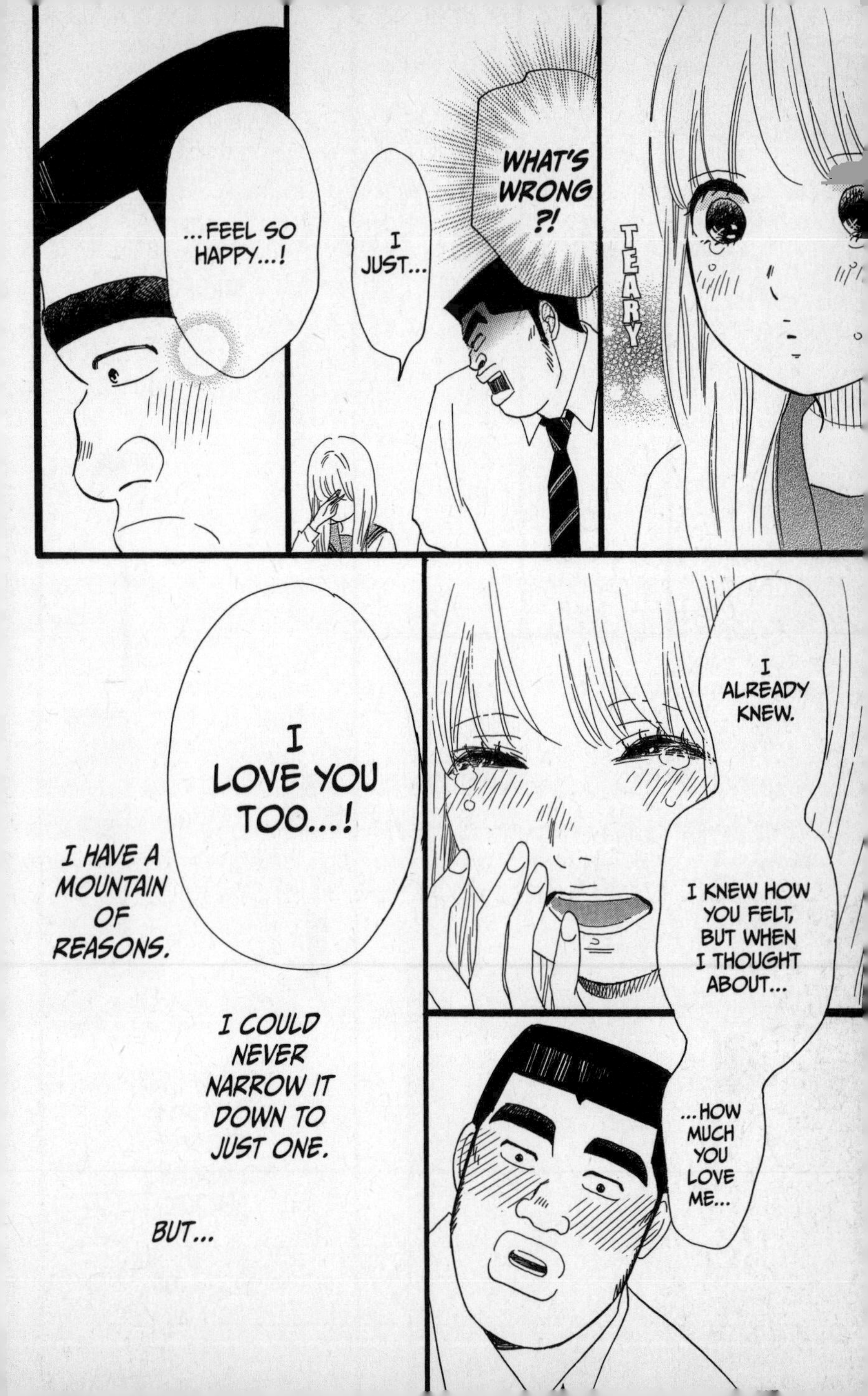
TEARY
WHAT'S WRONG?!
I JUST...
...FEEL SO HAPPY...!
I ALREADY KNEW.
I KNEW HOW YOU FELT, BUT WHEN I THOUGHT ABOUT...
...HOW MUCH YOU LOVE ME...
I LOVE YOU TOO...!
I HAVE A MOUNTAIN OF REASONS.
I COULD NEVER NARROW IT DOWN TO JUST ONE.
BUT...

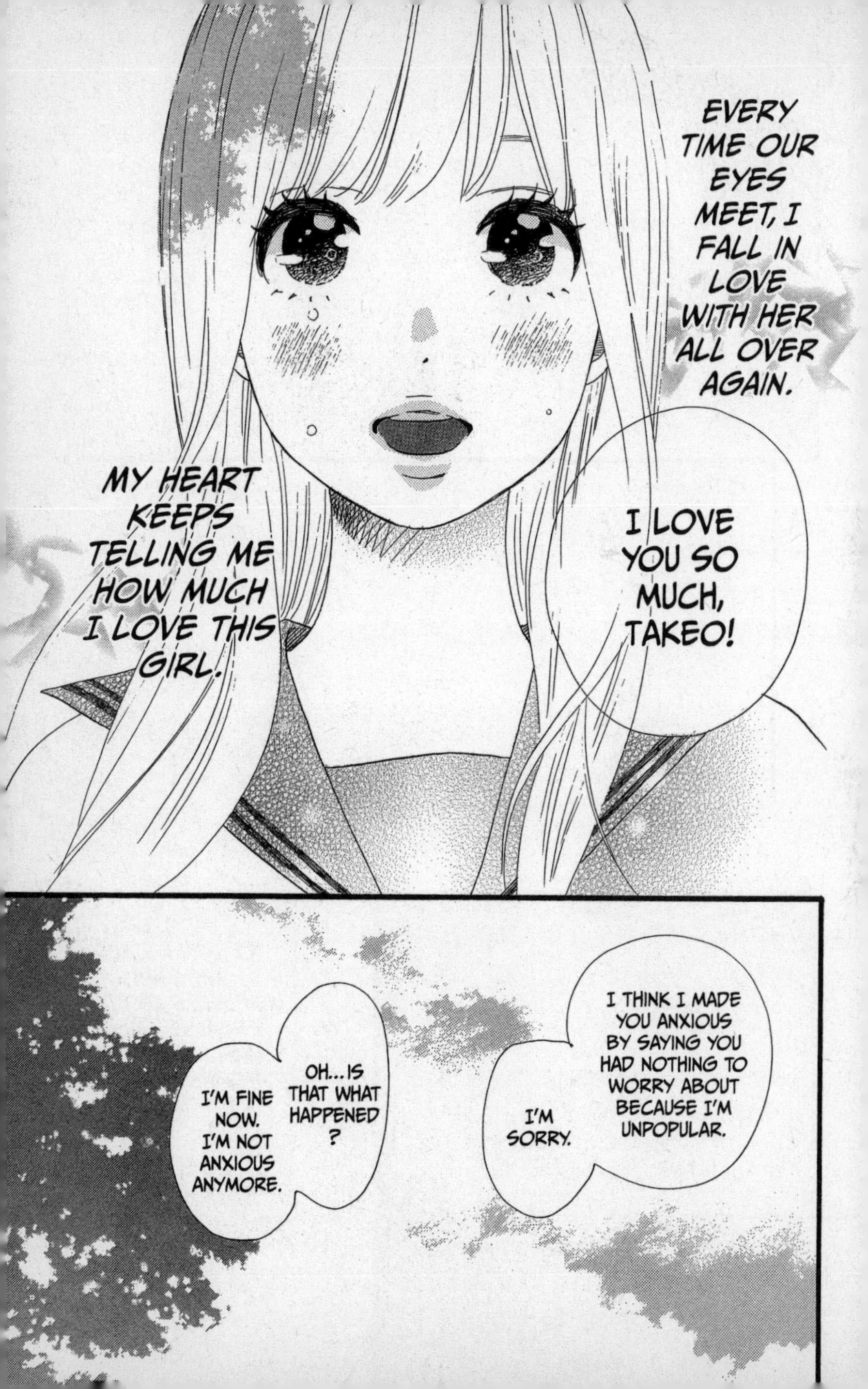
EVERY TIME OUR EYES MEET, I FALL IN LOVE WITH HER ALL OVER AGAIN.
I LOVE YOU SO MUCH, TAKEO!
MY HEART KEEPS TELLING ME HOW MUCH I LOVE THIS GIRL.
I THINK I MADE YOU ANXIOUS BY SAYING YOU HAD NOTHING TO WORRY ABOUT BECAUSE I'M UNPOPULAR.
I'M SORRY.
OH...IS THAT WHAT HAPPENED?
I'M FINE NOW. I'M NOT ANXIOUS ANYMORE.

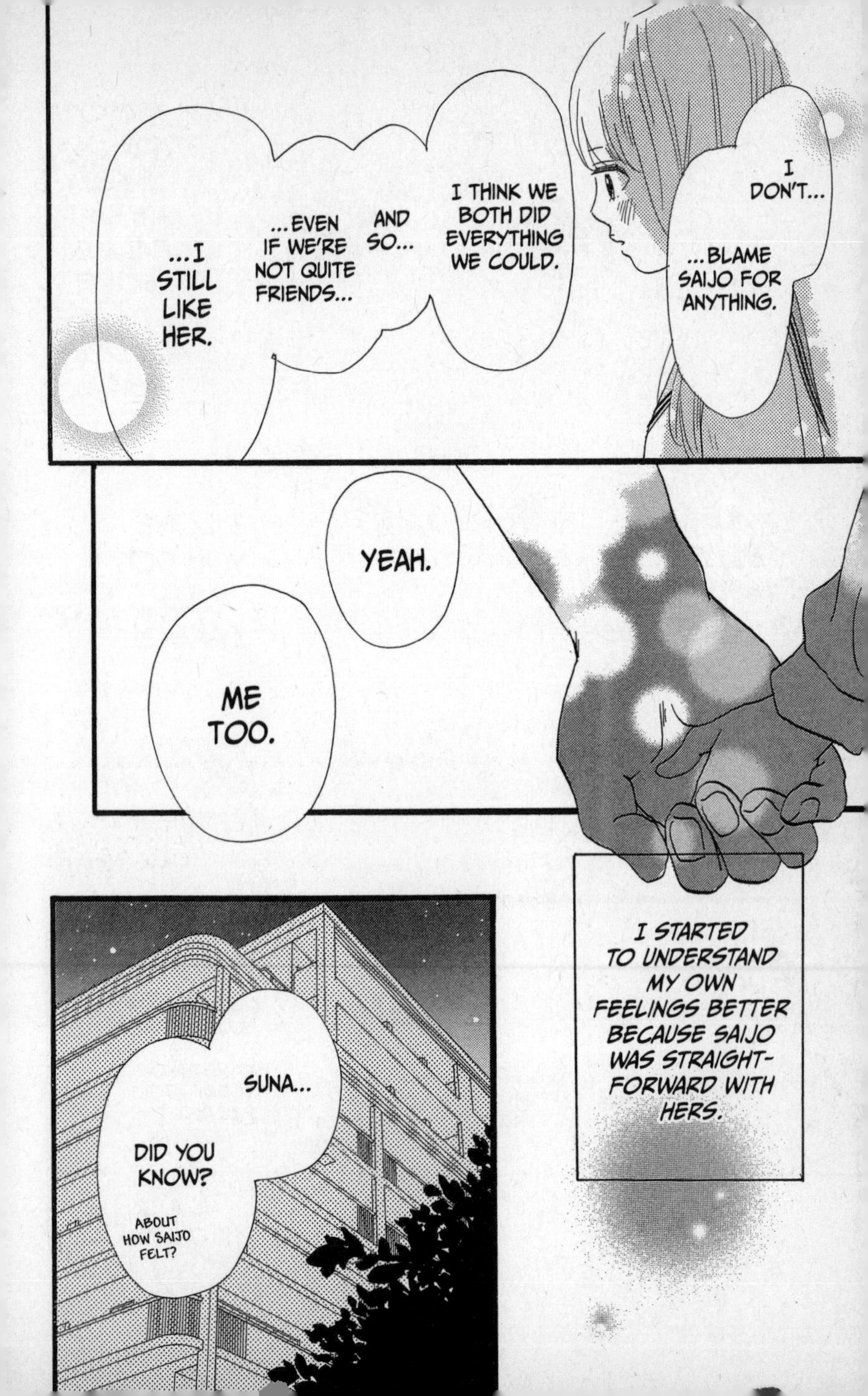
I DON'T...
...BLAME SAIJO FOR ANYTHING.
I THINK WE BOTH DID EVERYTHING WE COULD.
AND SO...
...EVEN IF WE'RE NOT QUITE FRIENDS...
...I STILL LIKE HER.
YEAH.
ME TOO.
I STARTED TO UNDERSTAND MY OWN FEELINGS BETTER BECAUSE SAIJO WAS STRAIGHT-FORWARD WITH HERS.
SUNA...
DID YOU KNOW?
ABOUT HOW SAIJO FELT?

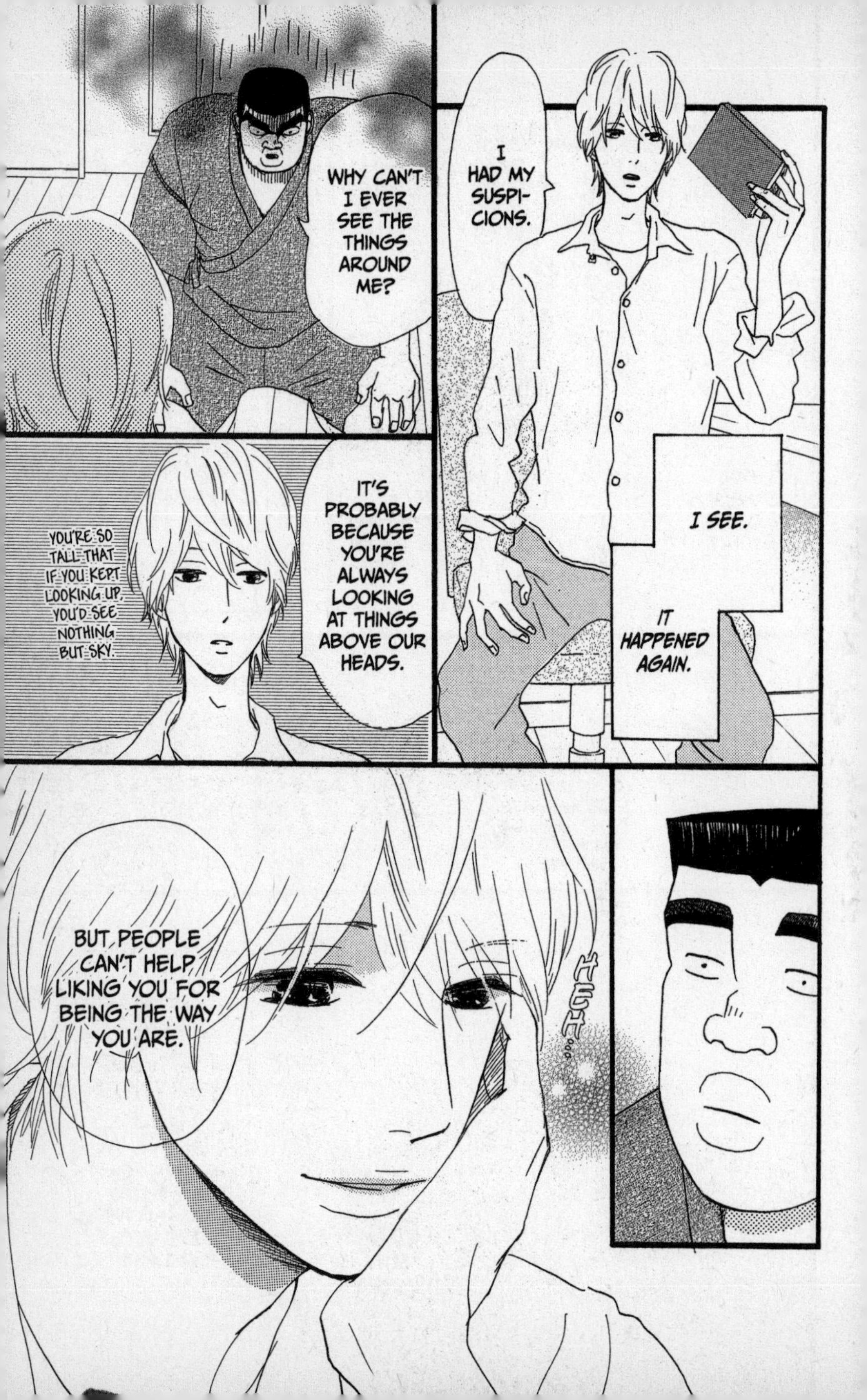
I HAD MY SUSPICIONS.
I SEE.
IT HAPPENED AGAIN.
WHY CAN'T I EVER SEE THE THINGS AROUND ME?
IT'S PROBABLY BECAUSE YOU'RE ALWAYS LOOKING AT THINGS ABOVE OUR HEADS.
YOU'RE SO TALL THAT IF YOU KEPT LOOKING UP, YOU'D SEE NOTHING BUT SKY.
HEH...
BUT PEOPLE CAN'T HELP LIKING YOU FOR BEING THE WAY YOU ARE.

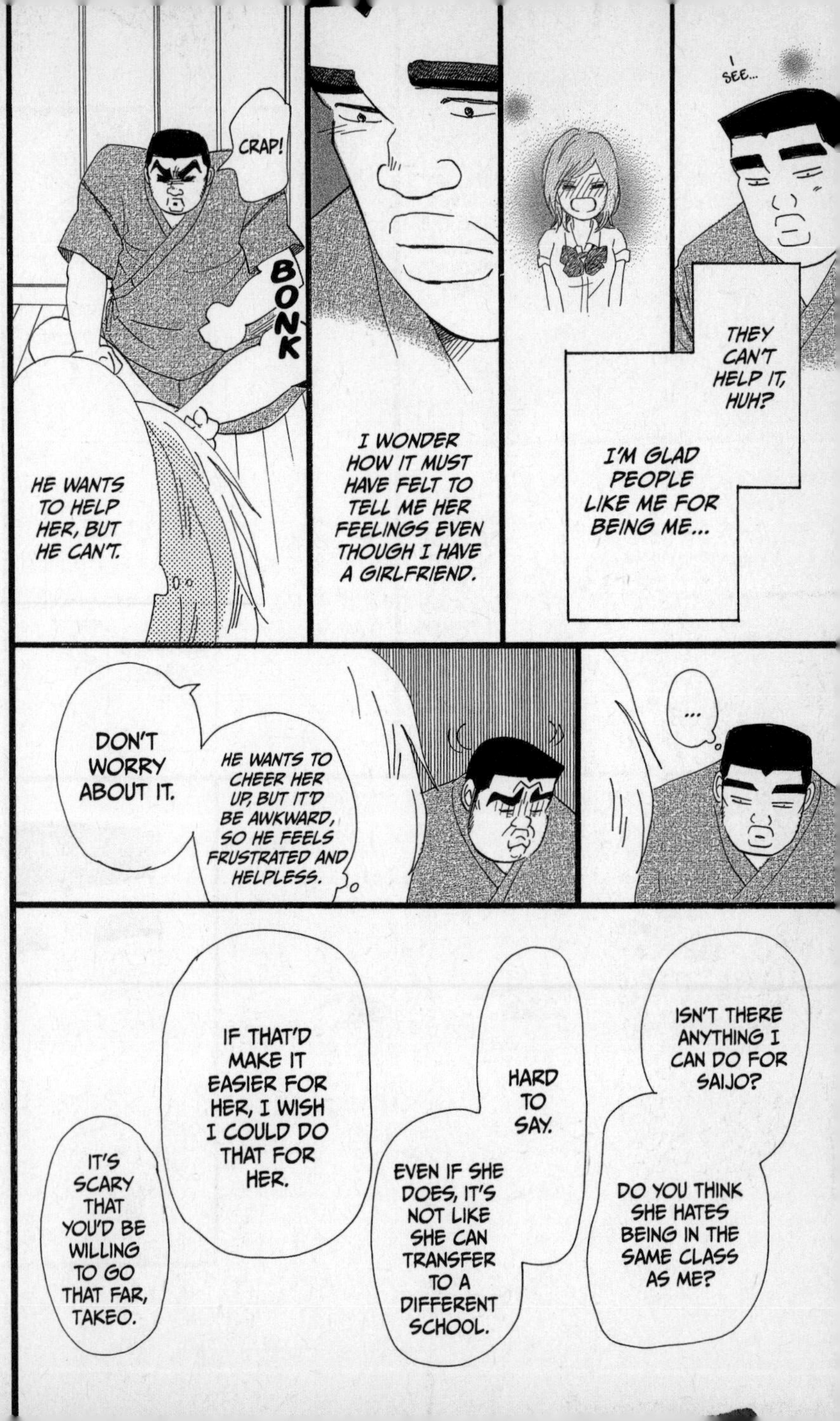
I SEE...
THEY CAN'T HELP IT, HUH?
I'M GLAD PEOPLE LIKE ME FOR BEING ME...
I WONDER HOW IT MUST HAVE FELT TO TELL ME HER FEELINGS EVEN THOUGH I HAVE A GIRLFRIEND.
CRAP!
BONK
HE WANTS TO HELP HER, BUT HE CAN'T.
...
HE WANTS TO CHEER HER UP, BUT IT'D BE AWKWARD, SO HE FEELS FRUSTRATED AND HELPLESS.
DON'T WORRY ABOUT IT.
ISN'T THERE ANYTHING I CAN DO FOR SAIJO?
DO YOU THINK SHE HATES BEING IN THE SAME CLASS AS ME?
HARD TO SAY.
EVEN IF SHE DOES, IT'S NOT LIKE SHE CAN TRANSFER TO A DIFFERENT SCHOOL.
IF THAT'D MAKE IT EASIER FOR HER, I WISH I COULD DO THAT FOR HER.
IT'S SCARY THAT YOU'D BE WILLING TO GO THAT FAR, TAKEO.

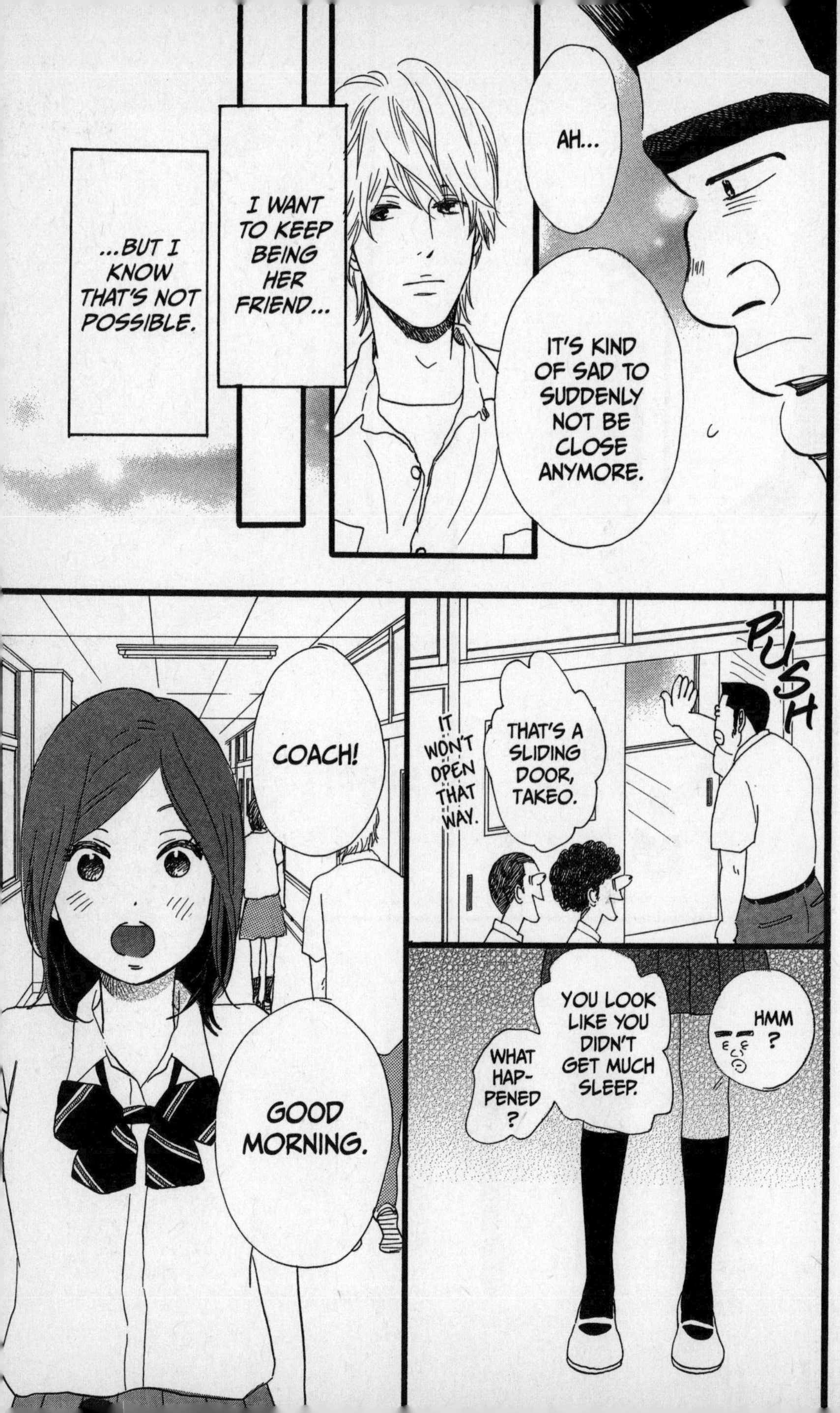
AH...
IT'S KIND OF SAD TO SUDDENLY NOT BE CLOSE ANYMORE.
I WANT TO KEEP BEING HER FRIEND...
...BUT I KNOW THAT'S NOT POSSIBLE.
PUSH
THAT'S A SLIDING DOOR, TAKEO.
IT WON'T OPEN THAT WAY.
HMM?
YOU LOOK LIKE YOU DIDN'T GET MUCH SLEEP.
WHAT HAPPENED?
COACH!
GOOD MORNING.

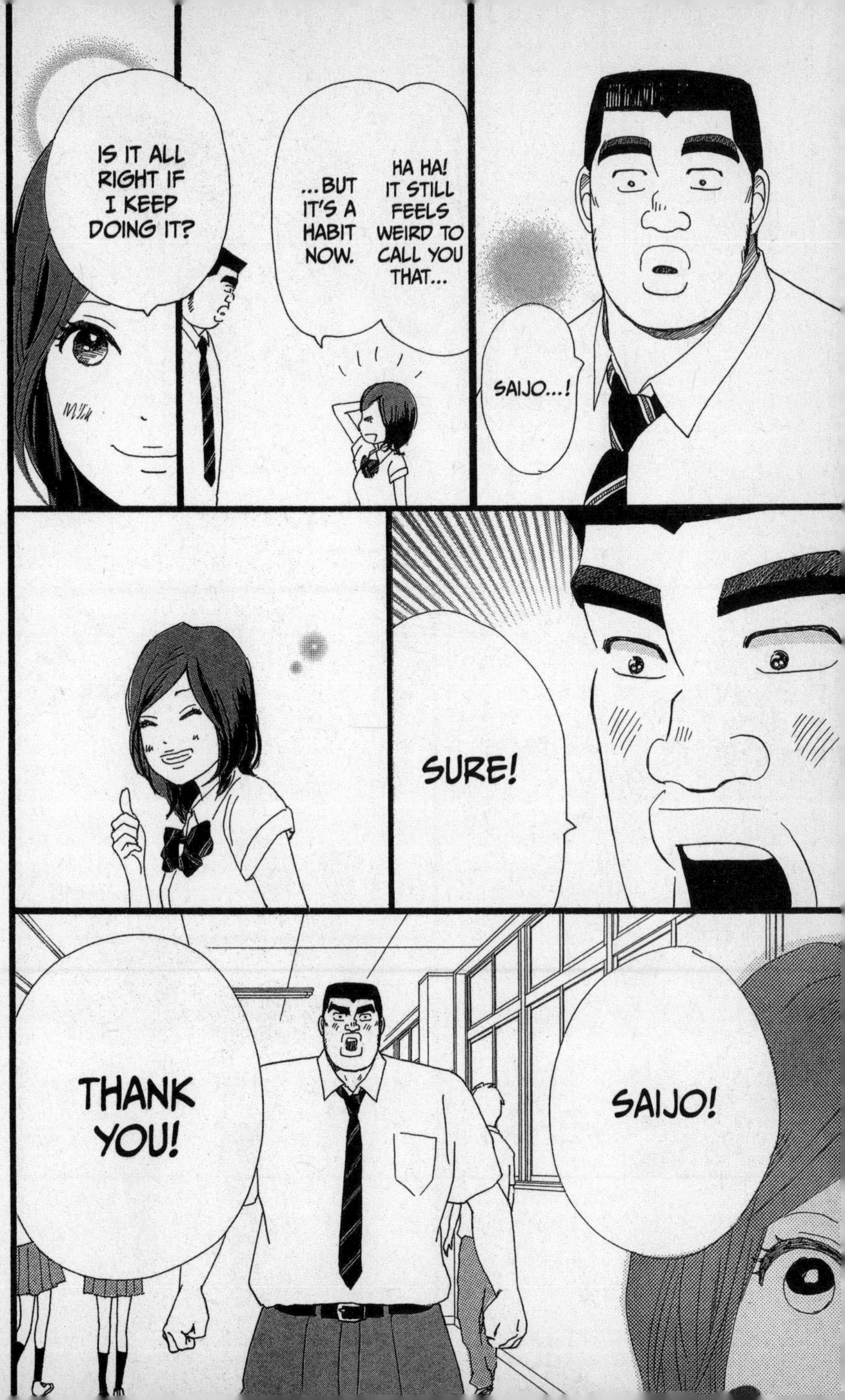
SAIJO...!
HA HA! IT STILL FEELS WEIRD TO CALL YOU THAT...
...BUT IT'S A HABIT NOW.
IS IT ALL RIGHT IF I KEEP DOING IT?
SURE!
SAIJO!
THANK YOU!

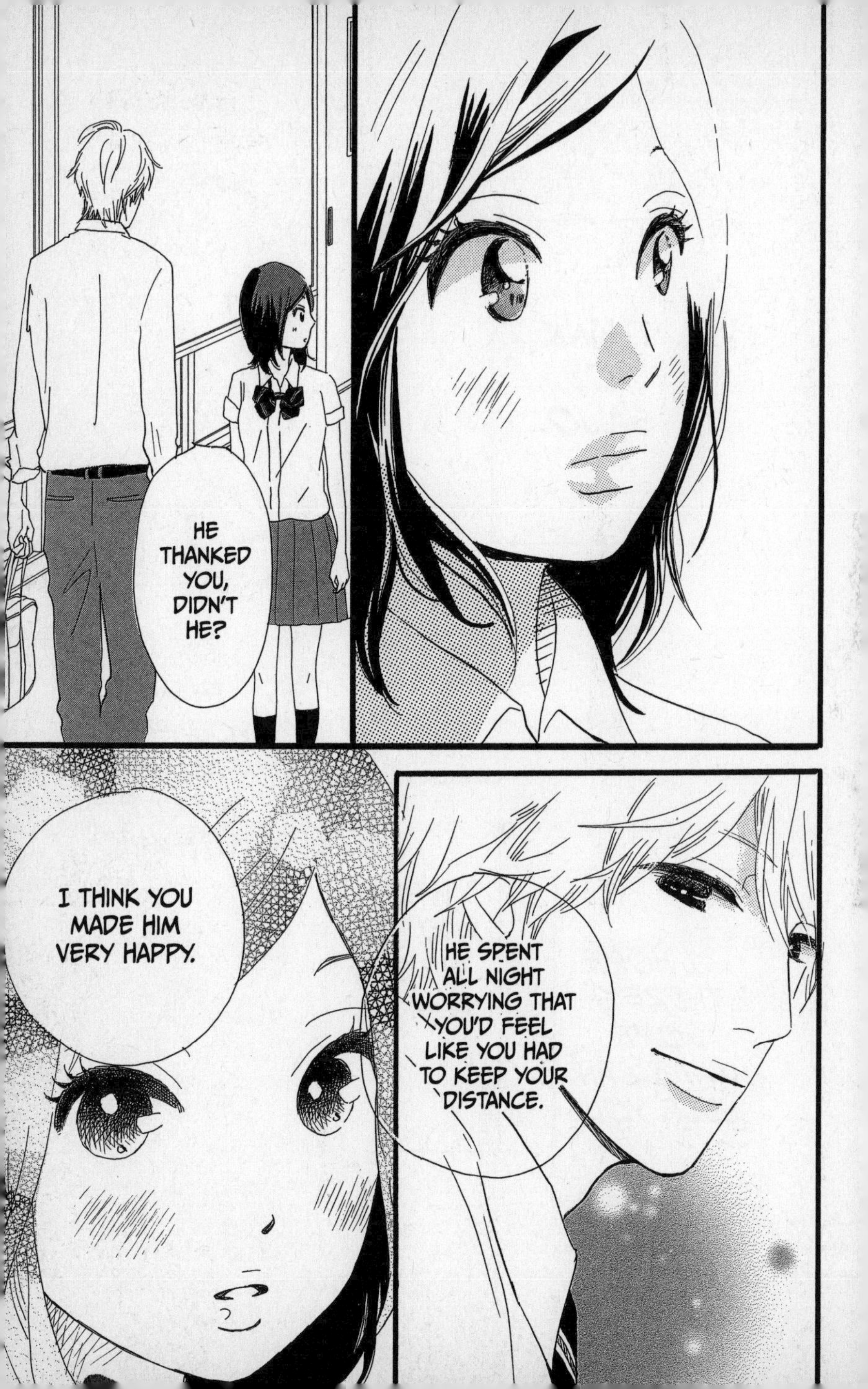
HE THANKED YOU, DIDN'T HE?
HE SPENT ALL NIGHT WORRYING THAT YOU'D FEEL LIKE YOU HAD TO KEEP YOUR DISTANCE.
I THINK YOU MADE HIM VERY HAPPY.

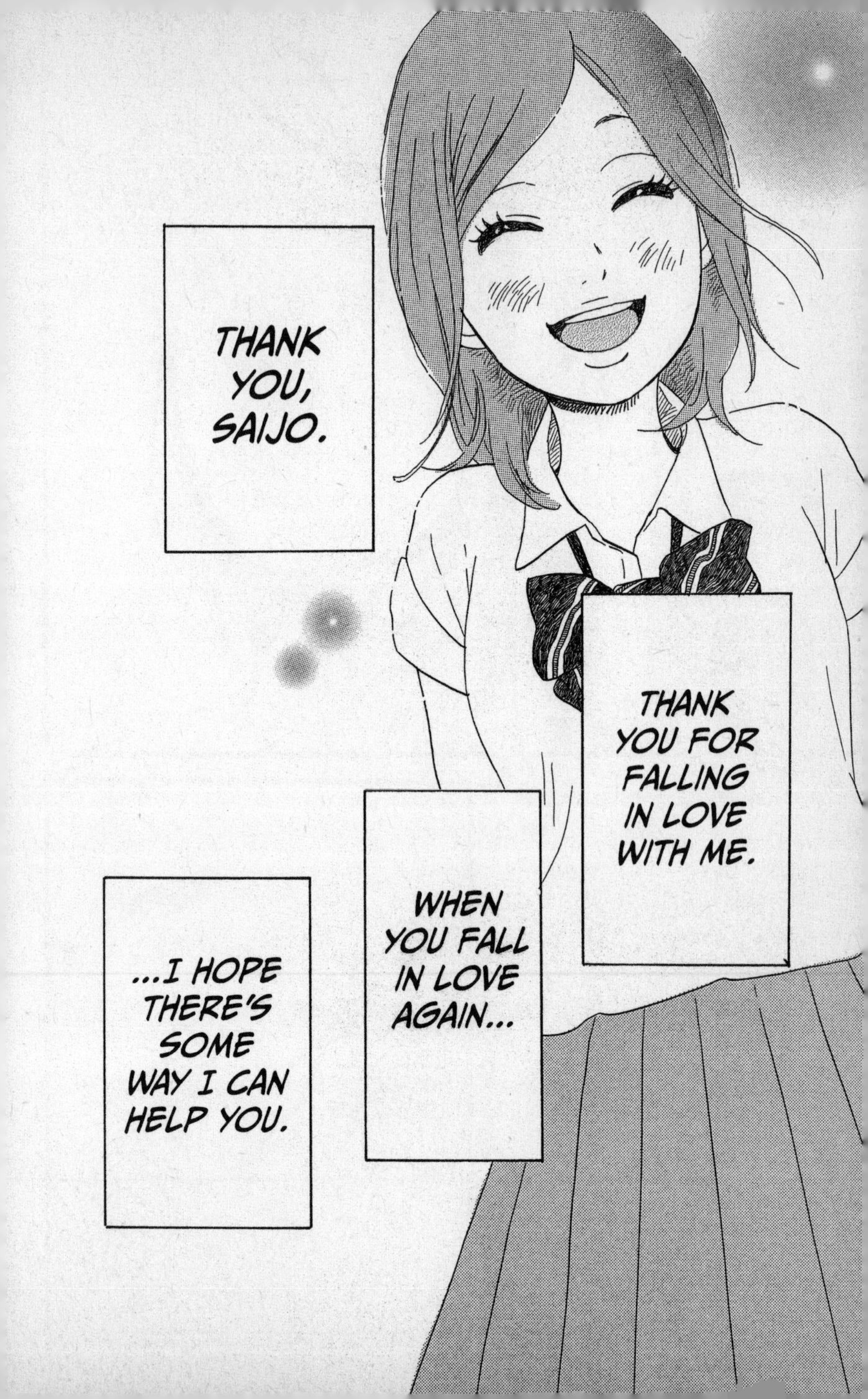
THANK YOU, SAIJO.
THANK YOU FOR FALLING IN LOVE WITH ME.
WHEN YOU FALL IN LOVE AGAIN...
...I HOPE THERE'S SOME WAY I CAN HELP YOU.

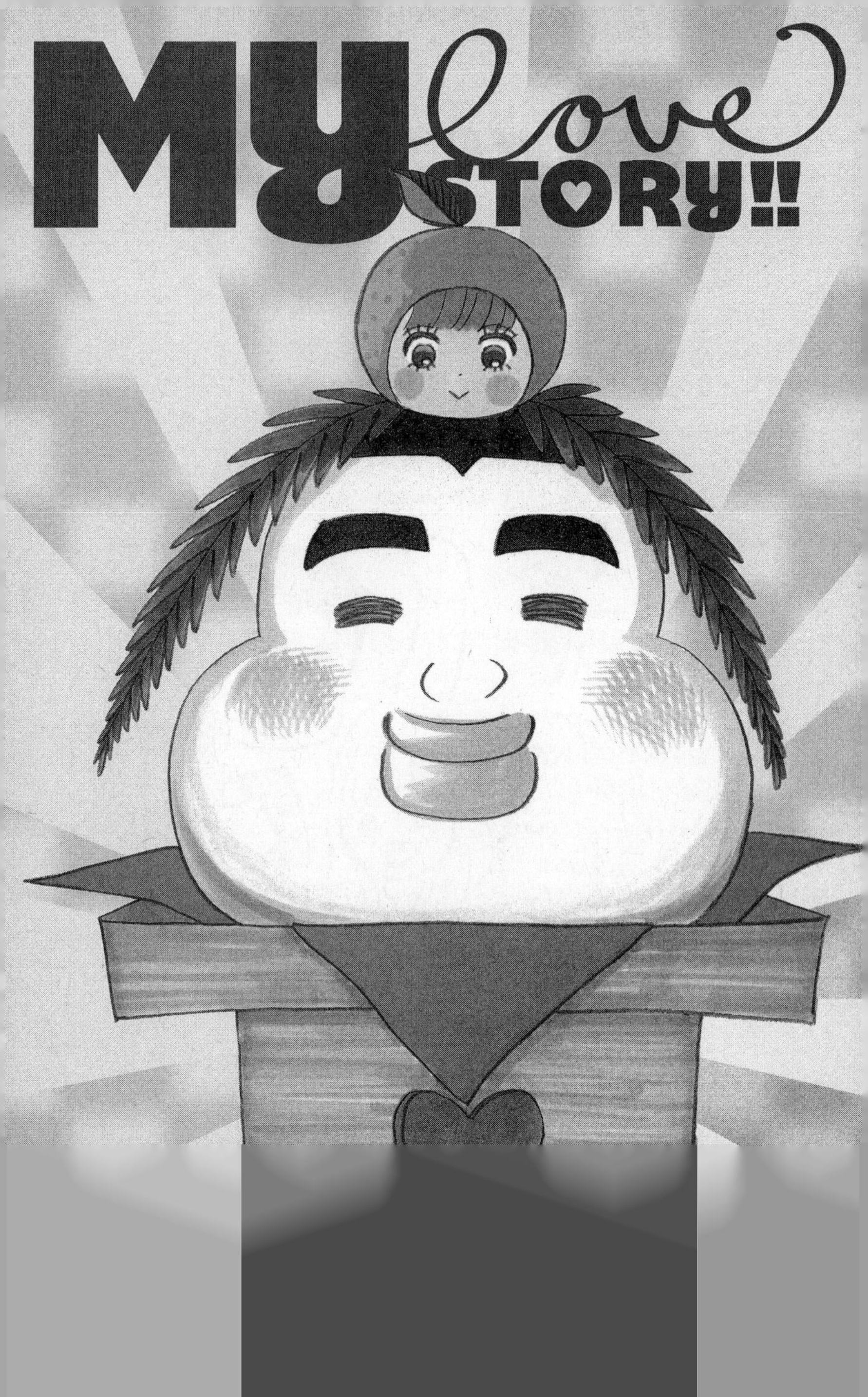
MY love STORY!!

THANK YOU FOR EVERYTHING!

Thank you for picking up *My Love Story!!* volume 5. I've made it this far through your support, so thank you very much! I don't know what the cover is going to be like, so as I'm writing this, I'm excited to find out how it'll look!

Last year *Bessatsu Margaret* made all kinds of special merchandise, like a pillow that feels like you're resting on Takeo's arm or a tissue box that has Sunakawa handing you tissues...

I usually don't know anything about them, so when I look in the magazine or my editor sends me one, I go, "What is this?!" and have a good laugh. I wouldn't call it cute, but it's very amusing. I guess it's cute.

Things like that aren't always available, so if you have a chance, try to enter to win them! I do sometimes.

Hope to see you in the next volume!

THANK YOU ♡

VERY MUCH!

Thank you for every- thing, Aruko!

KAZUNE KAWAHARA

This manuscript is all done digitally, but I get the feeling that doesn't mean much.

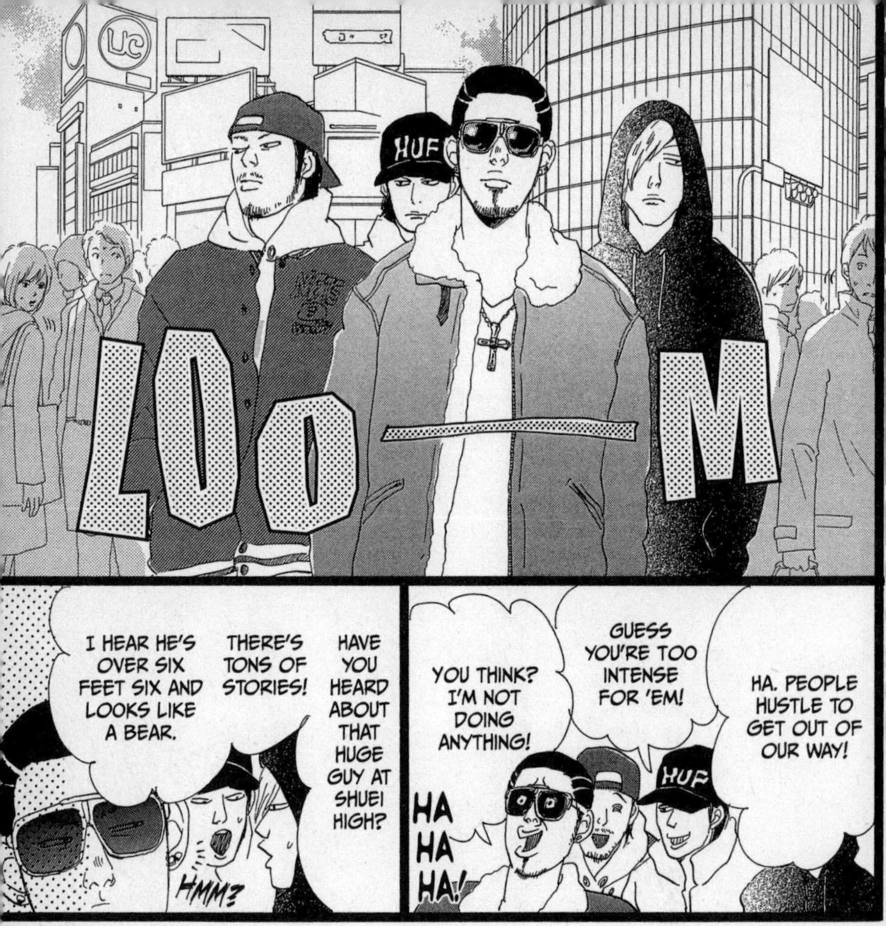
LOO—M
HA. PEOPLE HUSTLE TO GET OUT OF OUR WAY!
GUESS YOU'RE TOO INTENSE FOR 'EM!
YOU THINK? I'M NOT DOING ANYTHING!
HA HA HA!
HAVE YOU HEARD ABOUT THAT HUGE GUY AT SHUEI HIGH?
THERE'S TONS OF STORIES!
I HEAR HE'S OVER SIX FEET SIX AND LOOKS LIKE A BEAR.
HMM?

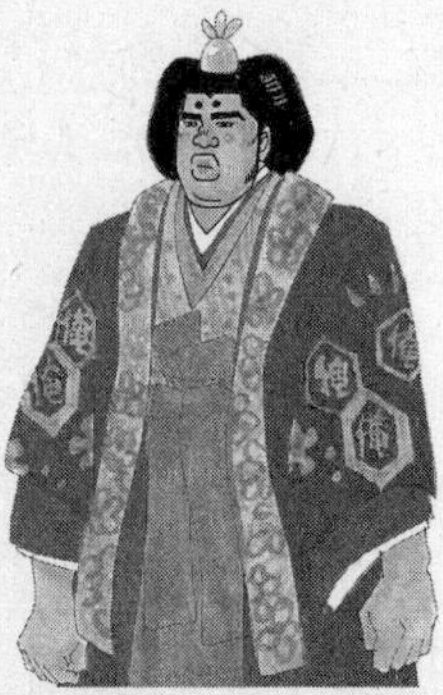

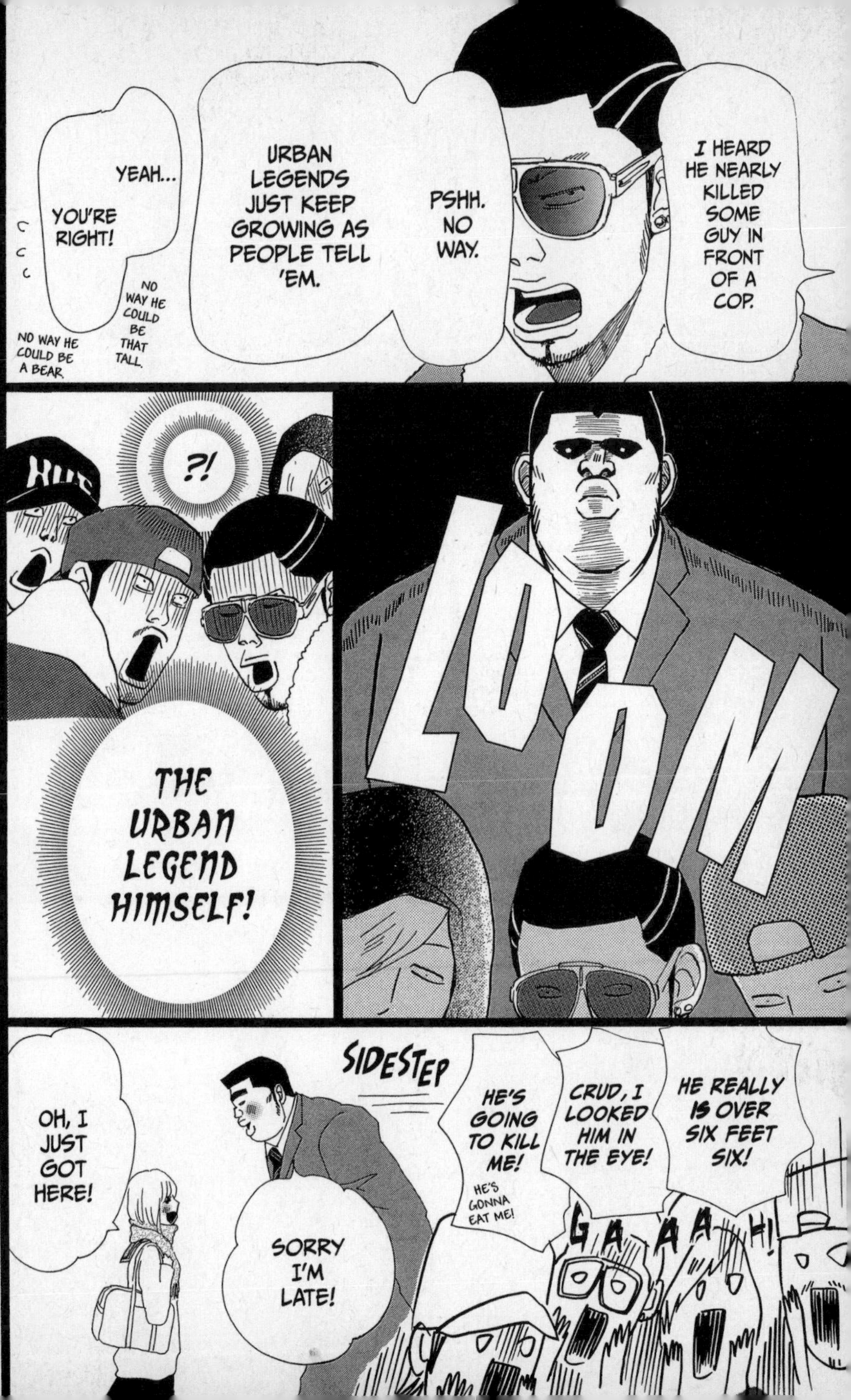
I HEARD HE NEARLY KILLED SOME GUY IN FRONT OF A COP.
PSHH. NO WAY.
URBAN LEGENDS JUST KEEP GROWING AS PEOPLE TELL 'EM.
YEAH... YOU'RE RIGHT!
NO WAY HE COULD BE THAT TALL.
NO WAY HE COULD BE A BEAR
LOOM
?!
THE URBAN LEGEND HIMSELF!
HE REALLY IS OVER SIX FEET SIX!
CRUD, I LOOKED HIM IN THE EYE!
HE'S GOING TO KILL ME!
HE'S GONNA EAT ME!
GAAAH!
SIDESTEP
SORRY I'M LATE!
OH, I JUST GOT HERE!

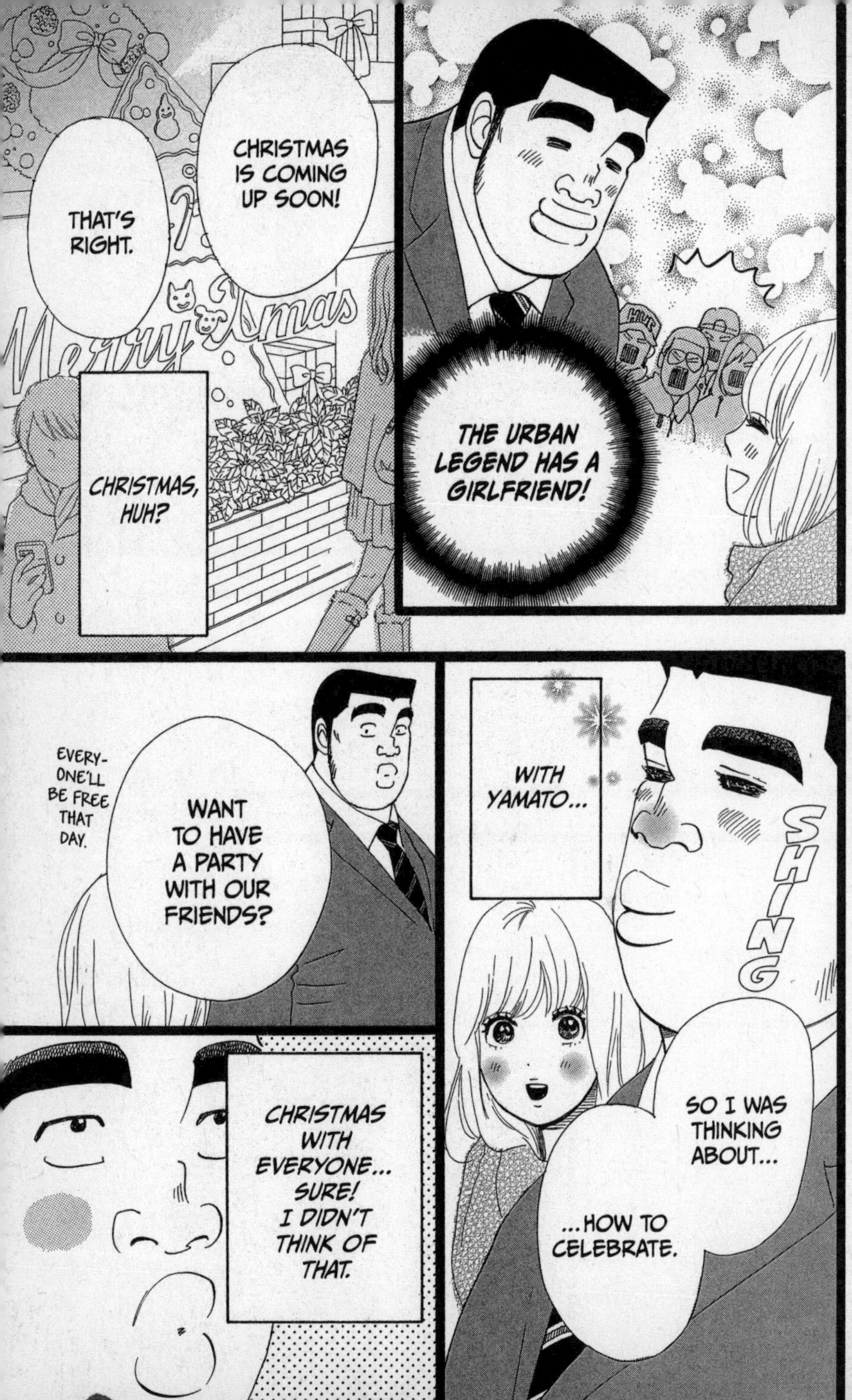
THE URBAN LEGEND HAS A GIRLFRIEND!
CHRISTMAS IS COMING UP SOON!
THAT'S RIGHT.
Merry Xmas
CHRISTMAS, HUH?
WITH YAMATO...
SHING
SO I WAS THINKING ABOUT...
...HOW TO CELEBRATE.
WANT TO HAVE A PARTY WITH OUR FRIENDS?
EVERY-ONE'LL BE FREE THAT DAY.
CHRISTMAS WITH EVERYONE... SURE! I DIDN'T THINK OF THAT.

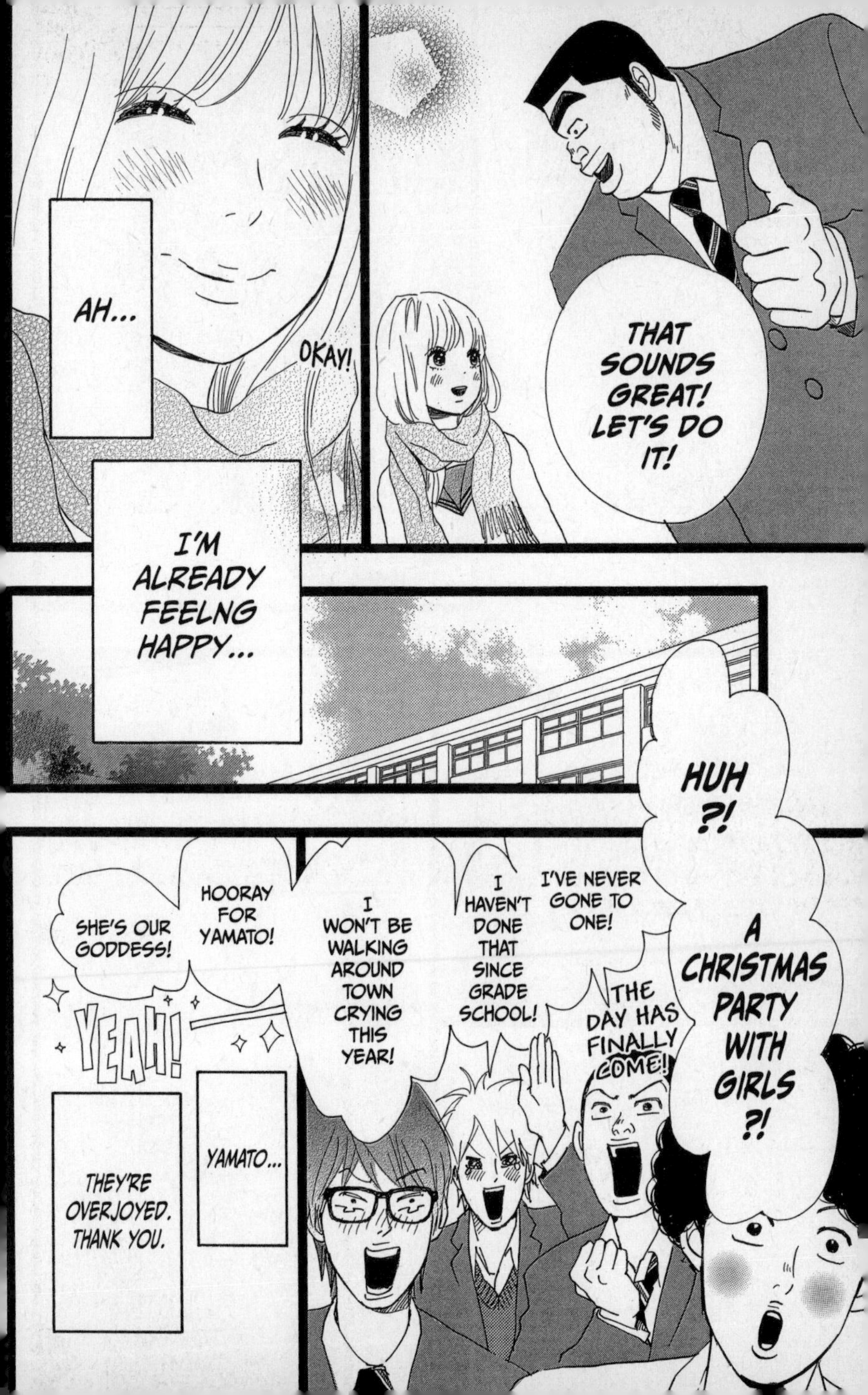
THAT SOUNDS GREAT! LET'S DO IT!
OKAY!
AH...
I'M ALREADY FEELNG HAPPY...
HUH ?!
A CHRISTMAS PARTY WITH GIRLS ?!
THE DAY HAS FINALLY COME!
I'VE NEVER GONE TO ONE!
I HAVEN'T DONE THAT SINCE GRADE SCHOOL!
I WON'T BE WALKING AROUND TOWN CRYING THIS YEAR!
HOORAY FOR YAMATO!
SHE'S OUR GODDESS!
YEAH!
YAMATO...
THEY'RE OVERJOYED. THANK YOU.

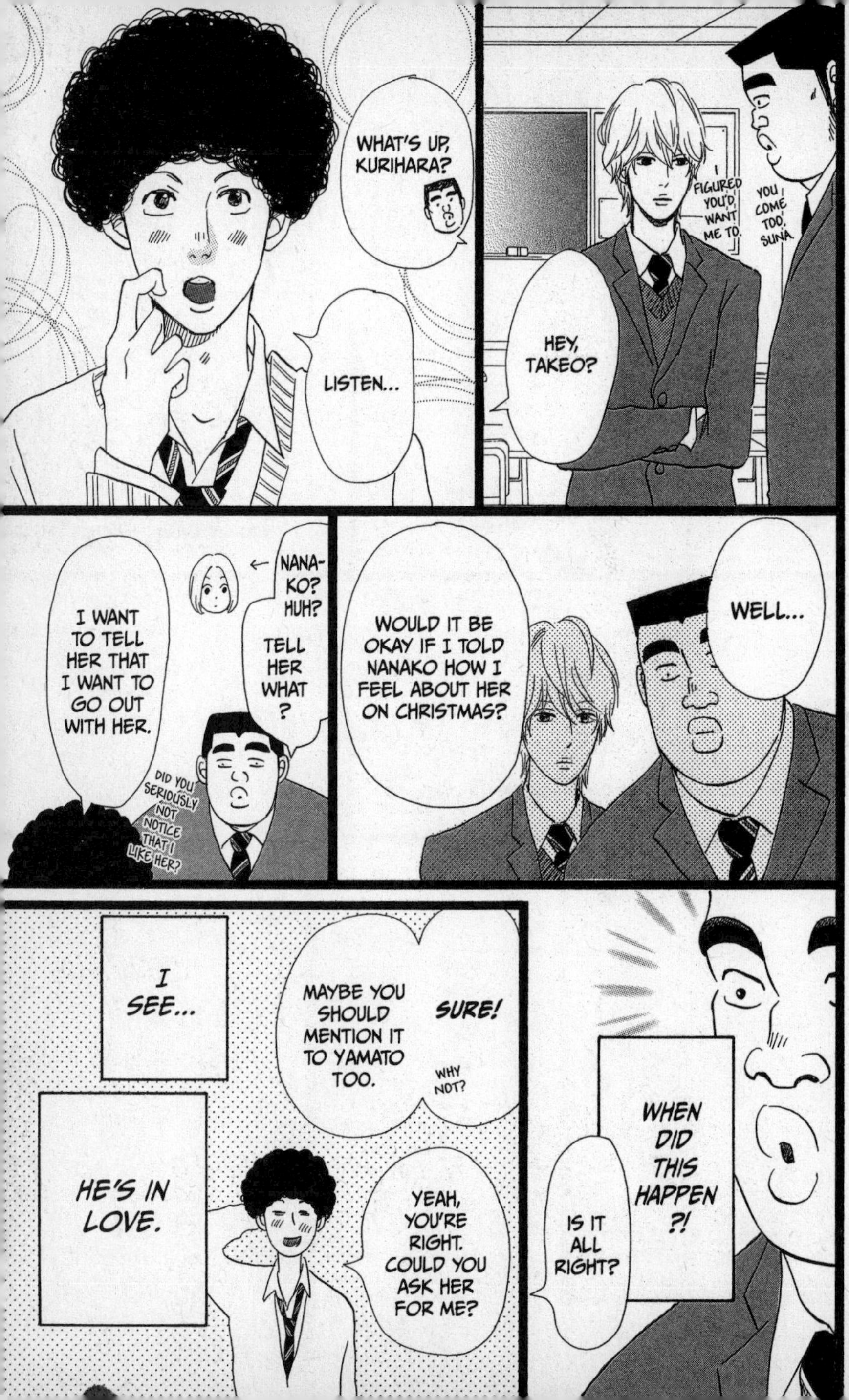
YOU COME TOO, SUNA.
I FIGURED YOU'D WANT ME TO.
HEY, TAKEO?
WHAT'S UP, KURIHARA?
LISTEN...
WELL...
WOULD IT BE OKAY IF I TOLD NANAKO HOW I FEEL ABOUT HER ON CHRISTMAS?
NANA-KO? HUH?
TELL HER WHAT?
I WANT TO TELL HER THAT I WANT TO GO OUT WITH HER.
DID YOU SERIOUSLY NOT NOTICE THAT I LIKE HER?
WHEN DID THIS HAPPEN?!
IS IT ALL RIGHT?
SURE!
WHY NOT?
MAYBE YOU SHOULD MENTION IT TO YAMATO TOO.
I SEE...
YEAH, YOU'RE RIGHT. COULD YOU ASK HER FOR ME?
HE'S IN LOVE.

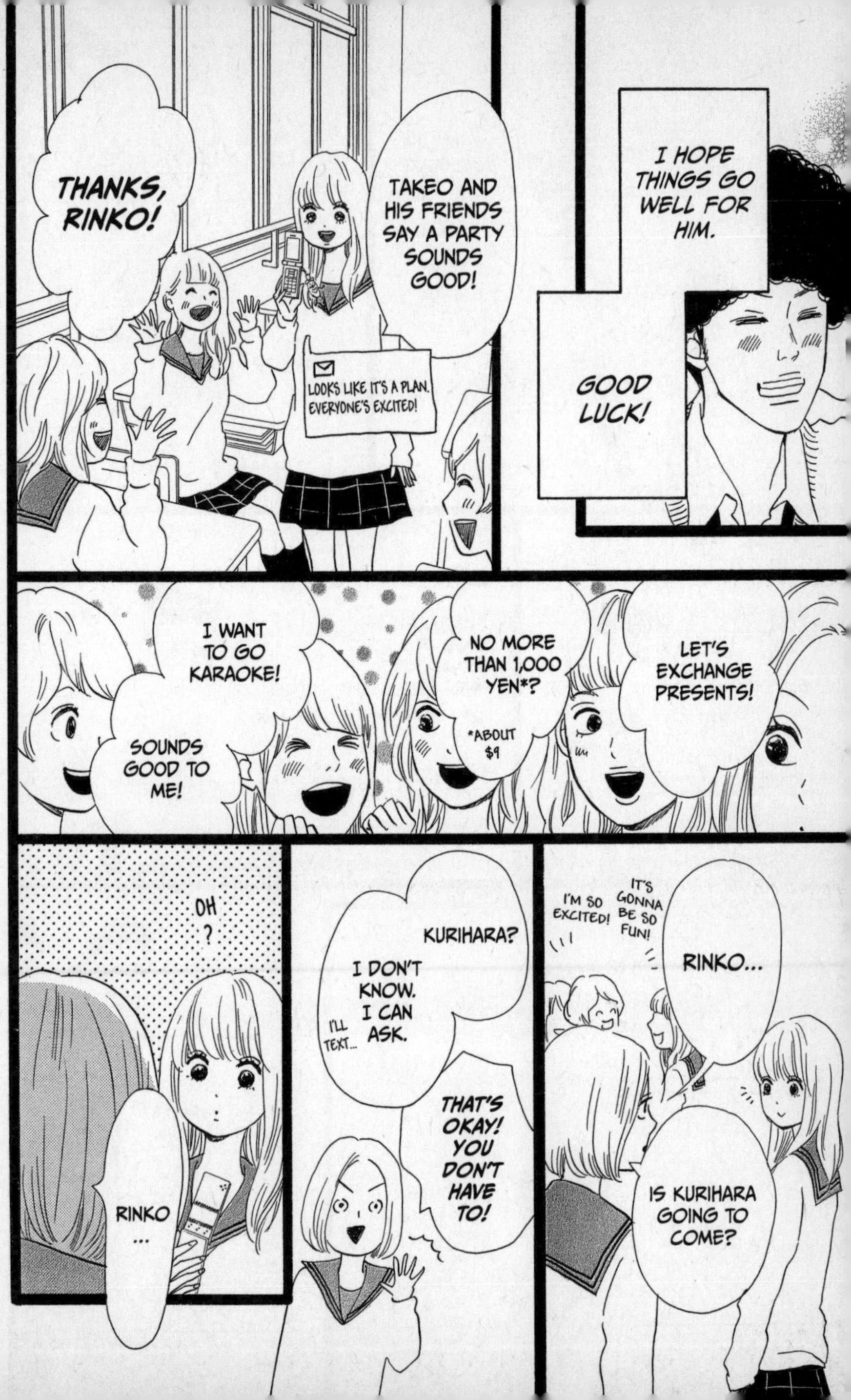
I HOPE THINGS GO WELL FOR HIM.
GOOD LUCK!
TAKEO AND HIS FRIENDS SAY A PARTY SOUNDS GOOD!
LOOKS LIKE IT'S A PLAN. EVERYONE'S EXCITED!
THANKS, RINKO!
LET'S EXCHANGE PRESENTS!
NO MORE THAN 1,000 YEN*?
*ABOUT $9
I WANT TO GO KARAOKE!
SOUNDS GOOD TO ME!
IT'S GONNA BE SO FUN!
I'M SO EXCITED!
RINKO...
IS KURIHARA GOING TO COME?
KURIHARA?
I DON'T KNOW. I CAN ASK.
I'LL TEXT...
THAT'S OKAY! YOU DON'T HAVE TO!
OH ?
RINKO ...

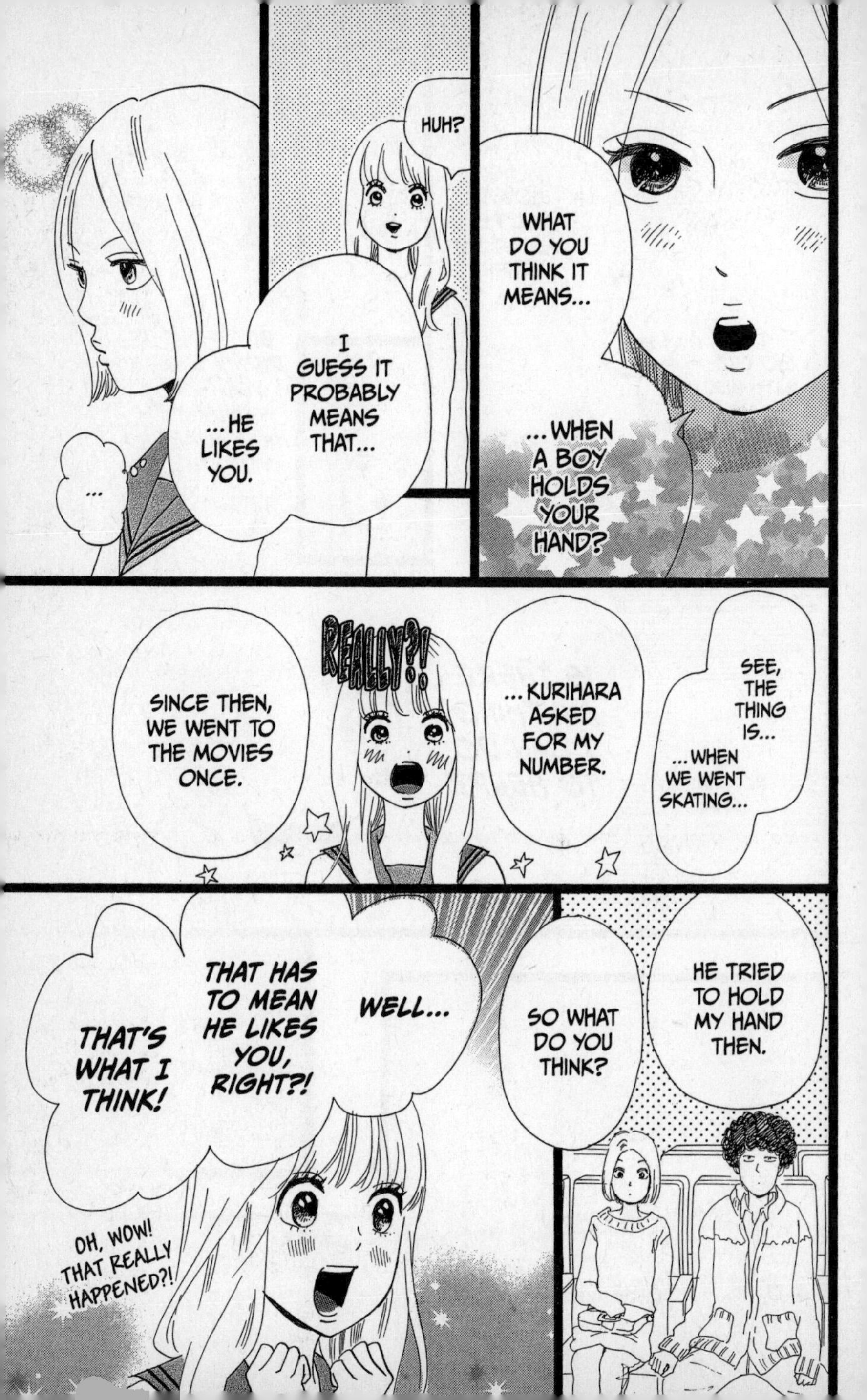
WHAT DO YOU THINK IT MEANS...
...WHEN A BOY HOLDS YOUR HAND?
HUH?
I GUESS IT PROBABLY MEANS THAT...
...HE LIKES YOU.
...
SEE, THE THING IS...
...WHEN WE WENT SKATING...
...KURIHARA ASKED FOR MY NUMBER.
REALLY?!
SINCE THEN, WE WENT TO THE MOVIES ONCE.
HE TRIED TO HOLD MY HAND THEN.
SO WHAT DO YOU THINK?
WELL...
THAT HAS TO MEAN HE LIKES YOU, RIGHT?!
THAT'S WHAT I THINK!
OH, WOW! THAT REALLY HAPPENED?!

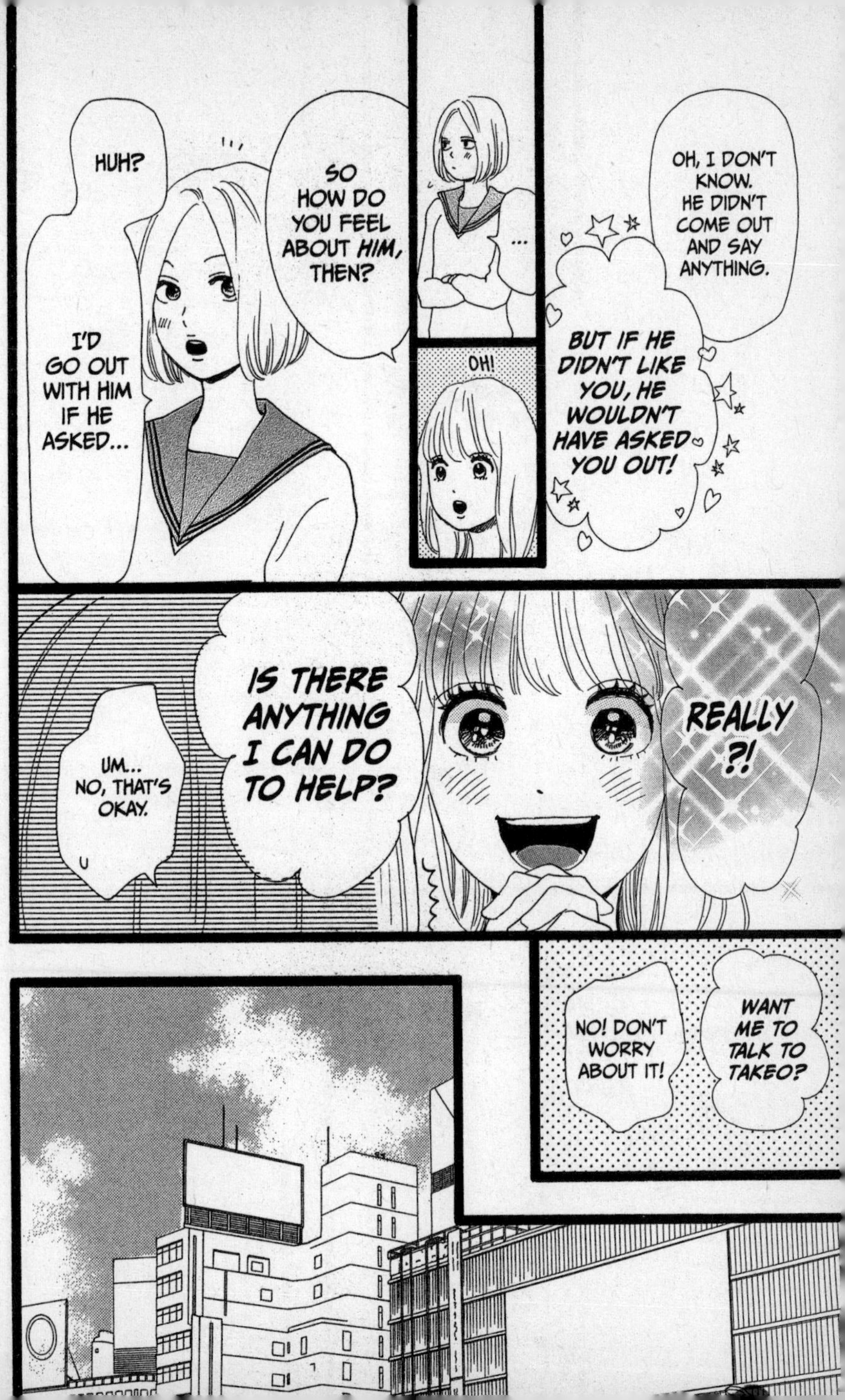
OH, I DON'T KNOW. HE DIDN'T COME OUT AND SAY ANYTHING.
...
BUT IF HE DIDN'T LIKE YOU, HE WOULDN'T HAVE ASKED YOU OUT!
OH!
SO HOW DO YOU FEEL ABOUT *HIM*, THEN?
HUH?
I'D GO OUT WITH HIM IF HE ASKED...
REALLY ?!
IS THERE ANYTHING I CAN DO TO HELP?
UM... NO, THAT'S OKAY.
WANT ME TO TALK TO TAKEO?
NO! DON'T WORRY ABOUT IT!

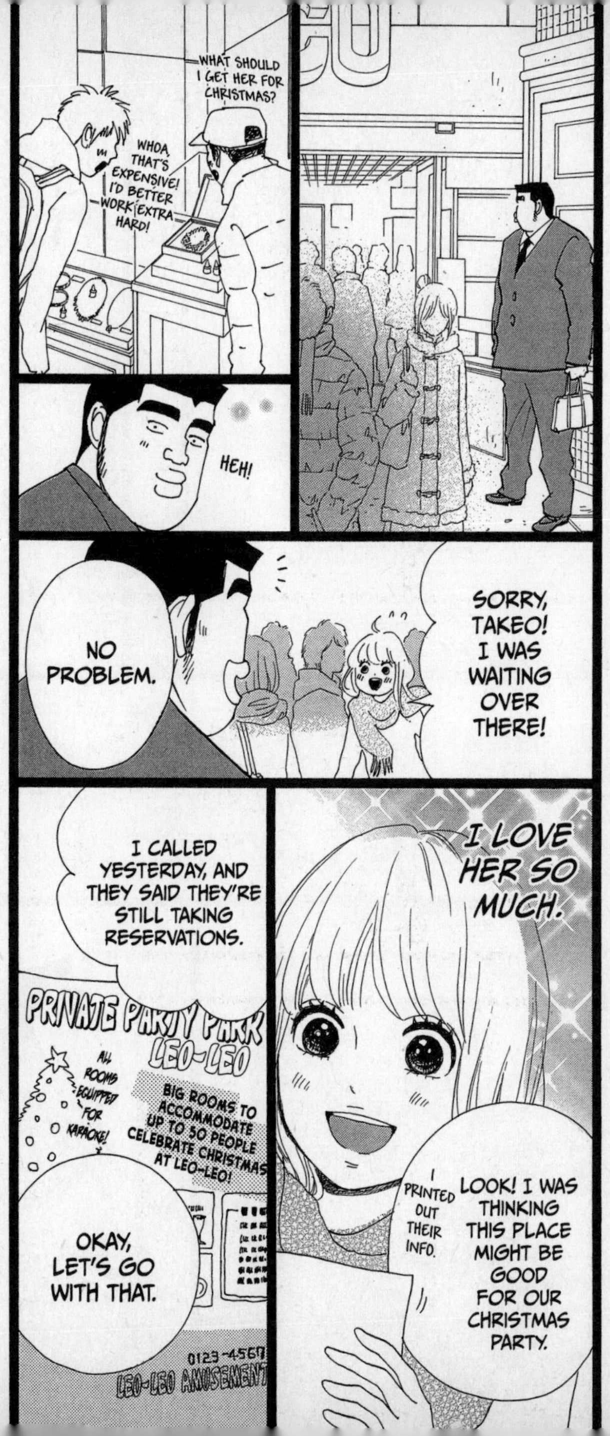
WHAT SHOULD I GET HER FOR CHRISTMAS?
WHOA, THAT'S EXPENSIVE! I'D BETTER WORK EXTRA HARD!
HEH!
SORRY, TAKEO! I WAS WAITING OVER THERE!
NO PROBLEM.
I LOVE HER SO MUCH.
LOOK! I WAS THINKING THIS PLACE MIGHT BE GOOD FOR OUR CHRISTMAS PARTY.
I PRINTED OUT THEIR INFO.
I CALLED YESTERDAY, AND THEY SAID THEY'RE STILL TAKING RESERVATIONS.
PRIVATE PARTY PARK LEO-LEO
ALL ROOMS EQUIPPED FOR KARAOKE!
BIG ROOMS TO ACCOMMODATE UP TO 50 PEOPLE CELEBRATE CHRISTMAS AT LEO-LEO!
0123-4567
LEO-LEO AMUSEMENT
OKAY, LET'S GO WITH THAT.

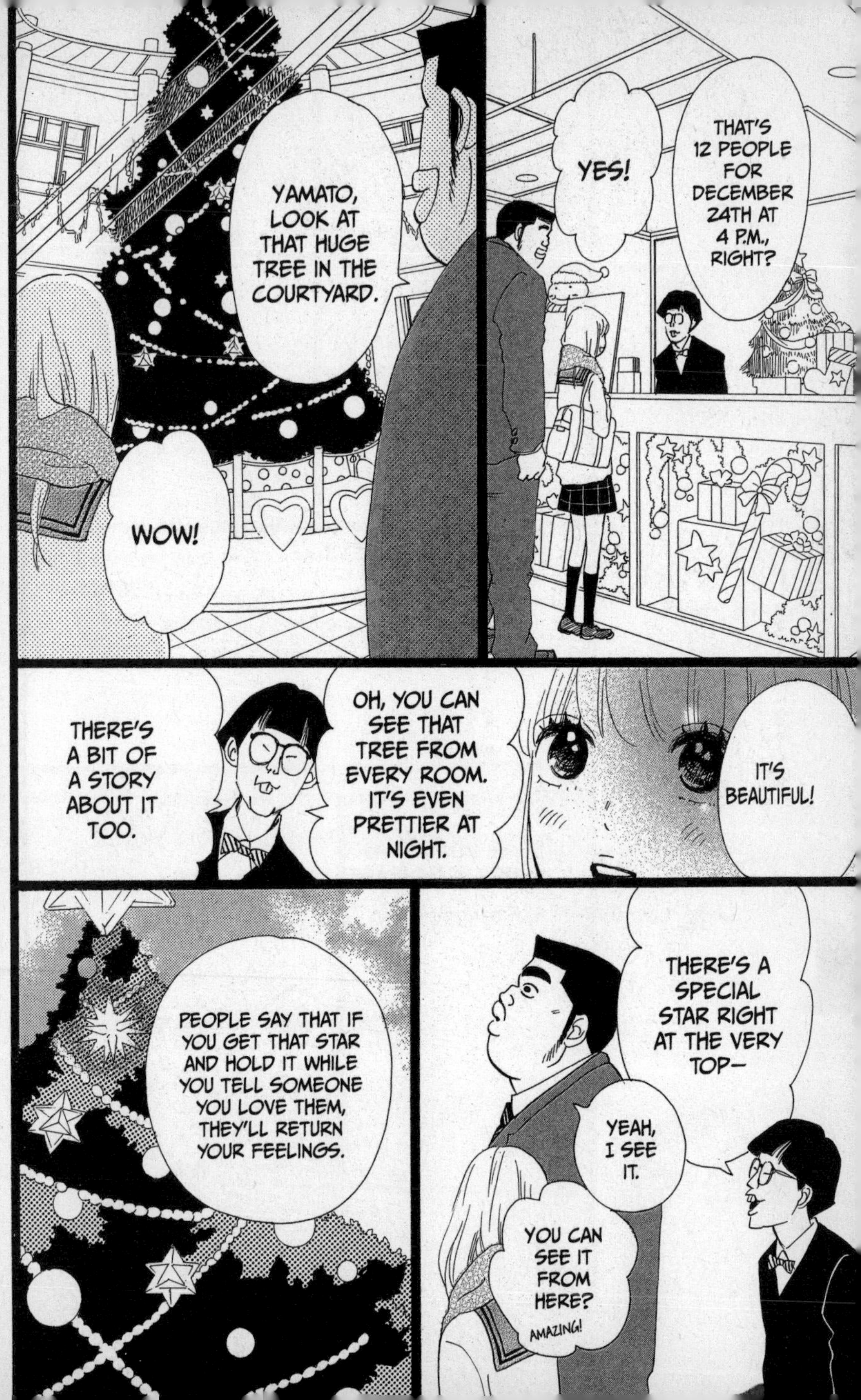
THAT'S 12 PEOPLE FOR DECEMBER 24TH AT 4 P.M., RIGHT?
YES!
YAMATO, LOOK AT THAT HUGE TREE IN THE COURTYARD.
WOW!
IT'S BEAUTIFUL!
OH, YOU CAN SEE THAT TREE FROM EVERY ROOM. IT'S EVEN PRETTIER AT NIGHT.
THERE'S A BIT OF A STORY ABOUT IT TOO.
THERE'S A SPECIAL STAR RIGHT AT THE VERY TOP—
YEAH, I SEE IT.
YOU CAN SEE IT FROM HERE?
AMAZING!
PEOPLE SAY THAT IF YOU GET THAT STAR AND HOLD IT WHILE YOU TELL SOMEONE YOU LOVE THEM, THEY'LL RETURN YOUR FEELINGS.

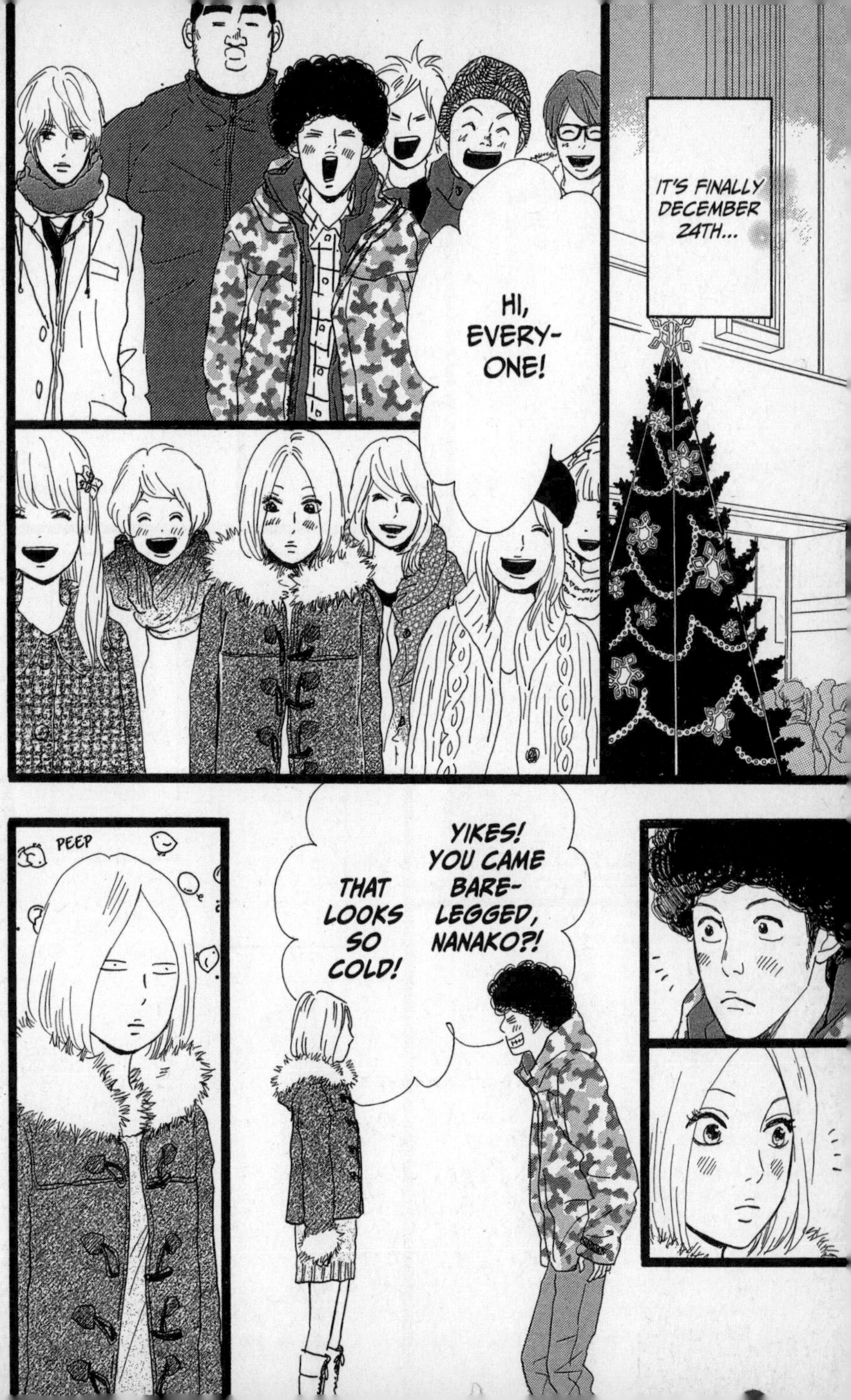
IT'S FINALLY DECEMBER 24TH...
HI, EVERYONE!
YIKES! YOU CAME BARE-LEGGED, NANAKO?!
THAT LOOKS SO COLD!
PEEP

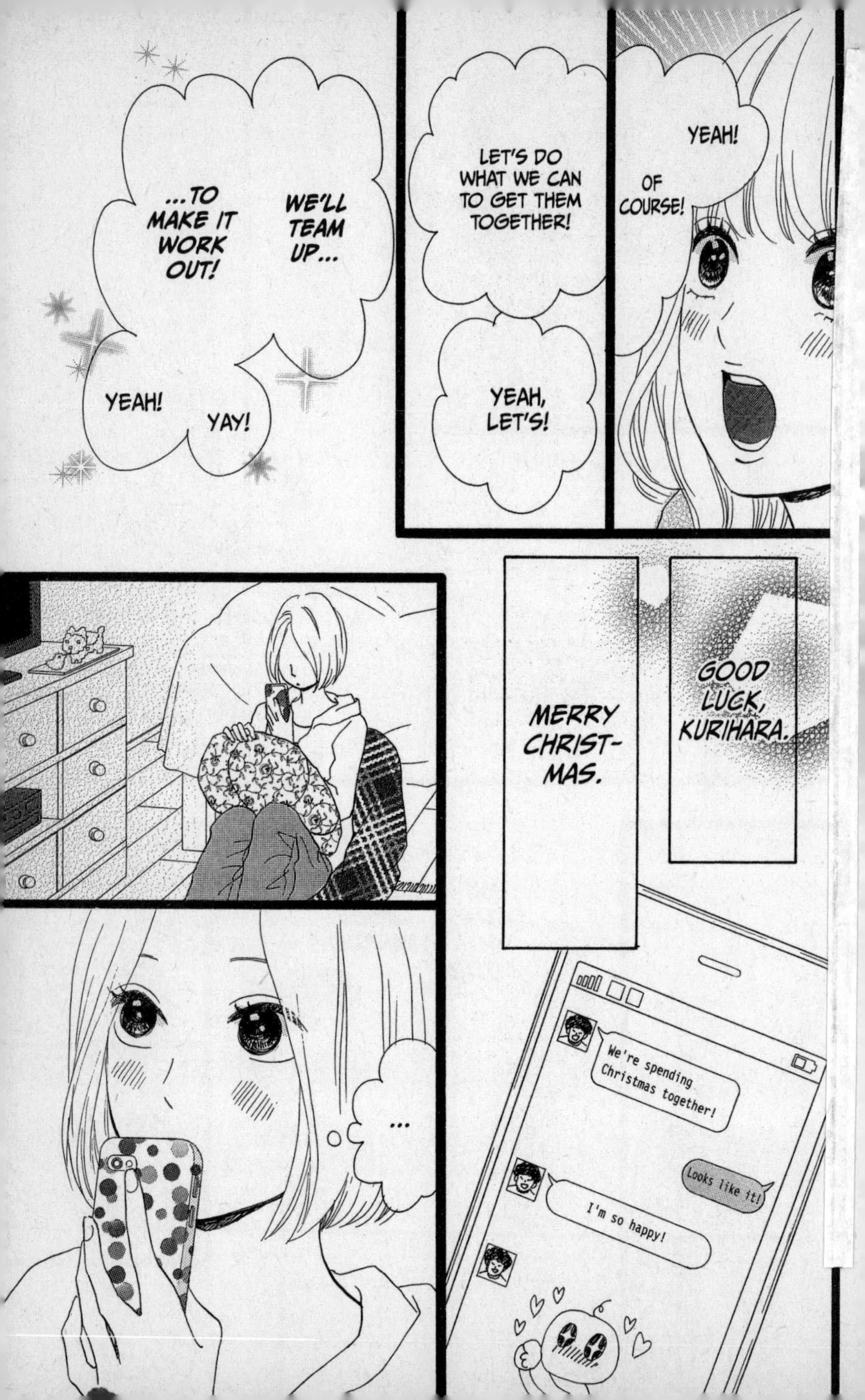
YEAH!
OF COURSE!
LET'S DO WHAT WE CAN TO GET THEM TOGETHER!
YEAH, LET'S!
WE'LL TEAM UP...
...TO MAKE IT WORK OUT!
YEAH!
YAY!
GOOD LUCK, KURIHARA.
MERRY CHRIST-MAS.
We're spending Christmas together!
Looks like it!
I'm so happy!
...

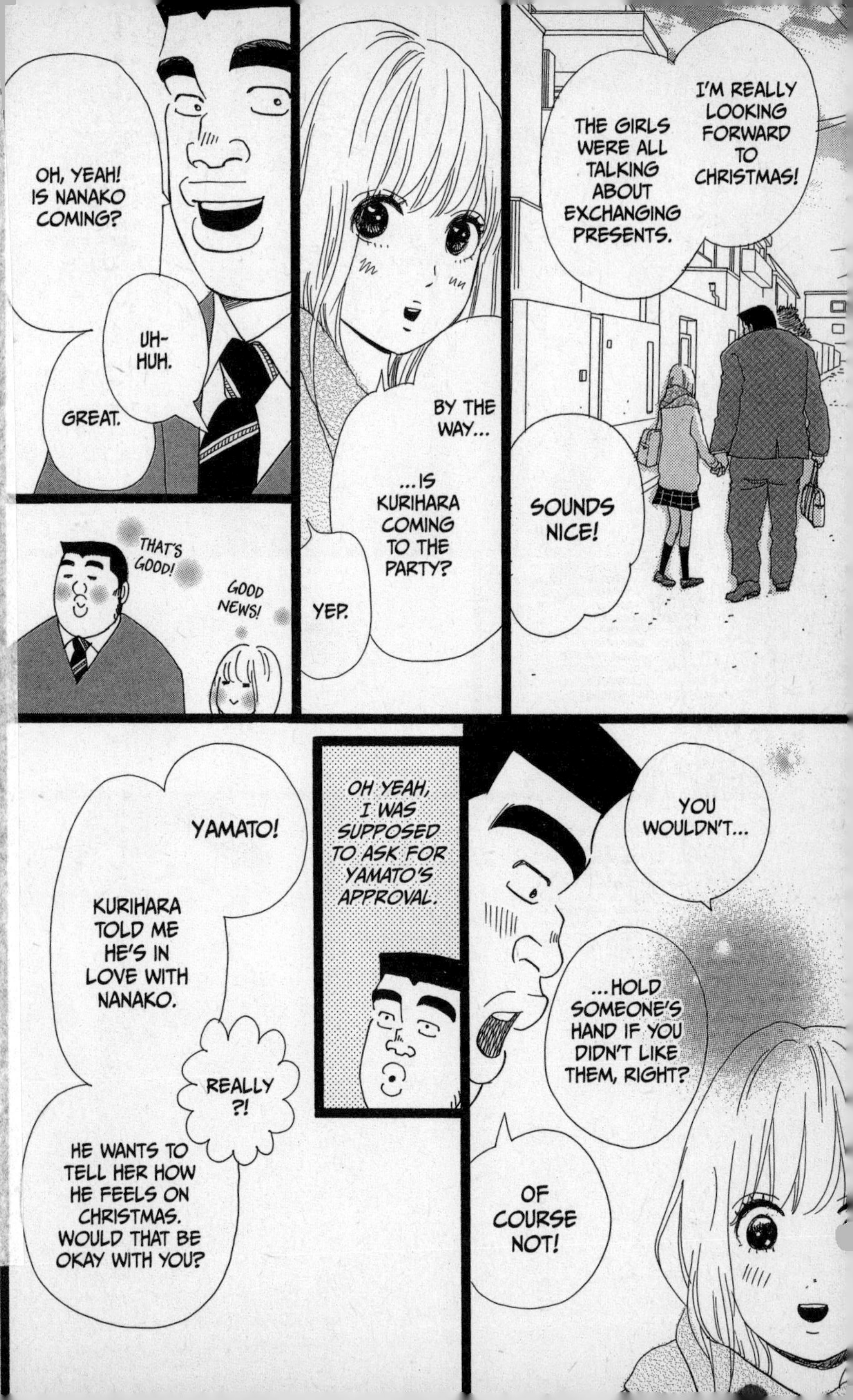
I'M REALLY LOOKING FORWARD TO CHRISTMAS!
THE GIRLS WERE ALL TALKING ABOUT EXCHANGING PRESENTS.
SOUNDS NICE!
BY THE WAY...
...IS KURIHARA COMING TO THE PARTY?
YEP.
OH, YEAH! IS NANAKO COMING?
UH-HUH.
GREAT.
THAT'S GOOD!
GOOD NEWS!
YOU WOULDN'T...
...HOLD SOMEONE'S HAND IF YOU DIDN'T LIKE THEM, RIGHT?
OF COURSE NOT!
OH YEAH, I WAS SUPPOSED TO ASK FOR YAMATO'S APPROVAL.
YAMATO!
KURIHARA TOLD ME HE'S IN LOVE WITH NANAKO.
REALLY ?!
HE WANTS TO TELL HER HOW HE FEELS ON CHRISTMAS. WOULD THAT BE OKAY WITH YOU?

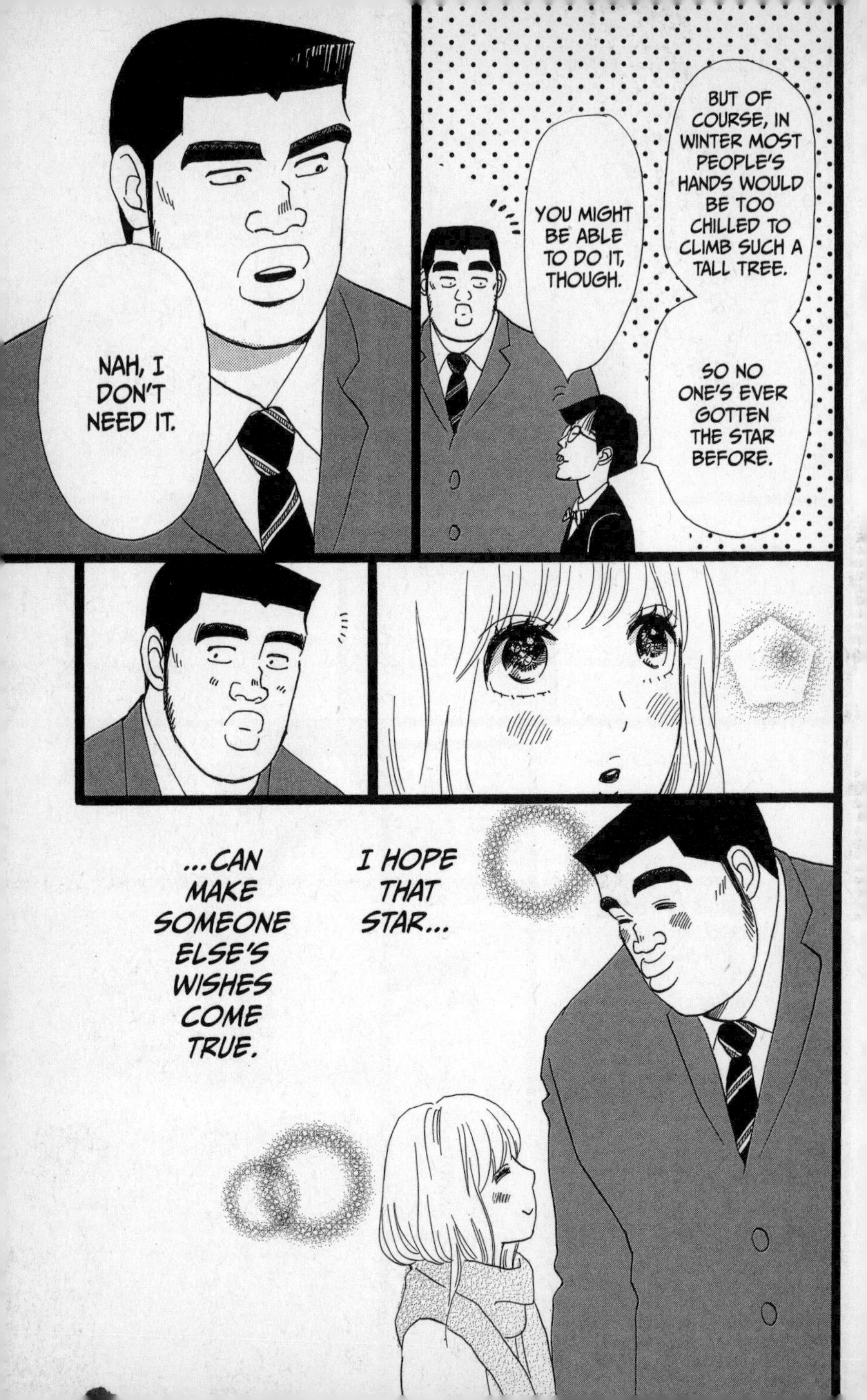
BUT OF COURSE, IN WINTER MOST PEOPLE'S HANDS WOULD BE TOO CHILLED TO CLIMB SUCH A TALL TREE.
SO NO ONE'S EVER GOTTEN THE STAR BEFORE.
YOU MIGHT BE ABLE TO DO IT, THOUGH.
NAH, I DON'T NEED IT.
I HOPE THAT STAR...
...CAN MAKE SOMEONE ELSE'S WISHES COME TRUE.

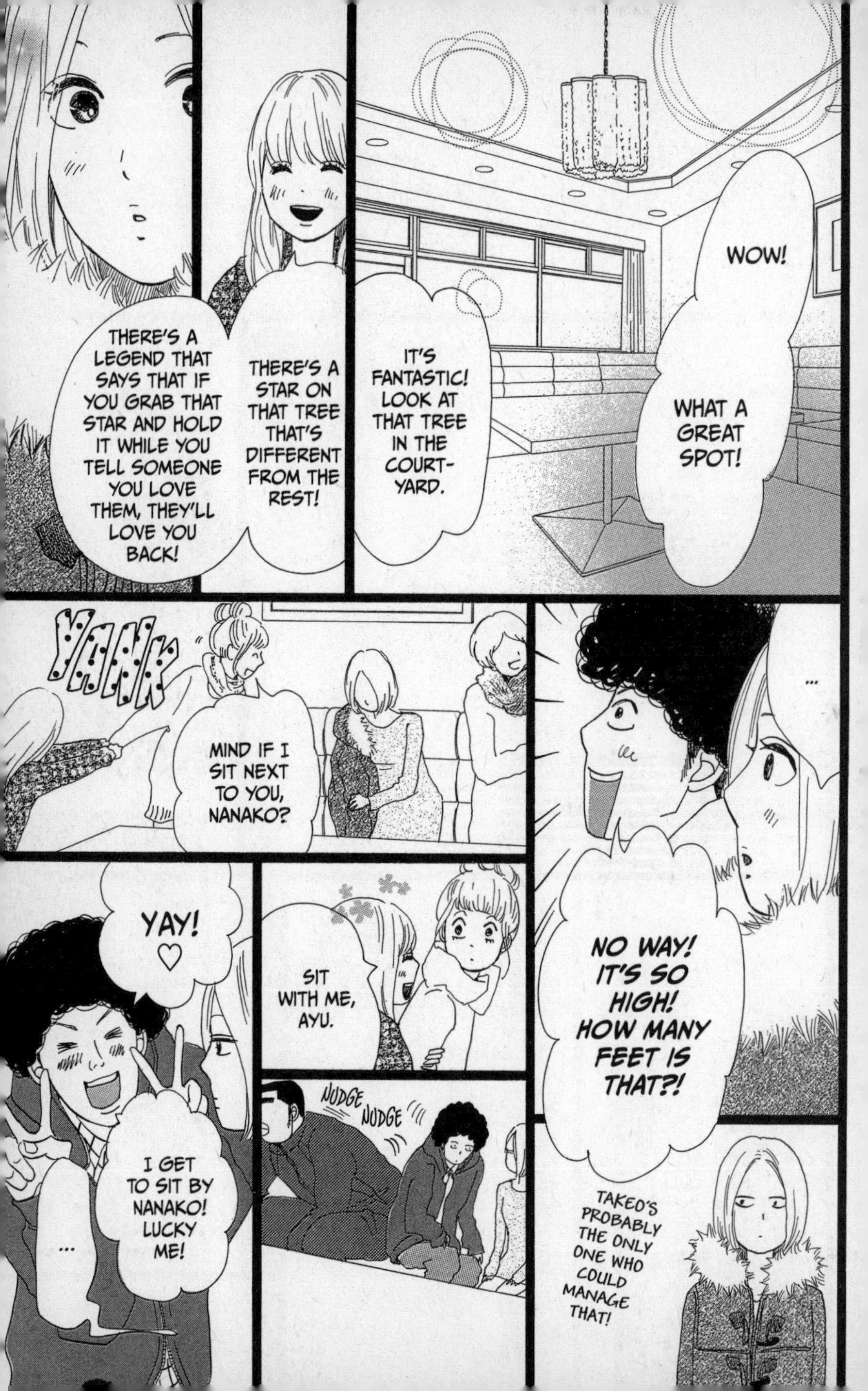
WOW!
WHAT A GREAT SPOT!
IT'S FANTASTIC! LOOK AT THAT TREE IN THE COURT-YARD.
THERE'S A STAR ON THAT TREE THAT'S DIFFERENT FROM THE REST!
THERE'S A LEGEND THAT SAYS THAT IF YOU GRAB THAT STAR AND HOLD IT WHILE YOU TELL SOMEONE YOU LOVE THEM, THEY'LL LOVE YOU BACK!
...
NO WAY! IT'S SO HIGH! HOW MANY FEET IS THAT?!
YANK
MIND IF I SIT NEXT TO YOU, NANAKO?
SIT WITH ME, AYU.
NUDGE NUDGE
YAY! ♡
I GET TO SIT BY NANAKO! LUCKY ME!
...
TAKEO'S PROBABLY THE ONLY ONE WHO COULD MANAGE THAT!

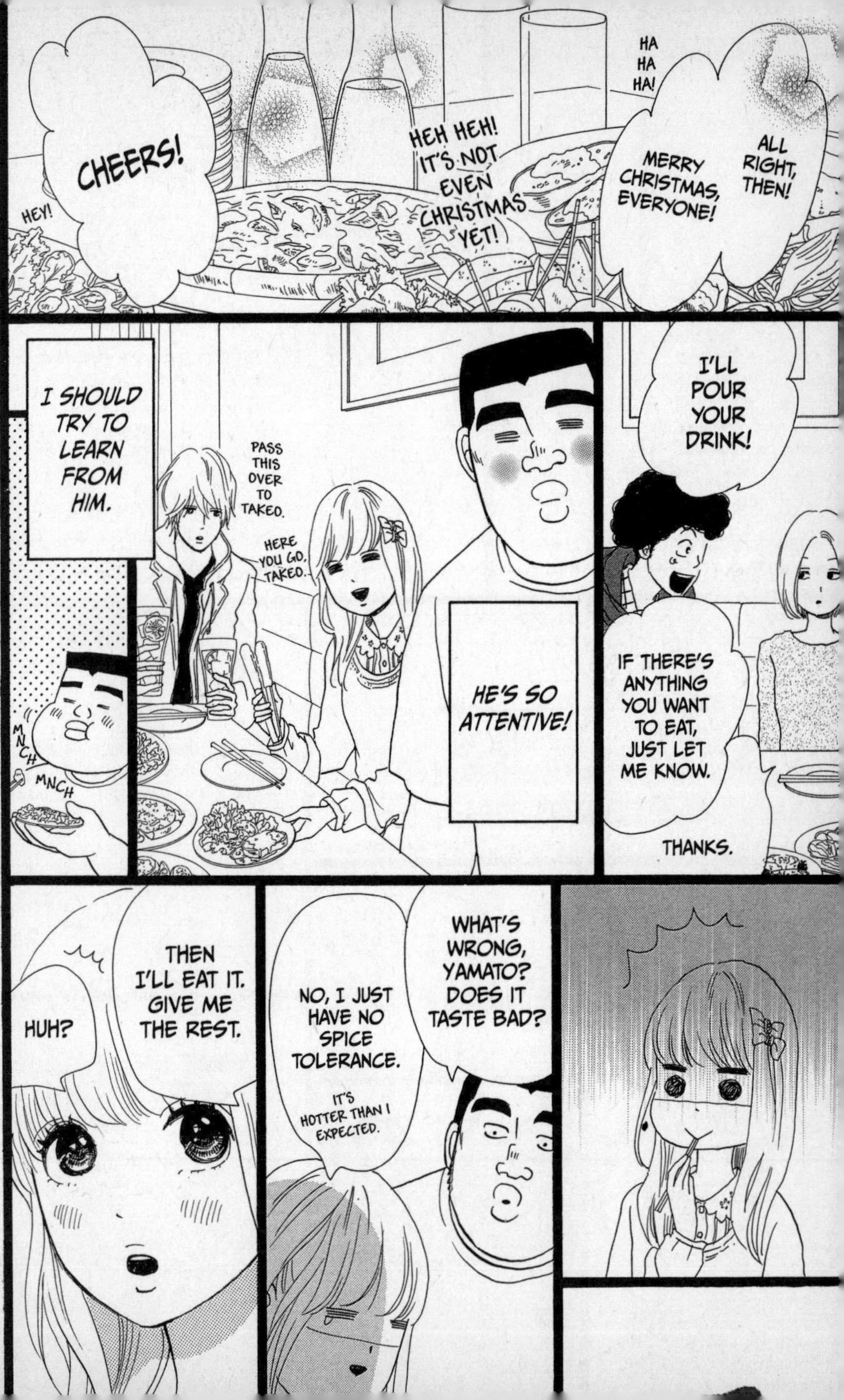
HA HA HA!
ALL RIGHT, THEN!
MERRY CHRISTMAS, EVERYONE!
HEH HEH! IT'S NOT EVEN CHRISTMAS YET!
CHEERS!
HEY!
I'LL POUR YOUR DRINK!
IF THERE'S ANYTHING YOU WANT TO EAT, JUST LET ME KNOW.
THANKS.
PASS THIS OVER TO TAKEO.
HERE YOU GO, TAKEO.
HE'S SO ATTENTIVE!
I SHOULD TRY TO LEARN FROM HIM.
MNCH
MNCH
WHAT'S WRONG, YAMATO? DOES IT TASTE BAD?
NO, I JUST HAVE NO SPICE TOLERANCE.
IT'S HOTTER THAN I EXPECTED.
THEN I'LL EAT IT. GIVE ME THE REST.
HUH?

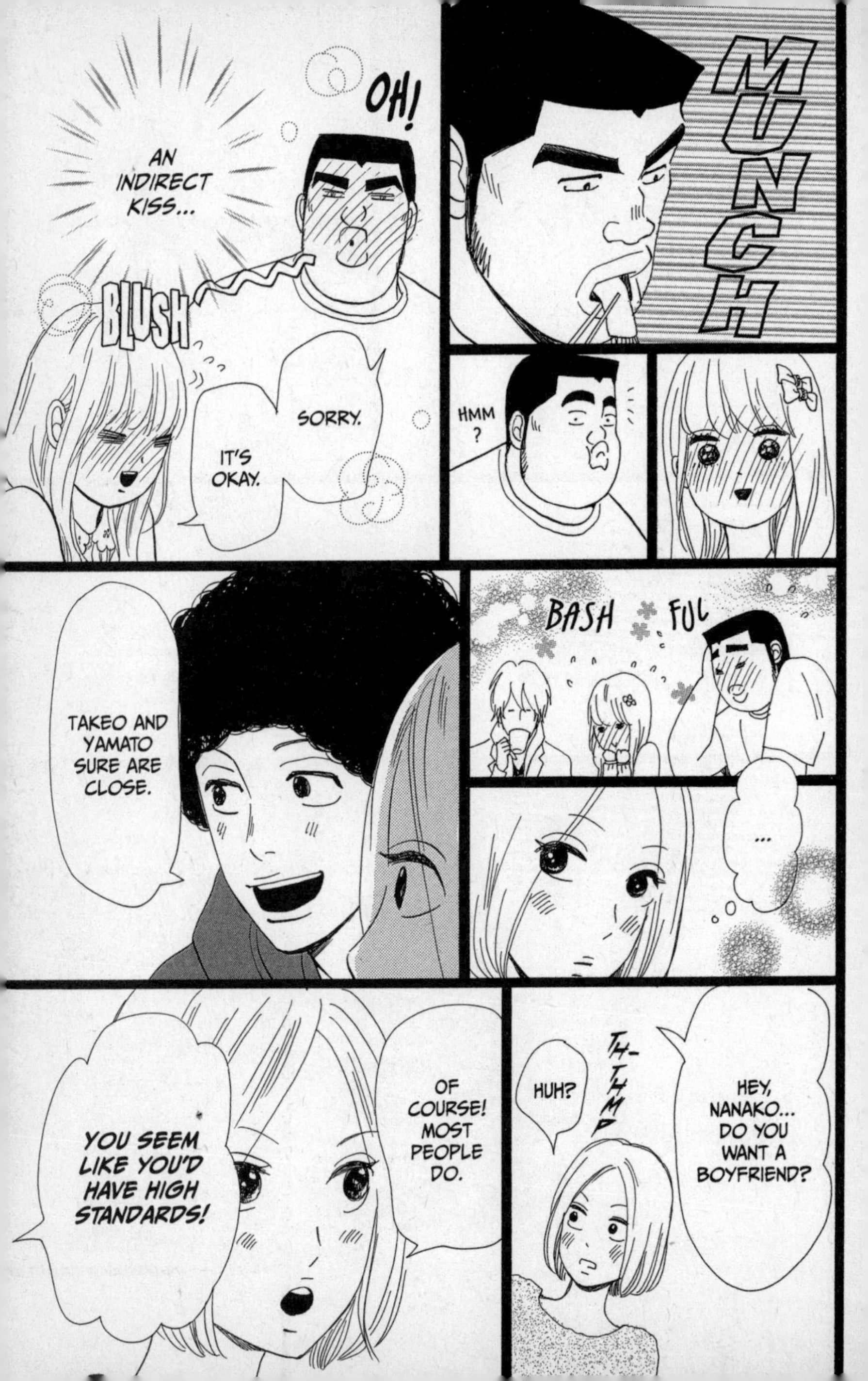
MUNCH
HMM?
OH!
AN INDIRECT KISS...
BLUSH
SORRY.
IT'S OKAY.
BASH FUL
...
TAKEO AND YAMATO SURE ARE CLOSE.
HEY, NANAKO... DO YOU WANT A BOYFRIEND?
TH-THMP
HUH?
OF COURSE! MOST PEOPLE DO.
YOU SEEM LIKE YOU'D HAVE HIGH STANDARDS!

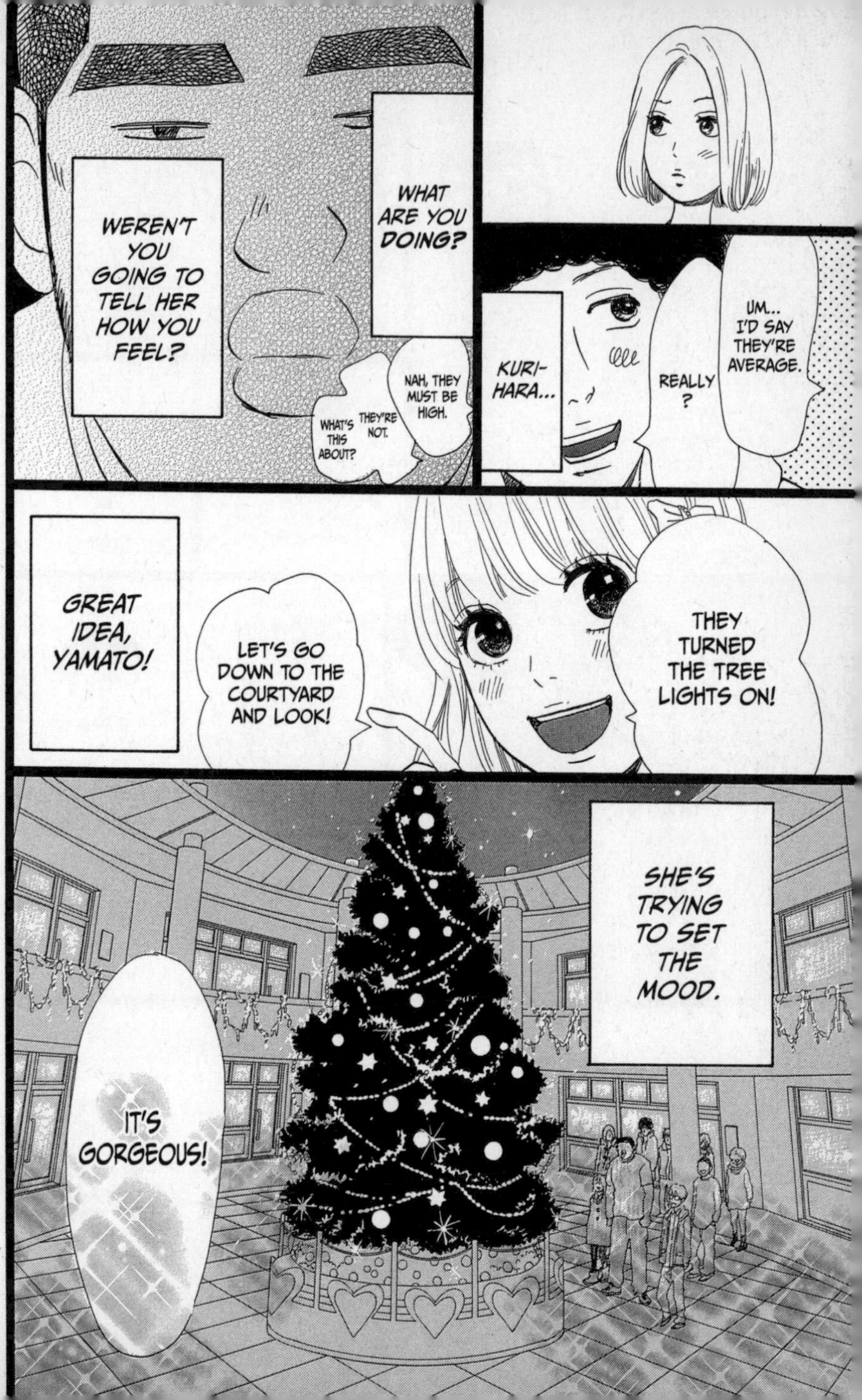

UM.. I'D SAY THEY'RE AVERAGE.
REALLY?
KURI-HARA...
WHAT ARE YOU DOING?
NAH, THEY MUST BE HIGH.
THEY'RE NOT.
WHAT'S THIS ABOUT?
WEREN'T YOU GOING TO TELL HER HOW YOU FEEL?
THEY TURNED THE TREE LIGHTS ON!
LET'S GO DOWN TO THE COURTYARD AND LOOK!
GREAT IDEA, YAMATO!
SHE'S TRYING TO SET THE MOOD.
IT'S GORGEOUS!

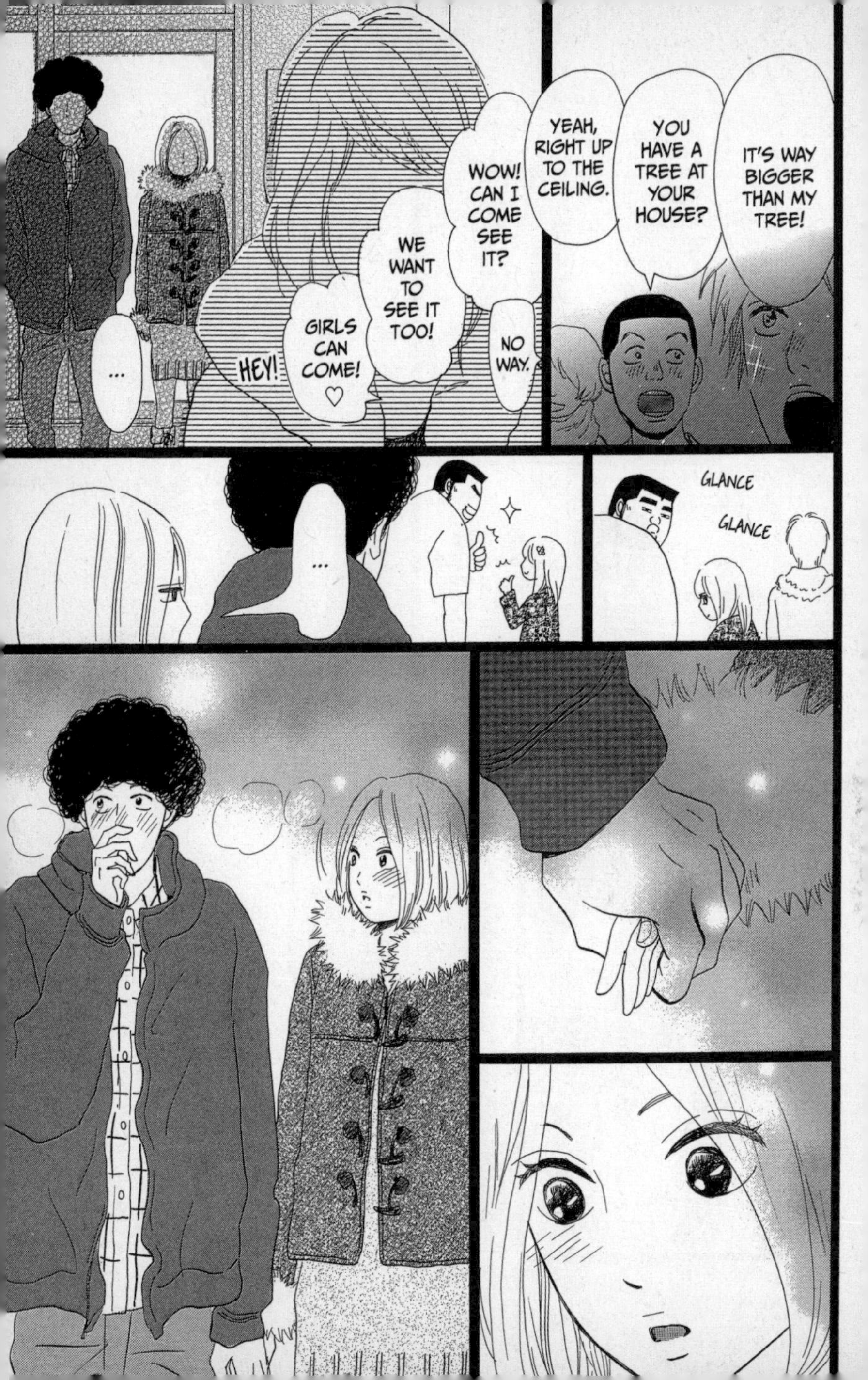
IT'S WAY BIGGER THAN MY TREE!
YOU HAVE A TREE AT YOUR HOUSE?
YEAH, RIGHT UP TO THE CEILING.
WOW! CAN I COME SEE IT?
NO WAY.
WE WANT TO SEE IT TOO!
GIRLS CAN COME! ♡
HEY!
...
GLANCE
GLANCE
...

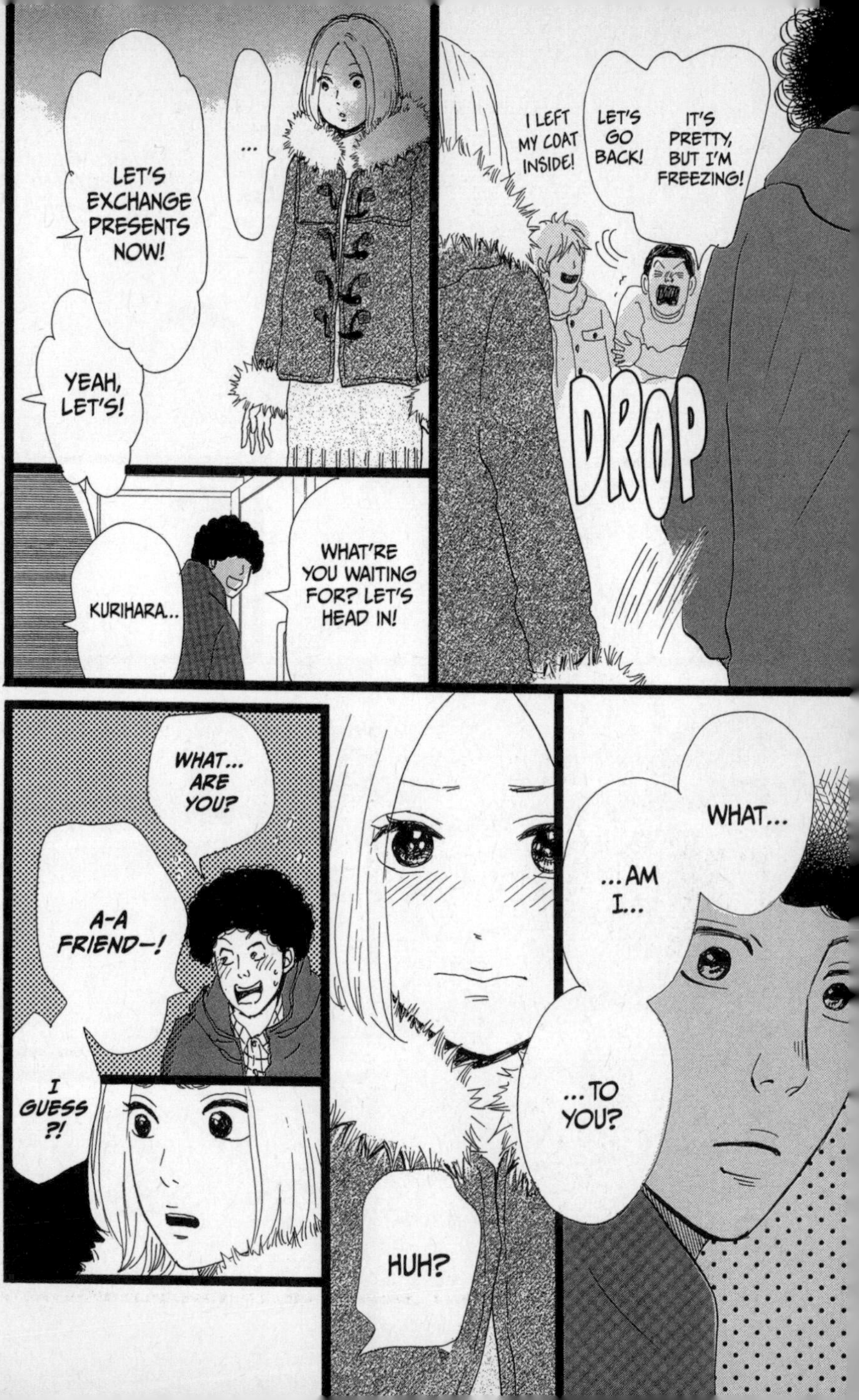
IT'S PRETTY, BUT I'M FREEZING!
LET'S GO BACK!
I LEFT MY COAT INSIDE!
DROP
...
LET'S EXCHANGE PRESENTS NOW!
YEAH, LET'S!
WHAT'RE YOU WAITING FOR? LET'S HEAD IN!
KURIHARA...
WHAT...
...AM I...
...TO YOU?
HUH?
WHAT... ARE YOU?
A-A FRIEND—!
I GUESS ?!

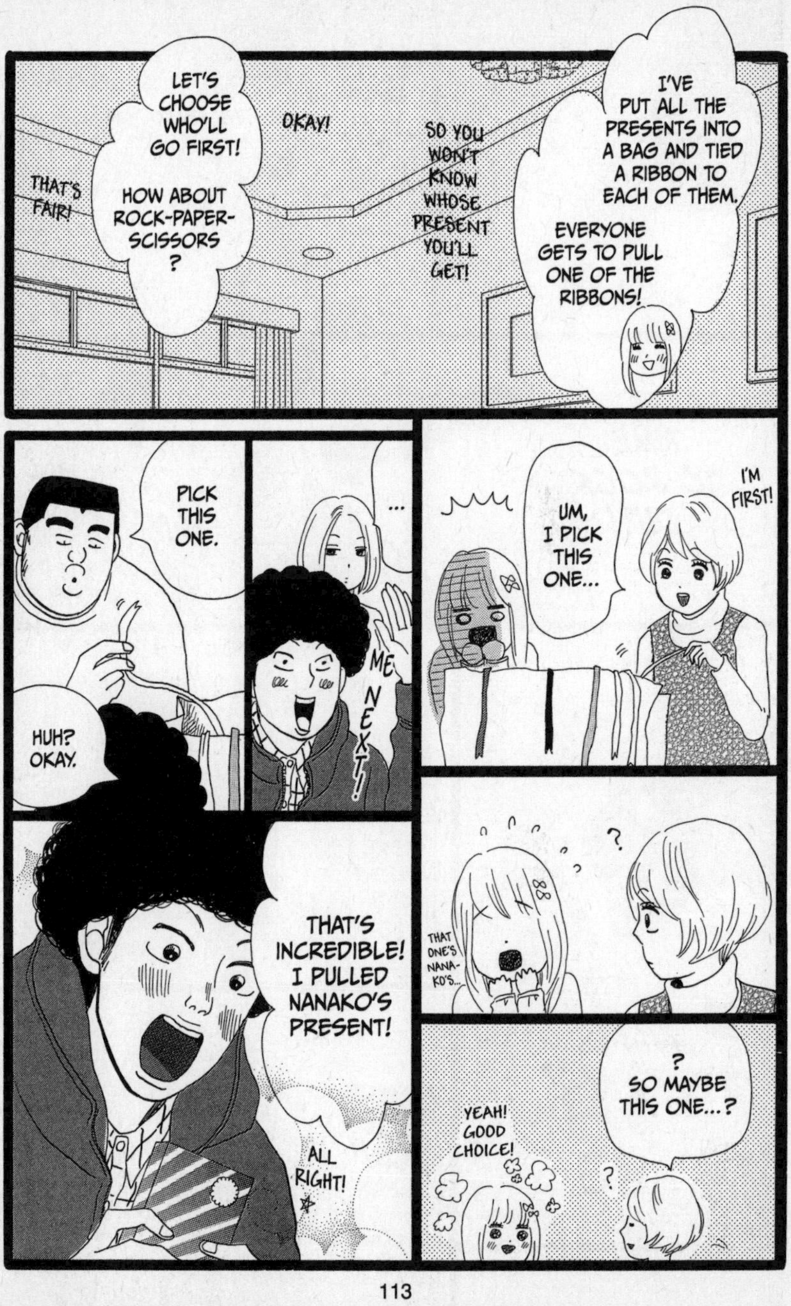
I'VE PUT ALL THE PRESENTS INTO A BAG AND TIED A RIBBON TO EACH OF THEM.
EVERYONE GETS TO PULL ONE OF THE RIBBONS!
SO YOU WON'T KNOW WHOSE PRESENT YOU'LL GET!
OKAY!
LET'S CHOOSE WHO'LL GO FIRST!
HOW ABOUT ROCK-PAPER-SCISSORS?
THAT'S FAIR!
I'M FIRST!
UM, I PICK THIS ONE...
THAT ONE'S NANAKO'S...
? SO MAYBE THIS ONE...?
YEAH! GOOD CHOICE!
...
ME NEXT!
PICK THIS ONE.
HUH? OKAY.
THAT'S INCREDIBLE! I PULLED NANAKO'S PRESENT!
ALL RIGHT!

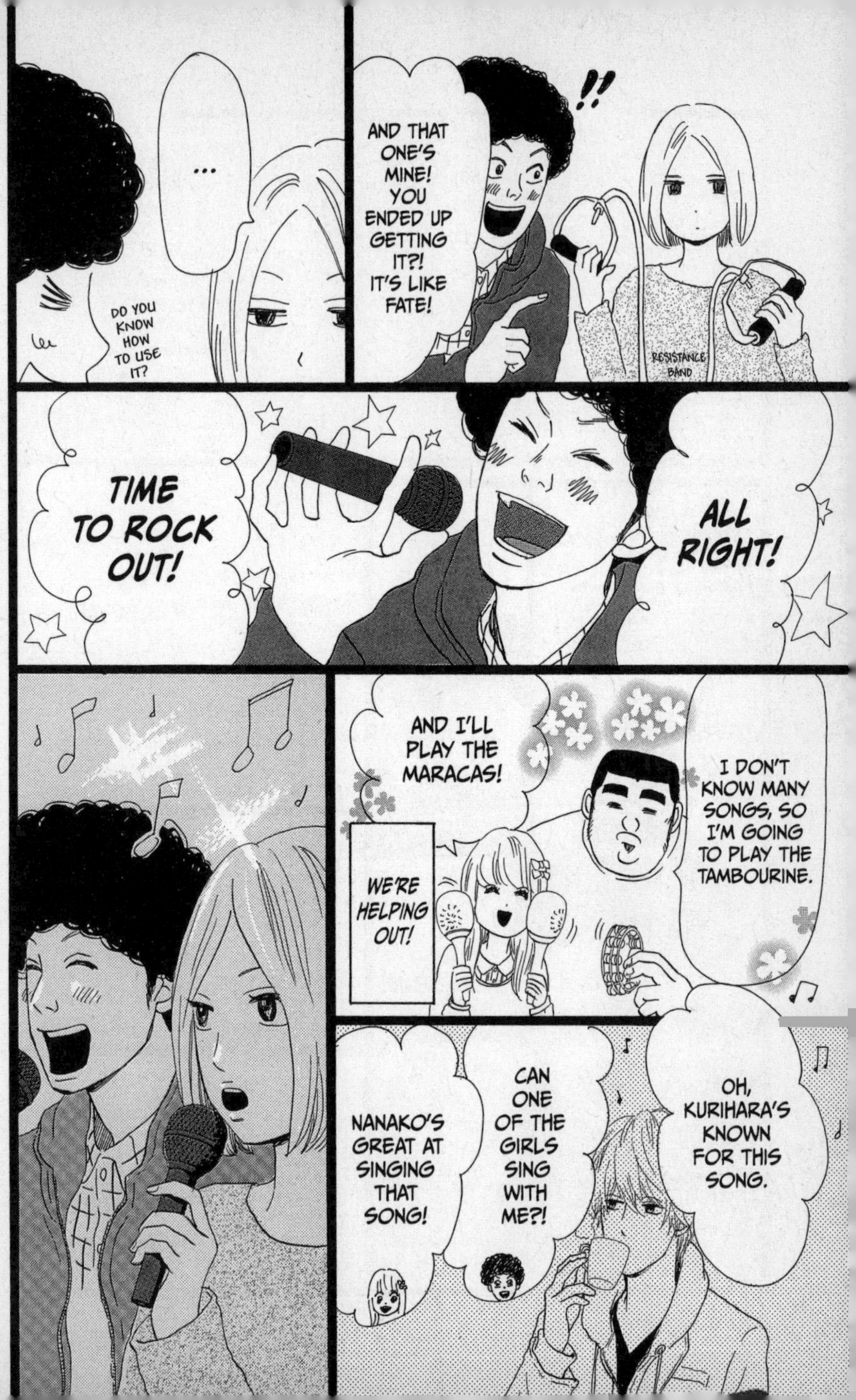
!!
AND THAT ONE'S MINE! YOU ENDED UP GETTING IT?! IT'S LIKE FATE!
RESISTANCE BAND
...
DO YOU KNOW HOW TO USE IT?
ALL RIGHT!
TIME TO ROCK OUT!
I DON'T KNOW MANY SONGS, SO I'M GOING TO PLAY THE TAMBOURINE.
AND I'LL PLAY THE MARACAS!
WE'RE HELPING OUT!
OH, KURIHARA'S KNOWN FOR THIS SONG.
CAN ONE OF THE GIRLS SING WITH ME?!
NANAKO'S GREAT AT SINGING THAT SONG!

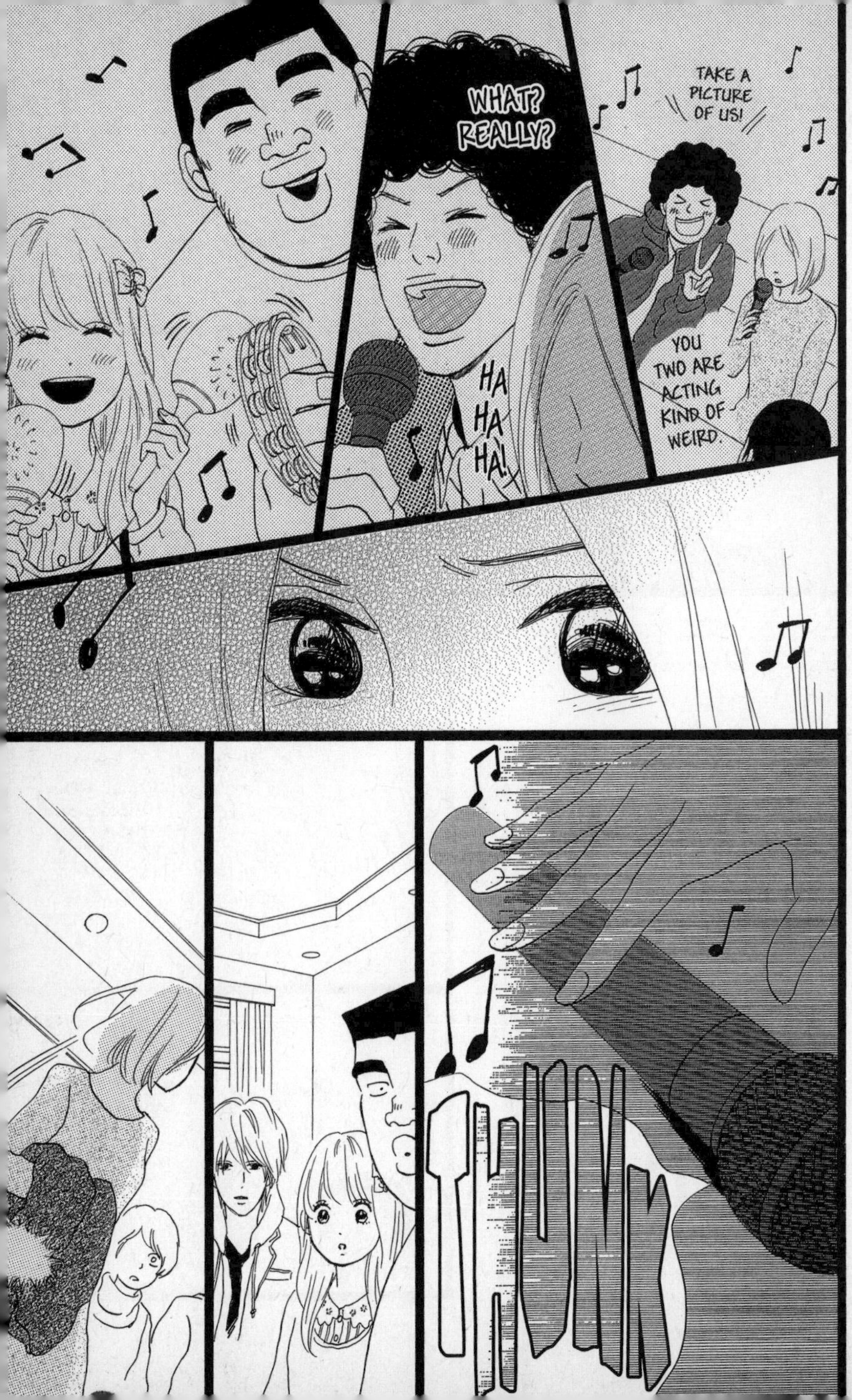
TAKE A PICTURE OF US!
YOU TWO ARE ACTING KIND OF WEIRD.
WHAT? REALLY?
HA HA HA!
THUNK

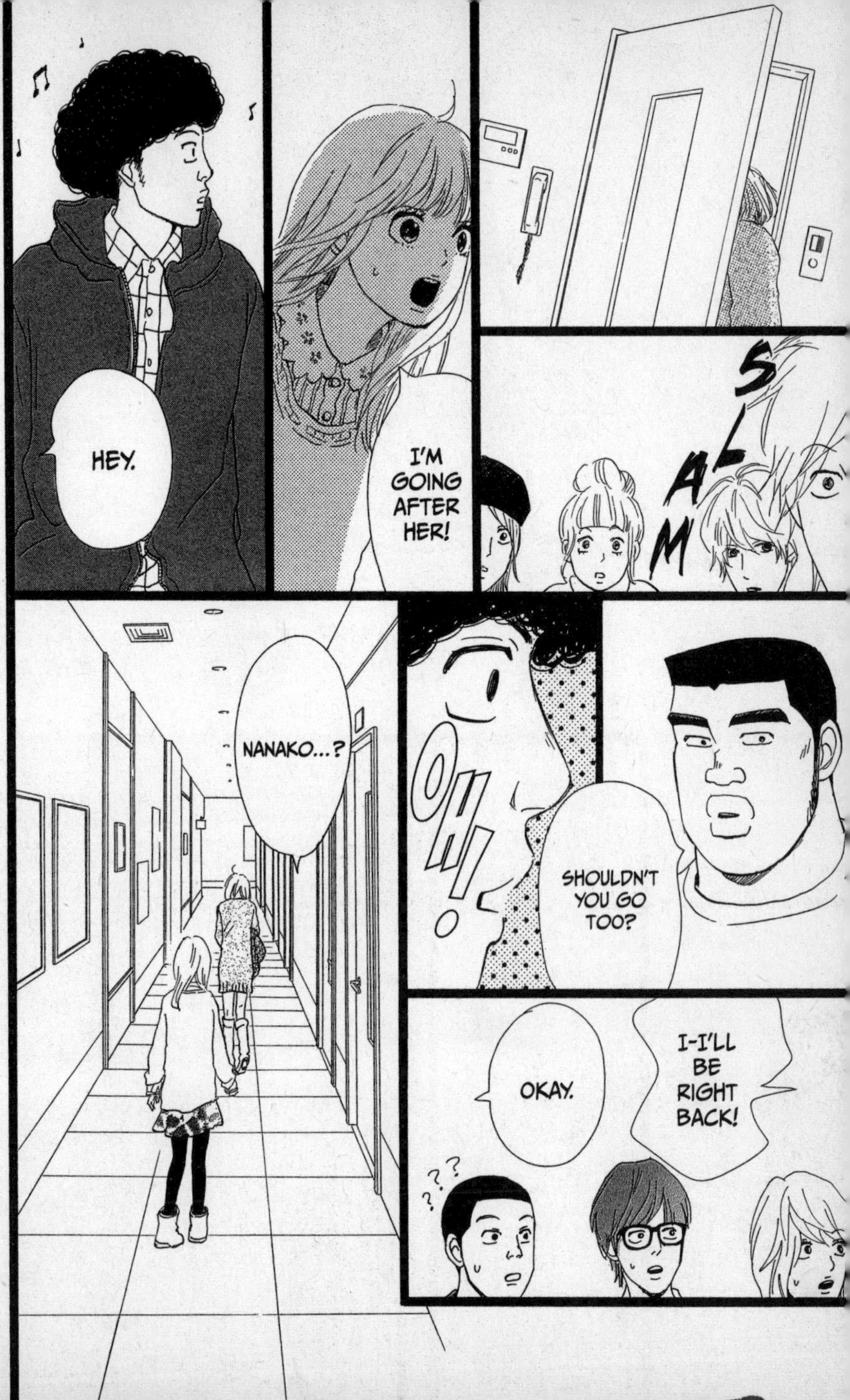
SLAM
I'M GOING AFTER HER!
HEY.
SHOULDN'T YOU GO TOO?
OH!
I-I'LL BE RIGHT BACK!
OKAY.
NANAKO...?

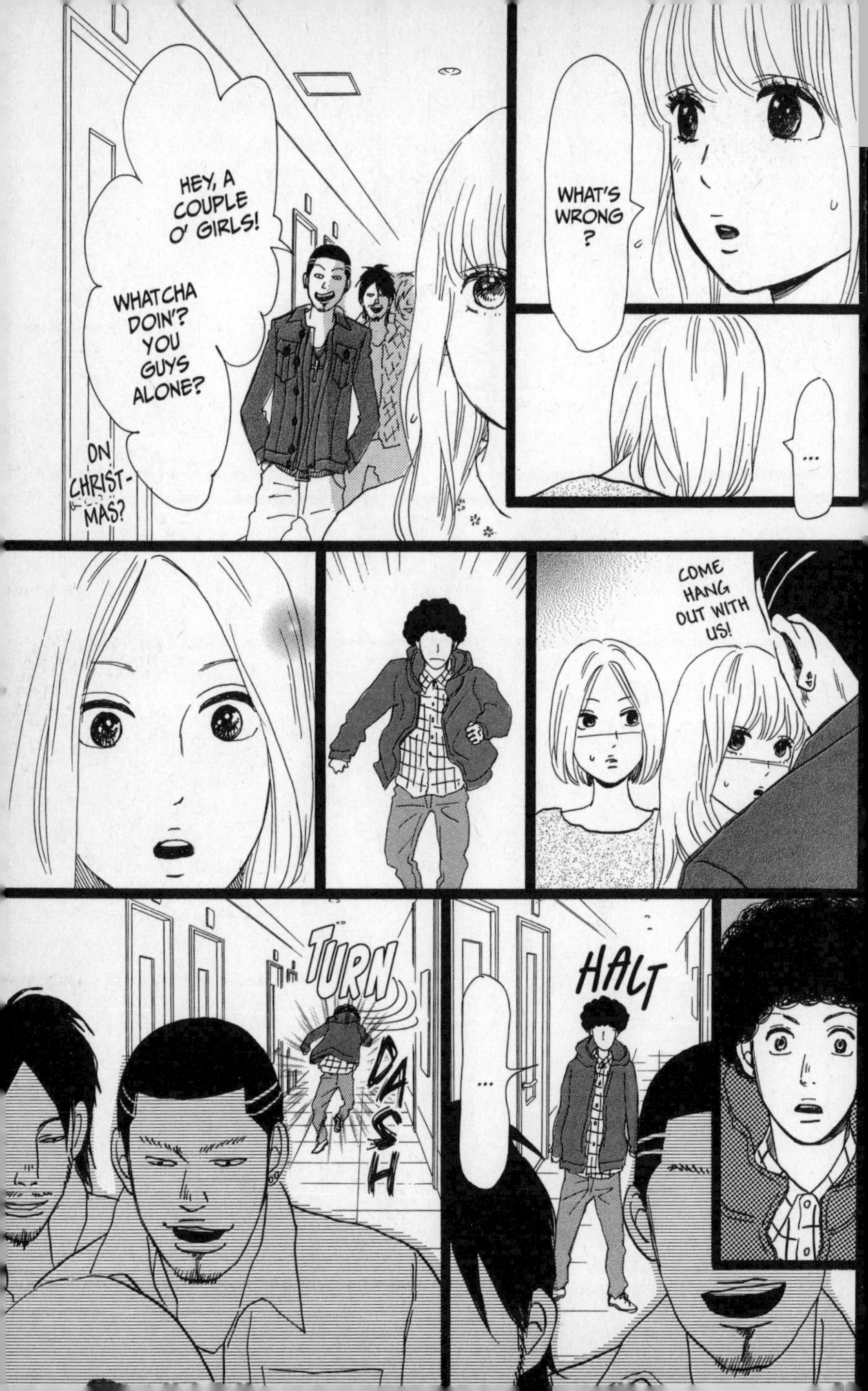
WHAT'S WRONG?
...
HEY, A COUPLE O' GIRLS!
WHATCHA DOIN'? YOU GUYS ALONE?
ON CHRISTMAS?
COME HANG OUT WITH US!
HALT
...
TURN
DASH

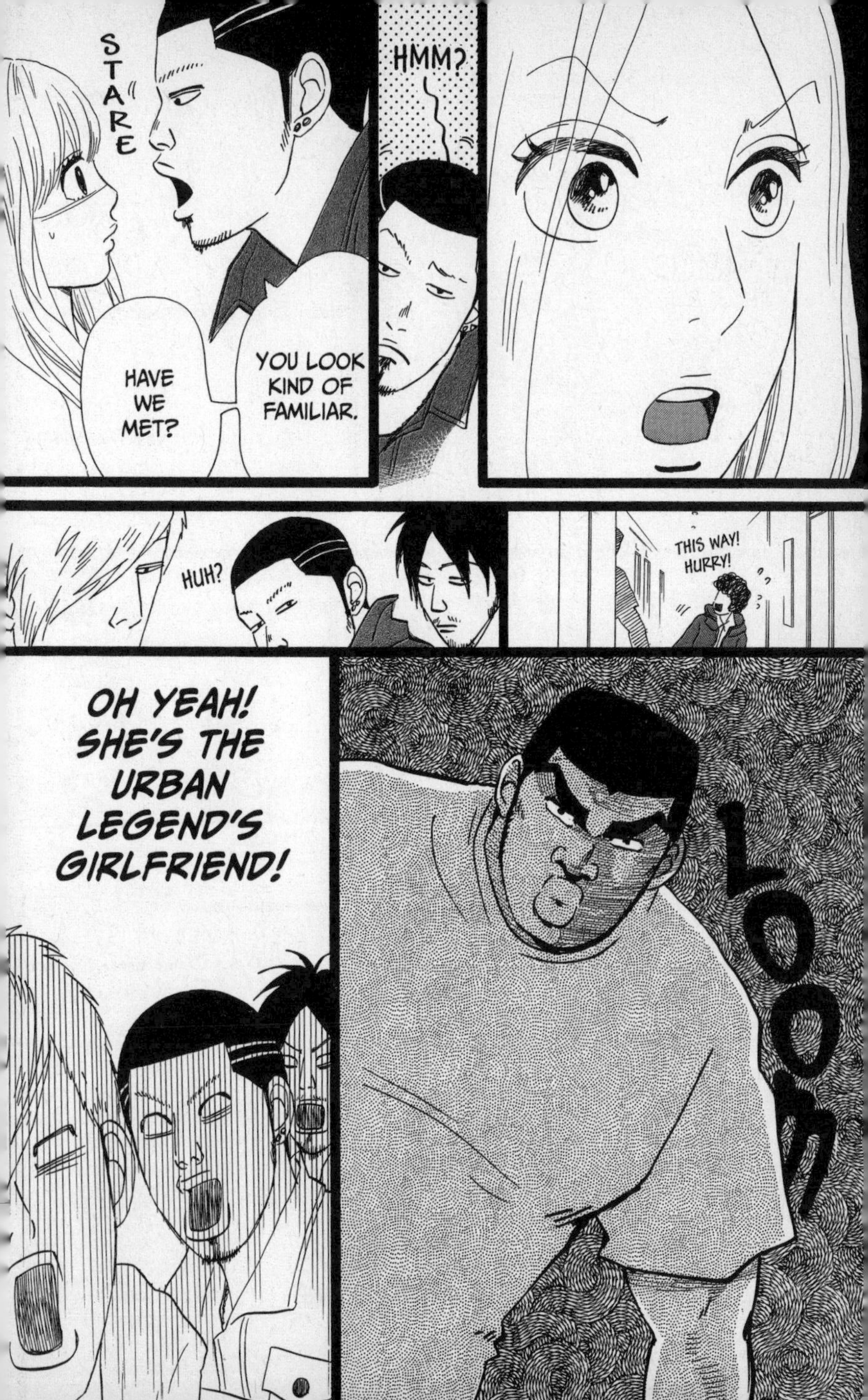
HMM?
STARE
YOU LOOK KIND OF FAMILIAR.
HAVE WE MET?
THIS WAY! HURRY!
HUH?
LOOM
OH YEAH! SHE'S THE URBAN LEGEND'S GIRLFRIEND!

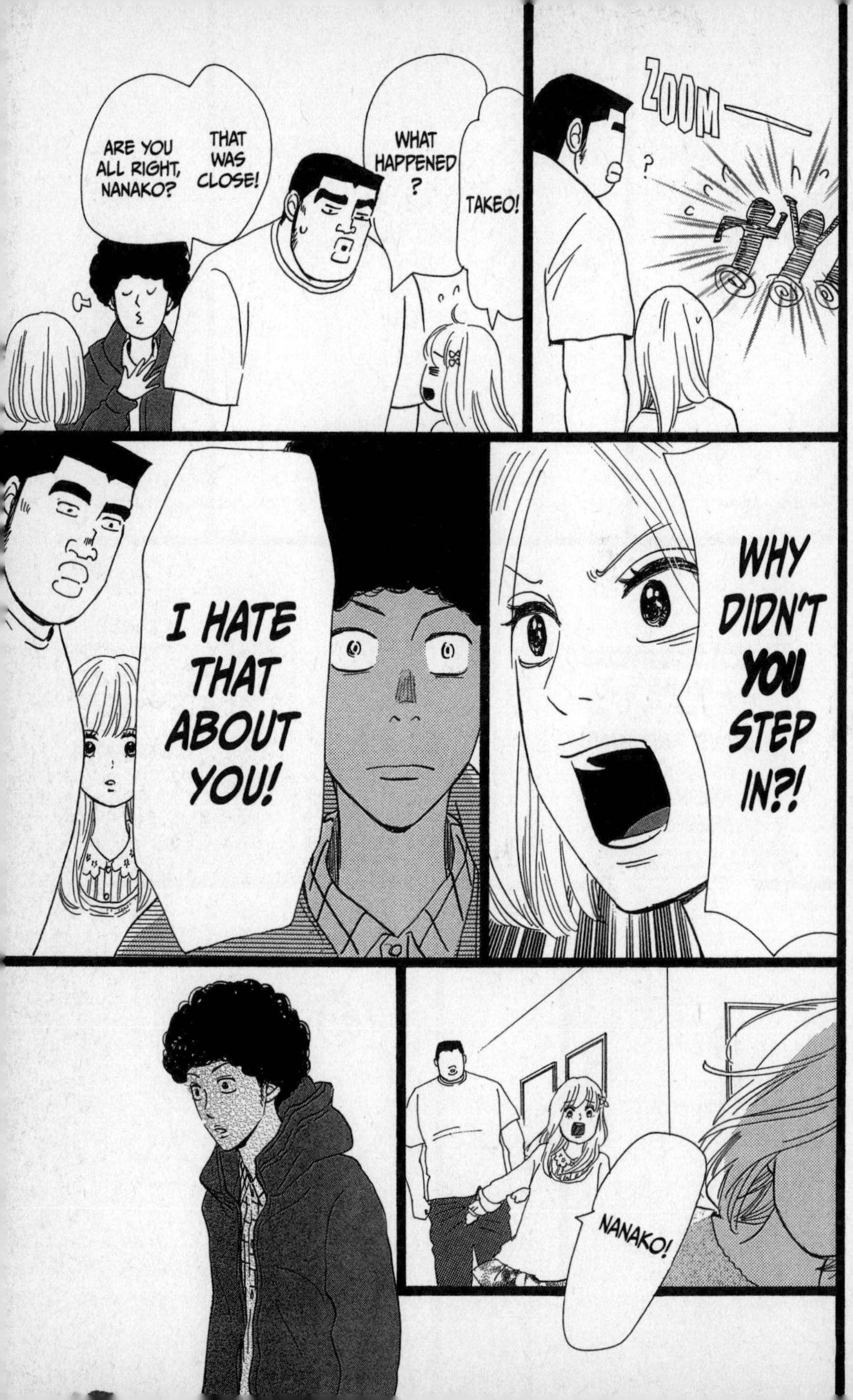
ZOOM
?
TAKEO!
WHAT HAPPENED?
THAT WAS CLOSE!
ARE YOU ALL RIGHT, NANAKO?
WHY DIDN'T YOU STEP IN?!
I HATE THAT ABOUT YOU!
NANAKO!

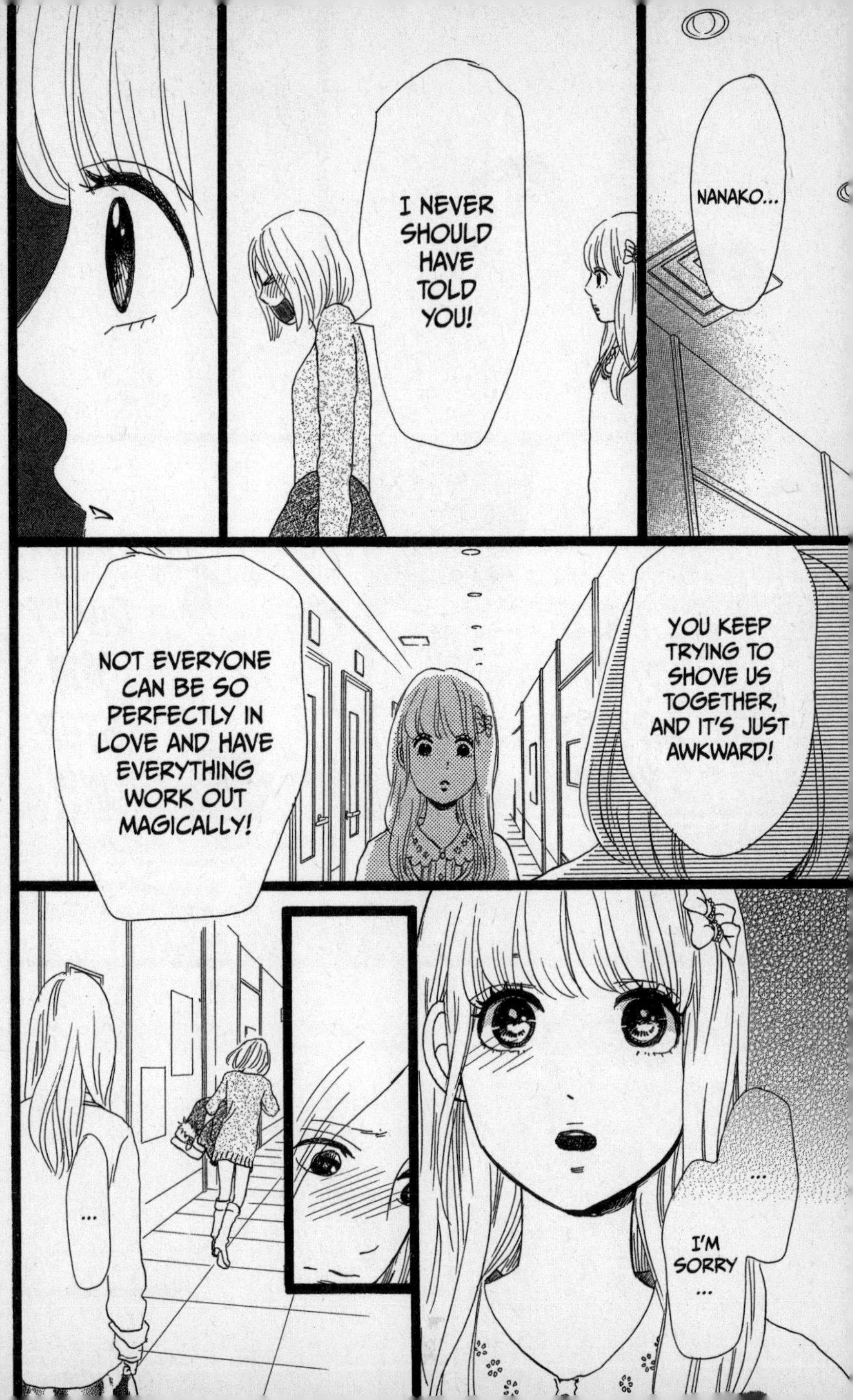
NANAKO...
I NEVER SHOULD HAVE TOLD YOU!
YOU KEEP TRYING TO SHOVE US TOGETHER, AND IT'S JUST AWKWARD!
NOT EVERYONE CAN BE SO PERFECTLY IN LOVE AND HAVE EVERYTHING WORK OUT MAGICALLY!
...
I'M SORRY ...
...

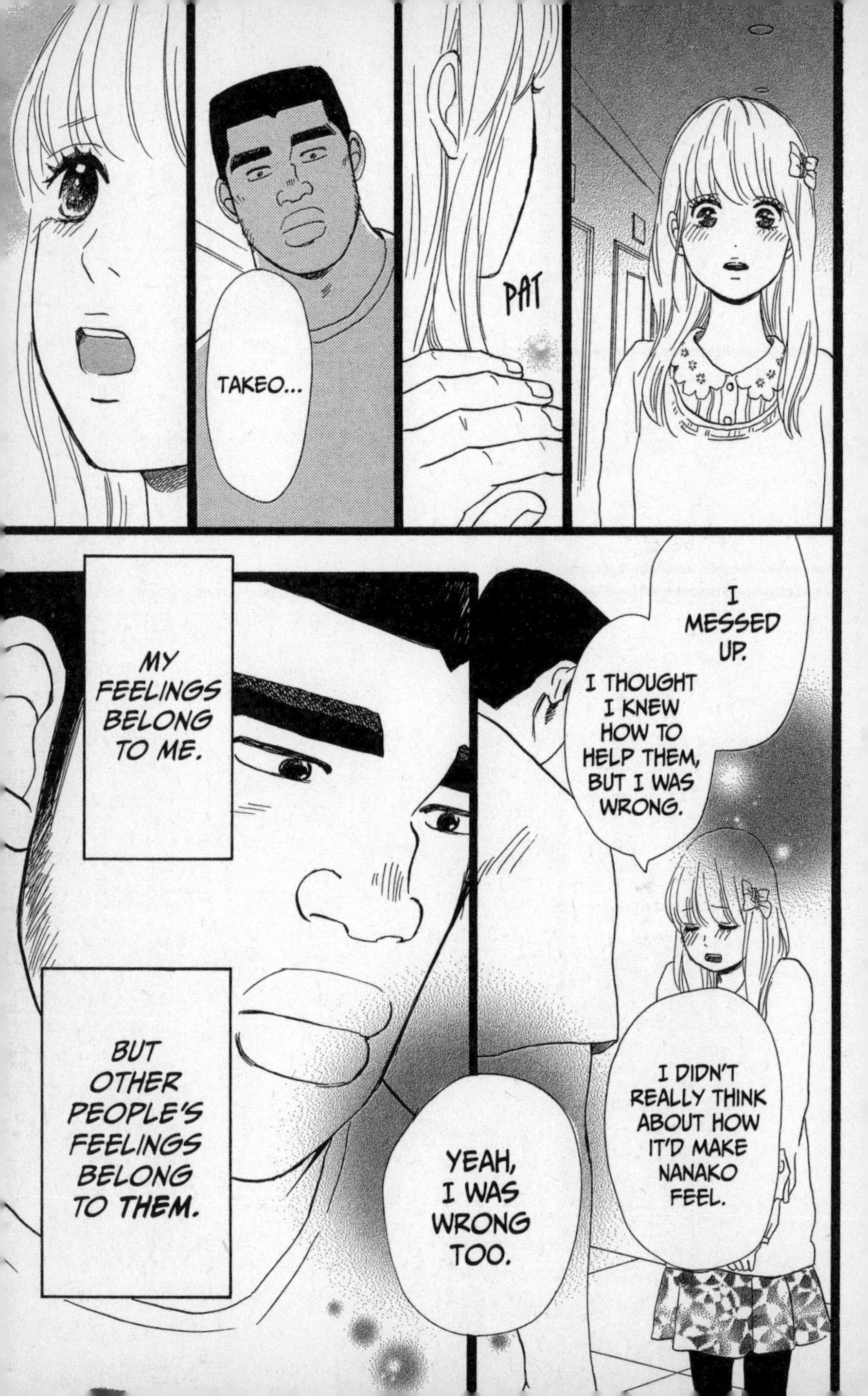
PAT
TAKEO...
I MESSED UP.
I THOUGHT I KNEW HOW TO HELP THEM, BUT I WAS WRONG.
I DIDN'T REALLY THINK ABOUT HOW IT'D MAKE NANAKO FEEL.
MY FEELINGS BELONG TO ME.
BUT OTHER PEOPLE'S FEELINGS BELONG TO THEM.
YEAH, I WAS WRONG TOO.

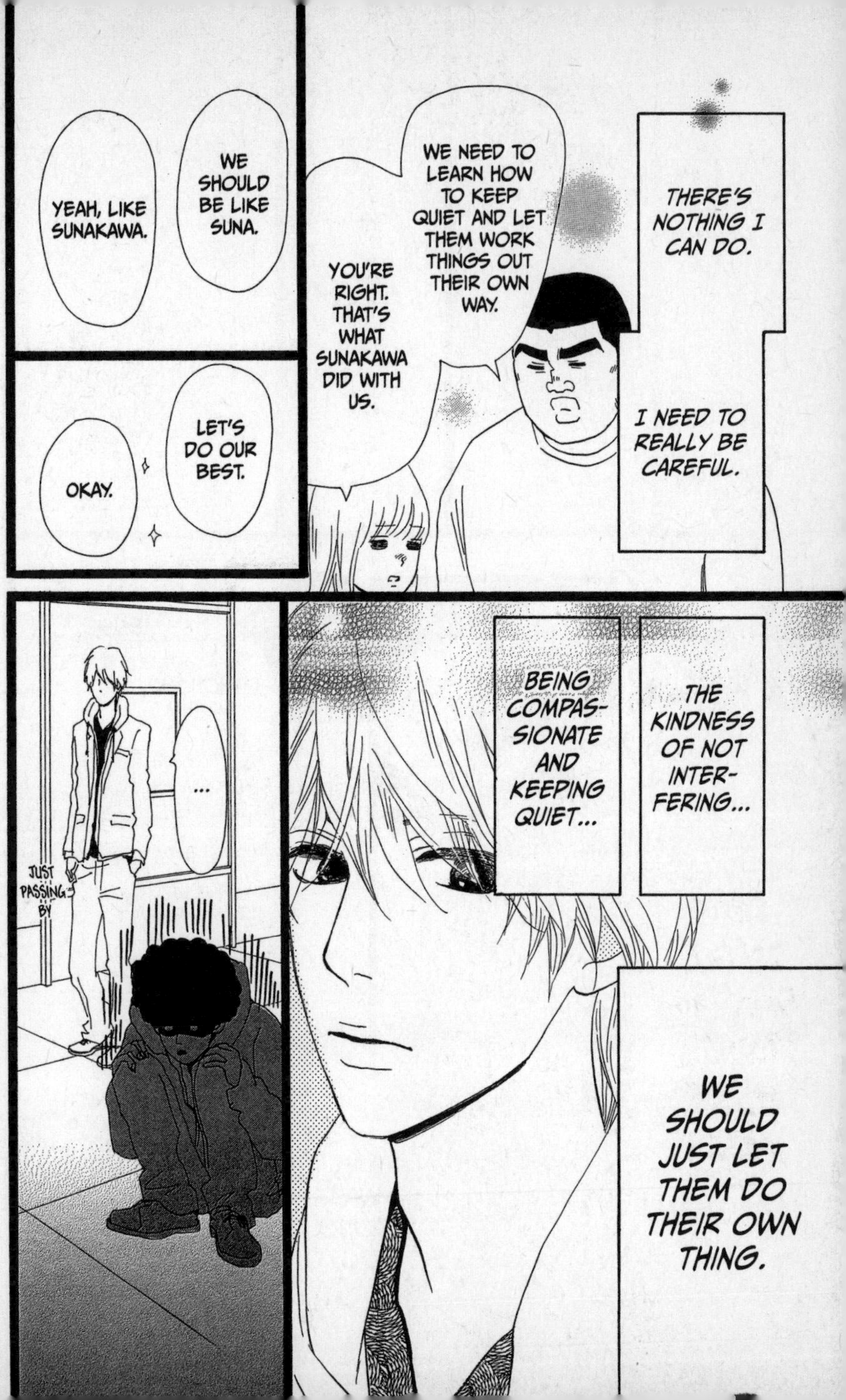
THERE'S NOTHING I CAN DO.
I NEED TO REALLY BE CAREFUL.
WE NEED TO LEARN HOW TO KEEP QUIET AND LET THEM WORK THINGS OUT THEIR OWN WAY.
YOU'RE RIGHT. THAT'S WHAT SUNAKAWA DID WITH US.
WE SHOULD BE LIKE SUNA.
YEAH, LIKE SUNAKAWA.
LET'S DO OUR BEST.
OKAY.
THE KINDNESS OF NOT INTER-FERING...
BEING COMPAS-SIONATE AND KEEPING QUIET...
WE SHOULD JUST LET THEM DO THEIR OWN THING.
...
JUST PASSING BY

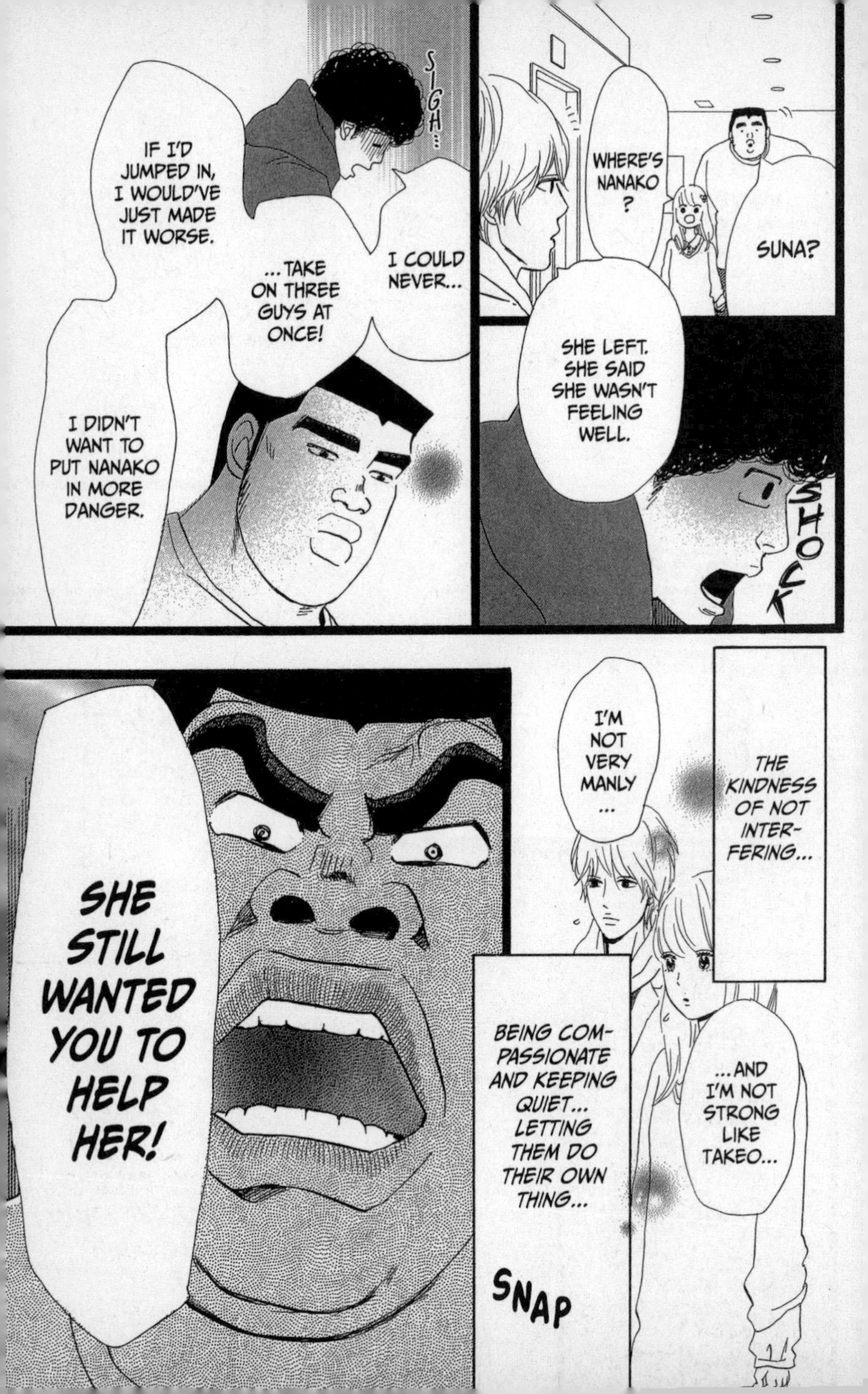
SUNA?
WHERE'S NANAKO ?
SHE LEFT. SHE SAID SHE WASN'T FEELING WELL.
SHOCK
SIGH...
I COULD NEVER...
...TAKE ON THREE GUYS AT ONCE!
IF I'D JUMPED IN, I WOULD'VE JUST MADE IT WORSE.
I DIDN'T WANT TO PUT NANAKO IN MORE DANGER.
THE KINDNESS OF NOT INTER-FERING...
I'M NOT VERY MANLY ...
...AND I'M NOT STRONG LIKE TAKEO...
BEING COM-PASSIONATE AND KEEPING QUIET... LETTING THEM DO THEIR OWN THING...
SNAP
SHE STILL WANTED YOU TO HELP HER!

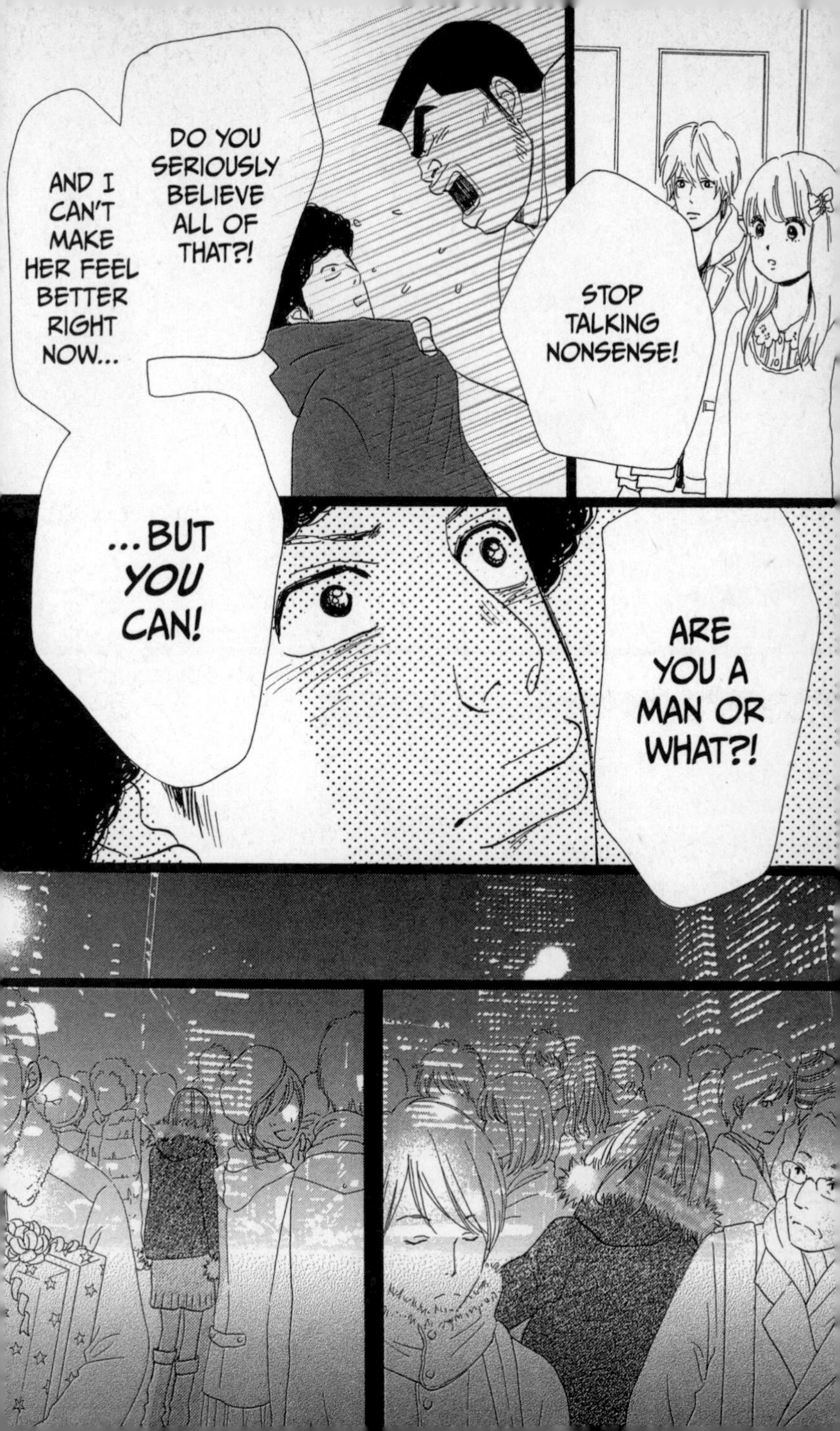
STOP TALKING NONSENSE!
DO YOU SERIOUSLY BELIEVE ALL OF THAT?!
AND I CAN'T MAKE HER FEEL BETTER RIGHT NOW...
...BUT *YOU* CAN!
ARE YOU A MAN OR WHAT?!

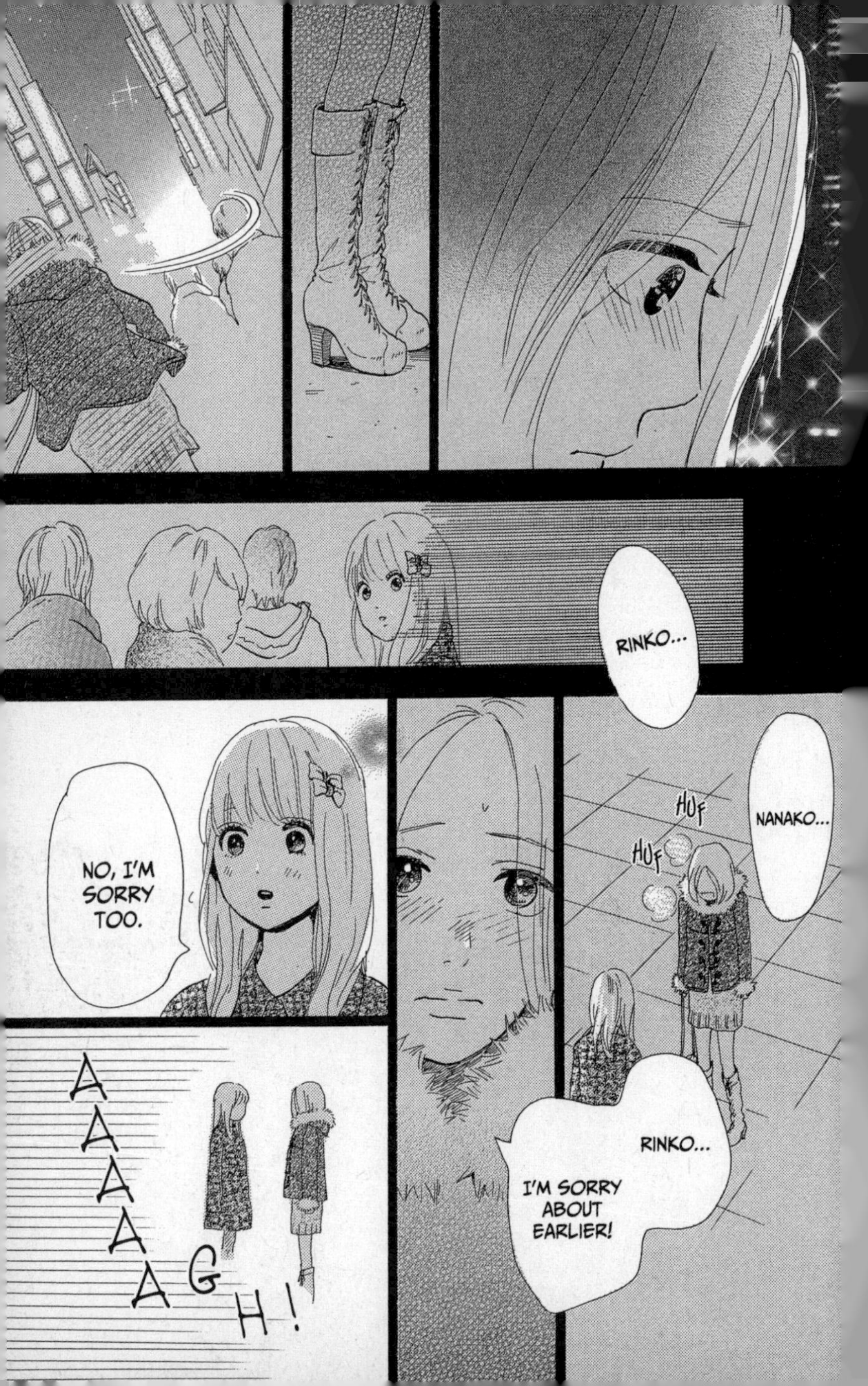
RINKO...
NANAKO...
HUF
HUF
RINKO...
I'M SORRY ABOUT EARLIER!
NO, I'M SORRY TOO.
AAAAAGH!

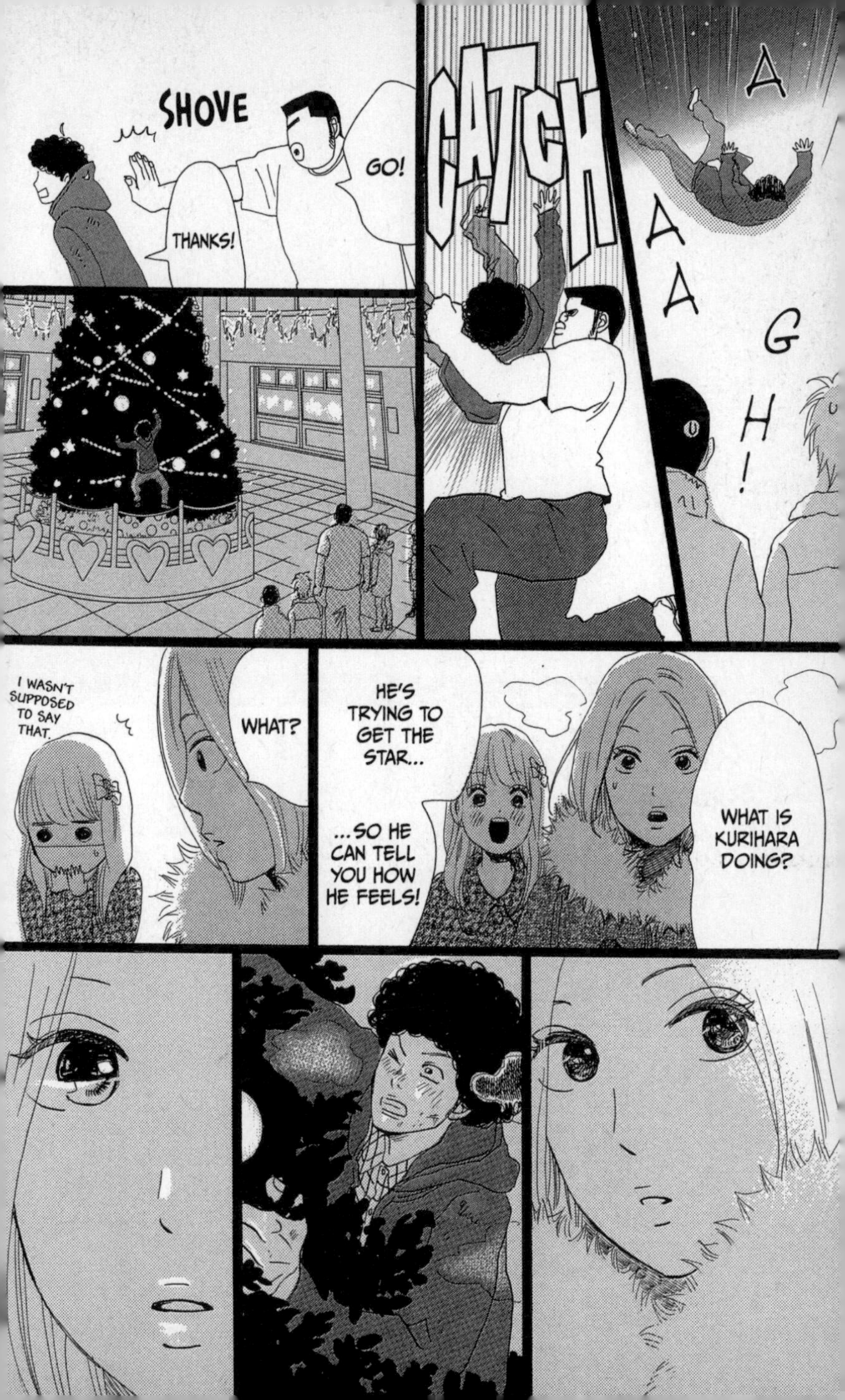
AAAGH!
CATCH
GO!
SHOVE
THANKS!
WHAT IS KURIHARA DOING?
HE'S TRYING TO GET THE STAR...
...SO HE CAN TELL YOU HOW HE FEELS!
WHAT?
I WASN'T SUPPOSED TO SAY THAT.

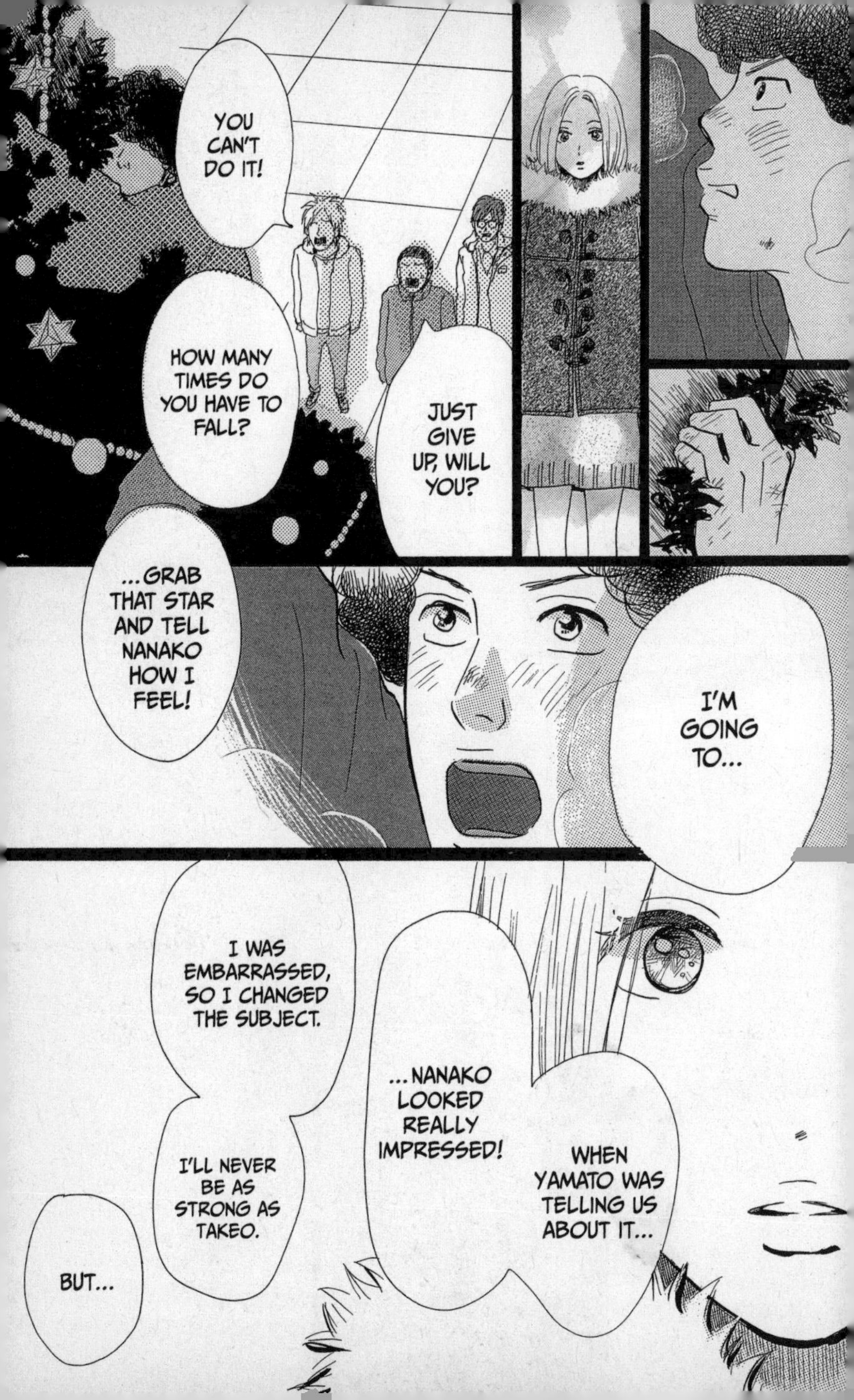
YOU CAN'T DO IT!
HOW MANY TIMES DO YOU HAVE TO FALL?
JUST GIVE UP, WILL YOU?
I'M GOING TO...
...GRAB THAT STAR AND TELL NANAKO HOW I FEEL!
WHEN YAMATO WAS TELLING US ABOUT IT...
...NANAKO LOOKED REALLY IMPRESSED!
I WAS EMBARRASSED, SO I CHANGED THE SUBJECT.
I'LL NEVER BE AS STRONG AS TAKEO.
BUT...

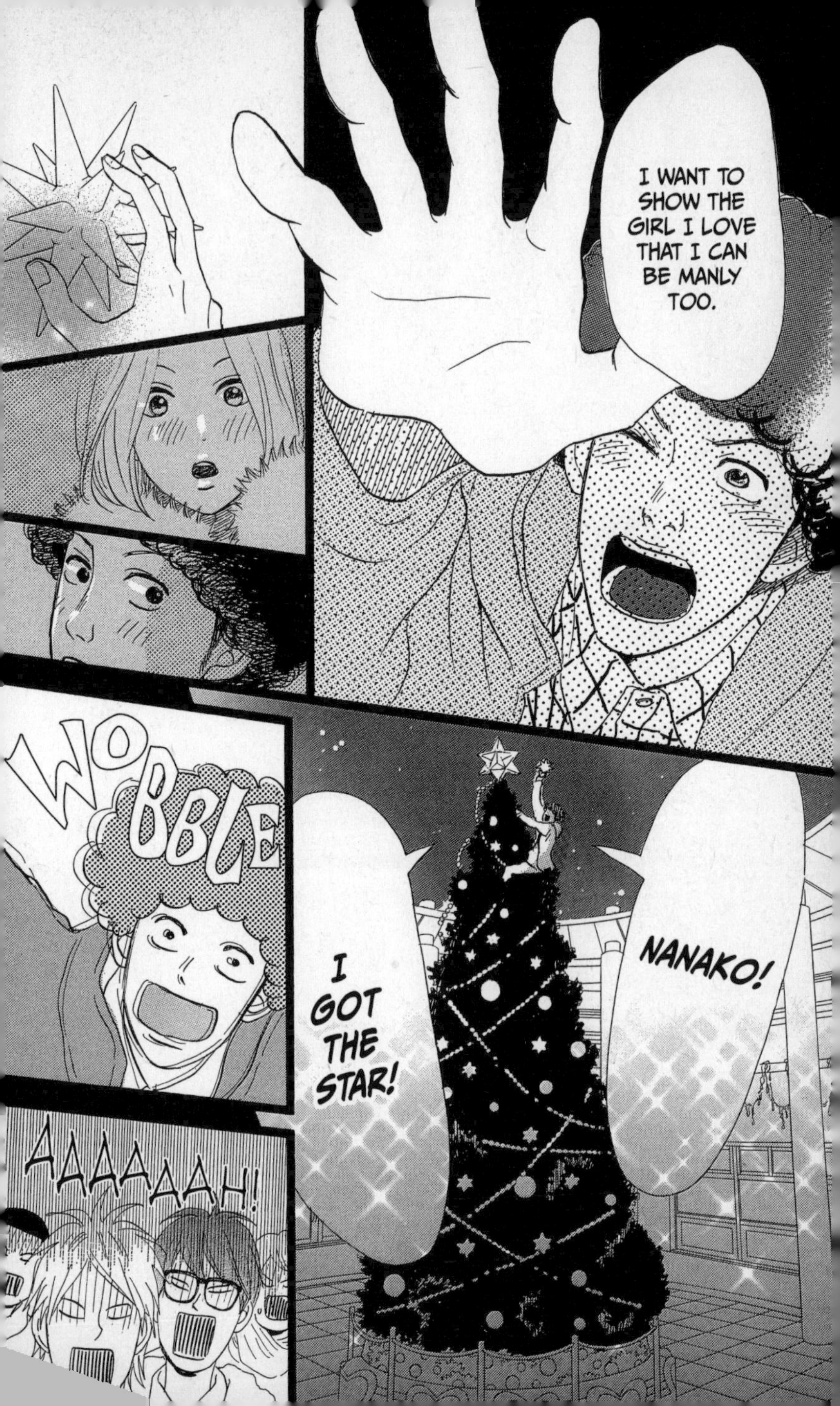
I WANT TO SHOW THE GIRL I LOVE THAT I CAN BE MANLY TOO.
NANAKO!
I GOT THE STAR!
WOBBLE
AAAAAAH!

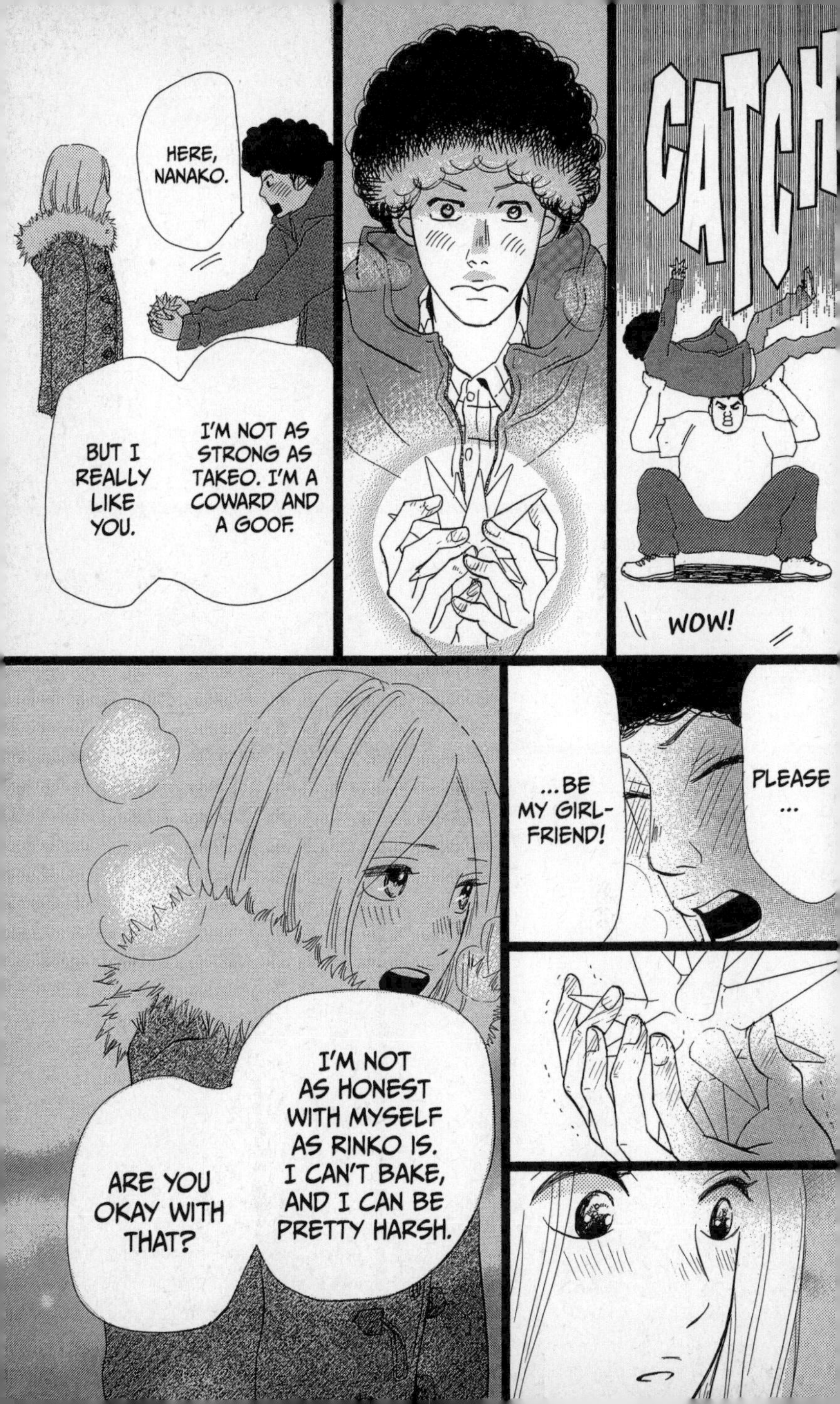
CATCH
WOW!
HERE, NANAKO.
I'M NOT AS STRONG AS TAKEO. I'M A COWARD AND A GOOF.
BUT I REALLY LIKE YOU.
PLEASE ...
...BE MY GIRL-FRIEND!
I'M NOT AS HONEST WITH MYSELF AS RINKO IS. I CAN'T BAKE, AND I CAN BE PRETTY HARSH.
ARE YOU OKAY WITH THAT?

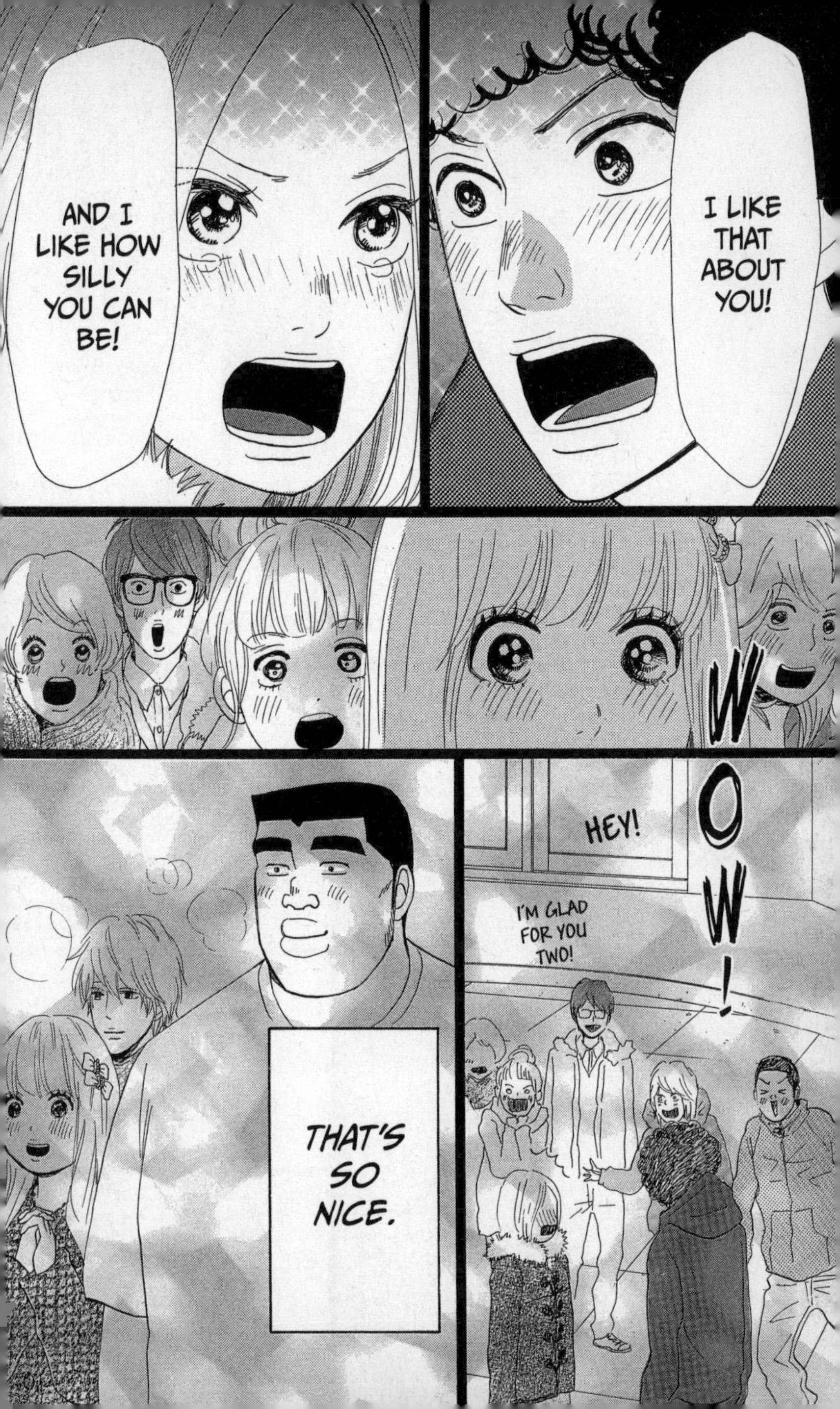
I LIKE THAT ABOUT YOU!
AND I LIKE HOW SILLY YOU CAN BE!
WOW!
HEY!
I'M GLAD FOR YOU TWO!
THAT'S SO NICE.

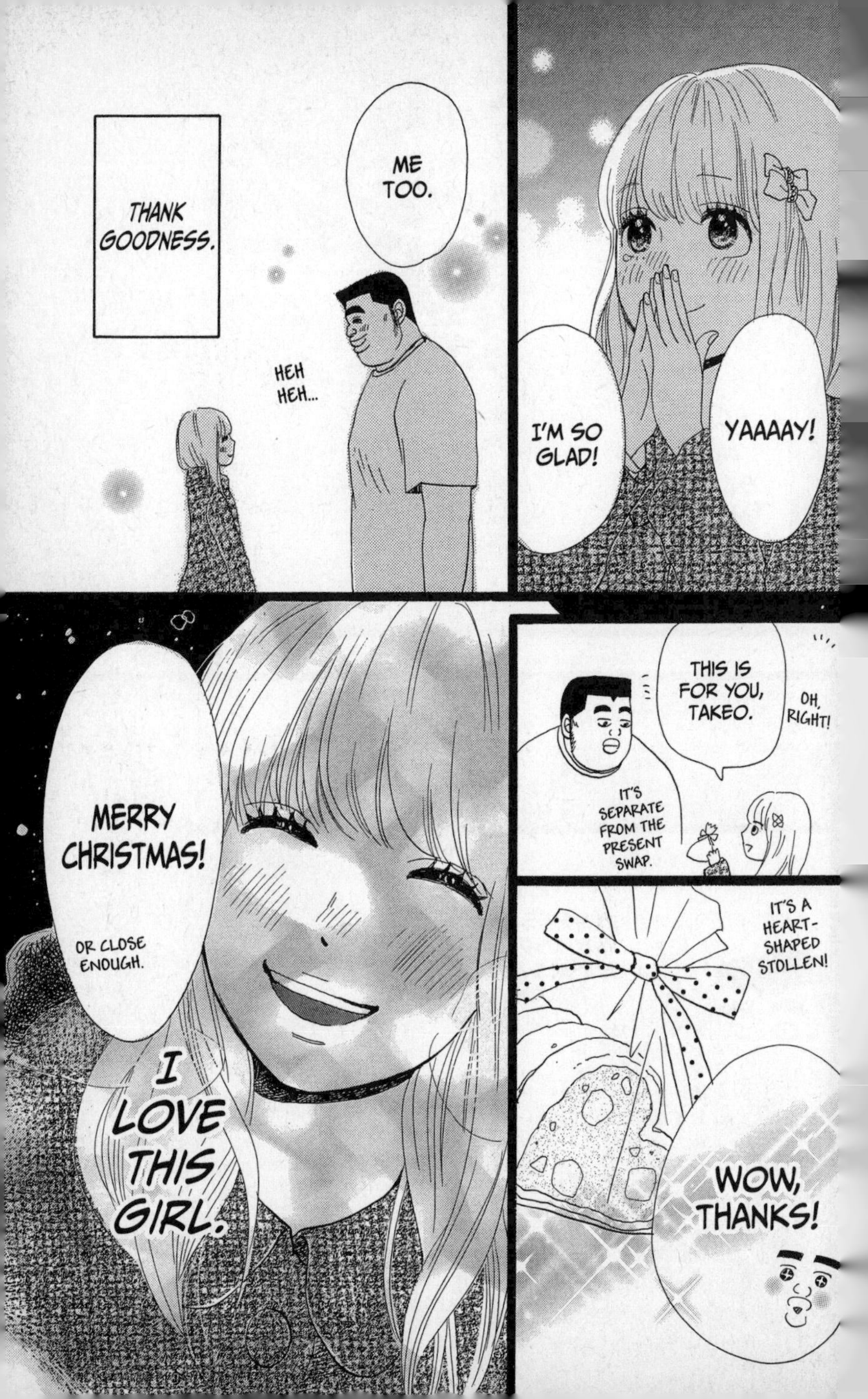
YAAAAY!
I'M SO GLAD!
ME TOO.
THANK GOODNESS.
HEH HEH...
OH, RIGHT!
THIS IS FOR YOU, TAKEO.
IT'S SEPARATE FROM THE PRESENT SWAP.
IT'S A HEART-SHAPED STOLLEN!
WOW, THANKS!
MERRY CHRISTMAS!
OR CLOSE ENOUGH.
I LOVE THIS GIRL.

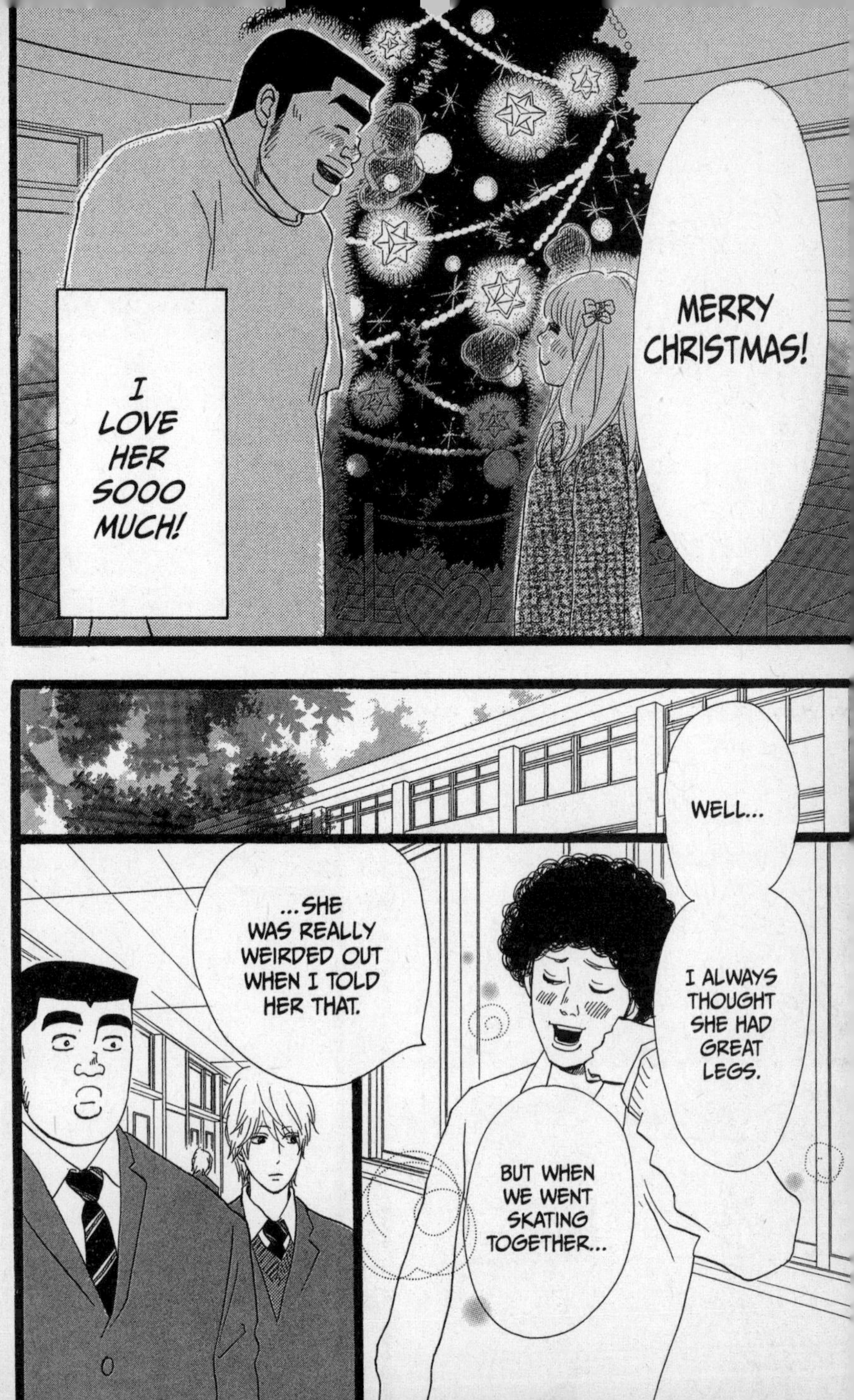
MERRY CHRISTMAS!
I LOVE HER SOOO MUCH!
WELL...
I ALWAYS THOUGHT SHE HAD GREAT LEGS.
BUT WHEN WE WENT SKATING TOGETHER...
...SHE WAS REALLY WEIRDED OUT WHEN I TOLD HER THAT.

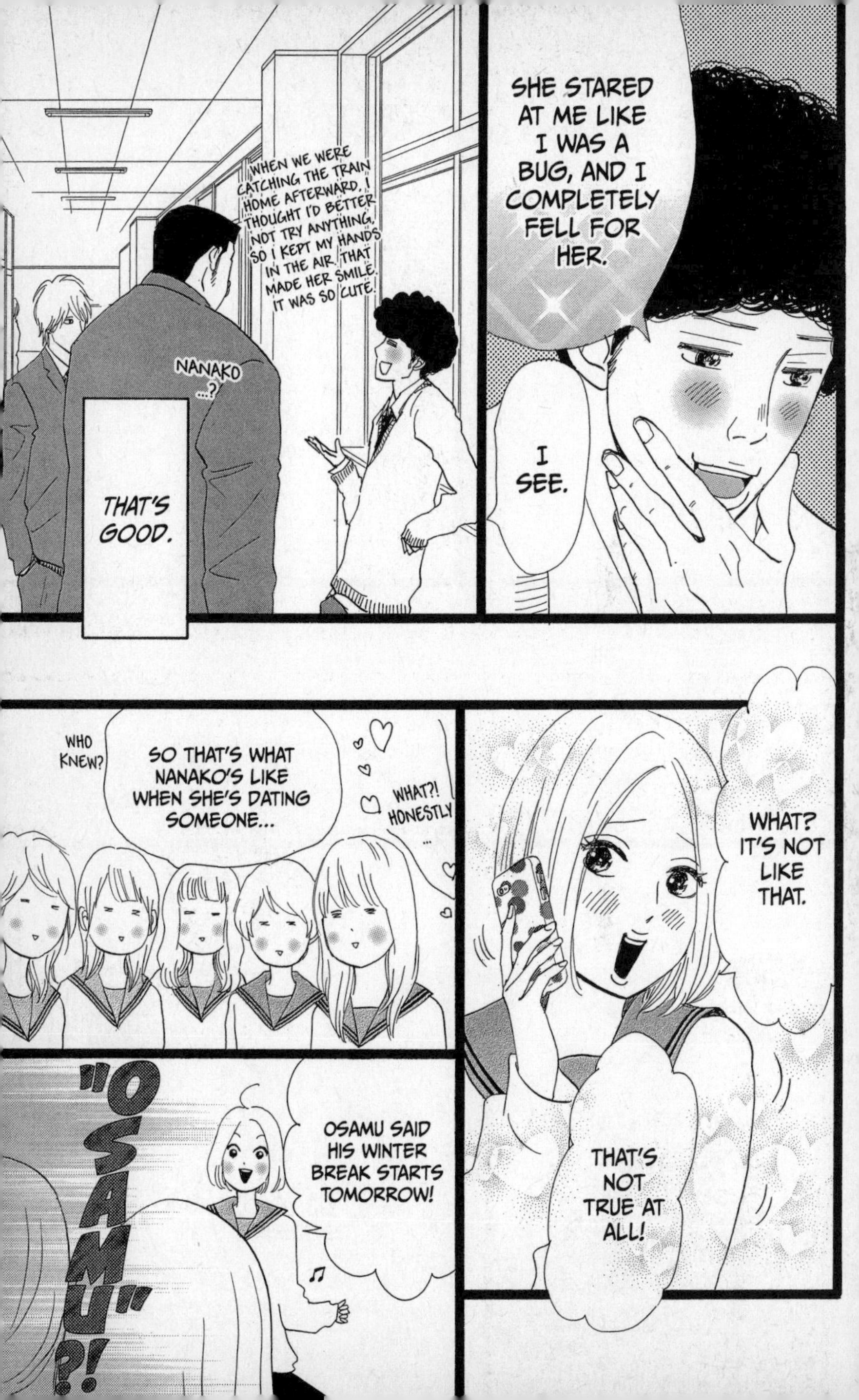
SHE STARED AT ME LIKE I WAS A BUG, AND I COMPLETELY FELL FOR HER.
I SEE.
WHEN WE WERE CATCHING THE TRAIN HOME AFTERWARD, I THOUGHT I'D BETTER NOT TRY ANYTHING, SO I KEPT MY HANDS IN THE AIR. THAT MADE HER SMILE. IT WAS SO CUTE.
NANAKO ...?
THAT'S GOOD.
WHAT? IT'S NOT LIKE THAT.
THAT'S NOT TRUE AT ALL!
WHAT?! HONESTLY ...
SO THAT'S WHAT NANAKO'S LIKE WHEN SHE'S DATING SOMEONE...
WHO KNEW?
OSAMU SAID HIS WINTER BREAK STARTS TOMORROW!
"OSAMU"?!

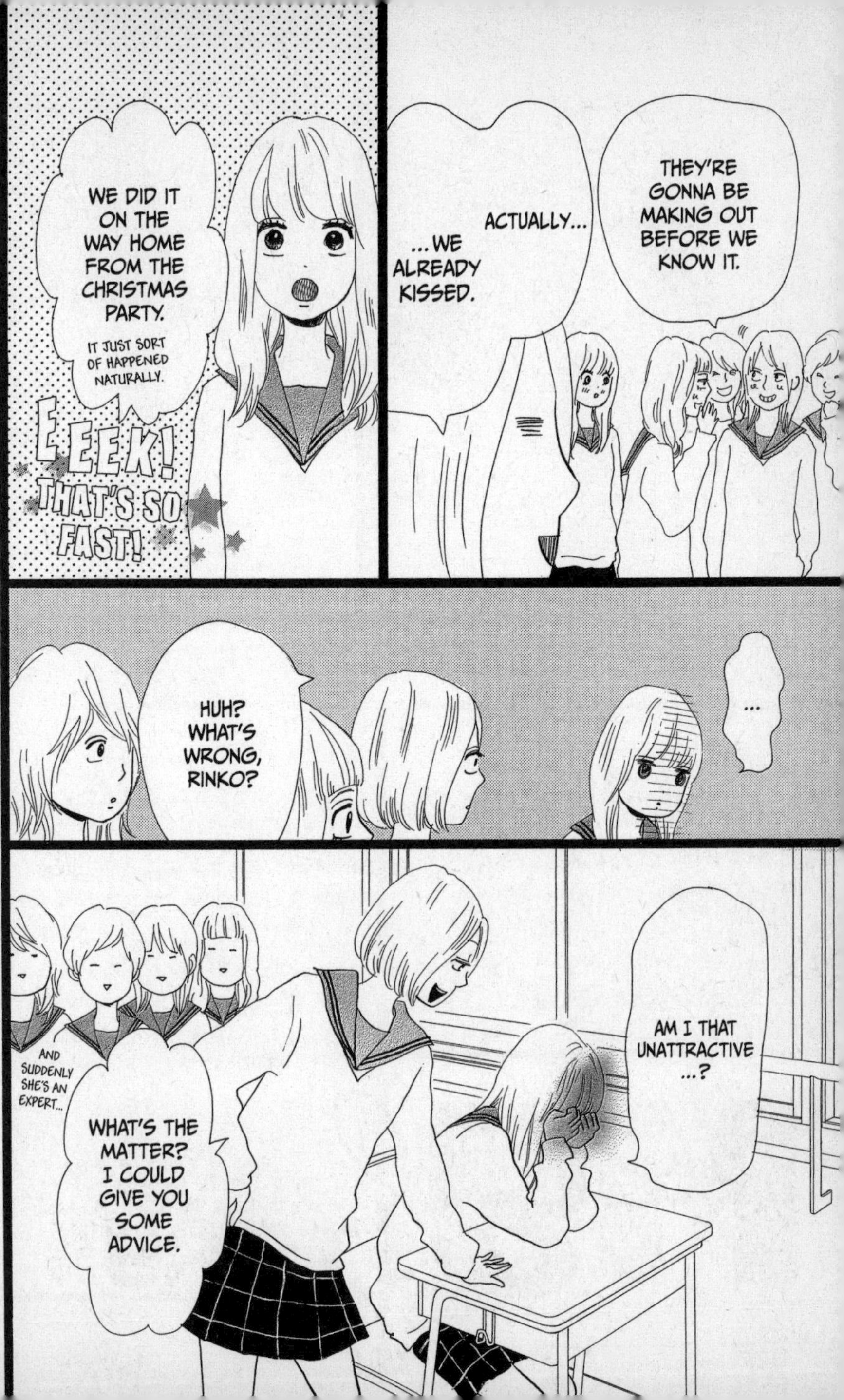
THEY'RE GONNA BE MAKING OUT BEFORE WE KNOW IT.
ACTUALLY...
...WE ALREADY KISSED.
WE DID IT ON THE WAY HOME FROM THE CHRISTMAS PARTY.
IT JUST SORT OF HAPPENED NATURALLY.
EEEK! THAT'S SO FAST!
...
HUH? WHAT'S WRONG, RINKO?
AM I THAT UNATTRACTIVE ...?
WHAT'S THE MATTER? I COULD GIVE YOU SOME ADVICE.
AND SUDDENLY SHE'S AN EXPERT...

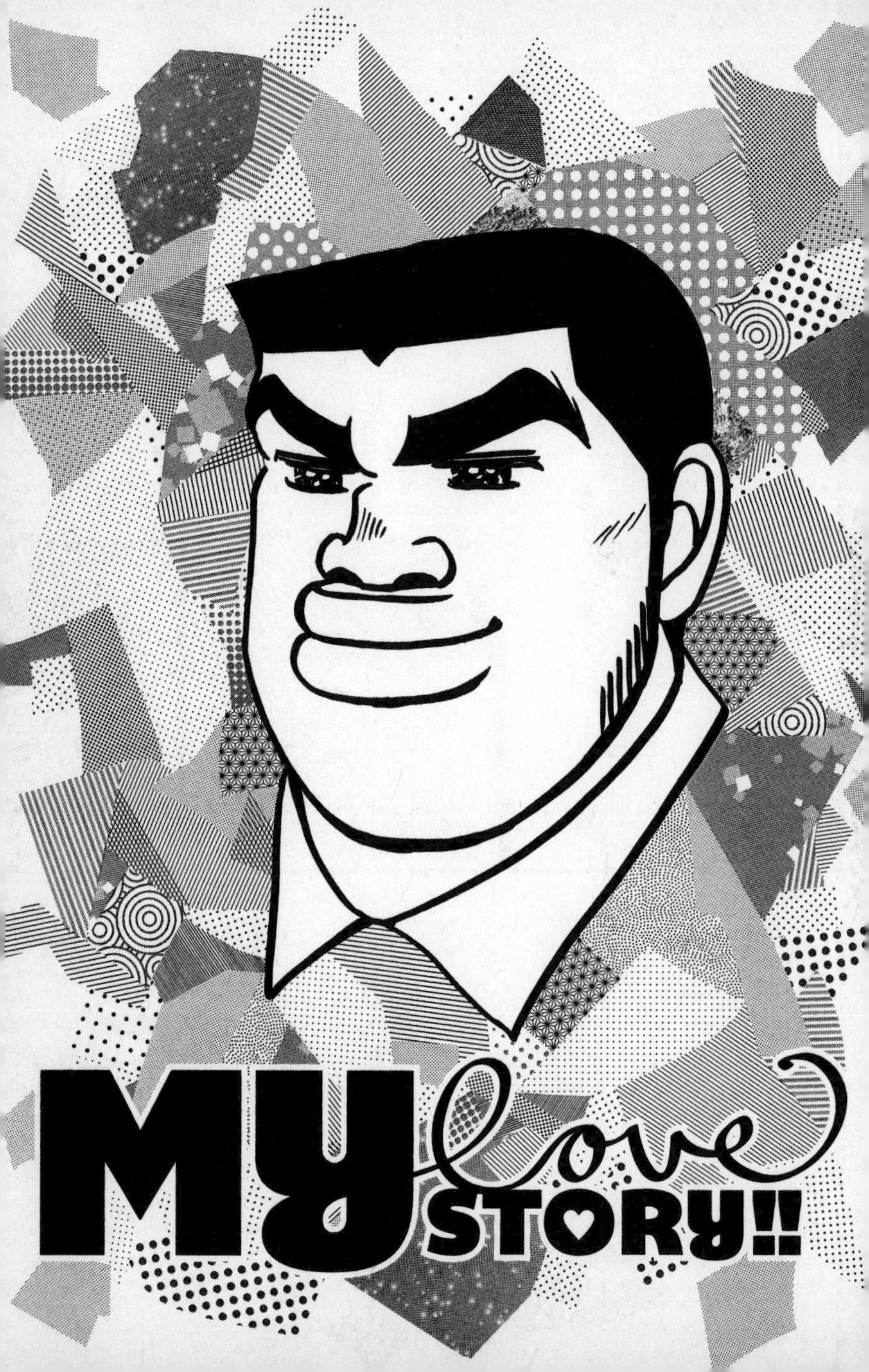
MY love STORY!!

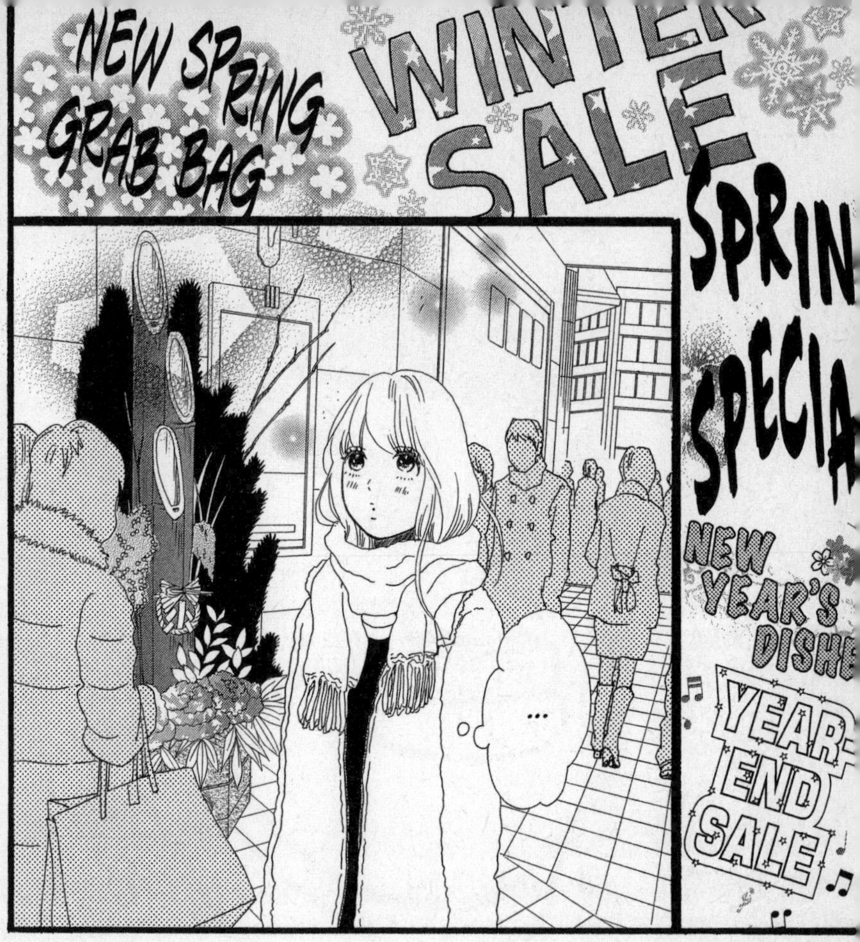
WINTER SALE
NEW SPRING GRAB BAG
SPRIN
SPECIA
NEW YEAR'S DISHE
YEAR-END SALE
...

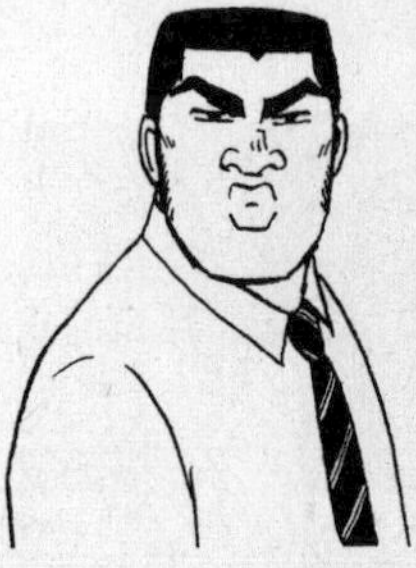

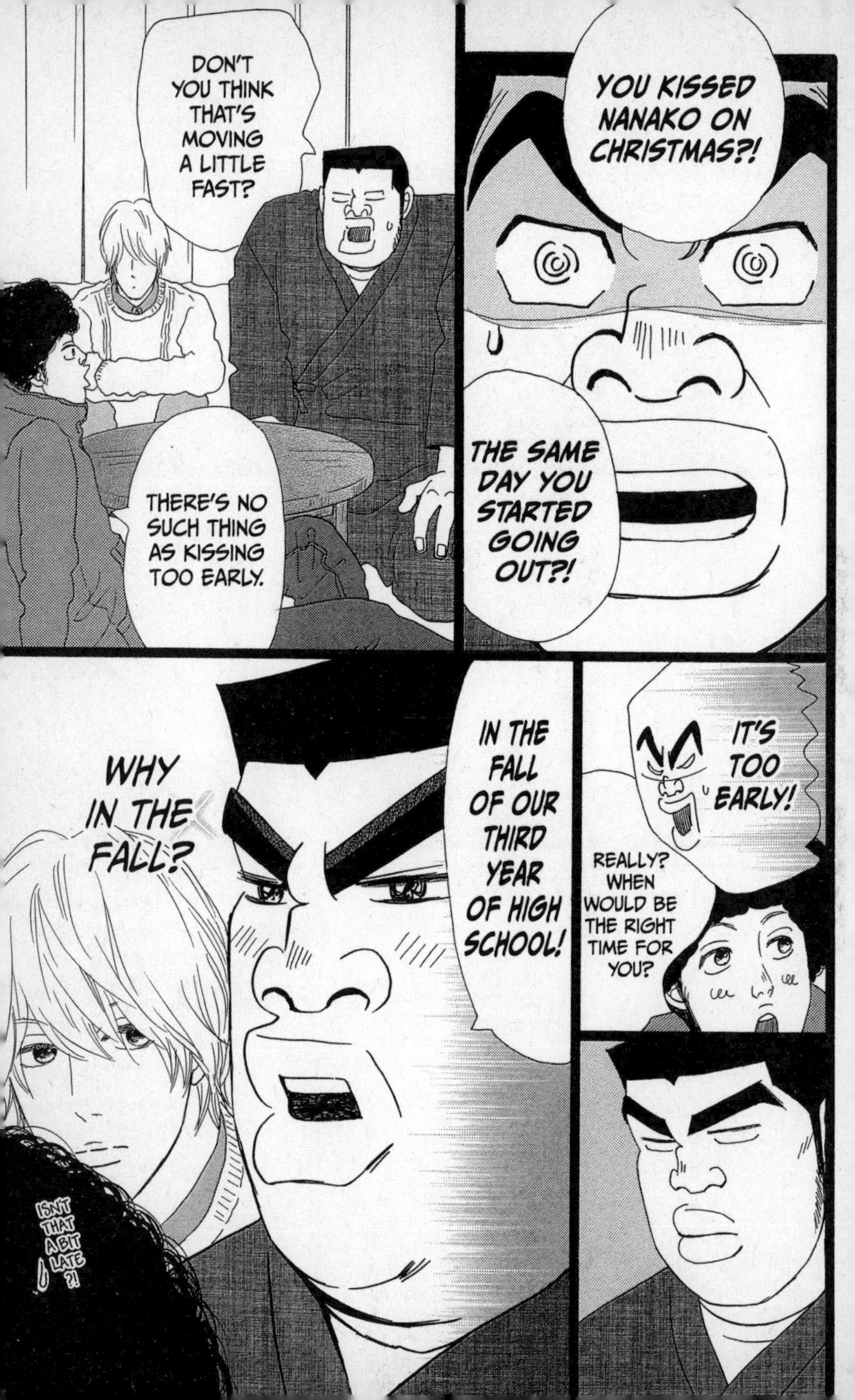
YOU KISSED NANAKO ON CHRISTMAS?!
THE SAME DAY YOU STARTED GOING OUT?!
DON'T YOU THINK THAT'S MOVING A LITTLE FAST?
THERE'S NO SUCH THING AS KISSING TOO EARLY.
IT'S TOO EARLY!
REALLY? WHEN WOULD BE THE RIGHT TIME FOR YOU?
IN THE FALL OF OUR THIRD YEAR OF HIGH SCHOOL!
WHY IN THE FALL?
ISN'T THAT A BIT LATE?!

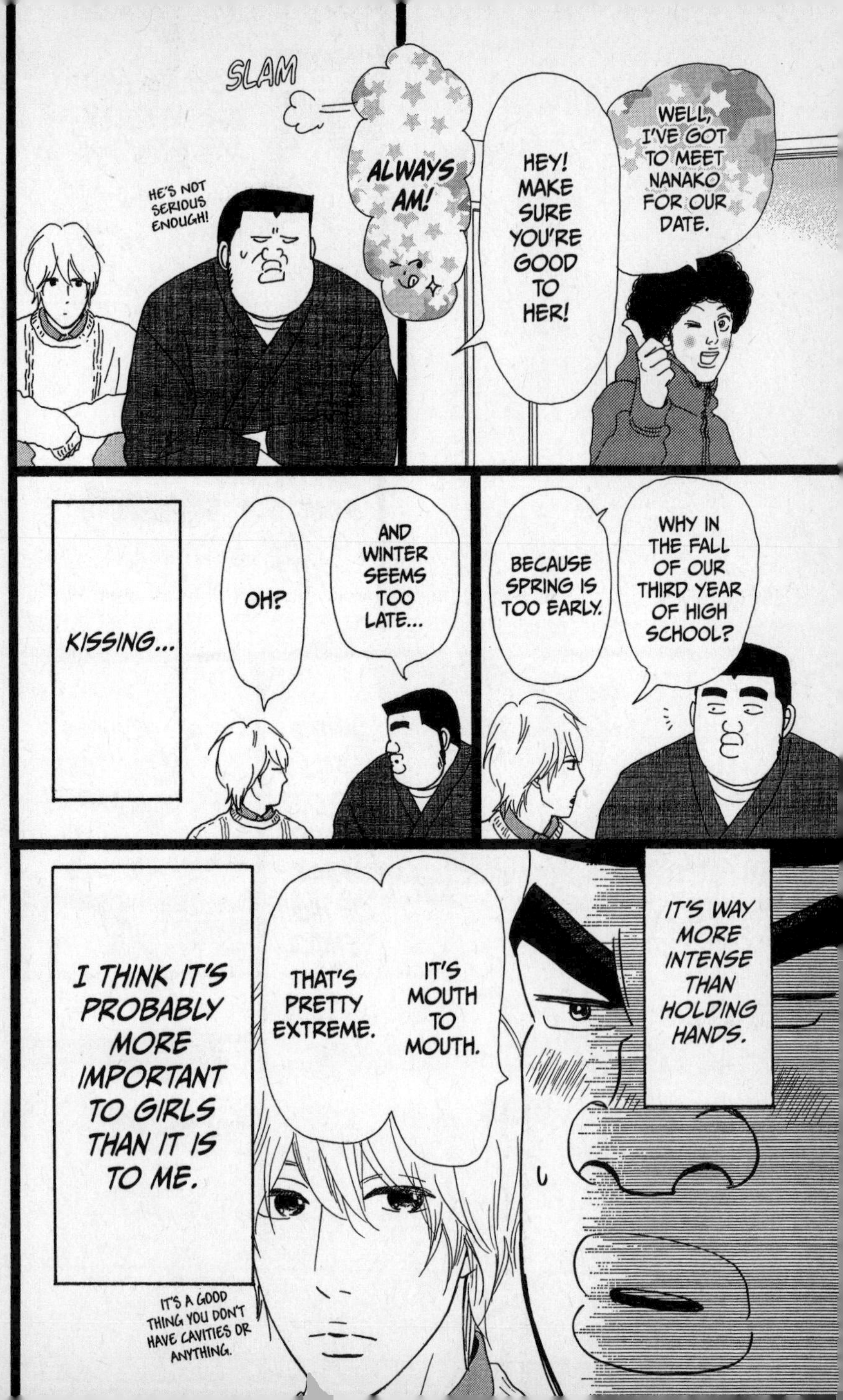
WELL, I'VE GOT TO MEET NANAKO FOR OUR DATE.
HEY! MAKE SURE YOU'RE GOOD TO HER!
ALWAYS AM!
SLAM
HE'S NOT SERIOUS ENOUGH!
WHY IN THE FALL OF OUR THIRD YEAR OF HIGH SCHOOL?
BECAUSE SPRING IS TOO EARLY.
AND WINTER SEEMS TOO LATE...
OH?
KISSING...
IT'S WAY MORE INTENSE THAN HOLDING HANDS.
IT'S MOUTH TO MOUTH.
THAT'S PRETTY EXTREME.
I THINK IT'S PROBABLY MORE IMPORTANT TO GIRLS THAN IT IS TO ME.
IT'S A GOOD THING YOU DON'T HAVE CAVITIES OR ANYTHING.

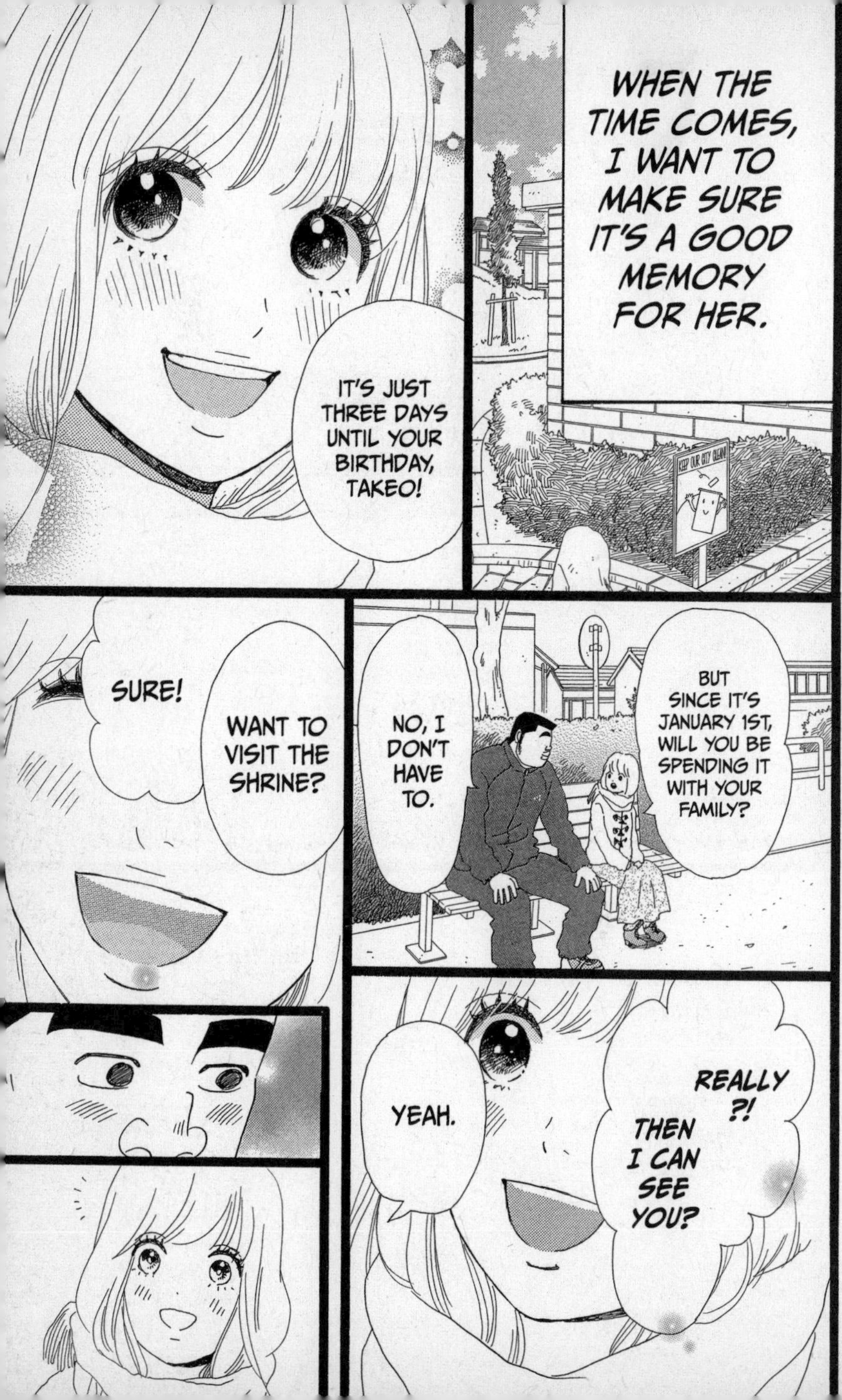
WHEN THE TIME COMES, I WANT TO MAKE SURE IT'S A GOOD MEMORY FOR HER.
IT'S JUST THREE DAYS UNTIL YOUR BIRTHDAY, TAKEO!
KEEP OUR CITY CLEAN!
BUT SINCE IT'S JANUARY 1ST, WILL YOU BE SPENDING IT WITH YOUR FAMILY?
NO, I DON'T HAVE TO.
REALLY?! THEN I CAN SEE YOU?
YEAH.
WANT TO VISIT THE SHRINE?
SURE!

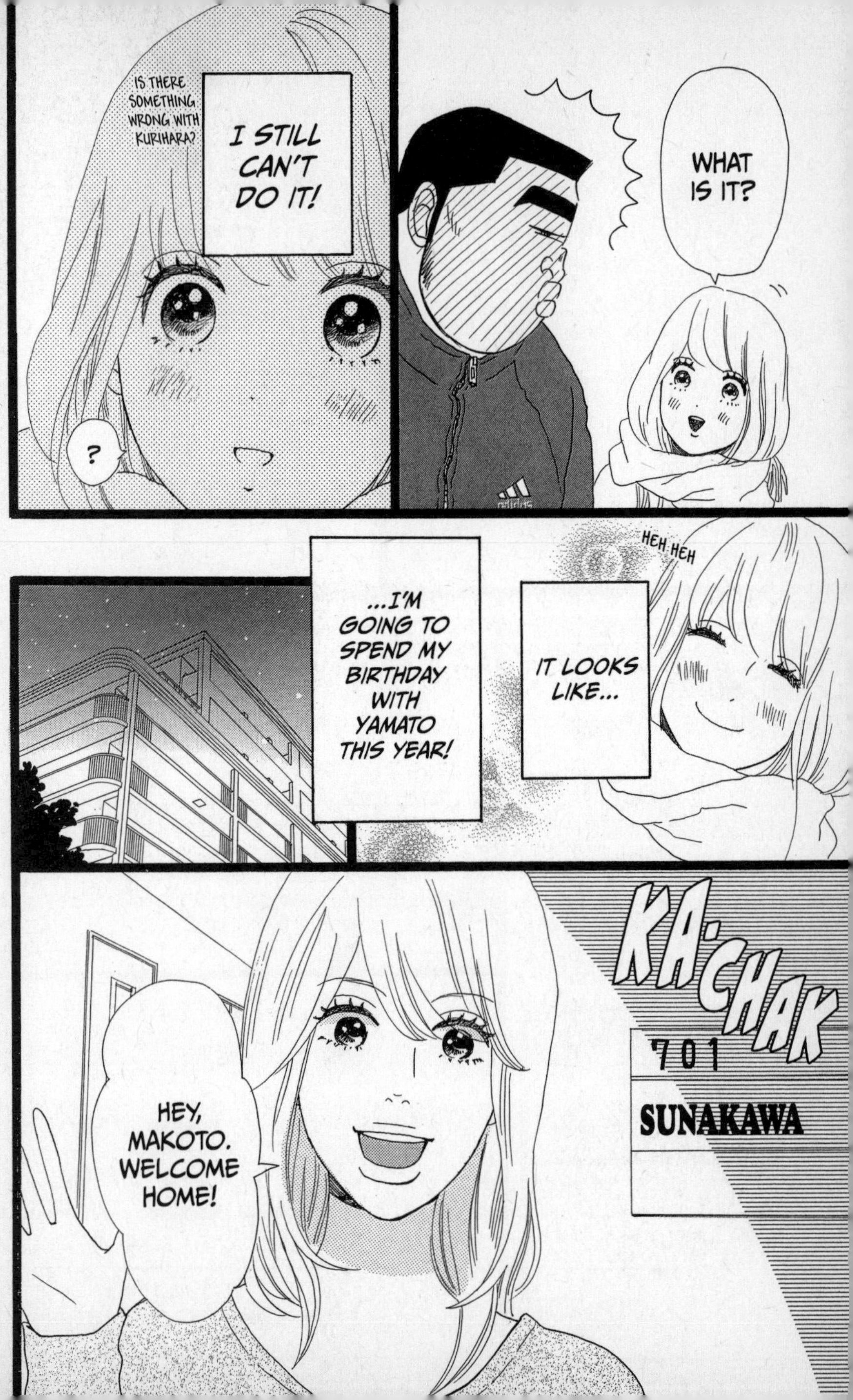
WHAT IS IT?
I STILL CAN'T DO IT!
IS THERE SOMETHING WRONG WITH KURIHARA?
?
HEH HEH
IT LOOKS LIKE...
...I'M GOING TO SPEND MY BIRTHDAY WITH YAMATO THIS YEAR!
KA-CHAK
701
SUNAKAWA
HEY, MAKOTO. WELCOME HOME!

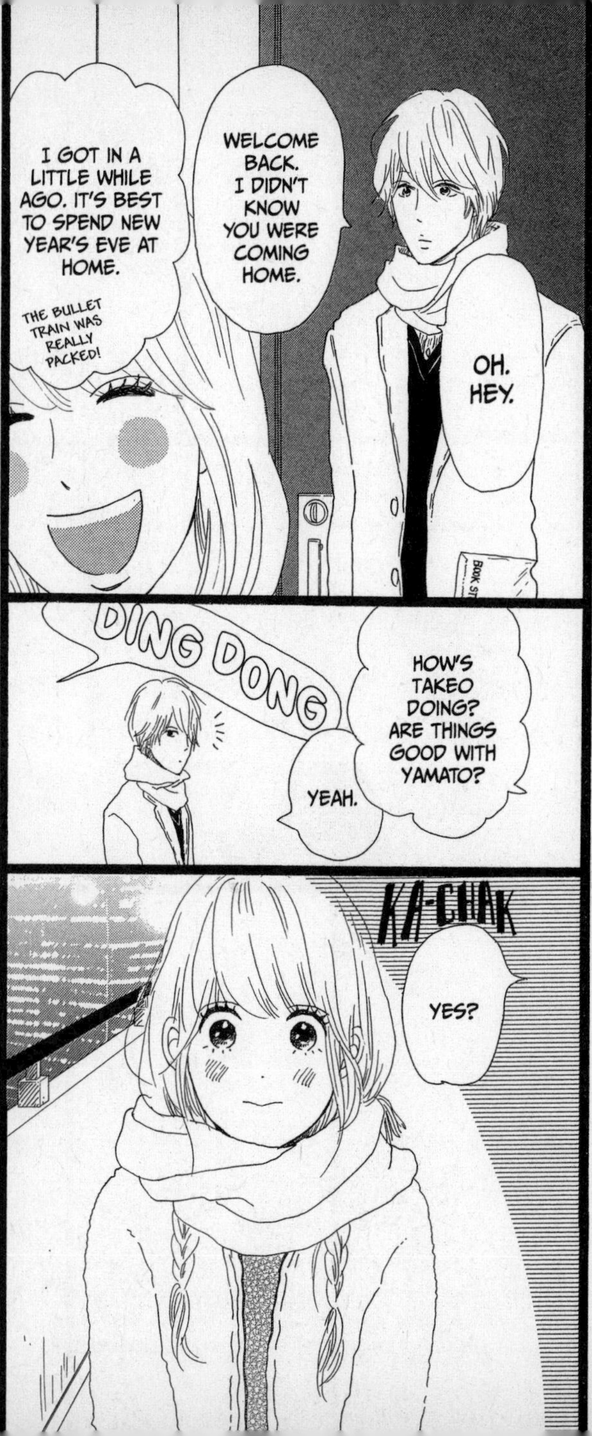
OH. HEY.
WELCOME BACK. I DIDN'T KNOW YOU WERE COMING HOME.
I GOT IN A LITTLE WHILE AGO. IT'S BEST TO SPEND NEW YEAR'S EVE AT HOME.
THE BULLET TRAIN WAS REALLY PACKED!
HOW'S TAKEO DOING? ARE THINGS GOOD WITH YAMATO?
YEAH.
DING DONG
KA-CHAK
YES?
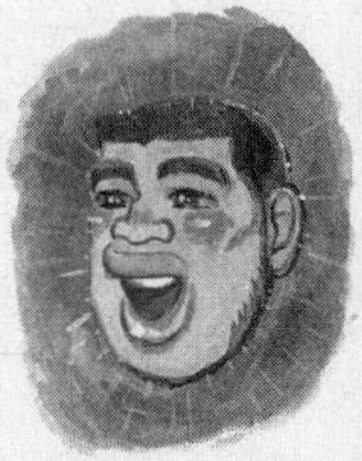

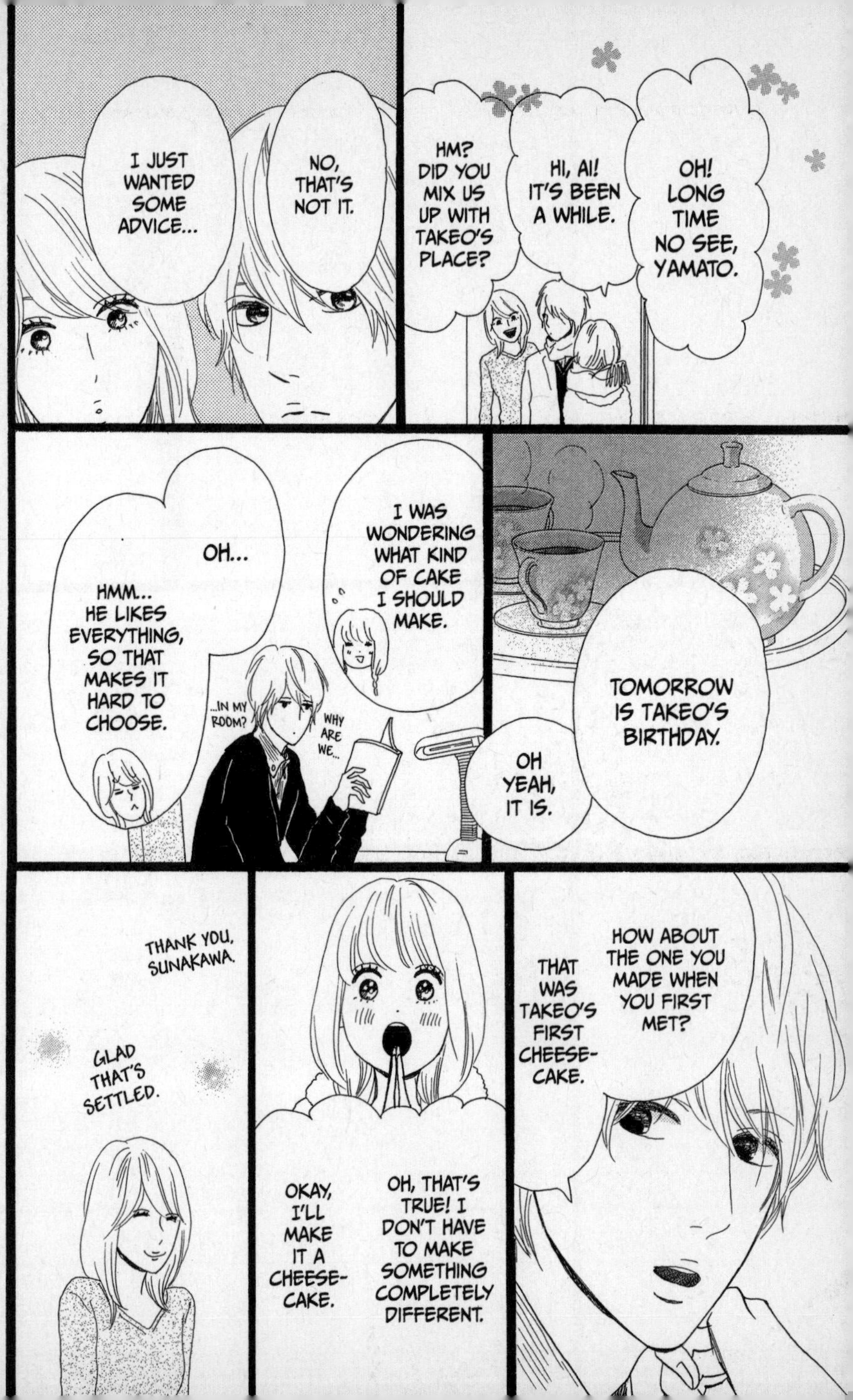
OH! LONG TIME NO SEE, YAMATO.
HI, AI! IT'S BEEN A WHILE.
HM? DID YOU MIX US UP WITH TAKEO'S PLACE?
NO, THAT'S NOT IT.
I JUST WANTED SOME ADVICE...
TOMORROW IS TAKEO'S BIRTHDAY.
OH YEAH, IT IS.
I WAS WONDERING WHAT KIND OF CAKE I SHOULD MAKE.
OH...
HMM... HE LIKES EVERYTHING, SO THAT MAKES IT HARD TO CHOOSE.
WHY ARE WE...
...IN MY ROOM?
HOW ABOUT THE ONE YOU MADE WHEN YOU FIRST MET?
THAT WAS TAKEO'S FIRST CHEESE-CAKE.
OH, THAT'S TRUE! I DON'T HAVE TO MAKE SOMETHING COMPLETELY DIFFERENT.
OKAY, I'LL MAKE IT A CHEESE-CAKE.
THANK YOU, SUNAKAWA.
GLAD THAT'S SETTLED.

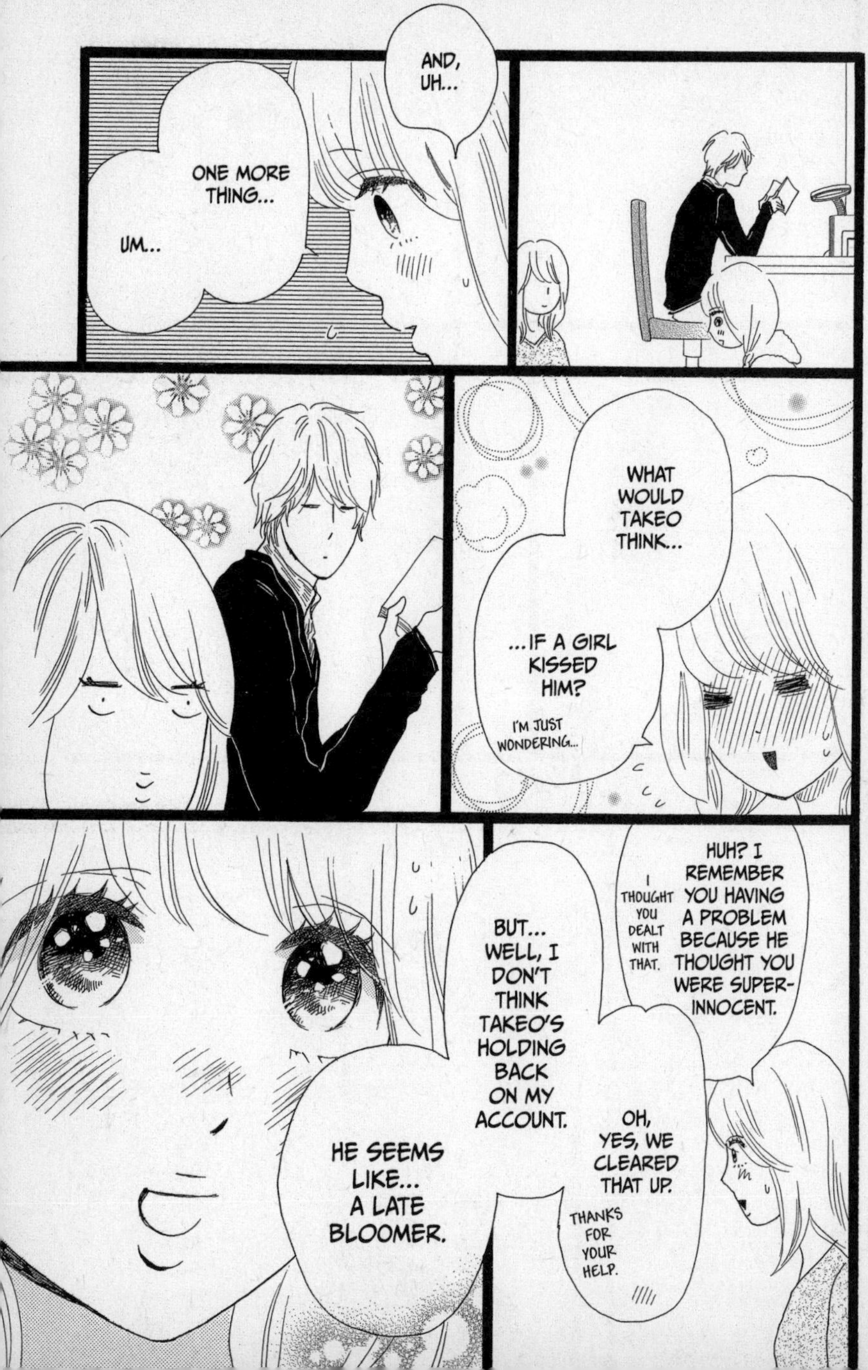
AND, UH...
ONE MORE THING...
UM...
WHAT WOULD TAKEO THINK...
...IF A GIRL KISSED HIM?
I'M JUST WONDERING...
HUH? I REMEMBER YOU HAVING A PROBLEM BECAUSE HE THOUGHT YOU WERE SUPER-INNOCENT.
I THOUGHT YOU DEALT WITH THAT.
OH, YES, WE CLEARED THAT UP.
THANKS FOR YOUR HELP.
BUT... WELL, I DON'T THINK TAKEO'S HOLDING BACK ON MY ACCOUNT.
HE SEEMS LIKE... A LATE BLOOMER.

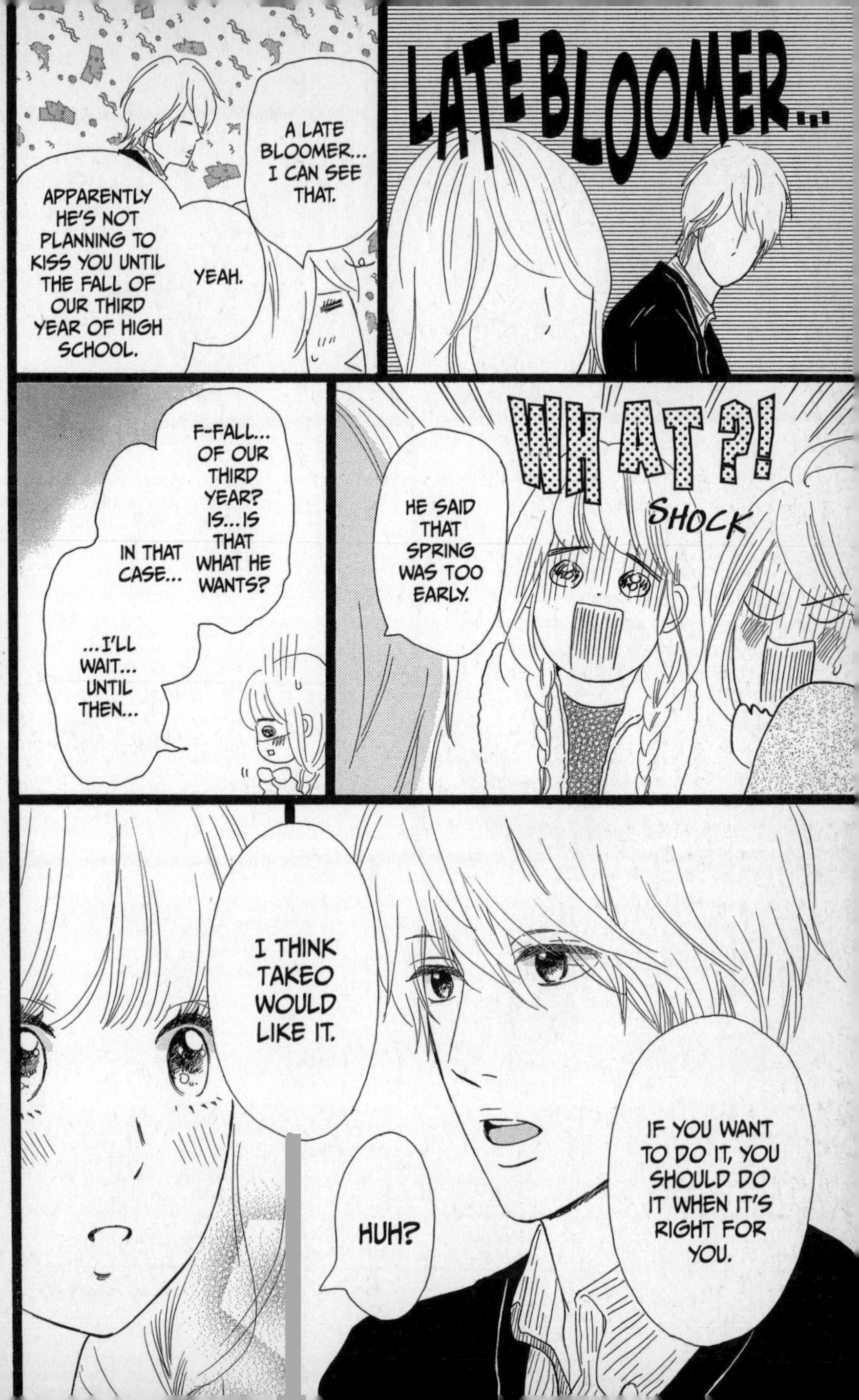
LATE BLOOMER...
A LATE BLOOMER... I CAN SEE THAT.
APPARENTLY HE'S NOT PLANNING TO KISS YOU UNTIL THE FALL OF OUR THIRD YEAR OF HIGH SCHOOL.
YEAH.
WHAT?!
SHOCK
HE SAID THAT SPRING WAS TOO EARLY.
F-FALL... OF OUR THIRD YEAR? IS...IS THAT WHAT HE WANTS?
IN THAT CASE...
...I'LL WAIT... UNTIL THEN...
IF YOU WANT TO DO IT, YOU SHOULD DO IT WHEN IT'S RIGHT FOR YOU.
HUH?
I THINK TAKEO WOULD LIKE IT.

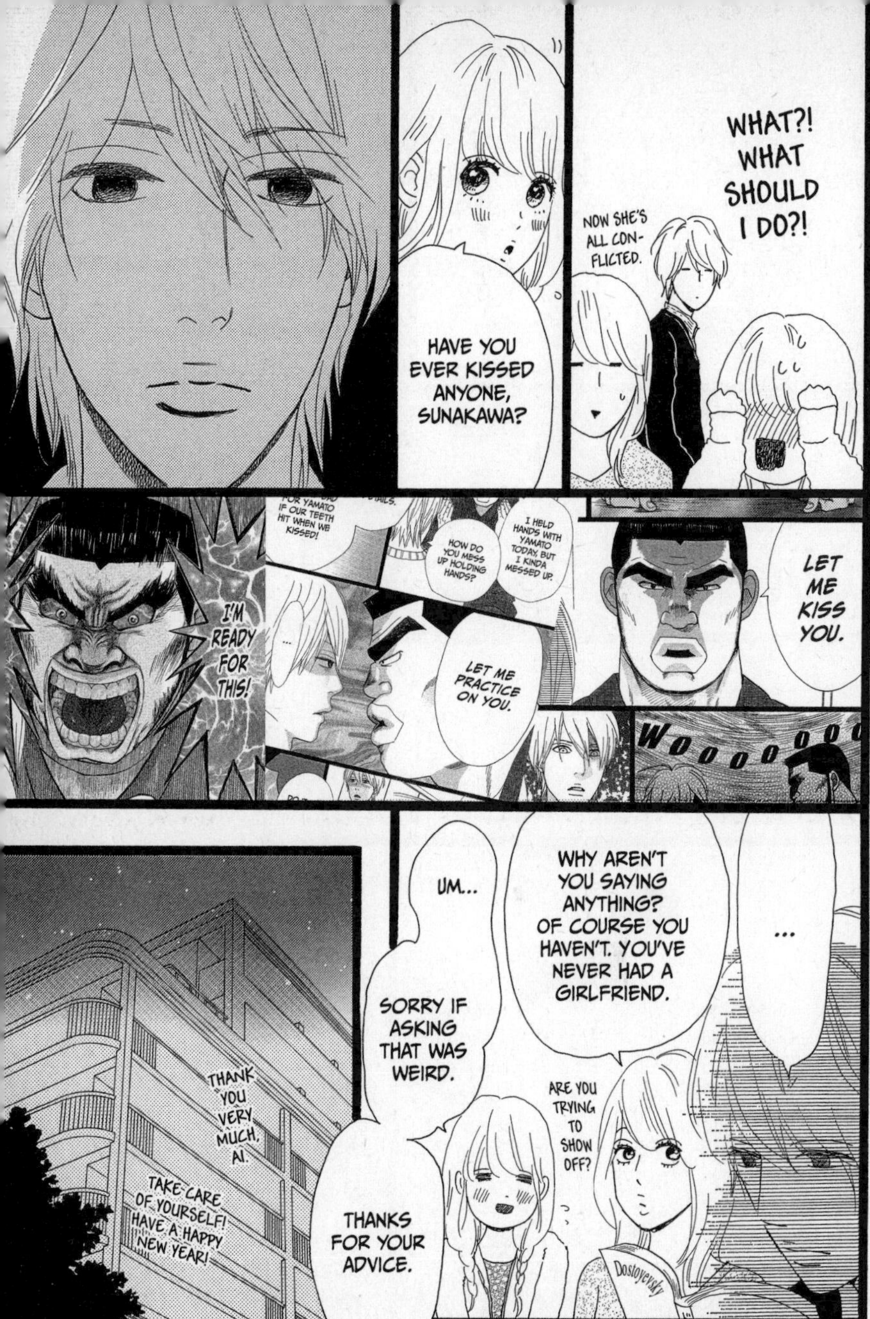
WHAT?! WHAT SHOULD I DO?!
NOW SHE'S ALL CON-FLICTED.
HAVE YOU EVER KISSED ANYONE, SUNAKAWA?
LET ME KISS YOU.
WOOOOOOOO
I HELD HANDS WITH YAMATO TODAY, BUT I KINDA MESSED UP.
HOW DO YOU MESS UP HOLDING HANDS?
IF OUR TEETH HIT WHEN WE KISSED!
LET ME PRACTICE ON YOU.
...
I'M READY FOR THIS!
...
WHY AREN'T YOU SAYING ANYTHING? OF COURSE YOU HAVEN'T. YOU'VE NEVER HAD A GIRLFRIEND.
UM...
ARE YOU TRYING TO SHOW OFF?
SORRY IF ASKING THAT WAS WEIRD.
THANKS FOR YOUR ADVICE.
Dostoyevsky
THANK YOU VERY MUCH, AI.
TAKE CARE OF YOURSELF! HAVE A HAPPY NEW YEAR!

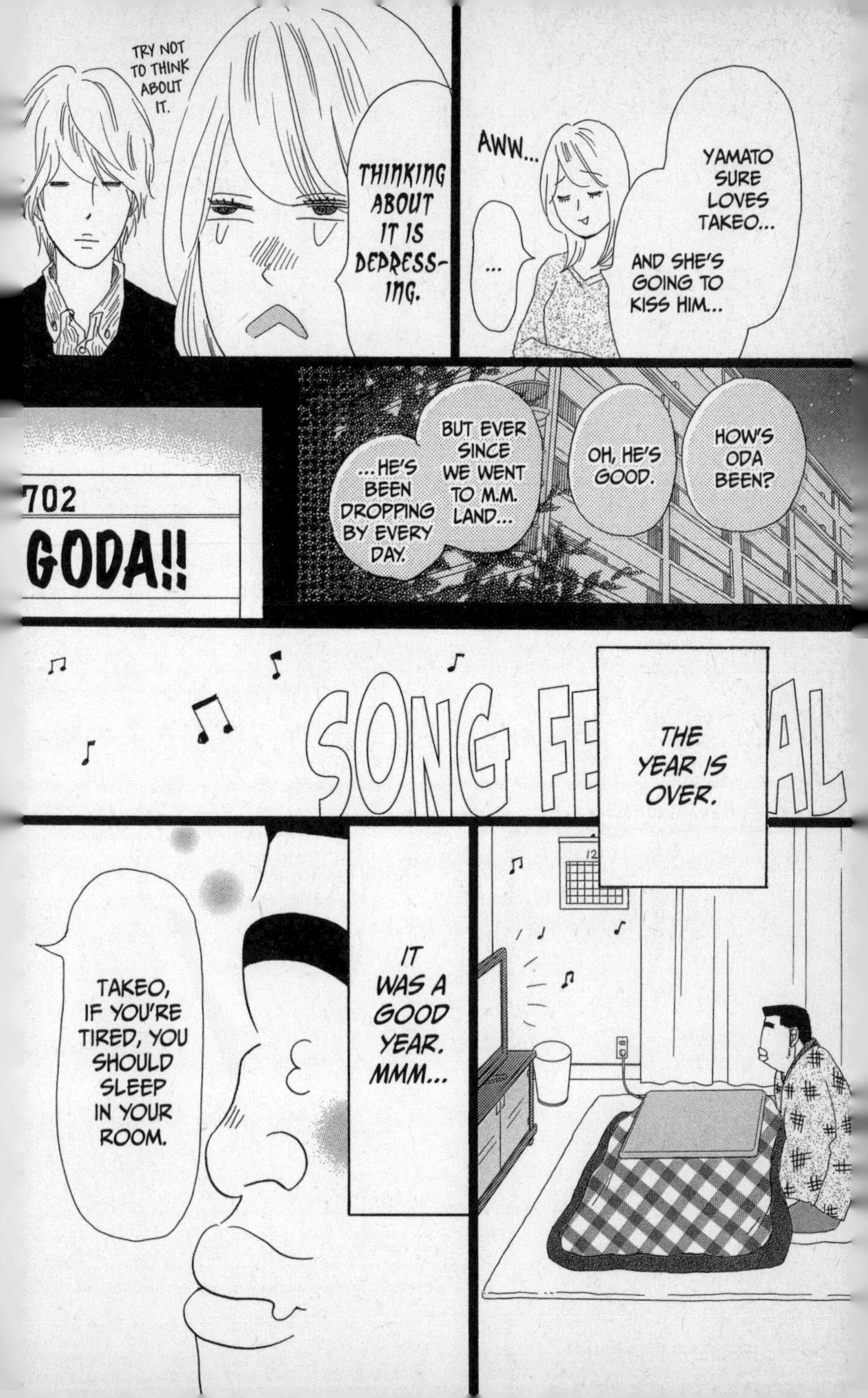
AWW...
YAMATO SURE LOVES TAKEO... AND SHE'S GOING TO KISS HIM...
...
THINKING ABOUT IT IS DEPRESS-ING.
TRY NOT TO THINK ABOUT IT.
HOW'S ODA BEEN?
OH, HE'S GOOD.
BUT EVER SINCE WE WENT TO M.M. LAND...
...HE'S BEEN DROPPING BY EVERY DAY.
702
GODA!!
THE YEAR IS OVER.
IT WAS A GOOD YEAR. MMM...
TAKEO, IF YOU'RE TIRED, YOU SHOULD SLEEP IN YOUR ROOM.

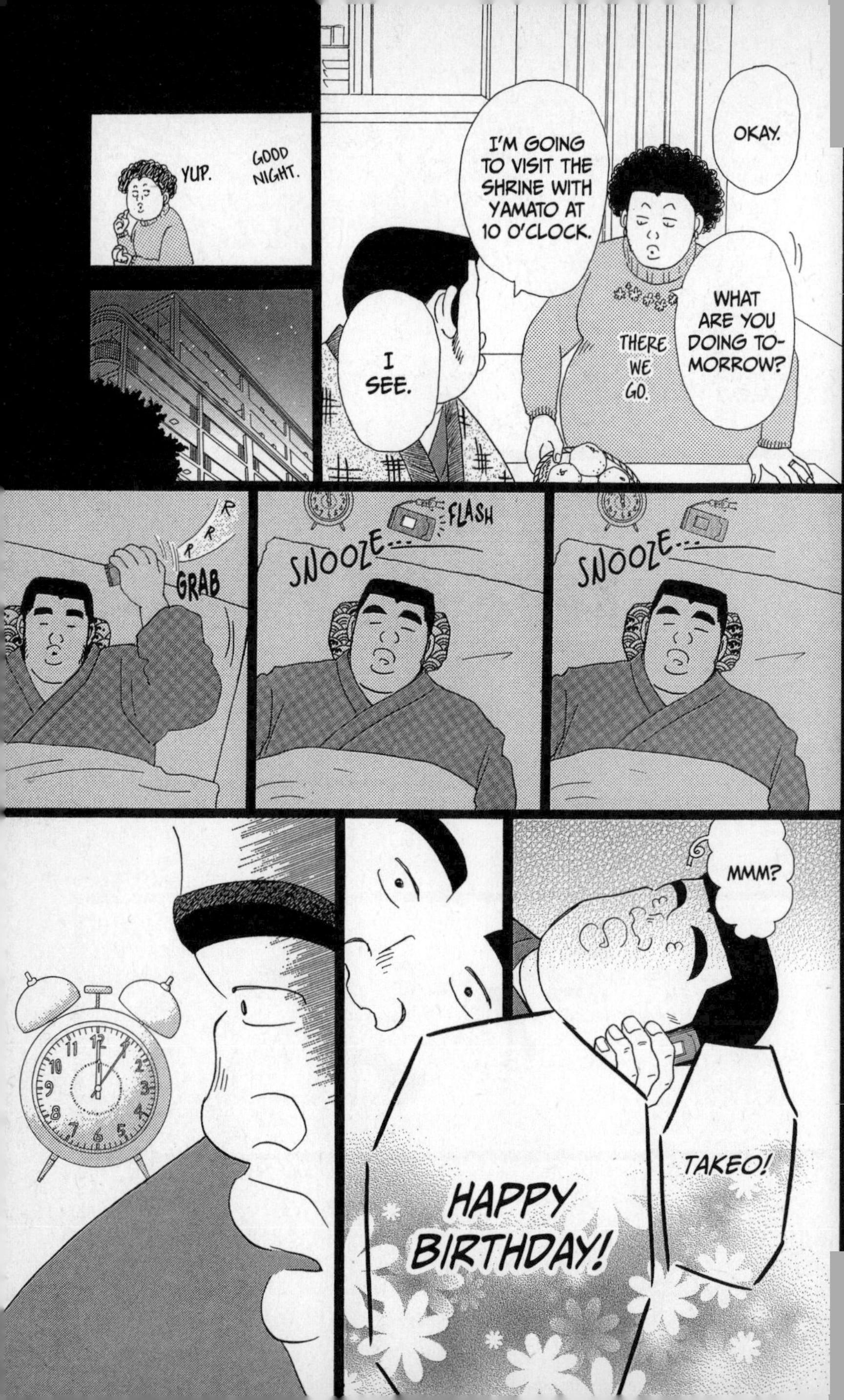
OKAY.
I'M GOING TO VISIT THE SHRINE WITH YAMATO AT 10 O'CLOCK.
WHAT ARE YOU DOING TO-MORROW?
THERE WE GO.
I SEE.
GOOD NIGHT.
YUP.
SNOOZE...
FLASH
SNOOZE...
RRR
GRAB
MMM?
TAKEO!
HAPPY BIRTHDAY!

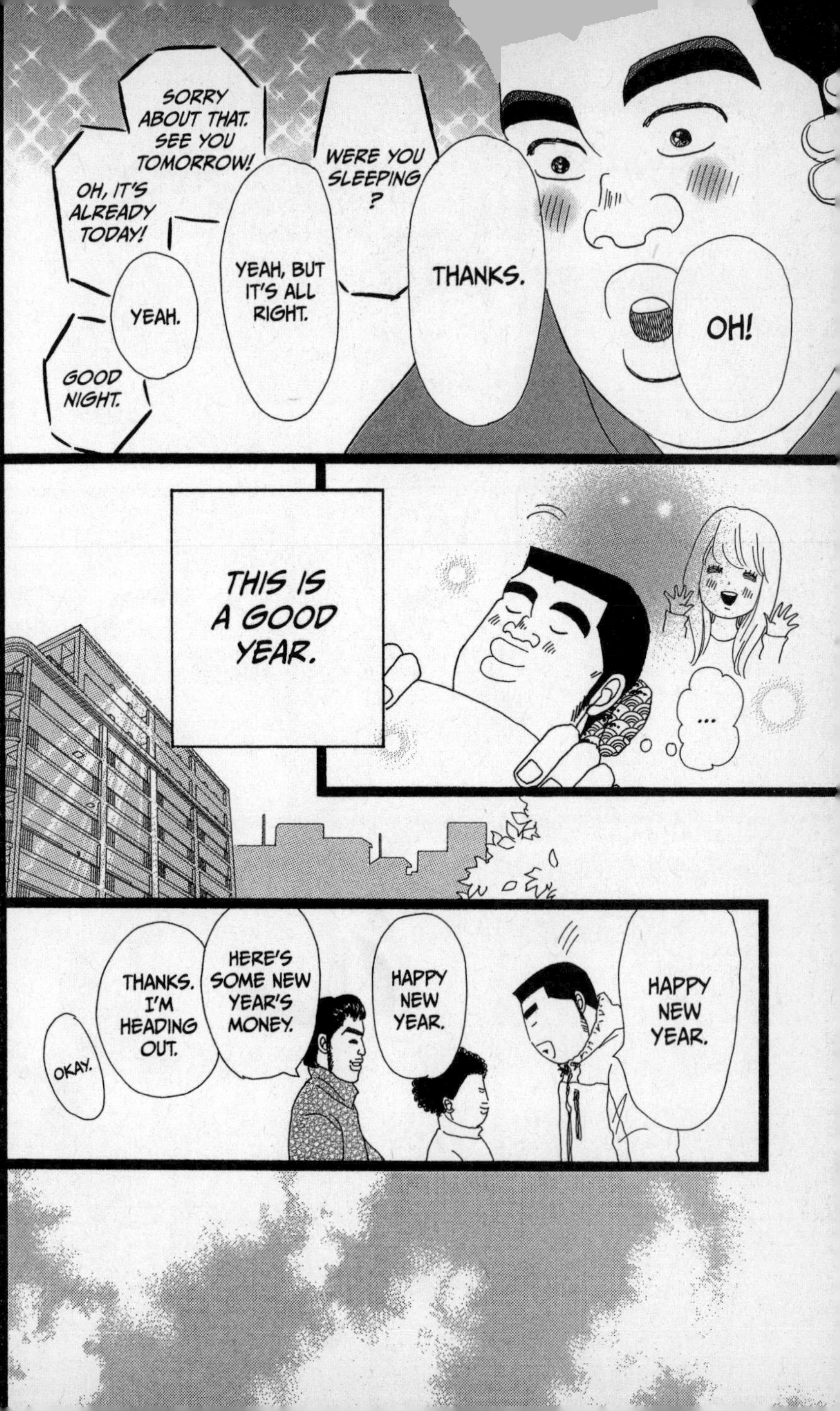
OH!
THANKS.
WERE YOU SLEEPING?
YEAH, BUT IT'S ALL RIGHT.
SORRY ABOUT THAT. SEE YOU TOMORROW!
OH, IT'S ALREADY TODAY!
YEAH.
GOOD NIGHT.
...
THIS IS A GOOD YEAR.
HAPPY NEW YEAR.
HAPPY NEW YEAR.
HERE'S SOME NEW YEAR'S MONEY.
THANKS. I'M HEADING OUT.
OKAY.

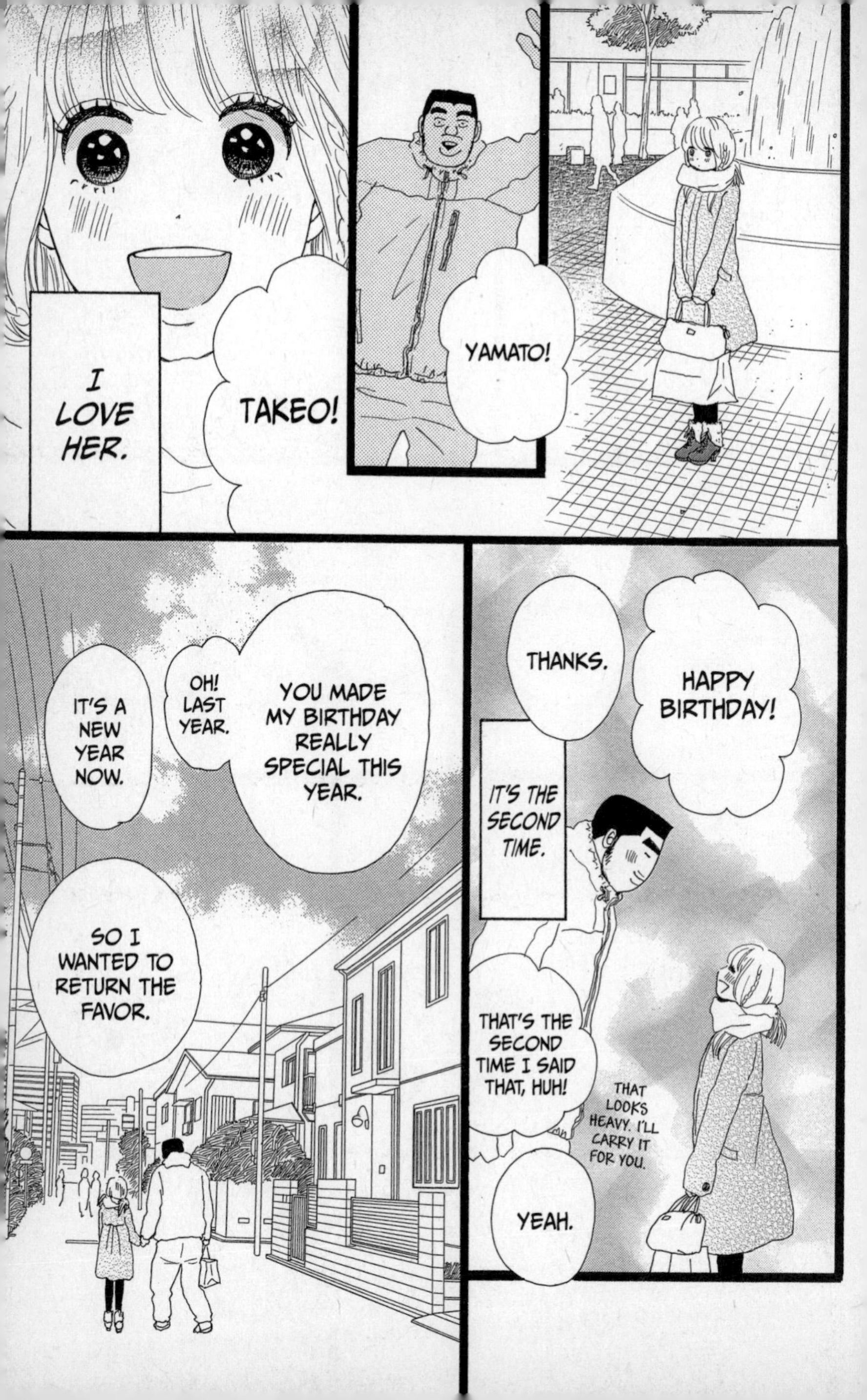
YAMATO!
TAKEO!
I LOVE HER.
HAPPY BIRTHDAY!
THANKS.
IT'S THE SECOND TIME.
THAT'S THE SECOND TIME I SAID THAT, HUH!
THAT LOOKS HEAVY. I'LL CARRY IT FOR YOU.
YEAH.
YOU MADE MY BIRTHDAY REALLY SPECIAL THIS YEAR.
OH! LAST YEAR.
IT'S A NEW YEAR NOW.
SO I WANTED TO RETURN THE FAVOR.

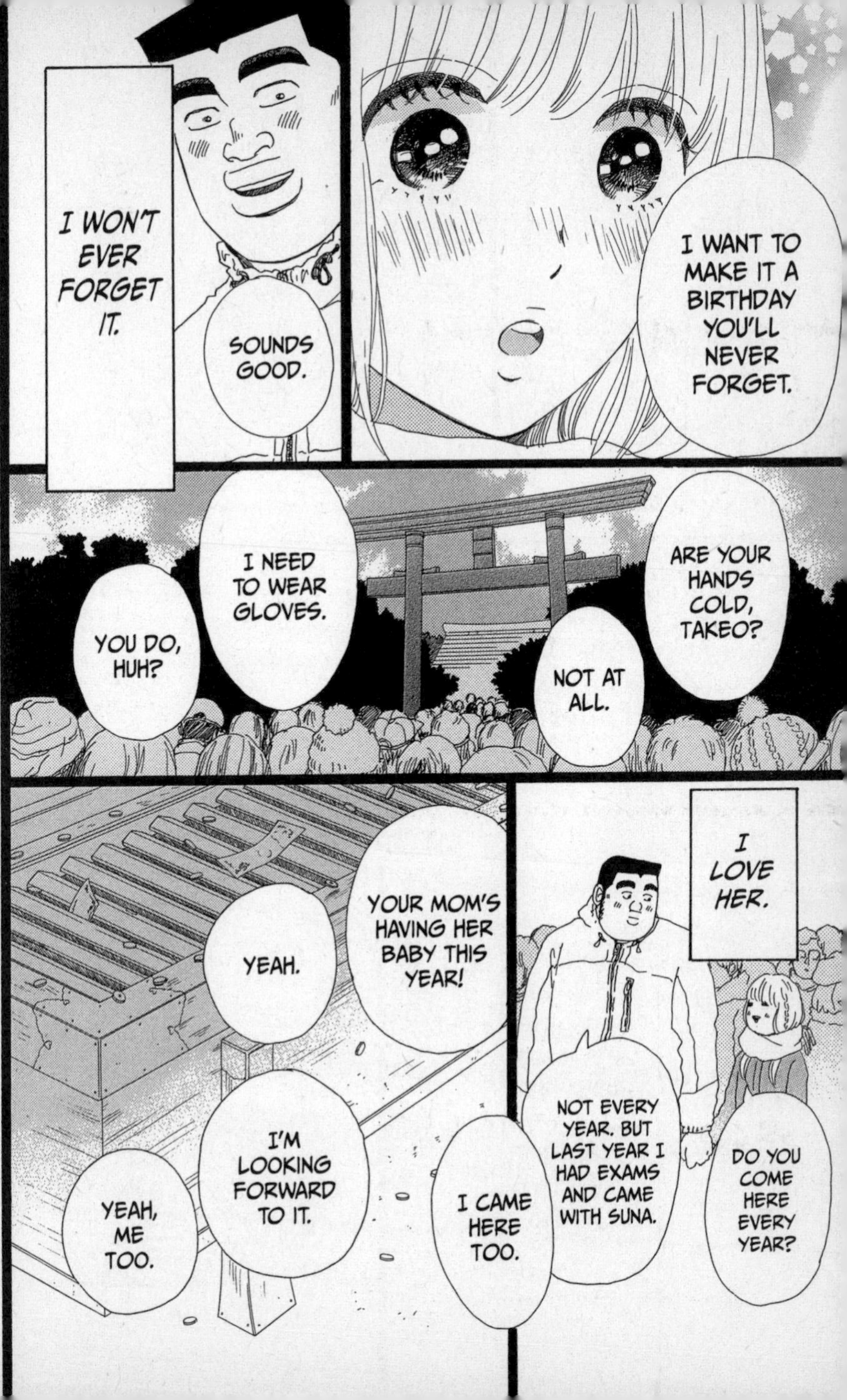
I WANT TO MAKE IT A BIRTHDAY YOU'LL NEVER FORGET.
SOUNDS GOOD.
I WON'T EVER FORGET IT.
ARE YOUR HANDS COLD, TAKEO?
NOT AT ALL.
I NEED TO WEAR GLOVES.
YOU DO, HUH?
I LOVE HER.
DO YOU COME HERE EVERY YEAR?
NOT EVERY YEAR. BUT LAST YEAR I HAD EXAMS AND CAME WITH SUNA.
I CAME HERE TOO.
YOUR MOM'S HAVING HER BABY THIS YEAR!
YEAH.
I'M LOOKING FORWARD TO IT.
YEAH, ME TOO.

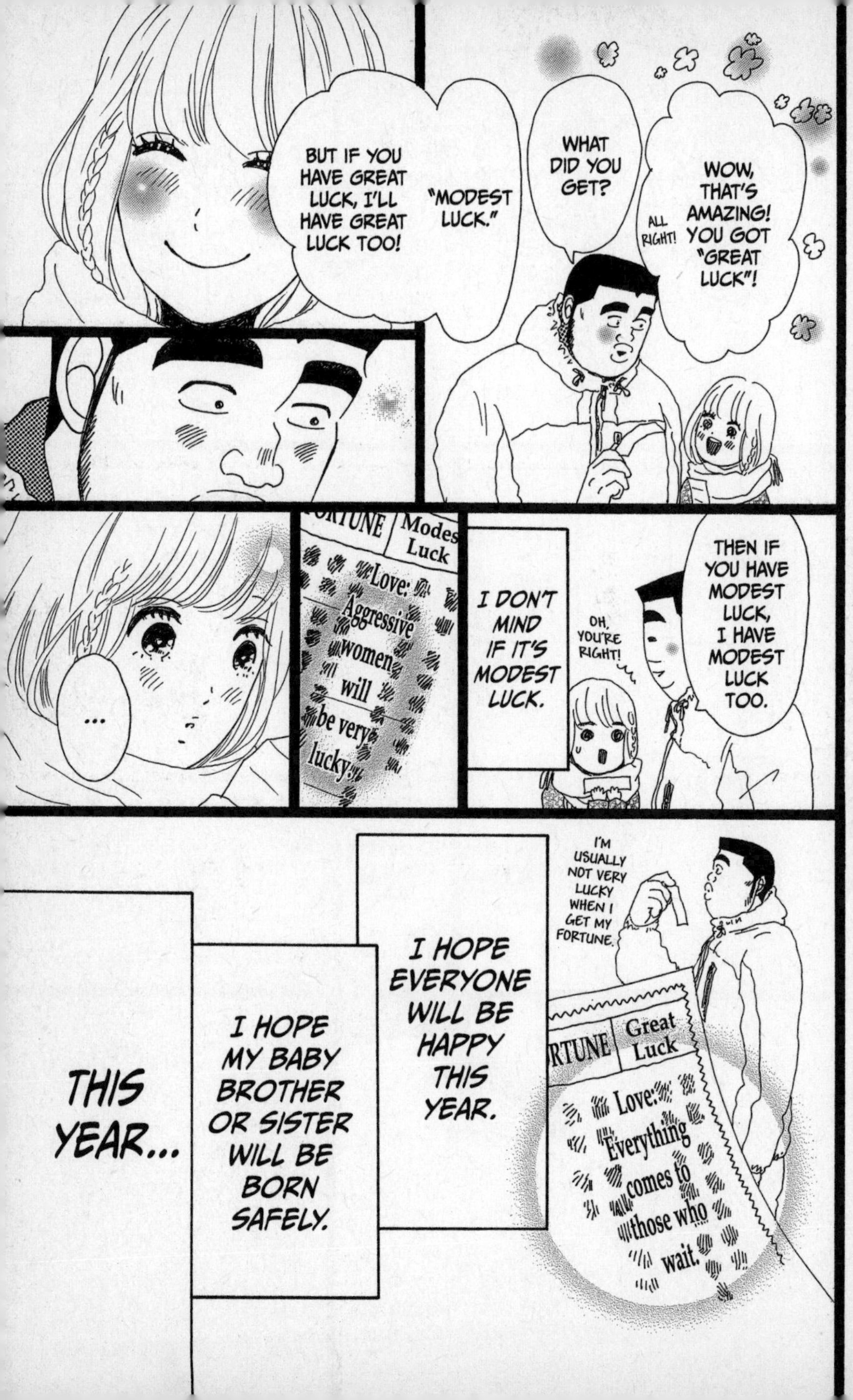
WOW, THAT'S AMAZING! YOU GOT "GREAT LUCK"!
ALL RIGHT!
WHAT DID YOU GET?
"MODEST LUCK."
BUT IF YOU HAVE GREAT LUCK, I'LL HAVE GREAT LUCK TOO!
THEN IF YOU HAVE MODEST LUCK, I HAVE MODEST LUCK TOO.
OH, YOU'RE RIGHT!
I DON'T MIND IF IT'S MODEST LUCK.
RTUNE
Modes Luck
Love: Aggressive women will be very lucky.
...
I'M USUALLY NOT VERY LUCKY WHEN I GET MY FORTUNE.
RTUNE
Great Luck
Love: Everything comes to those who wait.
I HOPE EVERYONE WILL BE HAPPY THIS YEAR.
I HOPE MY BABY BROTHER OR SISTER WILL BE BORN SAFELY.
THIS YEAR...

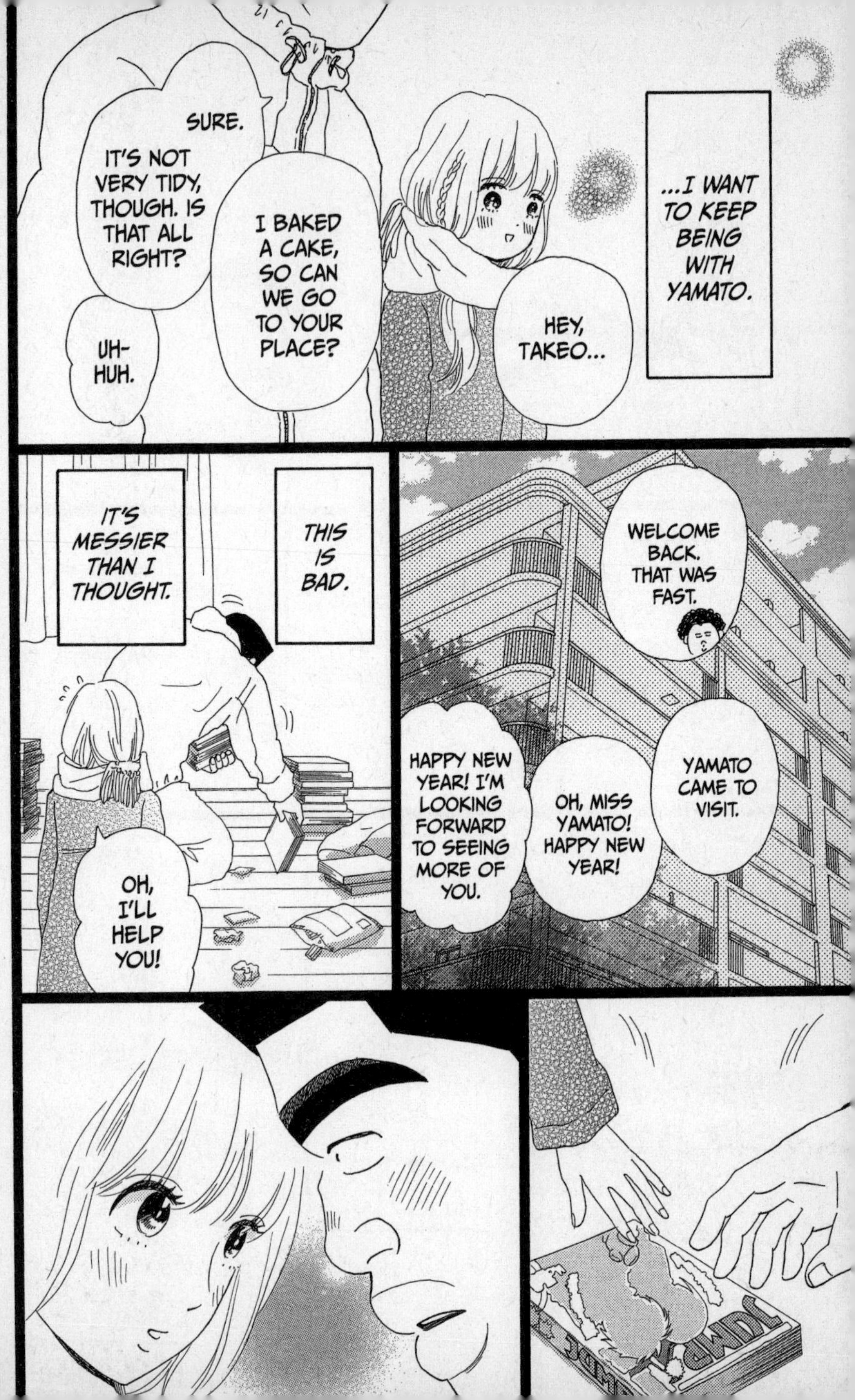
...I WANT TO KEEP BEING WITH YAMATO.
HEY, TAKEO...
I BAKED A CAKE, SO CAN WE GO TO YOUR PLACE?
SURE.
IT'S NOT VERY TIDY, THOUGH. IS THAT ALL RIGHT?
UH-HUH.
WELCOME BACK. THAT WAS FAST.
YAMATO CAME TO VISIT.
OH, MISS YAMATO! HAPPY NEW YEAR!
HAPPY NEW YEAR! I'M LOOKING FORWARD TO SEEING MORE OF YOU.
THIS IS BAD.
IT'S MESSIER THAN I THOUGHT.
OH, I'LL HELP YOU!

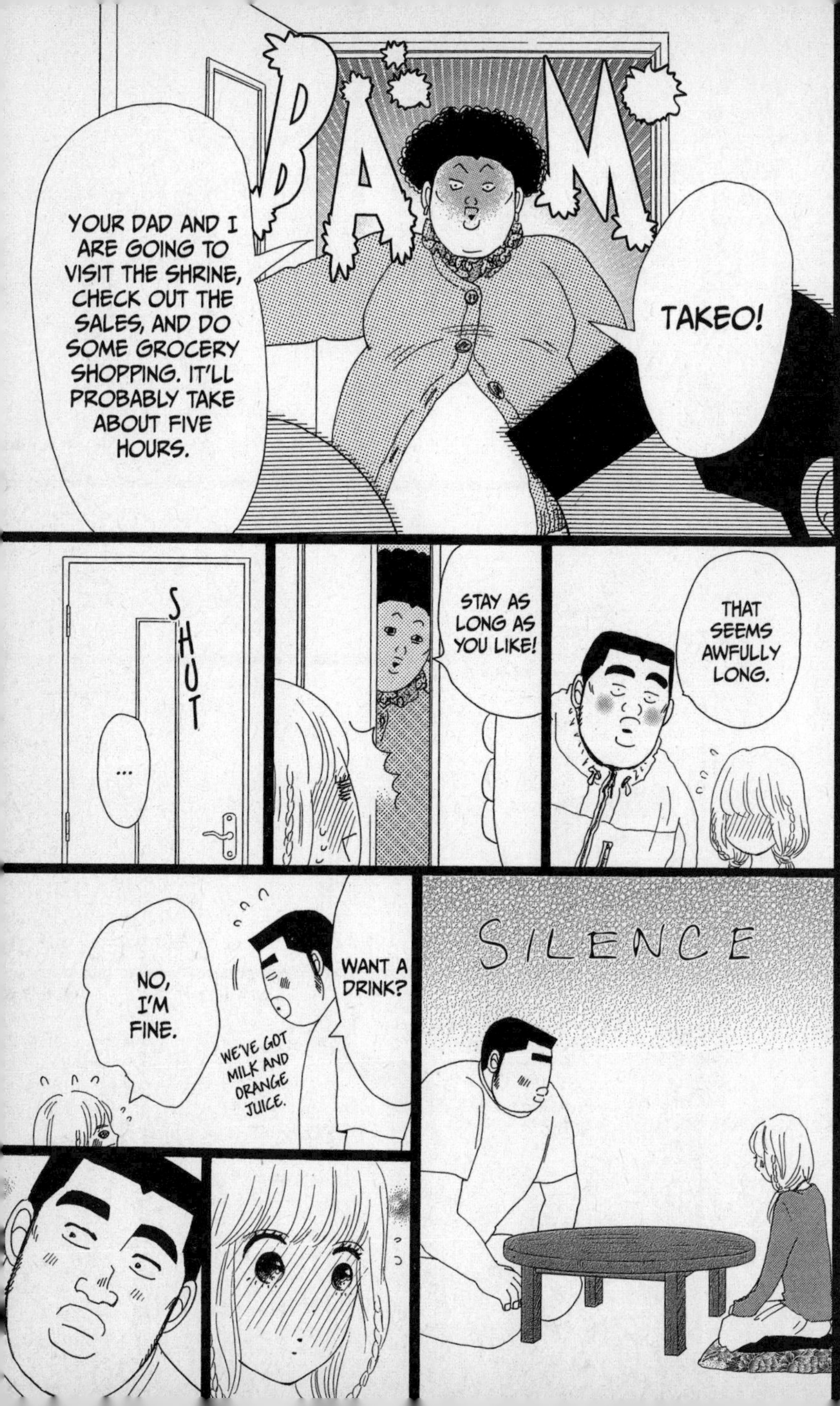
BAM
TAKEO!
YOUR DAD AND I ARE GOING TO VISIT THE SHRINE, CHECK OUT THE SALES, AND DO SOME GROCERY SHOPPING. IT'LL PROBABLY TAKE ABOUT FIVE HOURS.
THAT SEEMS AWFULLY LONG.
STAY AS LONG AS YOU LIKE!
SHUT
...
SILENCE
WANT A DRINK?
WE'VE GOT MILK AND ORANGE JUICE.
NO, I'M FINE.

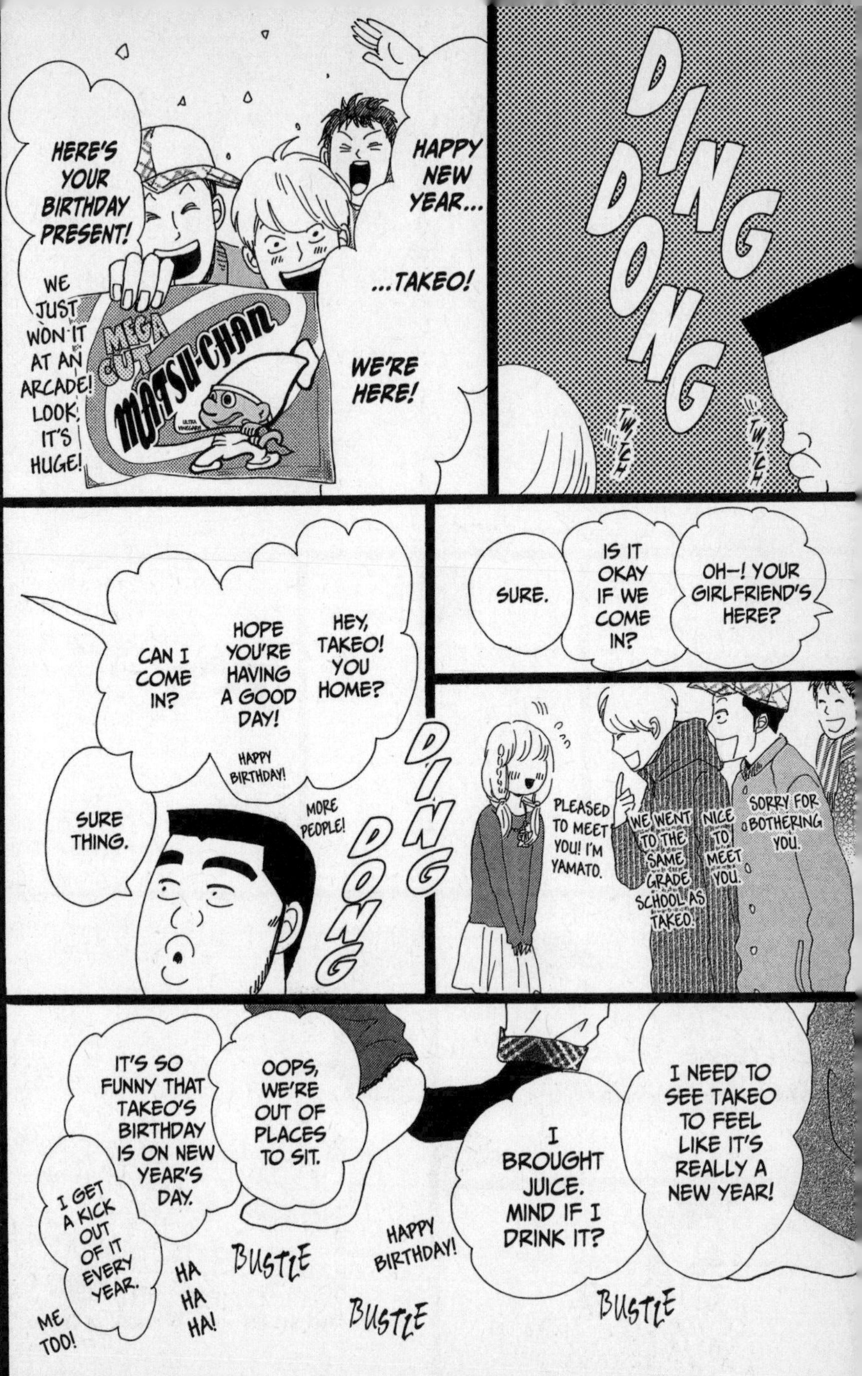
DING DONG
TWITCH
TWITCH
HAPPY NEW YEAR...
...TAKEO!
WE'RE HERE!
HERE'S YOUR BIRTHDAY PRESENT!
WE JUST WON IT AT AN ARCADE! LOOK, IT'S HUGE!
MEGA CUT
MATSU-CHAN
OH-! YOUR GIRLFRIEND'S HERE?
IS IT OKAY IF WE COME IN?
SURE.
SORRY FOR BOTHERING YOU.
NICE TO MEET YOU.
WE WENT TO THE SAME GRADE SCHOOL AS TAKEO.
PLEASED TO MEET YOU! I'M YAMATO.
DING DONG
HEY, TAKEO! YOU HOME?
HOPE YOU'RE HAVING A GOOD DAY!
CAN I COME IN?
HAPPY BIRTHDAY!
MORE PEOPLE!
SURE THING.
I NEED TO SEE TAKEO TO FEEL LIKE IT'S REALLY A NEW YEAR!
I BROUGHT JUICE. MIND IF I DRINK IT?
BUSTLE
HAPPY BIRTHDAY!
OOPS, WE'RE OUT OF PLACES TO SIT.
IT'S SO FUNNY THAT TAKEO'S BIRTHDAY IS ON NEW YEAR'S DAY.
BUSTLE
HA HA HA!
BUSTLE
I GET A KICK OUT OF IT EVERY YEAR.
ME TOO!

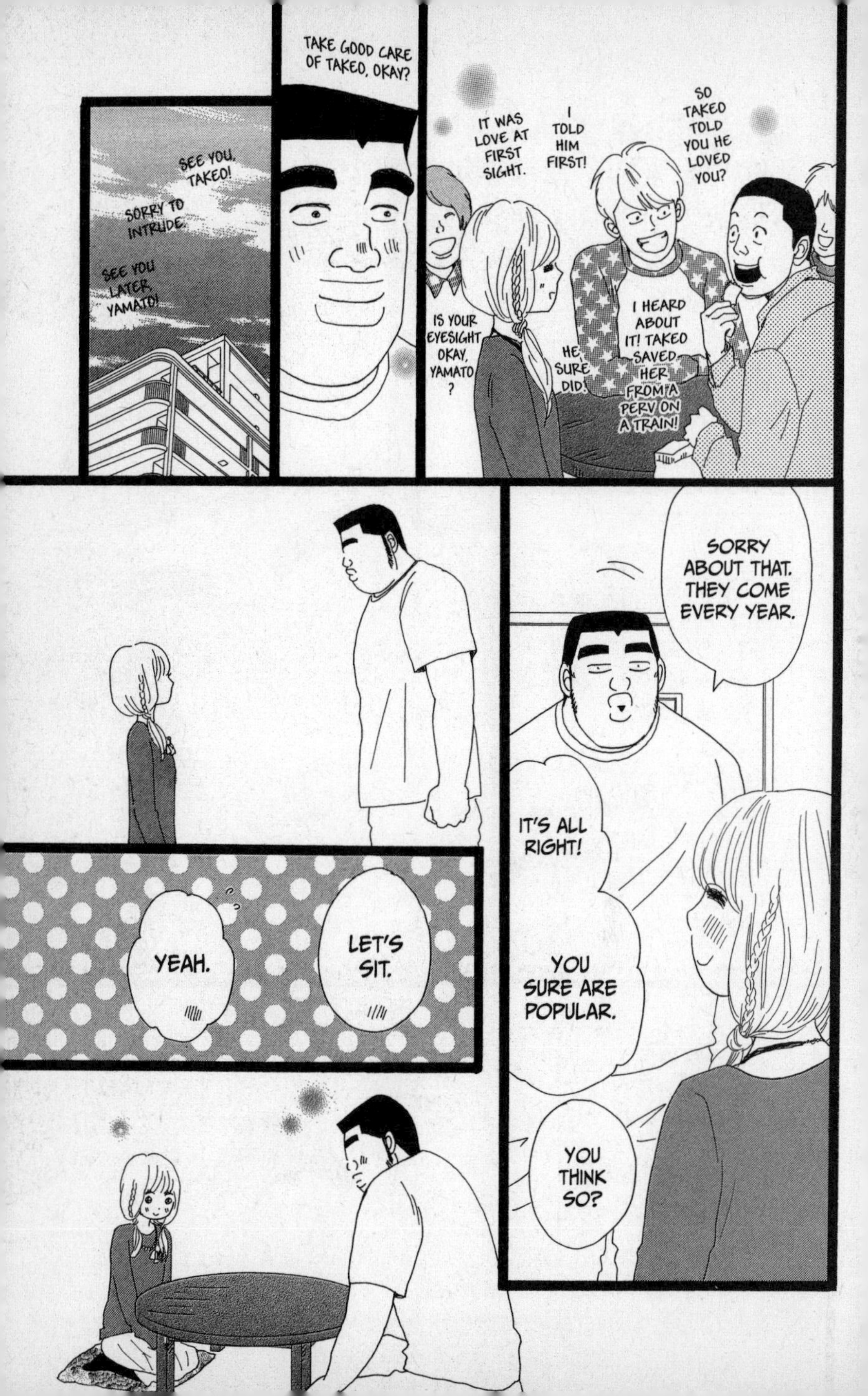
SO TAKEO TOLD YOU HE LOVED YOU?
I TOLD HIM FIRST!
IT WAS LOVE AT FIRST SIGHT.
I HEARD ABOUT IT! TAKEO SAVED HER FROM A PERV ON A TRAIN!
HE SURE DID!
IS YOUR EYESIGHT OKAY, YAMATO?
TAKE GOOD CARE OF TAKEO, OKAY?
SEE YOU, TAKEO!
SORRY TO INTRUDE.
SEE YOU LATER, YAMATO!
SORRY ABOUT THAT. THEY COME EVERY YEAR.
IT'S ALL RIGHT!
YOU SURE ARE POPULAR.
YOU THINK SO?
LET'S SIT.
YEAH.

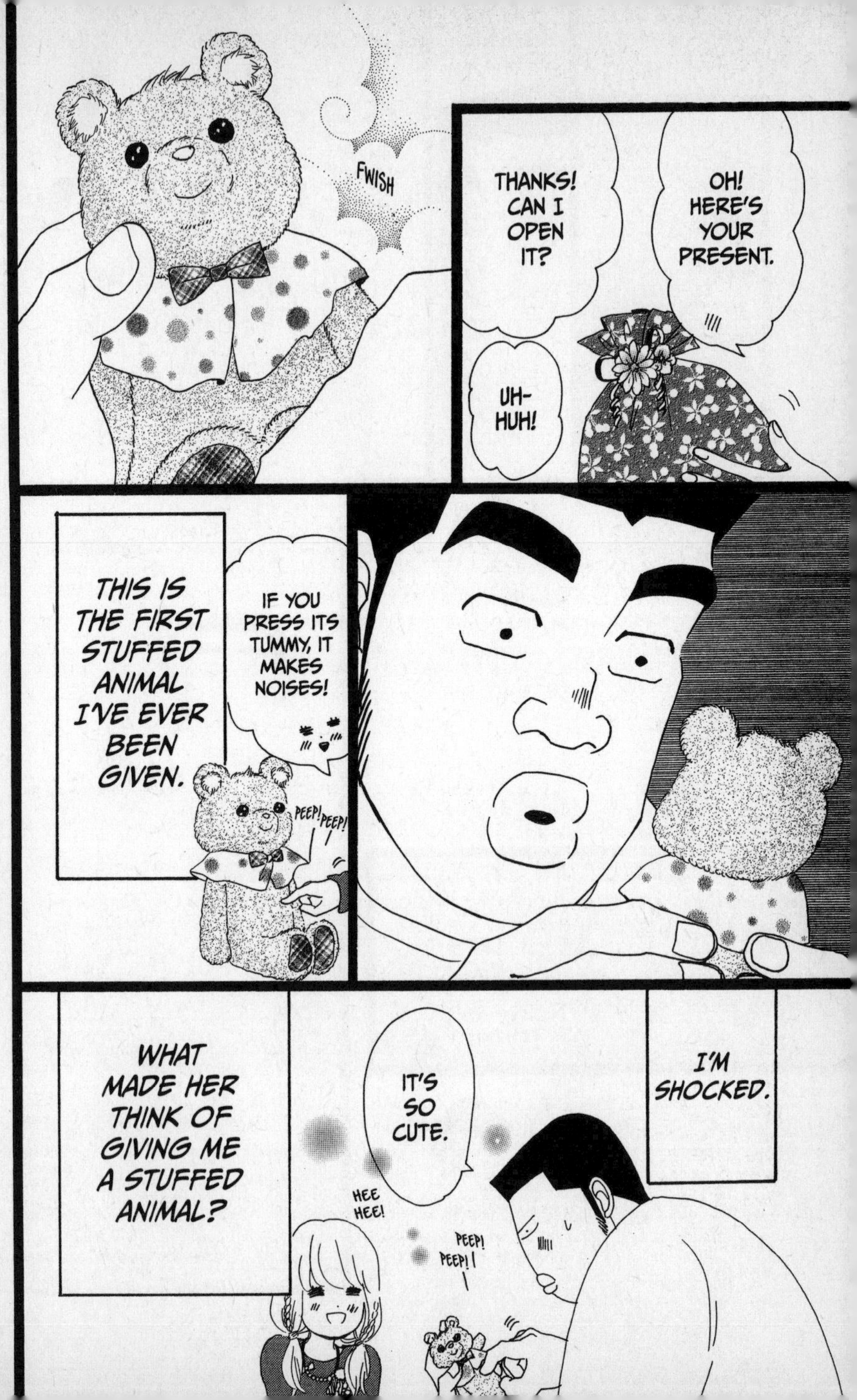
OH! HERE'S YOUR PRESENT.
THANKS! CAN I OPEN IT?
UH-HUH!
FWISH
IF YOU PRESS ITS TUMMY, IT MAKES NOISES!
THIS IS THE FIRST STUFFED ANIMAL I'VE EVER BEEN GIVEN.
PEEP! PEEP!
I'M SHOCKED.
IT'S SO CUTE.
PEEP! PEEP!
HEE HEE!
WHAT MADE HER THINK OF GIVING ME A STUFFED ANIMAL?

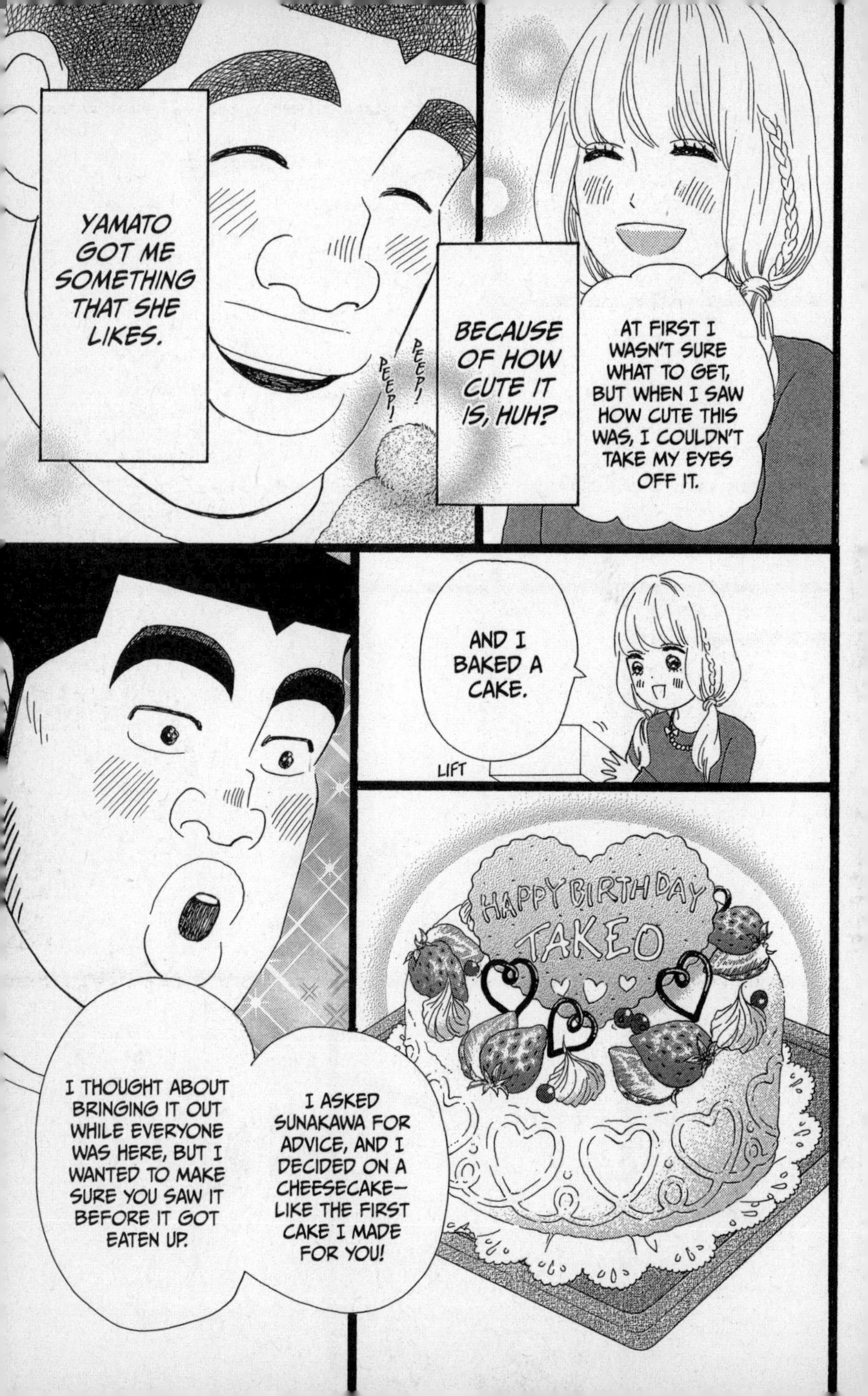
AT FIRST I WASN'T SURE WHAT TO GET, BUT WHEN I SAW HOW CUTE THIS WAS, I COULDN'T TAKE MY EYES OFF IT.
BECAUSE OF HOW CUTE IT IS, HUH?
YAMATO GOT ME SOMETHING THAT SHE LIKES.
PEEP!
PEEP!
AND I BAKED A CAKE.
LIFT
HAPPY BIRTHDAY TAKEO
I ASKED SUNAKAWA FOR ADVICE, AND I DECIDED ON A CHEESECAKE—LIKE THE FIRST CAKE I MADE FOR YOU!
I THOUGHT ABOUT BRINGING IT OUT WHILE EVERYONE WAS HERE, BUT I WANTED TO MAKE SURE YOU SAW IT BEFORE IT GOT EATEN UP.

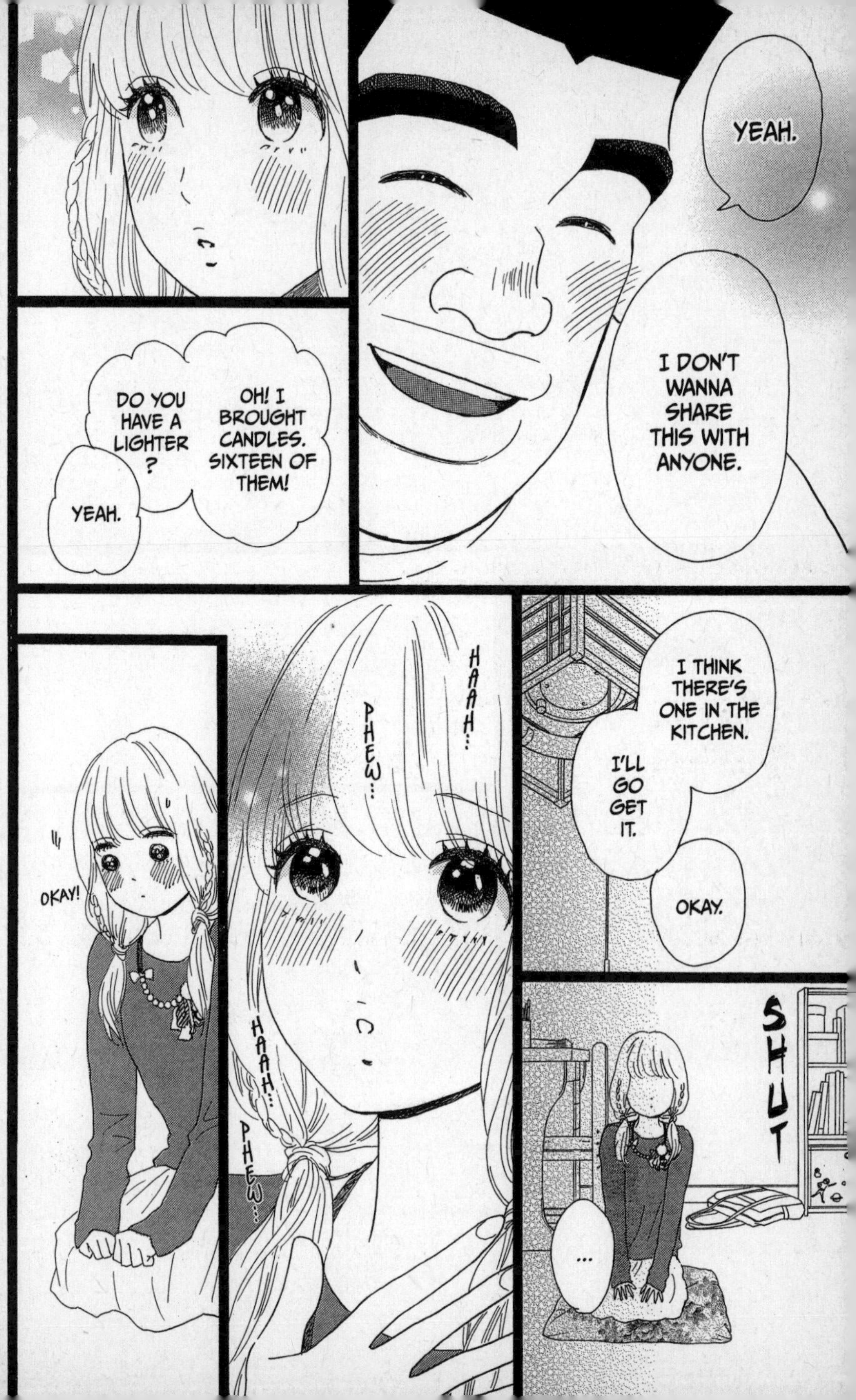
YEAH.
I DON'T WANNA SHARE THIS WITH ANYONE.
OH! I BROUGHT CANDLES. SIXTEEN OF THEM!
DO YOU HAVE A LIGHTER?
YEAH.
I THINK THERE'S ONE IN THE KITCHEN.
I'LL GO GET IT.
OKAY.
SHUT
...
HAAAH...
PHEW...
HAAAH...
PHEW...
OKAY!

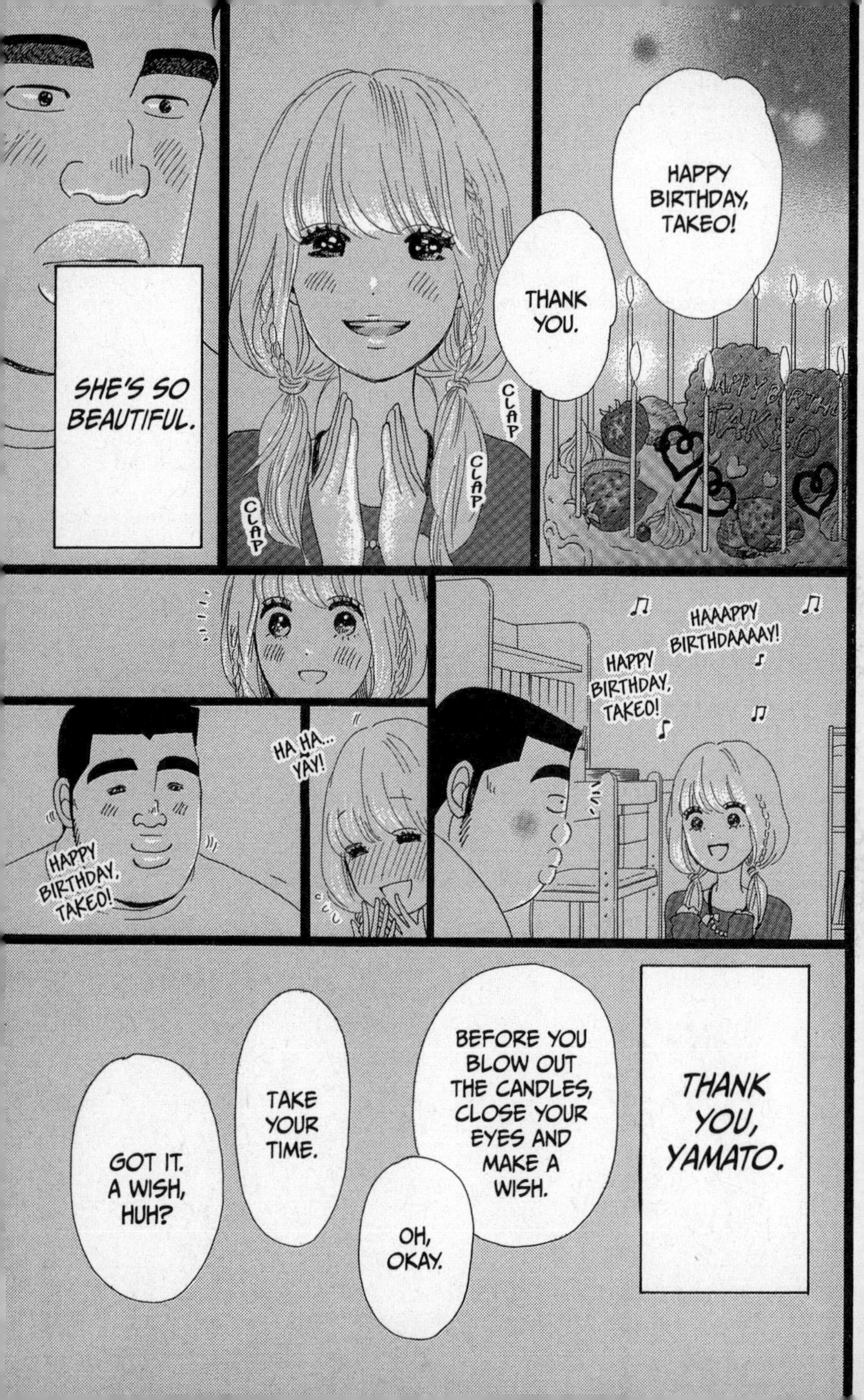
HAPPY BIRTHDAY, TAKEO!
THANK YOU.
CLAP
CLAP
CLAP
SHE'S SO BEAUTIFUL.
HAAAPPY BIRTHDAAAAY!
HAPPY BIRTHDAY, TAKEO!
HA HA... YAY!
HAPPY BIRTHDAY, TAKEO!
THANK YOU, YAMATO.
BEFORE YOU BLOW OUT THE CANDLES, CLOSE YOUR EYES AND MAKE A WISH.
OH, OKAY.
TAKE YOUR TIME.
GOT IT. A WISH, HUH?

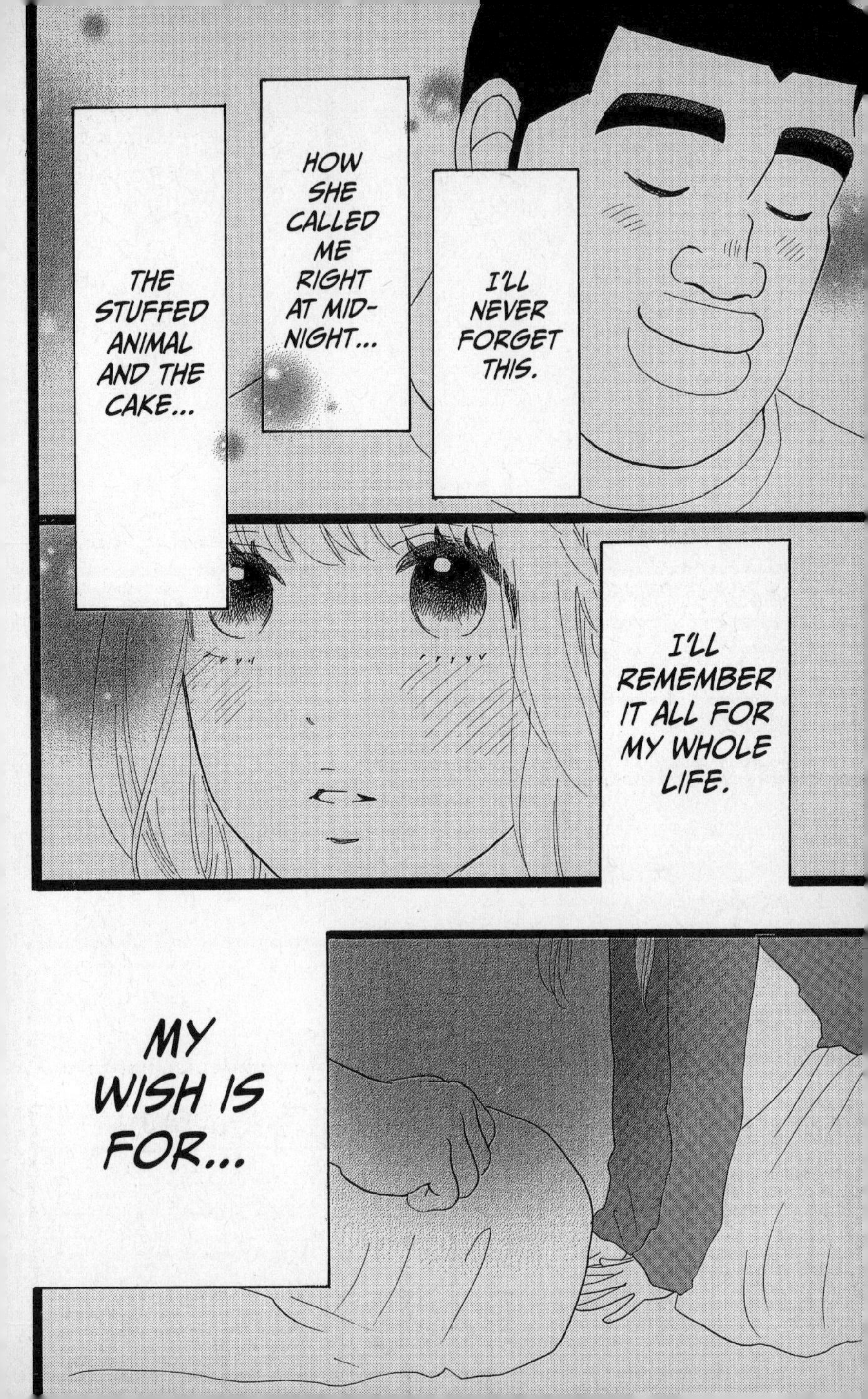
I'LL NEVER FORGET THIS.
HOW SHE CALLED ME RIGHT AT MID-NIGHT...
THE STUFFED ANIMAL AND THE CAKE...
I'LL REMEMBER IT ALL FOR MY WHOLE LIFE.
MY WISH IS FOR...

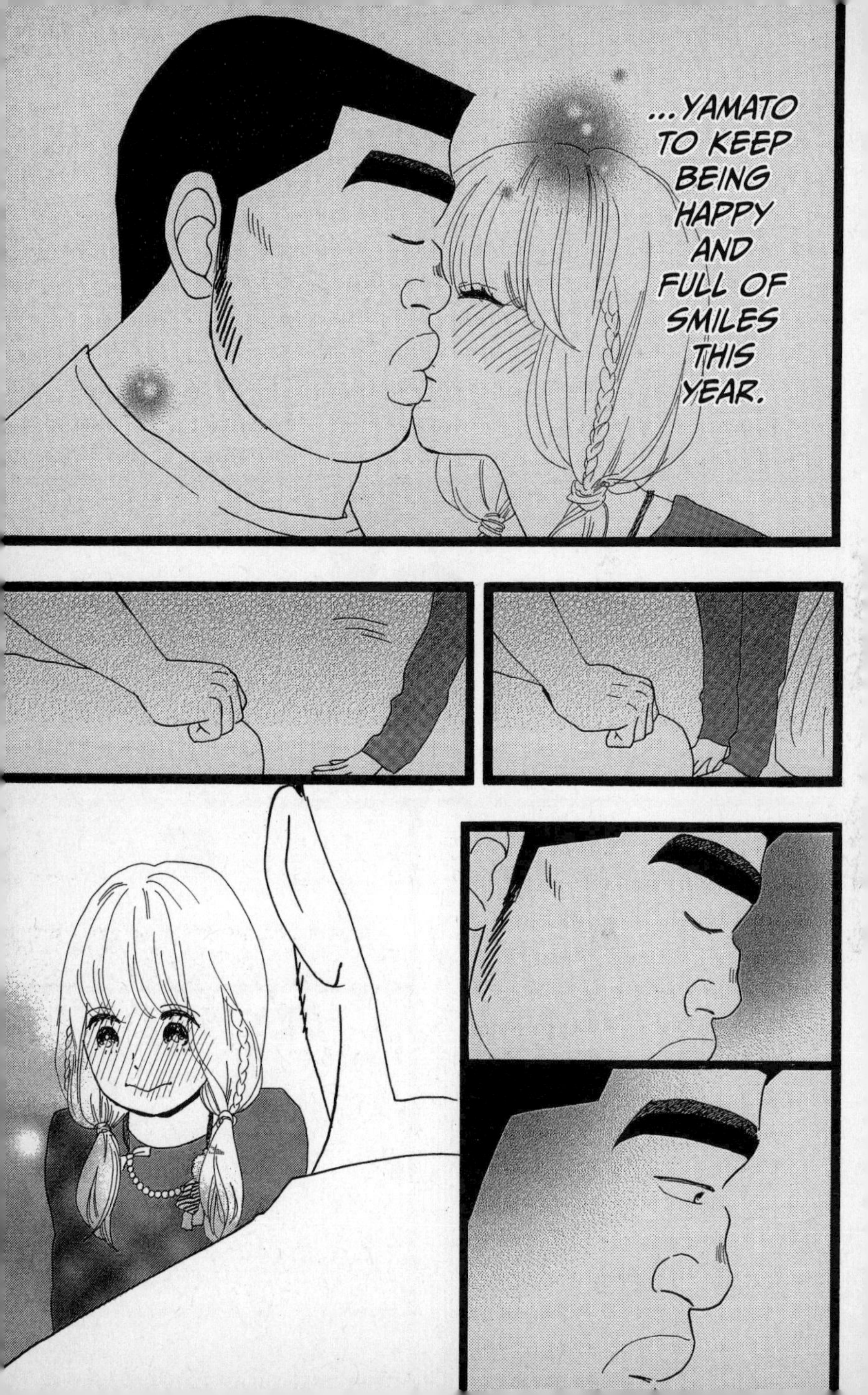
...YAMATO TO KEEP BEING HAPPY AND FULL OF SMILES THIS YEAR.

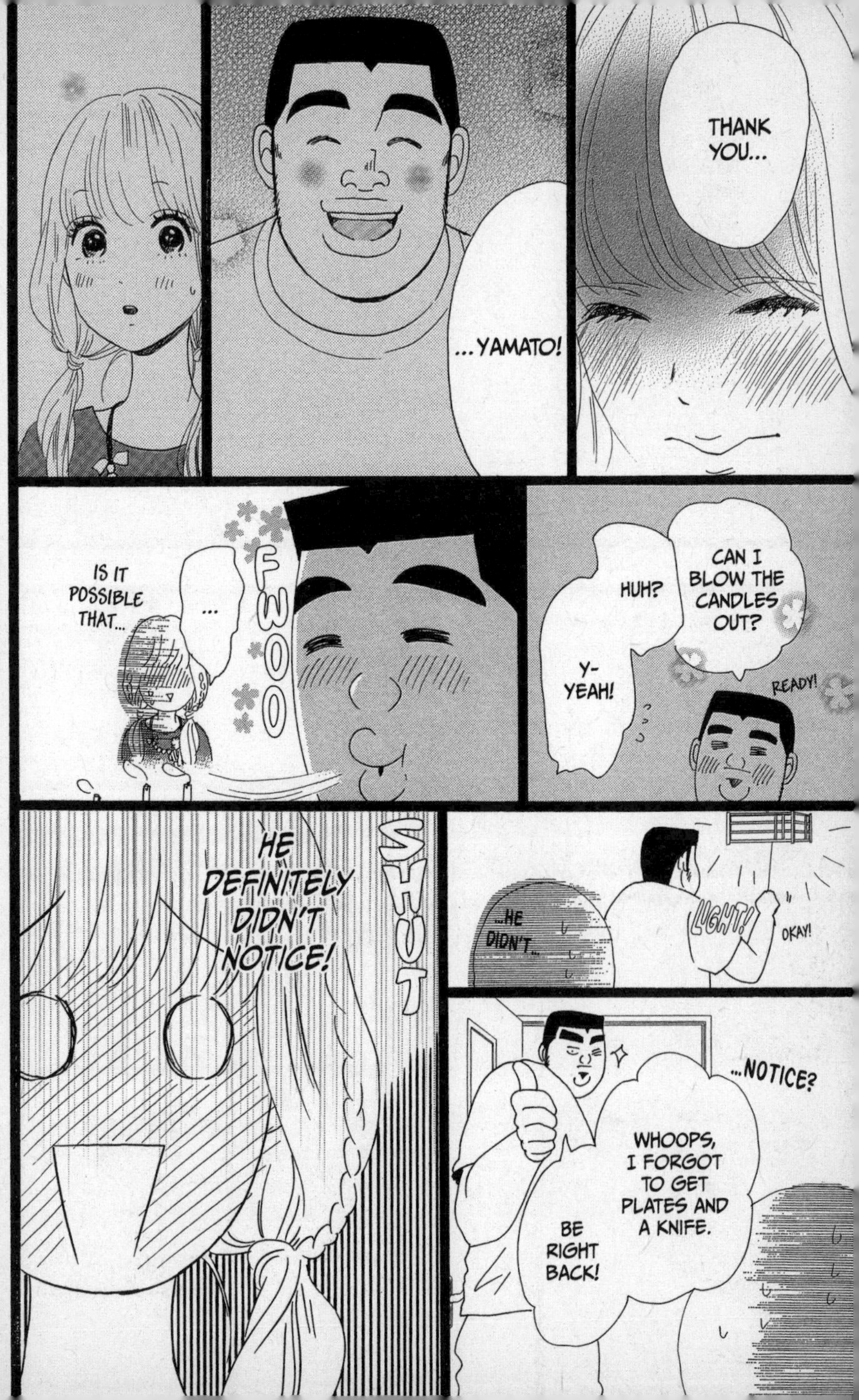
THANK YOU...
...YAMATO!
CAN I BLOW THE CANDLES OUT?
HUH?
Y-YEAH!
READY!
IS IT POSSIBLE THAT...
...
FWOO
OKAY!
LIGHT!
...HE DIDN'T...
...NOTICE?
WHOOPS, I FORGOT TO GET PLATES AND A KNIFE.
BE RIGHT BACK!
SHUT
HE DEFINITELY DIDN'T NOTICE!

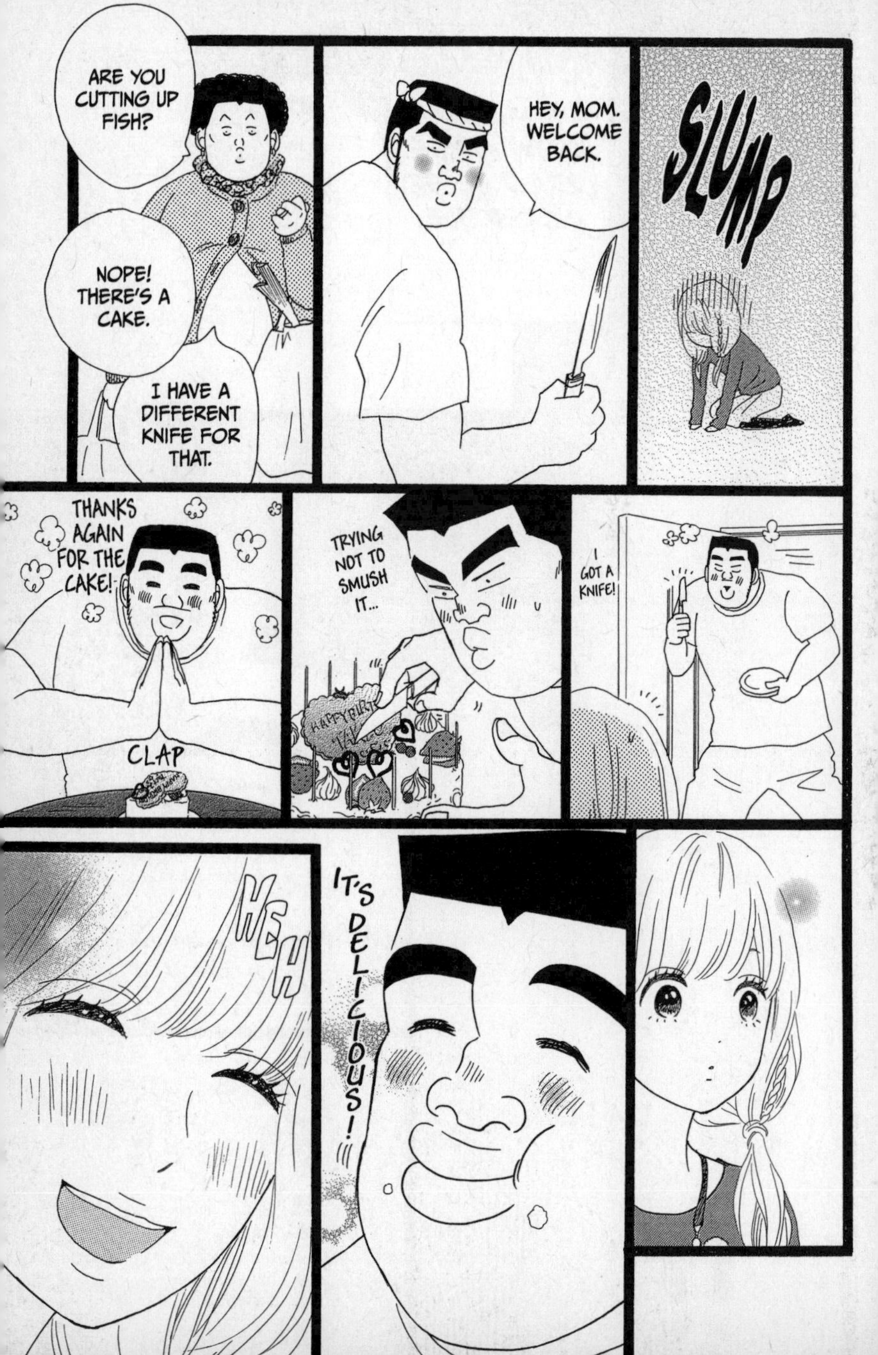
SLUMP
HEY, MOM. WELCOME BACK.
ARE YOU CUTTING UP FISH?
NOPE! THERE'S A CAKE.
I HAVE A DIFFERENT KNIFE FOR THAT.
I GOT A KNIFE!
TRYING NOT TO SMUSH IT...
THANKS AGAIN FOR THE CAKE!
CLAP
IT'S DELICIOUS!
HEH

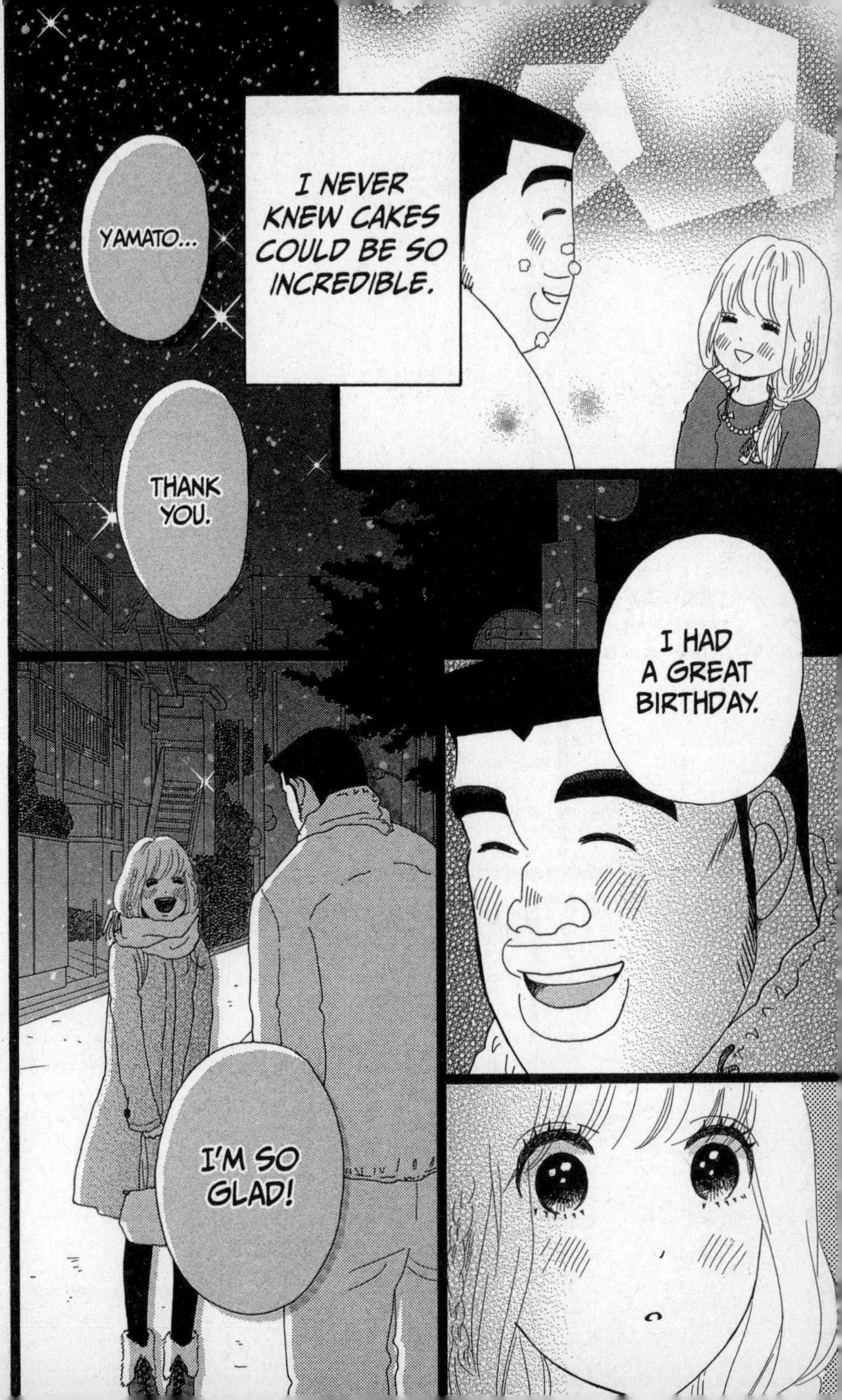
I NEVER KNEW CAKES COULD BE SO INCREDIBLE.
YAMATO...
THANK YOU.
I HAD A GREAT BIRTHDAY.
I'M SO GLAD!

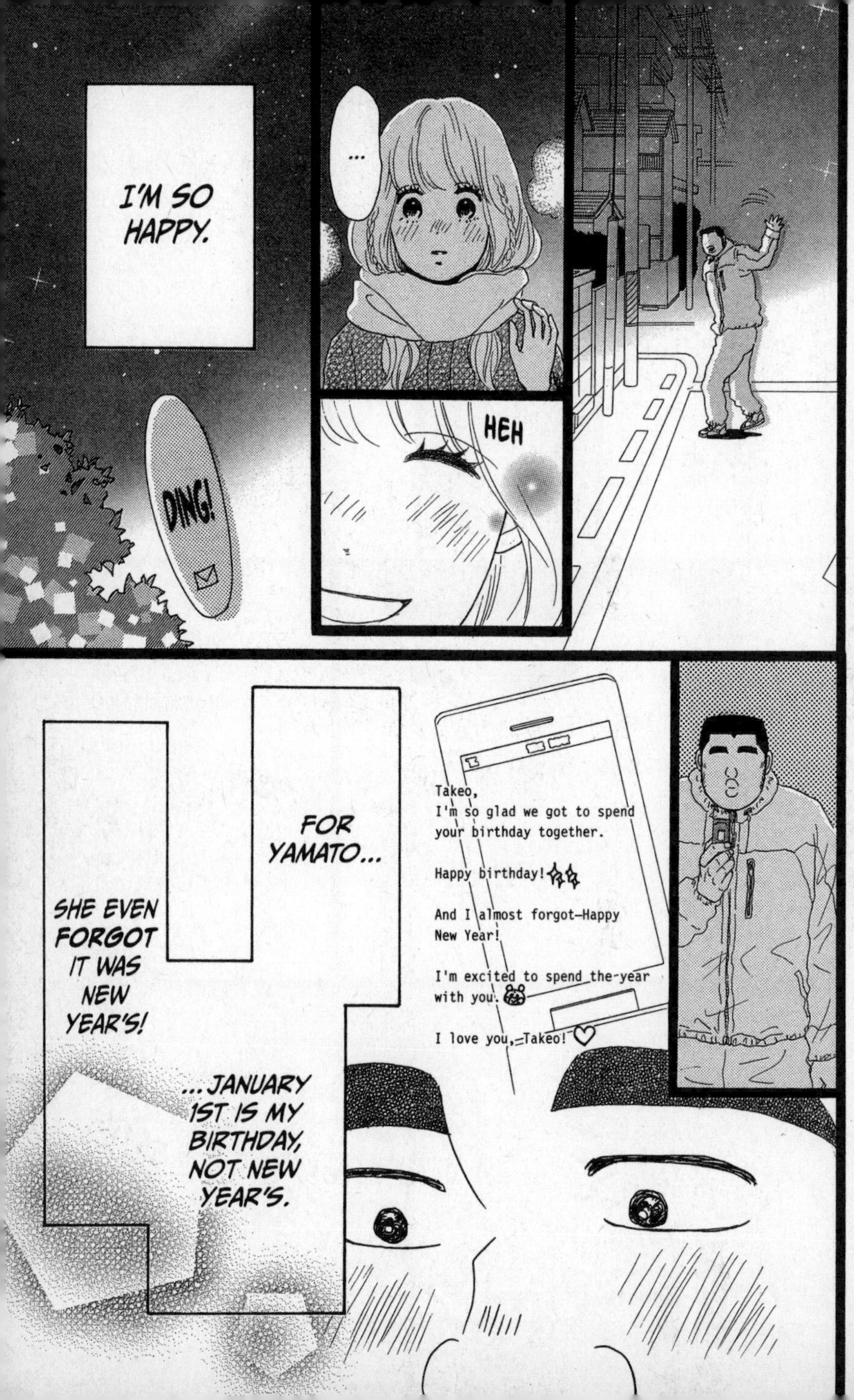
...
HEH
I'M SO HAPPY.
DING!
Takeo,
I'm so glad we got to spend your birthday together.
Happy birthday!
And I almost forgot—Happy New Year!
I'm excited to spend the year with you.
I love you, Takeo!
FOR YAMATO...
SHE EVEN FORGOT IT WAS NEW YEAR'S!
...JANUARY 1ST IS MY BIRTHDAY, NOT NEW YEAR'S.

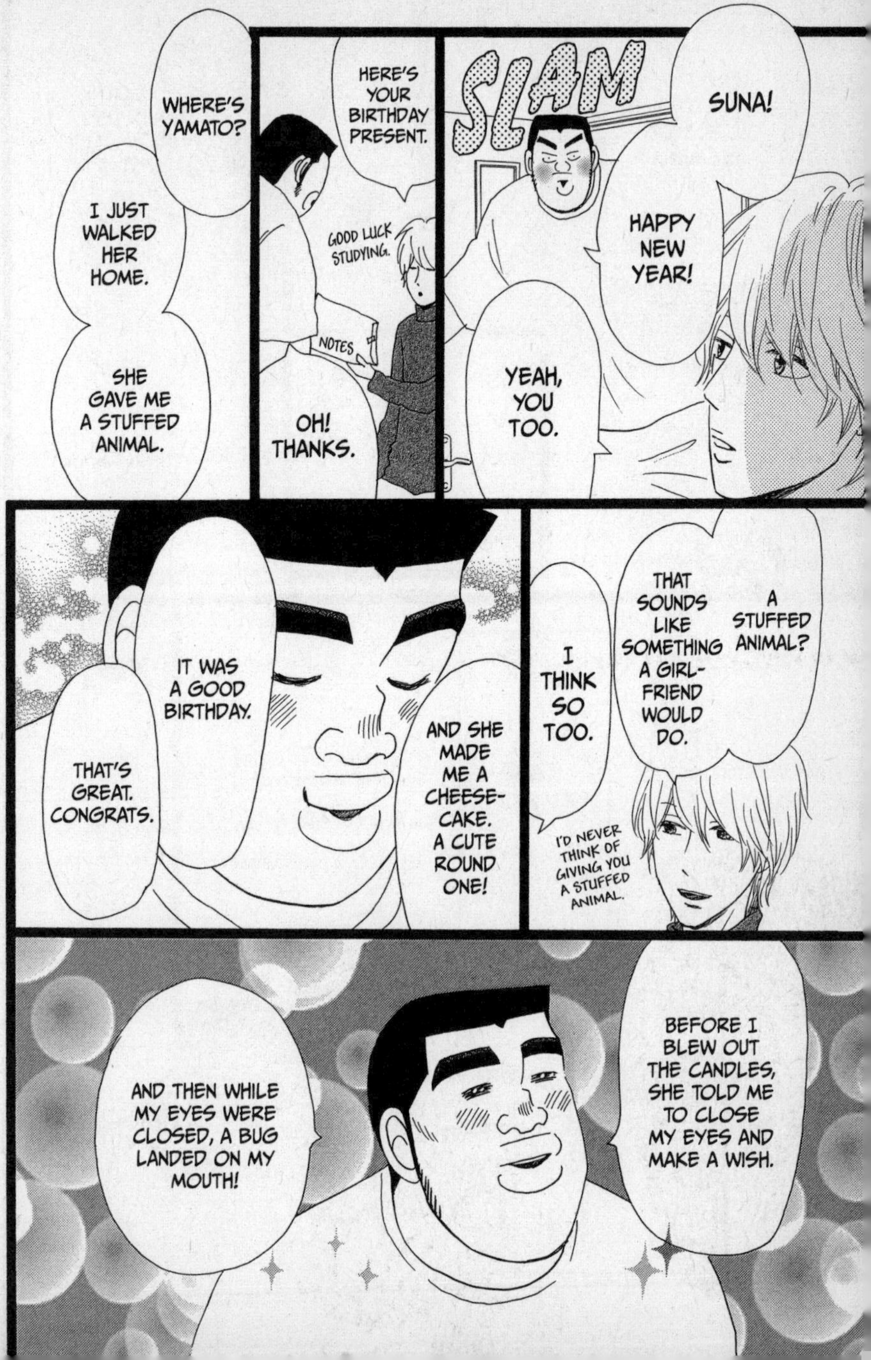
SLAM
SUNA!
HAPPY NEW YEAR!
YEAH, YOU TOO.
HERE'S YOUR BIRTHDAY PRESENT.
GOOD LUCK STUDYING.
NOTES
OH! THANKS.
WHERE'S YAMATO?
I JUST WALKED HER HOME.
SHE GAVE ME A STUFFED ANIMAL.
A STUFFED ANIMAL?
THAT SOUNDS LIKE SOMETHING A GIRL-FRIEND WOULD DO.
I THINK SO TOO.
I'D NEVER THINK OF GIVING YOU A STUFFED ANIMAL.
AND SHE MADE ME A CHEESE-CAKE. A CUTE ROUND ONE!
IT WAS A GOOD BIRTHDAY.
THAT'S GREAT. CONGRATS.
BEFORE I BLEW OUT THE CANDLES, SHE TOLD ME TO CLOSE MY EYES AND MAKE A WISH.
AND THEN WHILE MY EYES WERE CLOSED, A BUG LANDED ON MY MOUTH!

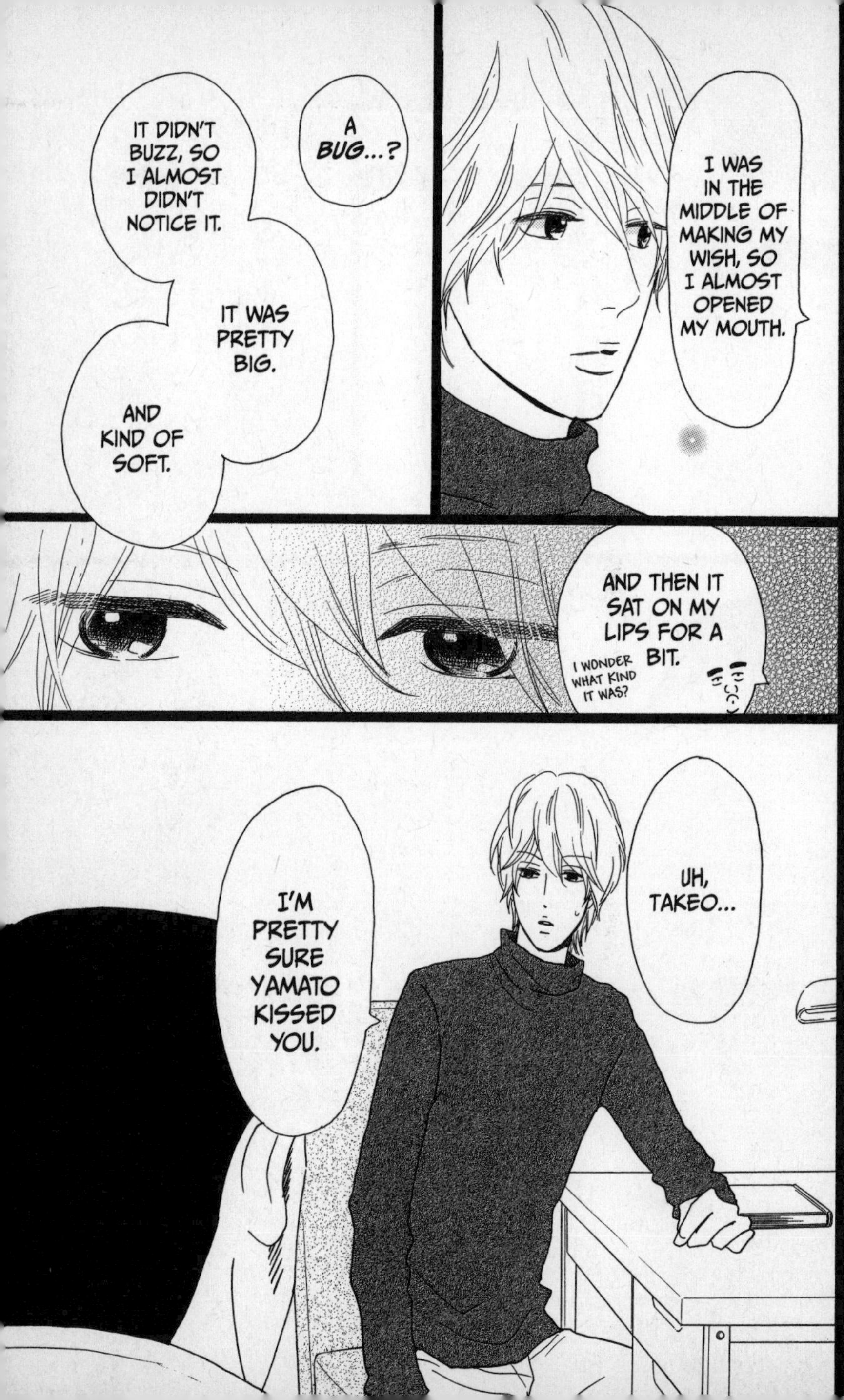
I WAS IN THE MIDDLE OF MAKING MY WISH, SO I ALMOST OPENED MY MOUTH.
A *BUG*...?
IT DIDN'T BUZZ, SO I ALMOST DIDN'T NOTICE IT.
IT WAS PRETTY BIG.
AND KIND OF SOFT.
AND THEN IT SAT ON MY LIPS FOR A BIT.
I WONDER WHAT KIND IT WAS?
UH, TAKEO...
I'M PRETTY SURE YAMATO KISSED YOU.

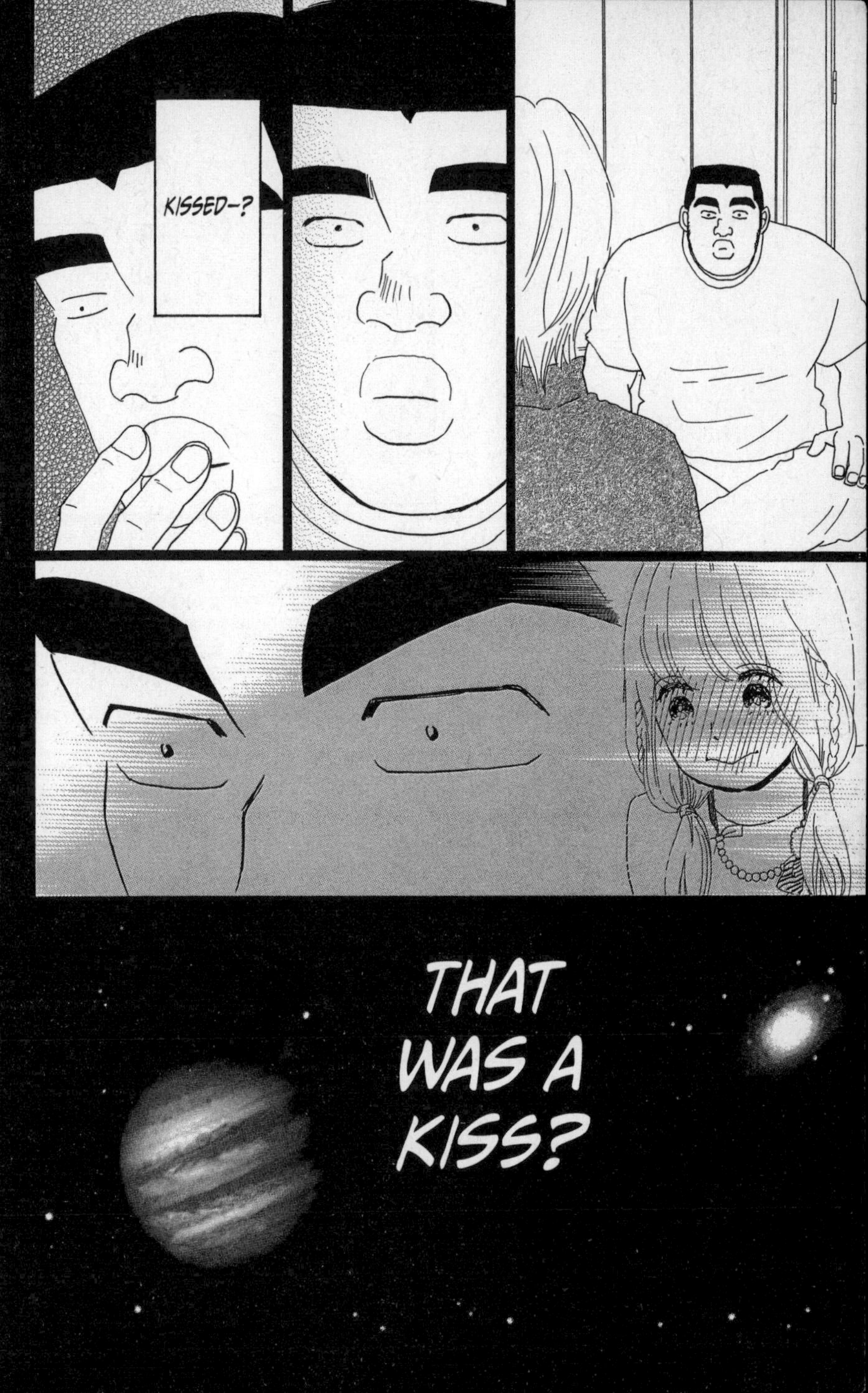
KISSED--?
THAT WAS A KISS?

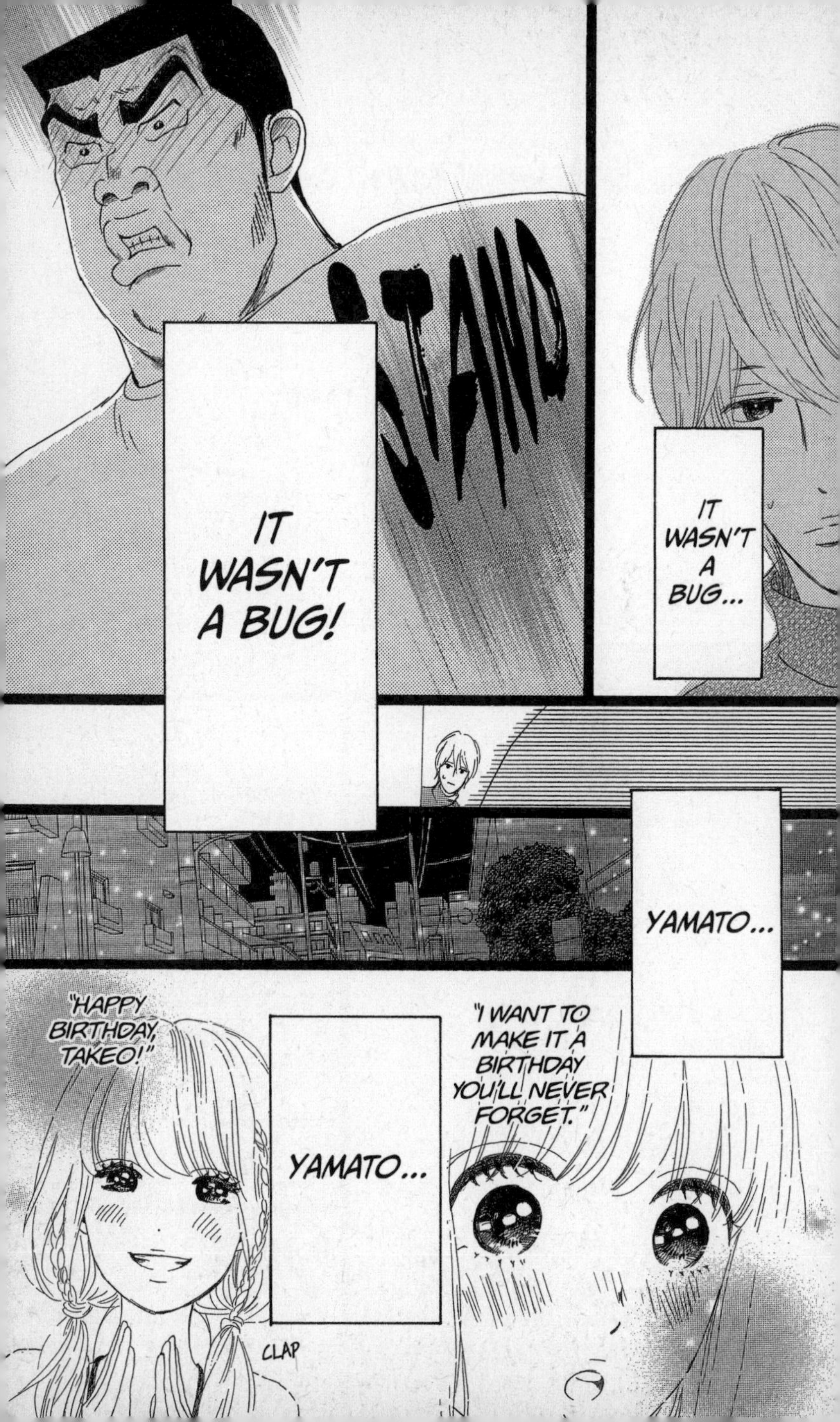

IT WASN'T A BUG...
STAND
IT WASN'T A BUG!
YAMATO...
"I WANT TO MAKE IT A BIRTHDAY YOU'LL NEVER FORGET."
YAMATO...
"HAPPY BIRTHDAY, TAKEO!"
CLAP

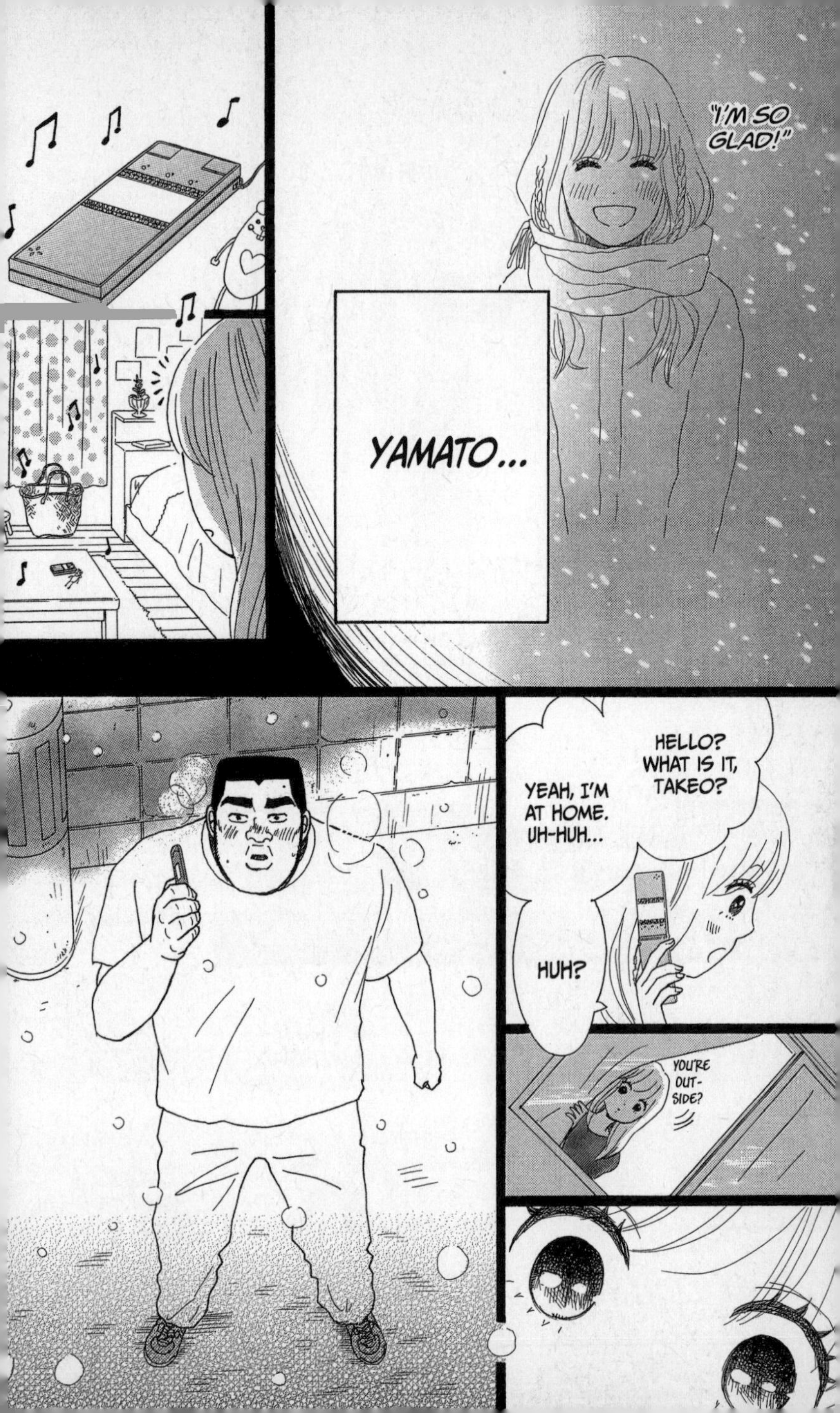
"I'M SO GLAD!"
YAMATO...
HELLO? WHAT IS IT, TAKEO?
YEAH, I'M AT HOME. UH-HUH...
HUH?
YOU'RE OUT-SIDE?

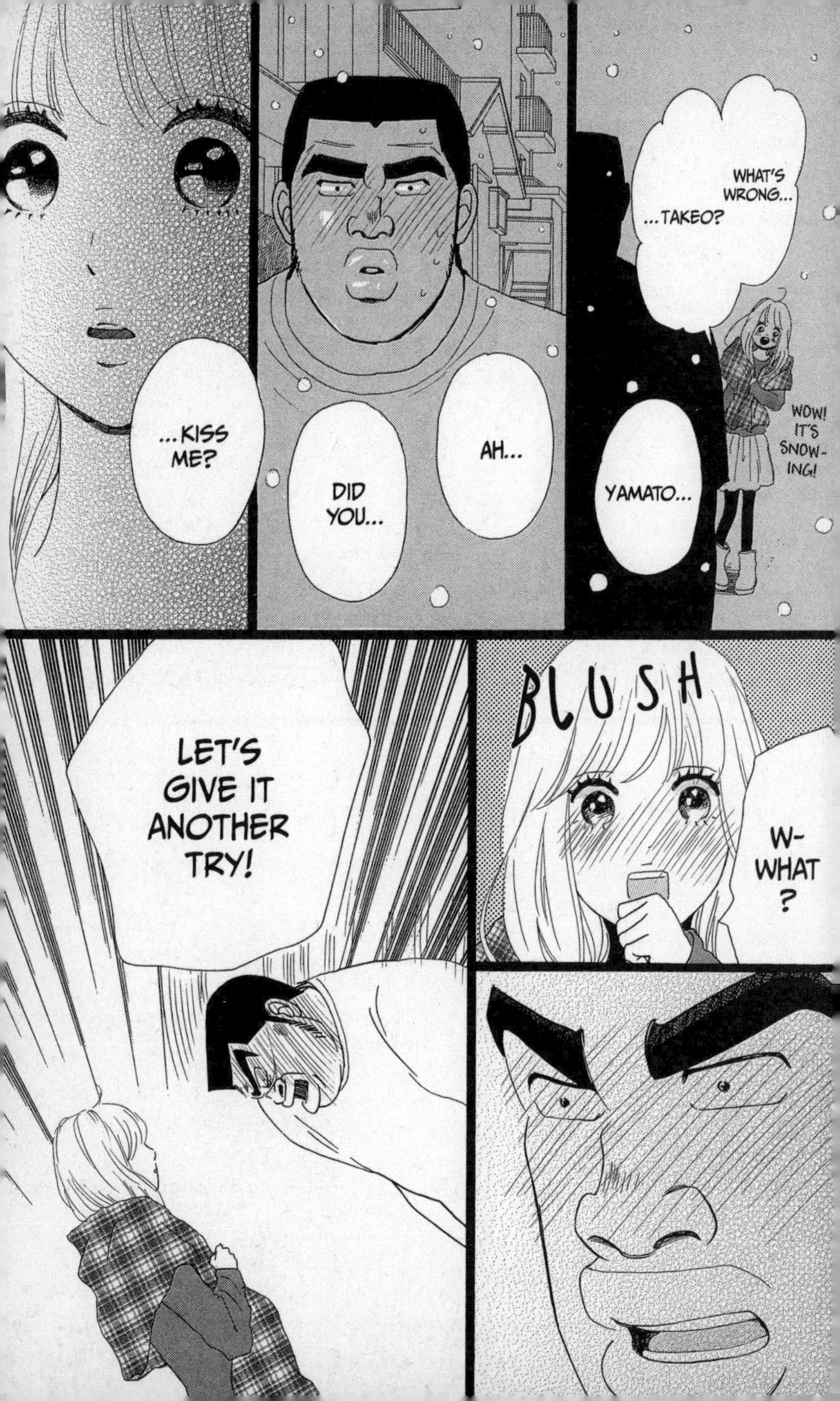
WHAT'S WRONG... ...TAKEO?
WOW! IT'S SNOW-ING!
YAMATO...
AH...
DID YOU...
...KISS ME?
BLUSH
W-WHAT?
LET'S GIVE IT ANOTHER TRY!

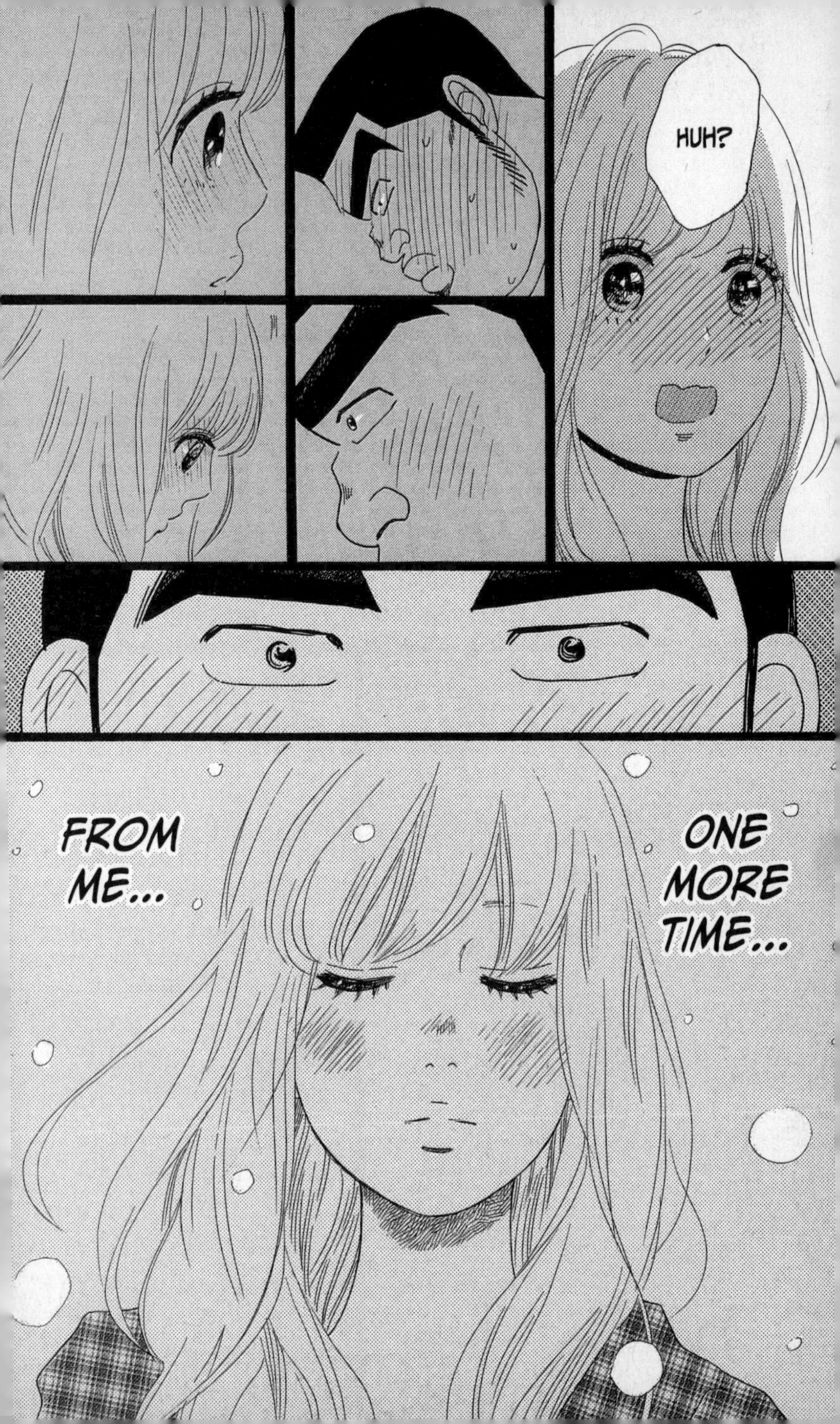
HUH?
ONE MORE TIME...
FROM ME...

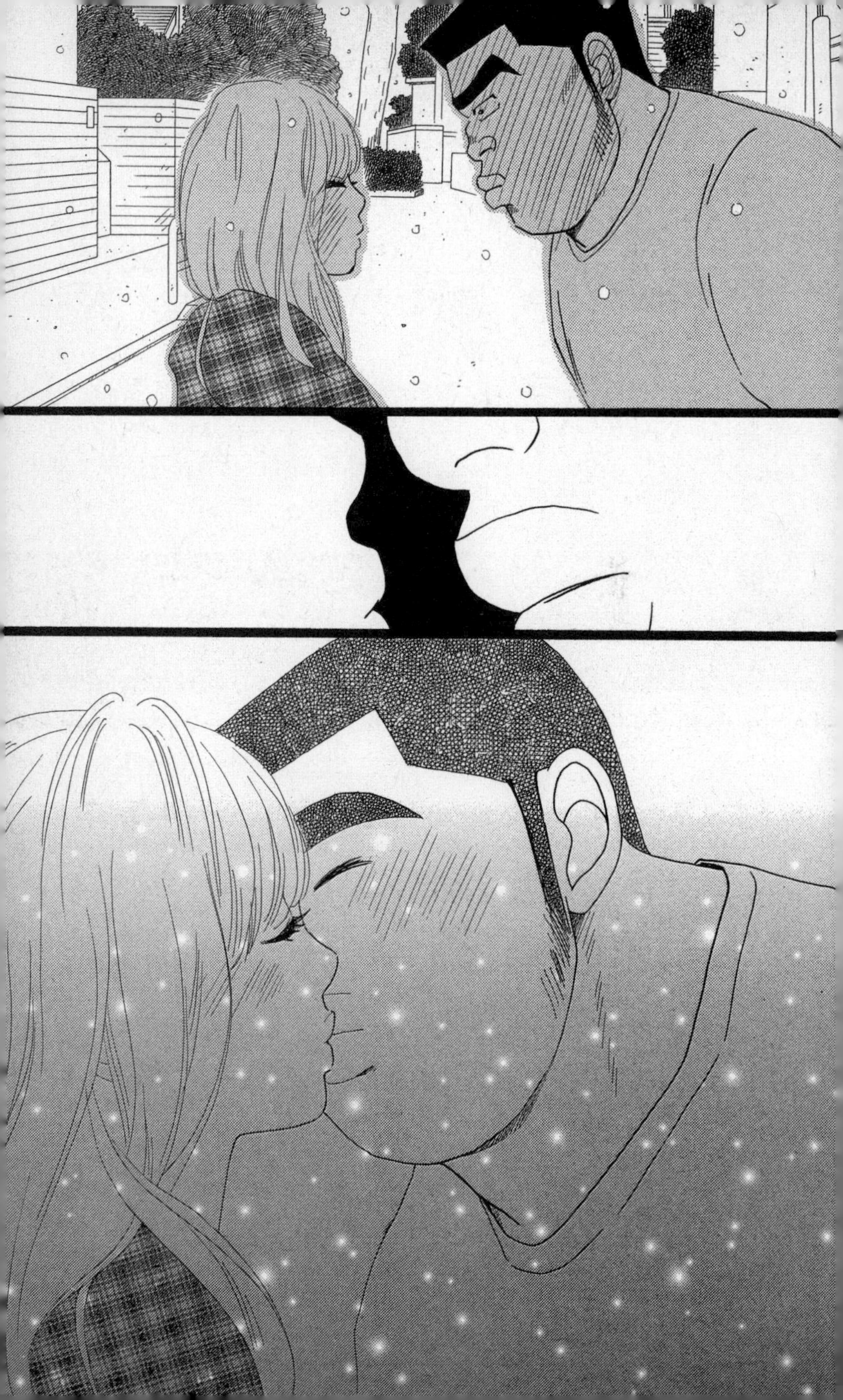

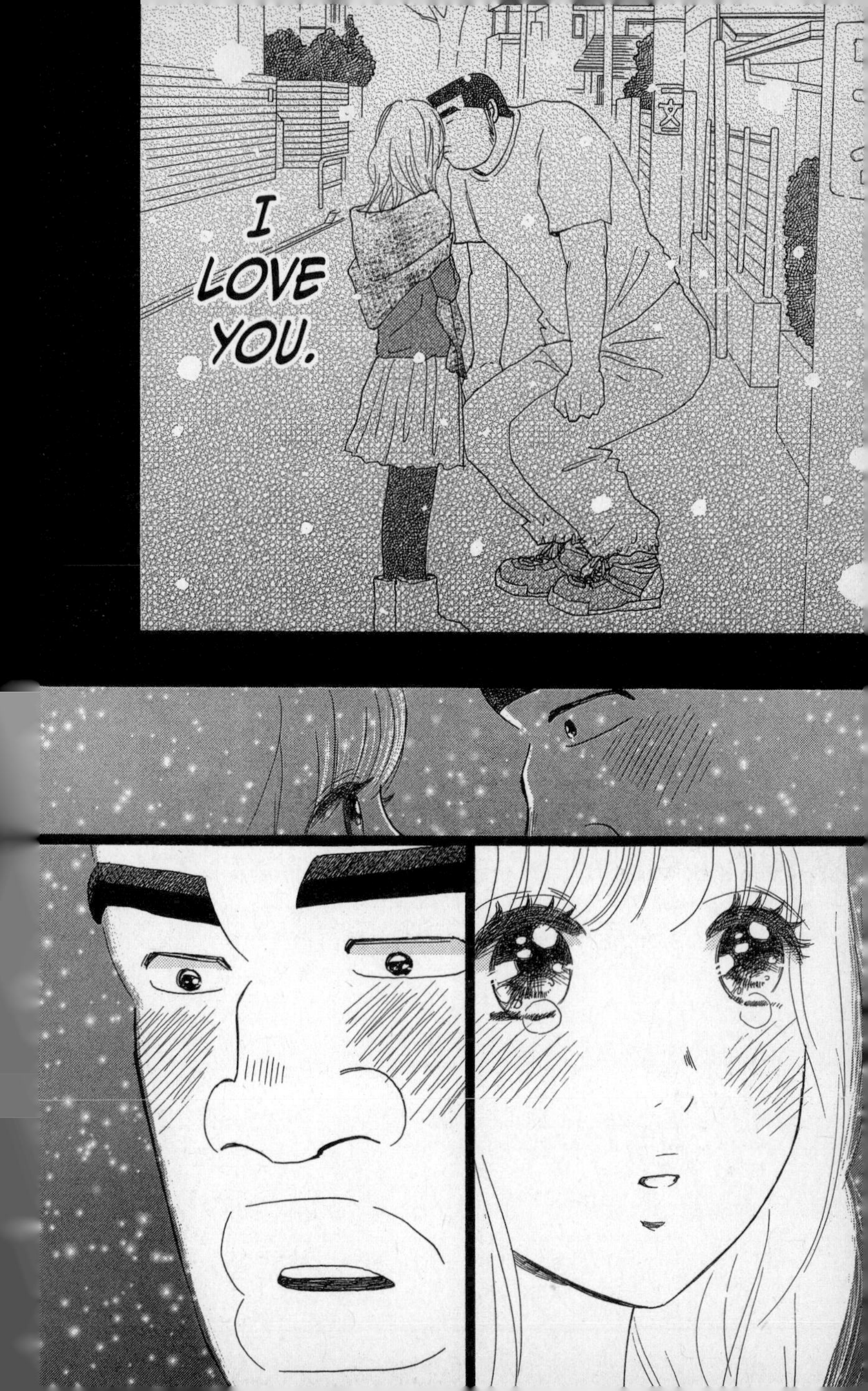
I LOVE YOU.

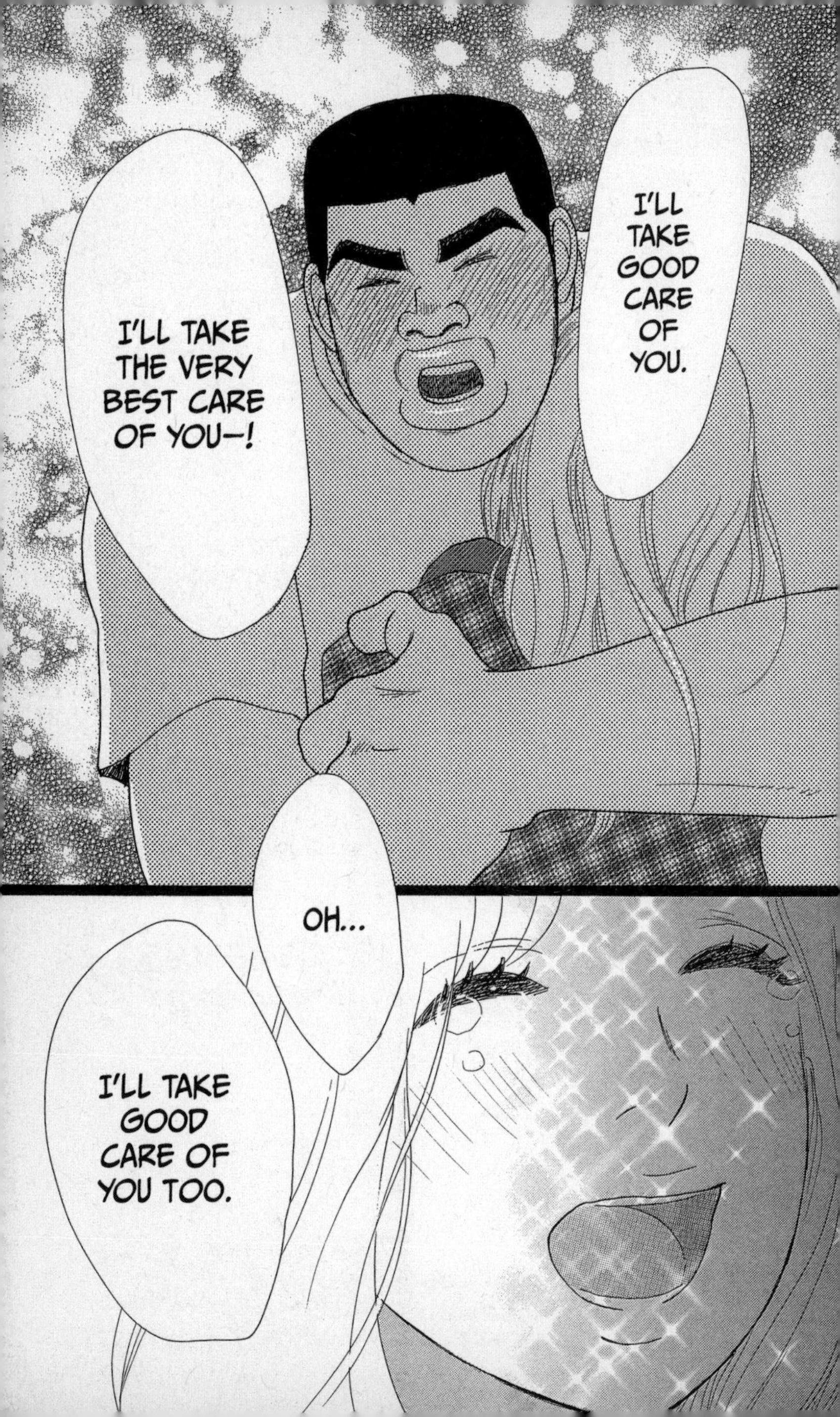
I'LL TAKE GOOD CARE OF YOU.
I'LL TAKE THE VERY BEST CARE OF YOU—!
OH...
I'LL TAKE GOOD CARE OF YOU TOO.

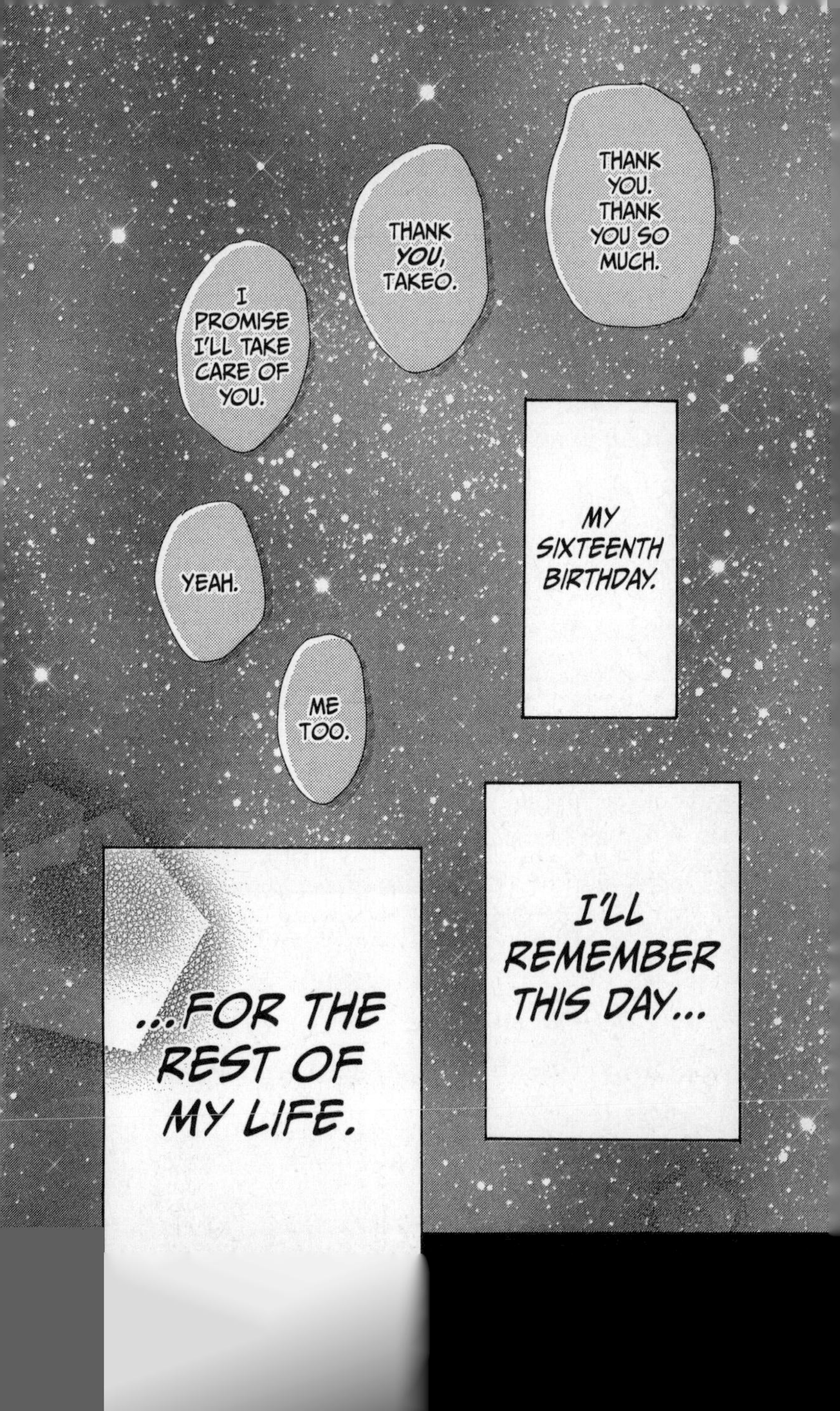
THANK YOU. THANK YOU SO MUCH.
THANK YOU, TAKEO.
I PROMISE I'LL TAKE CARE OF YOU.
MY SIXTEENTH BIRTHDAY.
YEAH.
ME TOO.
I'LL REMEMBER THIS DAY...
...FOR THE REST OF MY LIFE.

BONUS STORY!

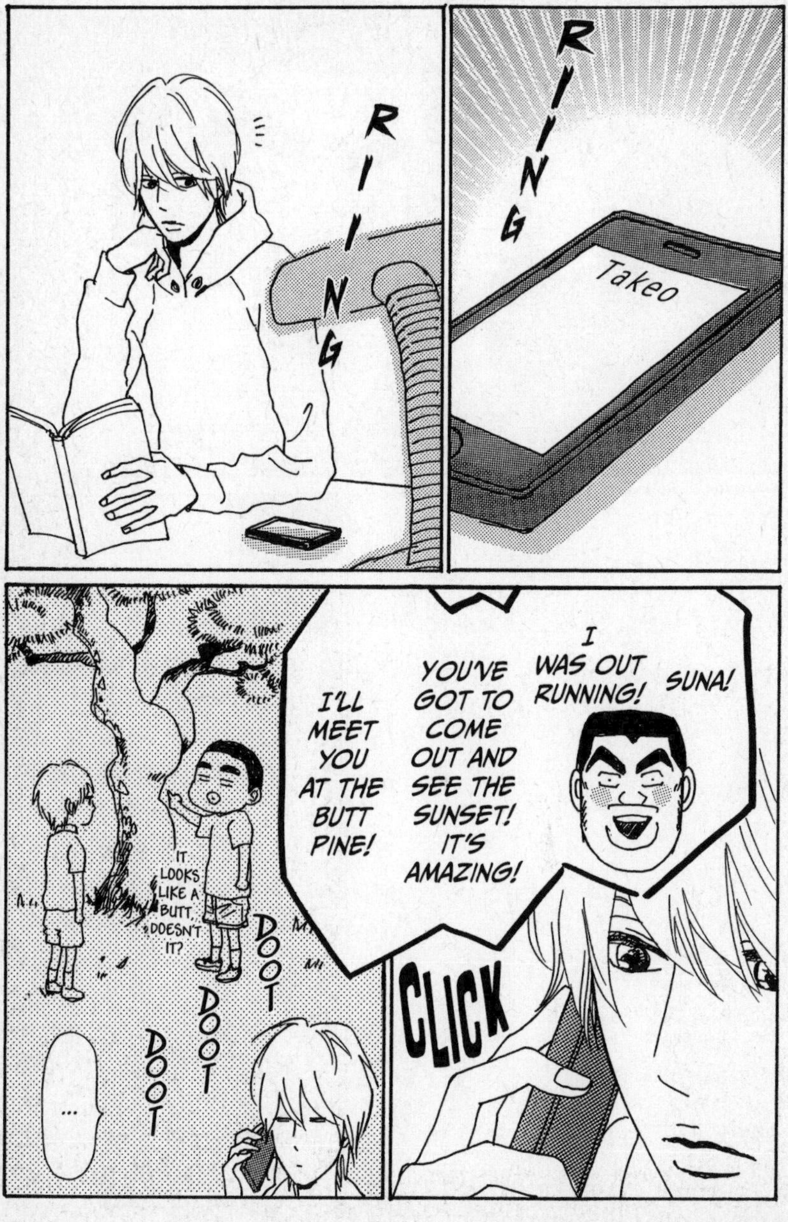
RIIING
Takeo
RIIING
SUNA!
I WAS OUT RUNNING!
YOU'VE GOT TO COME OUT AND SEE THE SUNSET! IT'S AMAZING!
I'LL MEET YOU AT THE BUTT PINE!
CLICK
IT LOOKS LIKE A BUTT, DOESN'T IT?
DOOT
DOOT
DOOT
...

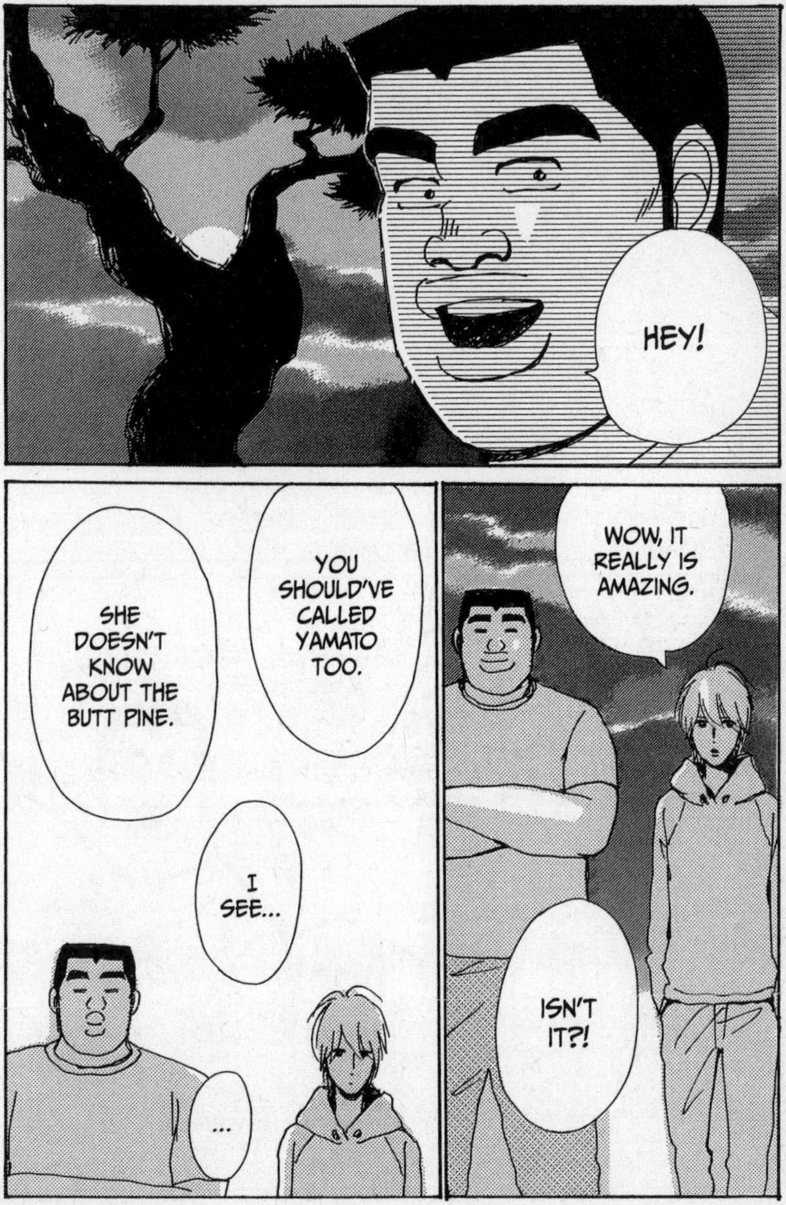
HEY!
WOW, IT REALLY IS AMAZING.
ISN'T IT?!
YOU SHOULD'VE CALLED YAMATO TOO.
SHE DOESN'T KNOW ABOUT THE BUTT PINE.
I SEE...
...

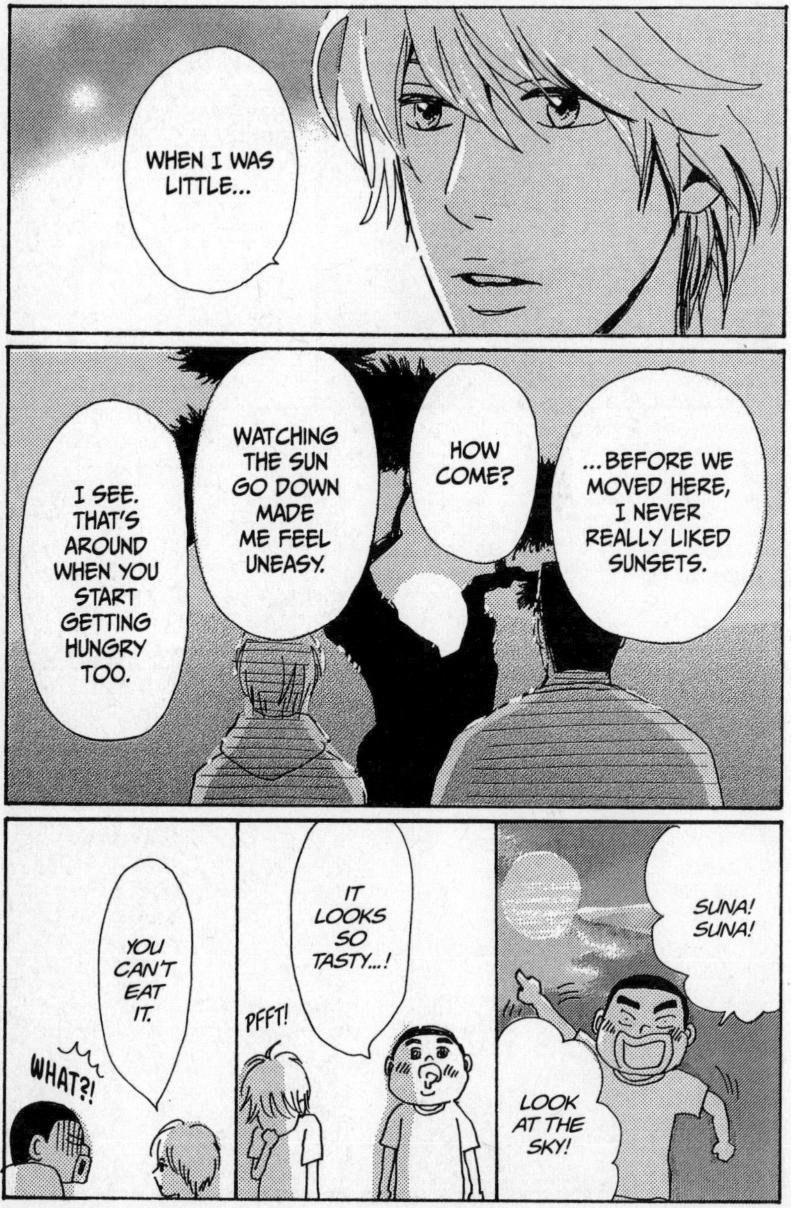
WHEN I WAS LITTLE...
...BEFORE WE MOVED HERE, I NEVER REALLY LIKED SUNSETS.
HOW COME?
WATCHING THE SUN GO DOWN MADE ME FEEL UNEASY.
I SEE. THAT'S AROUND WHEN YOU START GETTING HUNGRY TOO.
SUNA! SUNA!
LOOK AT THE SKY!
IT LOOKS SO TASTY...!
PFFT!
YOU CAN'T EAT IT.
WHAT?!

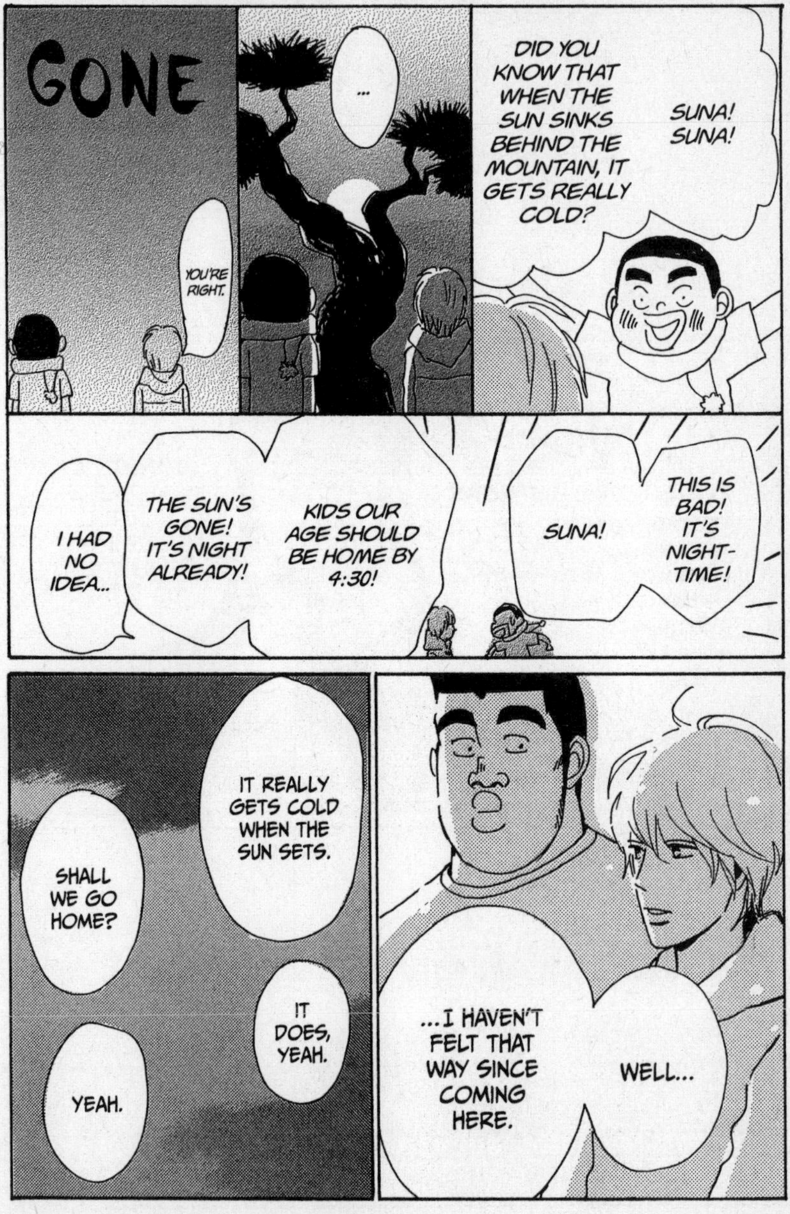
SUNA! SUNA!
DID YOU KNOW THAT WHEN THE SUN SINKS BEHIND THE MOUNTAIN, IT GETS REALLY COLD?
...
GONE
YOU'RE RIGHT.
THIS IS BAD! IT'S NIGHT-TIME!
SUNA!
KIDS OUR AGE SHOULD BE HOME BY 4:30!
THE SUN'S GONE! IT'S NIGHT ALREADY!
I HAD NO IDEA...
WELL...
...I HAVEN'T FELT THAT WAY SINCE COMING HERE.
IT REALLY GETS COLD WHEN THE SUN SETS.
IT DOES, YEAH.
SHALL WE GO HOME?
YEAH.

THE END

I'm so happy we're at volume 5! \(^o^)/ I just love manga, and I read them as I'm eating, before sleeping, and while working. I hope you read and enjoy *My Love Story!!* in your daily lives too. (^ω^)
– Kazune Kawahara

Ⓚ

ARUKO is from Ishikawa Prefecture in Japan and was born on July 26 (a Leo!). She made her manga debut with *Ame Nochi Hare* (Clear After the Rain). Her other works include *Yasuko to Kenji*, and her hobbies include laughing and getting lost.

KAZUNE KAWAHARA is from Hokkaido Prefecture in Japan and was born on March 11 (a Pisces!). She made her manga debut at age 18 with *Kare no Ichiban Sukina Hito* (His Most Favorite Person). Her best-selling shojo manga series *High School Debut* is available in North America from VIZ Media. Her hobby is interior redecorating.

It's volume 5! Thank you so much! Takeo...becomes more mature... I will work hard to keep up with him. I hope you keep on reading!
– Aruko

Ⓐ

MY LOVE STORY!!

Volume 5
Shojo Beat Edition

Story **KAZUNE KAWAHARA**
Art by **ARUKO**

English Adaptation ♡ **Ysabet Reinhardt MacFarlane**
Translation ♡ **JN Productions**
Touch-up Art & Lettering ♡ **Mark McMurray**
Design ♡ **Fawn Lau**
Editor ♡ **Amy Yu**

ORE MONOGATARI!!
© 2011 by Kazune Kawahara, Aruko
All rights reserved.
First published in Japan in 2011 by SHUEISHA Inc., Tokyo
English translation rights arranged by SHUEISHA Inc.

The stories, characters and incidents mentioned in
this publication are entirely fictional.

Printed in the U.S.A.

Published by VIZ Media, LLC
P.O. Box 77010
San Francisco, CA 94107

10 9 8 7 6 5 4 3 2 1
First printing, July 2015

PARENTAL ADVISORY
MY LOVE STORY!! is rated T for Teen and
is recommended for ages 13 and up. This
volume contains suggestive themes.
ratings.viz.com

www.viz.com

www.shojobeat.com

You may be reading the **wrong way!!**

IT'S TRUE: In keeping with the original Japanese comic format, this book reads from right to left—so action, sound effects, and word balloons are completely reversed. This preserves the orientation of the original artwork—plus, it's fun! Check out the diagram shown here to get the hang of things, and then turn to the other side of the book to get started!

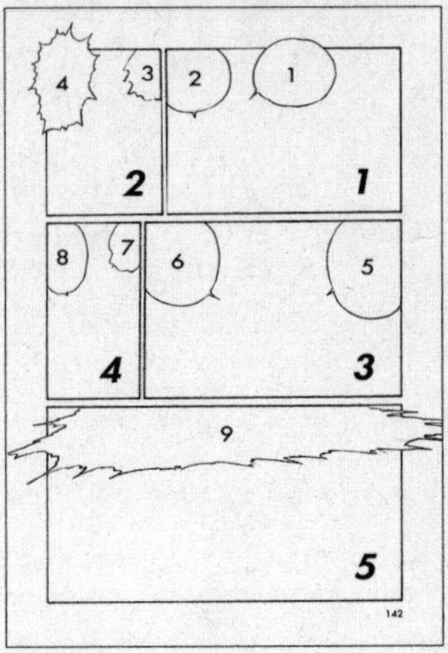
1
2
3
4
1
2
5
6
7
8
3
4
9
5
142

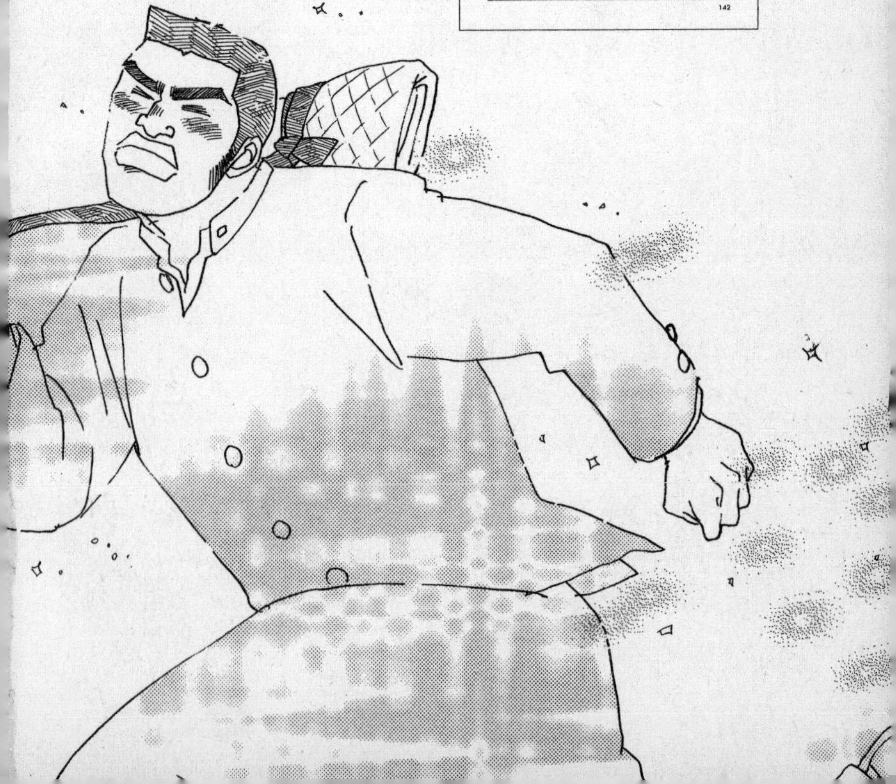